THE
BATTLE
FOR THE
RHINE

THE BATTLE FOR THE RHINE

THE BATTLE OF THE BULGE
AND THE
ARDENNES CAMPAIGN, 1944

ROBIN NEILLANDS

THE OVERLOOK PRESS
Woodstock & New York

This edition first published in the United States in 2007 by
The Overlook Press, Peter Mayer Publishers, Inc.
Woodstock & New York

WOODSTOCK:
One Overlook Drive
Woodstock, NY 12498
www.overlookpress.com
[for individual orders, bulk and special sales, contact our Woodstock office]

NEW YORK:
141 Wooster Street
New York, NY 10012

Library of Congress Cataloging-in-Publication Data

Neillands, Robin, 1935-2006.
The battle for the Rhine : the Battle of the Bulge and the
Ardennes campaign, 1944 / Robin Neillands.
p. cm.
Includes bibliographical references and index.
1. Ardennes, Battle of the, 1944-1945. I. Title
D756.5.A7N46 2007   940.54'219348—dc22   2006052736

Illustrations by Terry Brown
Cartography by Terry Brown and David Hoxley

Manufactured in the United States of America
ISBN-13 978-1-58567-787-0
10 9 8 7 6 5 4 3 2 1

This one is for Dr Nick Plowman and all the staff
at the Radiotherapy and Chemotherapy Departments
of the Cromwell Hospital, London,
with my grateful thanks.
I would never have completed it without them.

The success of a commander does not arise from following rules or models. It consists in an absolutely new comprehension of the dominant facts of the situation at the time and all the forces at work. Every great operation of war is unique. What is wanted is a profound appreciation of the actual event. There is no surer road to disaster than to imitate the plans of bygone heroes and fit them to a novel situation.

WINSTON S. CHURCHILL, *LIFE OF MARLBOROUGH*

CONTENTS

LIST OF MAPS AND ILLUSTRATIONS

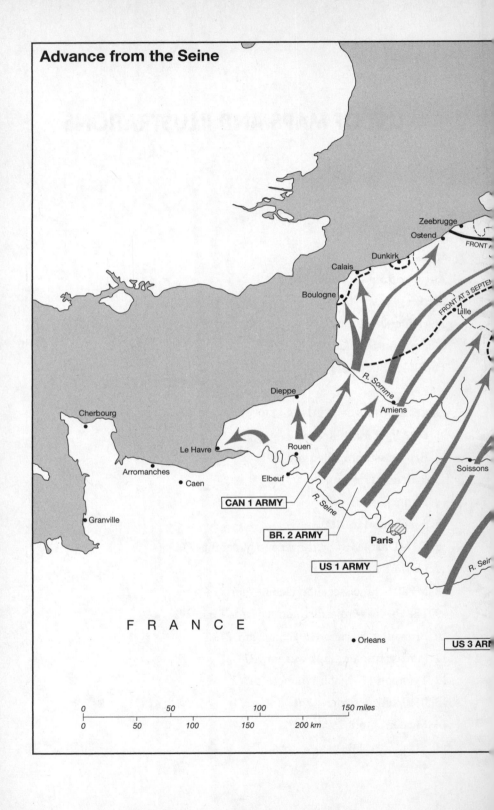

Advance from the Seine

Zeebrugge
Ostend
FRONT
Dunkirk
Calais
Boulogne
FRONT AT 3 SEPTEM
Lille
R. Somme
Dieppe
Amiens
Cherbourg
Le Havre
Rouen
Arromanches
Elbeuf
Soissons
Caen
CAN 1 ARMY
R. Seine
Granville
BR. 2 ARMY
Paris
US 1 ARMY
R. Seir

F R A N C E
Orleans
US 3 ARM

0		50		100		150 miles
0	50	100	150	200 km		

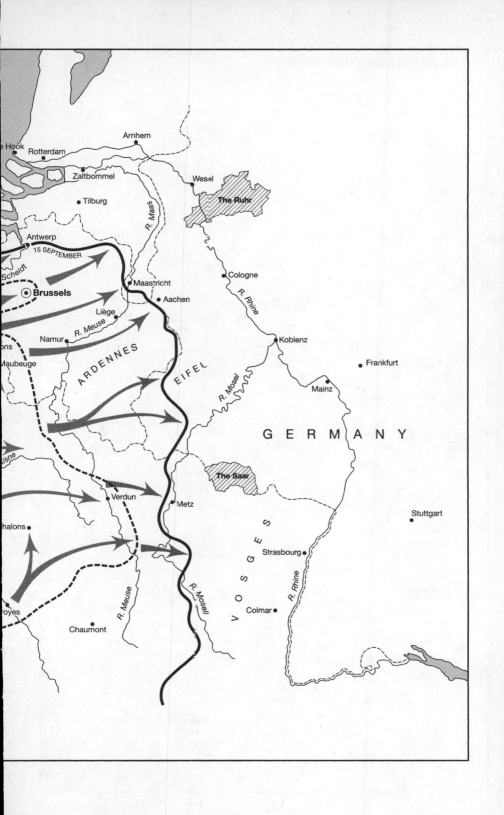

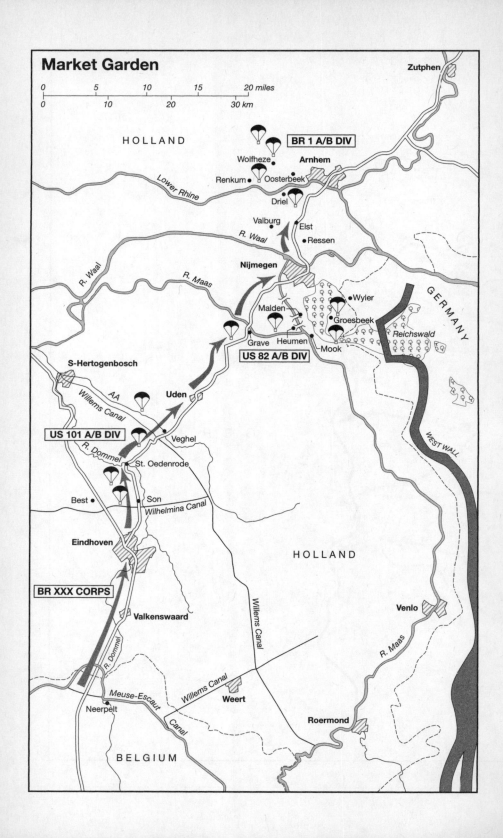

Market Garden

0 · · · 5 · · · 10 · · · 15 · · · 20 miles
0 · · · · 10 · · · · 20 · · · · 30 km

Zutphen

HOLLAND

BR 1 A/B DIV

Wolfheze
Arnhem

Renkum · Oosterbeek

Driel

Valburg

Elst

Ressen

R. Waal

Nijmegen

GERMANY

Wyler

Malden

Groesbeek

Grave · Heumen

Reichswald

US 82 A/B DIV

Mook

R. Waal

R. Maas

WEST WALL

S-Hertogenbosch

AA

Uden

Willems Canal

US 101 A/B DIV

R. Dommel

Veghel

St. Oedenrode

Best ·

Son

Wilhelmina Canal

HOLLAND

Eindhoven

BR XXX CORPS

Willems Canal

Venlo

Valkenswaard

R. Dommel

R. Maas

Meuse-Escaut Canal

Willems Canal

Weert

Neerpelt

Roermond

BELGIUM

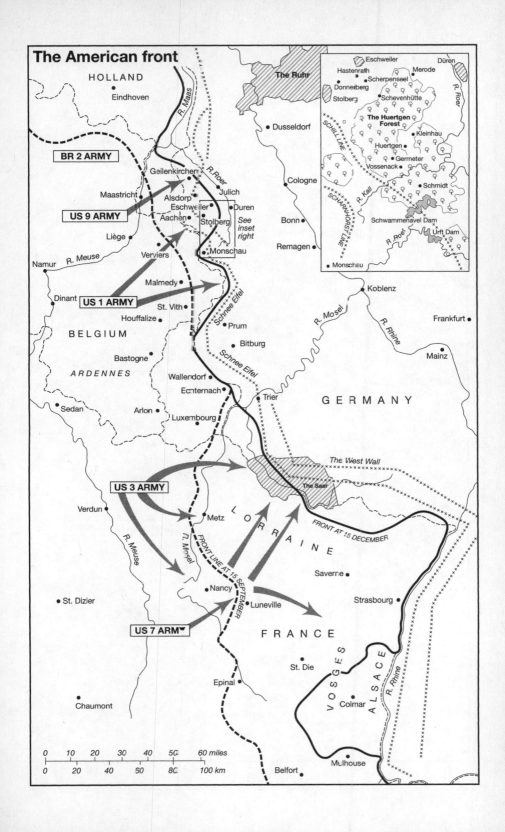

The American front

HOLLAND

The Ruhr

• Eindhoven

• Dusseldorf

Maastricht
Gailenkirchen
R. Roer
Julich
Alsdorp
Eschweiler
Duren
Aachen
Stolberg
See inset right

BR 2 ARMY

US 9 ARMY

• Liège

Verviers

• Cologne

• Bonn

• Remagen

Namur

R. Meuse

Monschau

US 1 ARMY

Malmedy

• Dinant

St. Vith

Houffalize

Schnee Eifel

Prum

• Koblenz

R. Mosel

R. Rhine

• Frankfurt

BELGIUM

• Bastogne

ARDENNES

• Bitburg

Schnee Eifel

Wallendorf

Ecternach

• Mainz

• Sedan

Arlon

Luxembourg

Trier

GERMANY

US 3 ARMY

The West Wall

• Verdun

R. Meuse

R. Mosel

• Metz

L O R R A I N E

The Saar

FRONT AT 15 DECEMBER

FRONT LINE AT 15 SEPTEMBER

• Saverne

• St. Dizier

Nancy

• Luneville

• Strasbourg

US 7 ARMY

F R A N C E

V O S G E S

A L S A C E

R. Rhine

• St. Die

• Epinal

• Chaumont

• Colmar

| 0 | 10 | 20 | 30 | 40 | 50 | 60 miles |
| 0 | 20 | 40 | 50 | 80 | 100 km | |

• Belfort

• Mulhouse

Inset (top right): The Huertgen Forest

Eschweiler
Hastenrath
Merode
Düren
Scherpenseel
Donnerberg
Schevenhütte
Stolberg
R. Roer

The Huertgen Forest

Kleinhau

Huertgen
Germeter
Vossenack
Schmidt

SCHILL LINE

R. Kall

SCHARNHORST LINE

Schwammenavel Dam

R. Roer

Urft Dam

• Monschau

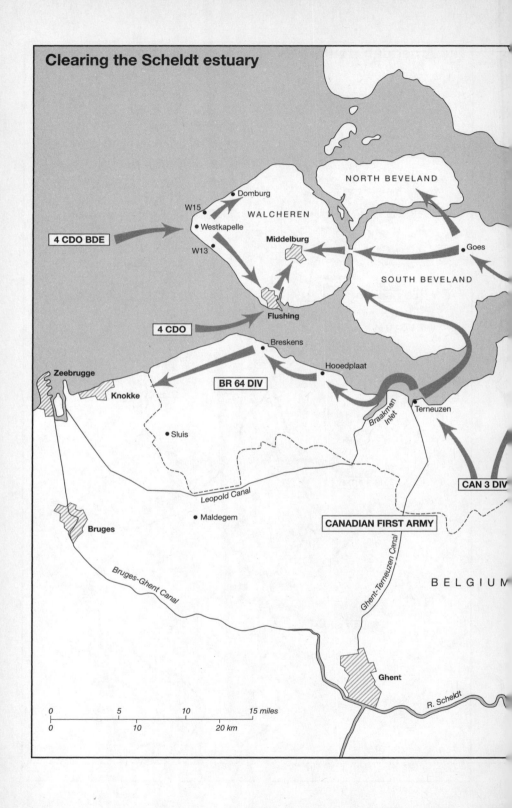

Clearing the Scheldt estuary

4 CDO BDE

Domburg
W15
Westkapelle
W13

WALCHEREN

Middelburg

NORTH BEVELAND

SOUTH BEVELAND

Goes

4 CDO

Flushing

Breskens

Hooedplaat

Terneuzen

Braakman Inlet

Zeebrugge

Knokke

BR 64 DIV

• Sluis

CAN 3 DIV

Leopold Canal

CANADIAN FIRST ARMY

• Maldegem

Bruges

Bruges-Ghent Canal

Ghent-Terneuzen Canal

BELGIUM

Ghent

R. Scheldt

0   5   10   15 miles
0   10   20 km

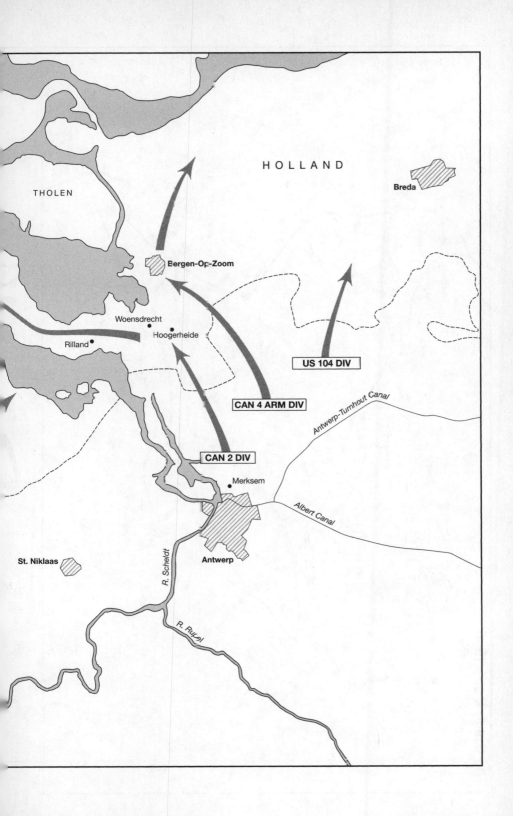

THOLEN

H O L L A N D

Breda

Bergen-Op-Zoom

Woensdrecht

Rilland

Hoogerheide

US 104 DIV

CAN 4 ARM DIV

CAN 2 DIV

Merksem

Antwerp-Turnhout Canal

Albert Canal

St. Niklaas

R. Scheldt

Antwerp

R. Rupel

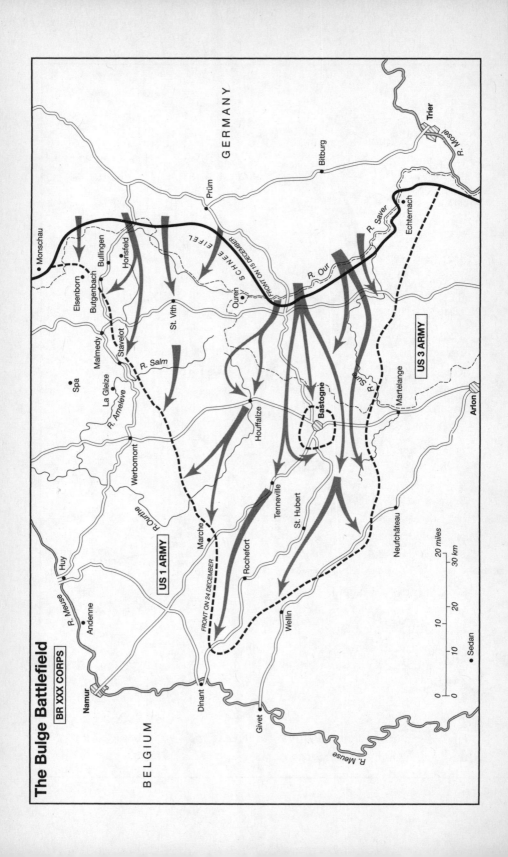

The Bulge Battlefield

BR XXX CORPS

GERMANY

Trier

R. Mosel

Bitburg

Prüm

R. Sayer

Echternach

S C H N E E   E I F E L

R. Our

Monschau

Eisenborn

Butgenbach

Bullingen

Honsfeld

Malmedy

Stavelot

R. Salm

St. Vith

Ouren

FRONT ON 15 DECEMBER

US 3 ARMY

Spa

La Gleize

R. Amel/eve

Werbomont

R. Ourthe

Houffalize

Bastogne

R. Sure

Martelange

Arlon

US 1 ARMY

Huy

R. Meuse

Andenne

Marche

Tenneville

St. Hubert

Rochefort

Neufchâteau

FRONT ON 24 DECEMBER

Namur

Dinant

Givet

Wellin

Sedan

R. Meuse

BELGIUM

0   10   20
0   10   20   30 km
20 miles

ACKNOWLEDGEMENTS

A great many people helped me with this book – as indeed they have done with all my other books. Whenever possible I have tried to include veteran accounts in my books and it is a sadness to note the number of veterans coming forward to advise on this one has shrunk considerably from those who came forward just a few years ago: all the more reason, then, to get their accounts of the Second World War into print before it is too late.

As ever, I have been able to rely on some stout-hearted supporters to keep me up to the mark. My thanks go, therefore, to Eric Garner, Royal Engineer sergeant, Chelsea Pensioner and *researcher extraordinaire,* for his assistance and mastery of the Internet. Next, to Major-General Julian Thompson, for reading the manuscript, for his many helpful comments and for lending me papers from his own book on the Parachute Regiment, *Ready for Anything.* Also to Major-General Ken Perkins for his encouragement and support; and my old 'oppo' Terry Brown, sometime of 42 Commando, Royal Marines, and a new colleague from the Oxford University Summer School, Paul McNicholls from Canada.

Among veteran organisations, I would like to thank the secretaries of the Normandy Veterans Association, especially Bob Smith of the Lincoln Branch, Mrs S. Rose of the Market Garden Veterans Association, and Major Ray Conningham of the Assault Glider Trust. Thanks also to the Royal Canadian Legion and the Royal British Legion.

Thanks must then go to Lord Carrington, General Sir David Fraser, Major George Thorne, and Major Frank Clark of the Guards Armoured Division, for their help with the chapters on Market Garden. Also to Major Charles Farrell of the 6th Guards Tank Brigade.

To Wally Harris, MM, for his help in tracking down veterans, and to Bill Hodkinson of the Jerboa Battery, 4th RHA, for his account of the advance through Belgium and on Market Garden; also to Sergeant Jack Lindley, MM, of the 2nd Lincolns. To Andrew Gibson-Watt, who has made a particular study of Market Garden. To Bob Smith of the 1st Lothians and Border Yeomanry. To Gordon Brennan and Les Wagar from Canada and to Doug Peterson of the 15 (S) Reconnaissance Regiment. To Bob Sudbury, on behalf of his father, who served in the Royal Canadian Artillery. To John Angus McDonald for sending me an account of the 3rd Canadian Infantry Division.

To David A. Taylor of the Lothians and Border Horse for permission to use extracts from his account of the advance on the Rhine with the 79th Armoured Division. To Bill Powell for his account of the fighting for the Walcheren causeway. To Gordon Mucklow of the 5th Duke of Cornwall's Light Infantry. To Sergeant Bill Heil, of the Canadian Armoured Carrier Regiment (the 'Kangaroos'). To Hans J. Wejers for his advice on SS units in Belgium. To Major F. Townsend of Liège, Belgium.

In the USA, to biographer and historian Carlo d'Este, to Professor Bob Berlin of the US Army Command and Staff College, Leavenworth, Kansas. To Jack Capell and Ralph Teeters of the US 4th Infantry Division for their accounts of the Battle of the Bulge. To Bill Everett of the US Seventh Army for his help with the story of Devers' 6th Army Group in the Vosges. To Zane Schlemmer of the 101st Airborne Division for his account of the Bulge fighting.

As always, thanks go to a wide range of museums, libraries and institutions: the National Army Museum and the Imperial War Museum, London; the National Archives, Kew; the Liddell Hart Centre for Military Archives, London; the ever-helpful staff of the London Library; and the various excellent museums at Arnhem and Bastogne.

And finally to my dear wife Judy, who kept me going in some difficult times and saw the work through.

ABOUT THIS BOOK

A commander likes to be popular but it isn't essential.
The essential thing is to win.

MAJOR-GENERAL JULIAN THOMPSON, CB, OBE

This is the fourth book I have written about the campaigns in France and North-West Europe between D-Day 1944 and VE Day, 1945. This is also the last one I shall write on the Second World War campaigns, and it is perhaps fortunate that I came to it when the others have been mulled over and the background to the events that took place between the Normandy breakout and the end of the Battle of the Bulge has already been explored. This book has proved the most difficult and the most complicated of the four and I am glad I came to it with a certain amount of experience under my belt.

My niche in the field of military history, such as it is, is as a 'myth buster'. I like to find a story and see if it is true, or entirely true, or partly composed of fact and partly of make-believe. I believe that in the period covered in this book, one glaring myth needs ventilating: the story of why Market Garden failed to achieve all it might have done, and why XXX Corps did not get to the Arnhem Bridge on D plus 2 of the operation, as they could have done. The chapters covering this part of the post-Normandy campaign make up the core of the book.

The previous books were not written in 'order of event'. *D-Day 1944,* written with Major Roderick de Normann, came in 1994, to mark the fiftieth anniversary of the Normandy landings. This was followed by *The Conquest of the Reich,* which picked up the Allied story after the Battle of the Bulge and carried it forward to VE Day. Then in 2002, came *The Battle of Normandy.* Copies of these books lie on my desk; I notice that each one is fatter than the last, the result of getting deeper into the subject and more involved with relevant events off the battlefield.

After writing about the Battle of Normandy it seemed logical to complete the task and bridge the gap between the end of the Normandy campaign in September 1944 and the end of the Battle of the Bulge in January 1945: so covering the post-Normandy period, when the Allied Armies were attempting to close on the Rhine. This task was undertaken before I fully realised how complicated and controversial the 1944 campaign for the Rhine had been.

Taken as a whole, the European war in the autumn and early winter of 1944–45 has been somewhat neglected by military historians. Perhaps this is because the campaign has no obvious end, or because British and Canadian attention has been attracted by the Battle of Arnhem, the Walcheren assault and the Battle of the Scheldt, while the Americans are drawn more to the epic Battle of the Bulge and the bitter struggles around Aachen and in the Huertgen Forest. For whatever reason, books on this period as a whole are a trifle thin on the ground. It is also possible, even probable, that the complex issues of the period have driven away many wise historians to more clear-cut conflicts.

The story of this time is not easy to unravel, but for this writer at least, the chief attraction of the period lies in its characters and its complexity. How to explain and evaluate the interlinked problems of command, terrain, logistics, strategy, policy, Anglo-US relations, press comment, Washington politics and, last but by no means least, the personalities and ambitions of the various Allied commanders, has kept me busy and fascinated for the last three years.

Looking back, the original idea was quite simple – to examine the various battles that took place in North-West Europe between the Normandy breakout and the end of the Bulge: Operation Market Garden, better known in Britain as the Battle of Arnhem, Aachen, the Huertgen Forest, Walcheren, the Scheldt, the Saar, Metz, Lorraine, the Colmar Pocket and the Bulge itself; and see how they contributed or detracted from the overall strategy of the campaign. At which point in the research I ran into difficulty. I was unable to see what exactly the strategy *was* for this campaign – indeed, this book might well be sub-titled *Battles in Search of a Strategy*.

If this seems odd, let me explain. While every military historian approaches the task in his or her own way, my method is to regard the strategy – best imagined as the overall plan for a particular campaign – as the blueprint for that campaign and the various battles as steps contributing towards the achievement of the campaign's objectives.

For example, during the Normandy campaign Allied strategy was always clear, though subject to change: change is understandable, for strategy is not set in stone. After the D-Day assault, the British Second Army would hold the left flank of the bridgehead, while the US First Army took the port of Cherbourg. In other words, the first strategic requirement for the two Allied armies in Normandy was to hold the left flank of the bridgehead and capture the port of Cherbourg. Other factors might intervene but nothing must detract from those two strategic aims, both of which were vital to the successful outcome of the entire campaign.

Then the strategy changed somewhat. Having taken Cherbourg, the US First Army must then secure the city of St Lô as the start line for the eventual breakout, while the British and Canadians, though still holding the eastern flank of the bridgehead secure, must also attract as many German panzer divisions as possible onto that eastern flank and wear them down in battles of attrition around Caen.

Finally, at the end of July, the US First Army, later joined by the Third Army, broke out in the West and combined with the British and Canadian forces to push the German armies – Seventh Army and Fifth Panzer Army – across the Seine in headlong retreat.

The point is that there was always a clear Allied strategy in Normandy. This overall strategy was worked out before D-Day by the British commander of 21st Army Group – and Ground Force Commander for the invasion phase of Operation Overlord – General Sir Bernard Law Montgomery, a man better known as 'Monty', and approved by the Supreme Allied Commander, General Dwight D. Eisenhower – known to all as 'Ike' – and this strategy duly delivered victory in the Normandy campaign.

My task in the Normandy book was therefore relatively simple – to slot the various battles of that campaign – at Villers-Bocage, Cherbourg, Caen, in the bocage, at St Lô, Hill 112, Vire, Mont Pinchon, Mortain, Falaise, together with Allied operations like Perch, Jupiter, Epsom, Goodwood, Cobra and the rest – into that strategy, and see how they contributed to the final outcome.

The Normandy campaign was not without its glitches and difficulties and accusation of incompetence, plus a goodly layer of self-serving myth. The various controversies about that campaign and those battles flourish to this day, but the strategy – the broad picture, the background to events, the basic plan – was always clear, at least to those at SHAEF not totally devoted to destroying the career and reputation of General Montgomery.

Not so the battles and events that took place during the battle for the Rhine between 1 September 1944 and the end of the Battle of the Bulge in January 1945. Study this period and a consistent, logical strategy to reach the Rhine – and perhaps end the war in 1944 – seems elusive. Indeed, the very phrase, 'The Battle for the Rhine', is my own construct, created to give some shape to the arguments and a title to the book.

The US Official History (*The Siegfried Line Campaign*, p. 39) records an order to General Gerow, commanding the V Corps in Hodges' First US Army, to *'penetrate the West Wall'*, the first step into Germany and towards the River Rhine. That order was issued on 11 September 1944: the first Allied troops actually crossed the Rhine six months later and they came from the 9th US Armored Division, which took the Rhine bridge at Remegen on 7 March 1945, just eight weeks before the war in Europe ended. Given the growing power of the Allied armies in Western Europe post D-Day 1944, what can account for this long delay? When all other factors are considered the answer must surely lie in the areas of command and strategy, and the first difficulty in writing this book arises from my failure to identify a clear, logical, consistent, strategic plan for this final 1944 campaign. Yes, the aim of the war was the defeat of Germany but the question constantly arises: what was the strategy *now*, the one that would contribute to that outcome in the immediate future? Unlike in Normandy, the strategic plan in North-West Europe seems continually confused by a wealth of options with no clear, sustained policy. This itself causes a problem. For without a grasp of the basic strategy – the means of attaining the aim – it is hard to answer the basic question: *'What are the generals – or, more often, the Allied Supreme Commander – trying to do here?'* Or, when considering some particular engagement, say the Huertgen Forest battles: '*Where is all this loss and bloodshed leading?'*

Attempting to answer these questions is one aim of this book. It is also an attempt to decide, among the welter of objectives and difficulties facing the Allied commanders, what clear, logical, course of action might have proved more effective and possibly ended the European War in 1944 or at least put the Allied armies – American, British, Canadian – in a better position to win it in 1945.

In seeking this last objective I have to be careful. Historians should not 'play general' and take it on themselves to dictate some course of action to former commanders. Hindsight is a wonderful gift and historians would be lost without it, but hindsight has its dangers. On the other hand, the spectator, especially from a distance, often sees more of the game. We can see the final outcome of events and judge how much of the contemporary controversy was necessary or relevant. Military operations are never easy and I am always sympathetic to the problems of the commanding generals: they bear great responsibilities and must make hard decisions in the knowledge that, good or bad, those decisions are sending men to their deaths.

Even so, one is entitled to expect a certain level of competence and foresight in a commander. He has to know his job. He has to understand the importance of such basic military principles as the selection and maintenance of the aim and the need for a concentration of force. At the same time he must not be dominated by doctrine or pre-established opinions. He must have a strong sense of priority and the ability – and courage – to make decisions based on a cold calculation of the available relevant facts, and hopefully, without one eye on the favourable judgement of posterity or the contemporary press.

This last point is relevant because posterity – and the press – has decided that the Supreme Allied Commander, General Dwight D. Eisenhower, who took over field command of the Allied armies in September 1944, was a very nice guy and therefore an outstanding general, while Field Marshal Sir Bernard Law Montgomery was a nasty piece of work of no particular competence and only good for set piece attacks. There is a certain amount of truth in both con-clusions – plus a considerable amount of myth – but in the context of a major war the relevance escapes me. Fighting men died while the generals bickered: arguing about who gets the eventual credit for a decision is less important than making the right decision in the first place.

However, strange though it may seem, the issue of popularity is important in the context of this campaign, which is one reason for covering that issue regularly in this book. Because Eisenhower was a nice guy, so runs one argument, criticism of his generalship can only be taken as a personal attack. No one has ever accused Montgomery of being a nice guy, but his generalship in the field is under constant attack, and on very little evidence. What is the relevance of pop-ularity in this context? Are these men up to the tasks they are charged with or not? As Major-General Julian Thompson points out, popularity is not important in a commander – what is important is that a general *must win*.

General Dwight Eisenhower – Ike – rightly emerged from the Second World

War as a wildly popular hero, a revered Allied Supreme Commander who eventually became President of the United States. No one can dispute his talents as
Supreme Commander... but whether Eisenhower was a successful *field
commander* in the campaigns after September 1944 is quite another matter. And
yet the question of popularity, which I would otherwise happily ignore, cannot
be dismissed because it was considered relevant *at the time*.

In the context of a war in which men were dying or being maimed in large
numbers every day, the editorial opinions expressed in the *Boston Globe* or the
Cleveland *Plain Dealer* about the conduct of the war seem less than important –
but they were read by the American public, who voted in the politicians, who
spoke to General George C. Marshall, the US Chief of Staff, and he passed
these comments on to Eisenhower and demanded action: specifically that the
American generals must run the European war and take full credit for the
eventual victory.

One must not be naive. It is too much to expect that a battlefield commander
can make his decisions solely on the basis of the factors immediately confronting
his command – the enemy, the ground, his own forces, the problems of weather
and supply. All too often, other factors, political or personal, have a tendency
to intervene and so it was here, during the post-Normandy campaign.

As we shall see in the ensuing pages, many extraneous factors set far from the
front line – the US Presidential elections of 1944, the views of George Marshall,
press comment in Britain and the USA, public opinion, various antipathies
between the nations and the commanders, the hunt for glory, recognition and
much more besides – had a direct bearing on the conduct of this campaign and
the controversies arising from it.

The Americans have a saying: '*Nice guys don't win ball games*', and very true it
is. In writing of other generals and campaigns I have noticed that the hard-
driving general is usually the one who wins the battle or campaign and does so
with fewer casualties – General Patton being an exception to the latter half of this
rule. Given the choice, front line soldiers would take the efficient martinet over
the amiable duffer every time. There is no apparent reason why a general cannot
be both competent and a nice guy, but the combination is rare. The US commanders liked General Sir Harold Alexander and would have much preferred
him to Montgomery, but an examination of General Alexander's performance
in Sicily and Italy leads one to the reluctant conclusion that, for all his charm,

General Alexander was lazy and somewhat short of 'grip' – the essential quality for any commander, consisting of the ability to issue clear orders and get them obeyed – qualities that, as we shall see, General Eisenhower often failed to display in adequate amounts. No one ever accused Montgomery of lacking 'grip'.

In the course of this book it will sometimes seem as if the generals devoted more energy to fighting among themselves than to fighting the enemy; and that the hatred they had for the enemy was as nothing to the loathing the US generals felt for Montgomery and the British. It all makes for a sad, frustrating, but fascinating story.

One final point. Reviewing my book on the Battle of Normandy, one critic said I had 'chosen to defend that unlikely hero, Field Marshal Montgomery'. This is probably true, since I believe Montgomery's contribution to the Normandy campaign has been grossly underrated. On the other hand, I would hesitate to describe myself, or let myself be described, as a Montgomery partisan. I am fully aware of the Field Marshal's numerous faults and personal failings, and know he had a unique talent for upsetting his superiors and colleagues. If I have defended him, it is because his professional reputation as a military commander has been under constant and bitter attack, mostly ill judged, and mostly from American historians, for the past six decades.

That damning reputation seems in need of reappraisal and while freely admitting Montgomery could be vastly irritating, frequently cautious in battle, and not above tampering with the truth in his subsequent account of events, I believe he was, nevertheless, a first-class general who has been persistently and unjustly traduced by people who were not fit to polish his boots. This may not be a popular view but, to echo General Thompson's comment yet again, historians should not seek popularity. It is rather more important to muster the facts, avoid bias as far as possible and – above all – be fair to the people involved. In attempting this task I have one considerable asset: a deep love of the United States and a profound admiration of the American soldier. I simply don't *do* chauvinism; I cannot see the point of it; and it flies in the face of my personal experience. I have had the privilege of meeting many American veterans in the course of my work: better men, finer soldiers and nicer people do not breathe.

I find I can manage all that while remaining proud of the fact that I am British and an equally strong admirer of that wonderful, dauntless, bloody-minded human being, the British soldier. To be quite frank, I can find very little difference between American and British soldiers apart from the fact that one likes tea and the other coffee, and if the old photographs are anything to go by, the British soldier stands a little closer to the razor while shaving.

This book will follow the Allied soldiers – American, British, Canadian, Dutch, French, Polish – in some of the hardest campaigns of the Second World War. Much of this book is about the generals, but the heroes are the men in the foxholes and trenches, in the tanks, and manning the guns: the fighting soldiers of the Allied armies, whose sufferings and sacrifices in the battles for the Rhine should never be forgotten.

1 · THE END IN NORMANDY

AUGUST 1944

If it ain't broke, don't fix it.

OLD AMERICAN PROVERB

The Battle of Normandy ended officially on 1 September 1944. That date also marked the end of the invasion phase, the three-month struggle to break out of the Normandy bridgehead formed after D-Day, and therefore of General Sir Bernard Montgomery's tenure as Allied Ground Force Commander. All in all, General Montgomery could look back on his time in that post with considerable satisfaction. Since 6 June, when the Allied Armies stormed the Normandy beaches, they had got ashore and stayed ashore and, having routed the German armies, were now in the process of pursuing a beaten foe towards the distant frontiers of Germany. Final victory was just round the corner... or so it seemed.

That was certainly the view of the Allied High Command. According to a SHAEF (Supreme Headquarters Allied Expeditionary Force) intelligence summary, issued on 26 August: 'The end of the war in Europe is in sight, almost within reach. The strength of the German Armies in the West has been shattered, Paris belongs to France again and the Allied Armies are streaming towards the frontiers of the Reich.'

These hopeful comments were borne out by the current progress of the Allied armies. By dawn on the morning of 1 September all these armies were across the Seine. To the west of Rouen, in the operational area of Montgomery's 21st Army Group, the six divisions of Lieutenant General Harry Crerar's First

Canadian Army was pushing hard for the Channel coast, though stoutly opposed by the German Fifteenth Army, a force which had largely escaped the debacle in Normandy and was tasked with defending the Channel ports.

On the right flank of the Canadians, Lieutenant General Sir Miles Dempsey's British Second Army, consisting of three armoured divisions and five infantry divisions, was thrusting north towards the Belgian frontier, with an armoured spearhead already at Amiens in Picardy, driving before it such shattered remnants of the Fifth Panzer Army as had managed to cross the Seine.

In the centre of the Allied advance, part of General Omar Bradley's 12th US Army Group, the US First Army of Lieutenant General Courtney Hodges, consisting of four armoured divisions and six infantry divisions, was advancing more slowly, but on a broader front, and had pushed beyond the River Aisne to Laon, its progress barely delayed by such bedraggled elements of the German Seventh Army as had managed to escape from Normandy. Away to the east of Paris, the second force in Bradley's Group, Lieutenant General George Patton's Third Army, consisting of two armoured divisions and four infantry divisions, had already reached the River Meuse and taken the city of Verdun, eighty miles east of Paris.

Patton's troops had made swift progress since crossing the Seine two weeks before, forging rapidly ahead in the face of slight opposition, but were about to encounter the German First Army, which had three panzer divisions and three panzer-grenadier divisions defending the city of Metz and the southern gateway to the Reich beyond the Saar.

Finally, further south in the Rhône valley, the troops of Lieutenant General Jacob Devers' 6th Army Group (the US Seventh Army – three armoured divisions and nine infantry divisions – and the First French Army – three armoured divisions and nine infantry divisions), was pressing north, driving back the German Nineteenth Army. The basic aim of all the Allied armies at this time was to push the pursuit, keeping the enemy on the run with no chance to rest, regroup or take up a defensive position. The enemy was in full retreat and the task now was to keep him retreating all the way back to Germany – and at the end of August 1944, this aim seemed attainable.

However, this rosy picture of Allied success fails to reveal the entire position. Some chronic problems were starting to arise, problems over supply and transport, and matters of strategy and command: problems that called for difficult and controversial decisions. Not all those Allied divisions were advancing: some had been stopped, or 'grounded', either because they had no fuel or their transport was needed to carry fuel forward to the rest.

The matter of logistics was coming into play, and not to the Allied advantage. As the Germans fell back, their supply lines were shortening, while those of the Allied armies grew ever more stretched: the problem of transport and supply was starting to rear its ugly head among the Allied staff, for unless the front line troops were supplied, how could this rapid advance continue?

Nor were the Germans routed. The German armies were certainly retreating, but when they turned at bay even a small kampfgruppe – perhaps an infantry company supported by a couple of tanks – was fully capable of giving the pursuers a bloody nose: a daily indication to their front line pursuers that the German Army could fight back, and would do so with increasing strength if given the chance to muster.

It therefore seemed that how soon the Allied armies would reach the frontiers of the Reich, and how soon the European war ended, would depend very largely on what happened in the next few days or weeks, not least on how – and rather more to the present purpose, how soon – the Supreme Allied Commander, General Eisenhower, addressed the crucial questions of command, strategy and supply for the post-Normandy campaign and decided on his policy for the next phase of the battle. If he got it right, victory in 1944 was considered possible, even probable; if he got it wrong, victory would certainly be delayed and more hard times lay ahead. Even with the enemy in full retreat, nothing could be taken for granted.

It is said that victory has a thousand fathers, while defeat is an orphan. The problem with victory is that the fathers quickly start wrangling over who should get the credit and what should happen next in order to exploit that victory and garner the laurels. Such problems, but most notably those arguments on how the Normandy victory should be exploited, were already exercising higher minds at Eisenhower's headquarters in the Cotentin and at Montgomery's tactical headquarters in the field. The strategy that had delivered victory in Normandy had run its course; another strategy would be needed to carry the armies to the German frontier and beyond.

The task of developing and implementing this new strategy lay with Eisenhower and with no one else. On 1 September 1944 he would replace

Montgomery as Ground Force Commander, adding that demanding portfolio to his already extensive responsibilities as Supreme Allied Commander in Europe. Even before taking over direct command of the Army Groups, Eisenhower's responsibilities were awesome. He was responsible to the Combined Chiefs of Staff in Washington and to his direct superior and mentor, General George C. Marshall, the US Chief of Staff. He was in regular contact with Winston Churchill, the British Prime Minister and Minister of Defence. He was responsible for the supply of his armies, the overall direction of the war in Western Europe, and the civil administration in the newly liberated territories – not least for feeding the French and enduring the demands of the Free French leader, General Charles de Gaulle. In 1944, all roads, all chains of command, led to Ike's headquarters at SHAEF – and now he had to exercise day-to-day command of three Allied Army Groups in the field. In this task he was hardly helped by Lieutenant General J. C. H. Lee, who actually ran the US Army logistic system to his own satisfaction.

Moreover, with the enemy in full retreat, decisions over future strategy and the issuing of orders for this new campaign could not wait. The Allied armies were already over the Seine and in hot pursuit of the retreating foe, heading in all directions, some north, some east, some north-east, each army pursuing the enemy to its front. This was fine as far as it went, but where was it all leading? Firm orders had to be issued governing the progress of future events in order to give some shape, some direction, and some strategic purpose to the present endeavours of the Allied armies. Local successes on their own are of little use: in order to exploit the successes of Normandy, the Allied armies had to be directed towards some common aim and not fight separate wars. Selecting a sound strategy for the next phase of the war in Western Europe was not going to be easy. The difficulties confronting the Allied Supreme Commander should not be underestimated.

The fundamental problem facing the Allies at the end of August was one of priority – of what to do next – and this issue concentrated in two main areas. At the moment the enemy was on the run and all the accumulated wisdom of military history dictated that he should be kept on the run. On the other hand, the looming problems of supply dictated that the Allied armies should stop and regroup, shortening their supply lines before another major advance: if they failed to solve the supply problem, they would probably grind to a halt anyway.

But if they halted they would be giving the enemy time to rest and regroup. Given time, the enemy would bring up more troops and either prepare fresh defensive positions or occupy the existing defensive positions on the German frontier – the West Wall or Siegfried Line. So here was the first point of decision: should the pursuit continue – if that were logistically possible – or should the Supreme Commander halt his armies on the line of the Seine, bring up supplies and shorten his supply lines before a further advance, knowing that such a pause would hand precious time back to the enemy?

The next dilemma concerned the need to decide on the best route from the Seine towards Germany. Whether the Supreme Commander opted for hot pursuit now or a set piece advance later, there were four possible roads to the Rhine. The first lay across the Flanders plain to the Lower Rhine and Holland, avoiding much of the German West Wall defences and paving a path to the industrial area of the Ruhr and Berlin. The second option was the traditional invasion route into Germany, through the Aachen Gap, north of the Ardennes towards Cologne and the Rhine. The third was to drive directly through the Ardennes, back up the route the Germans had taken in their blitzkrieg offensive of 1940. The last was to follow General Patton on the road east, entering Germany via Metz and the Saar industrial area and so to Frankfurt.

Each route offered advantages and disadvantages, but which one offered the best chance of a quick victory, always assuming one route alone was advisable? Should the Supreme Commander not go for two or even three routes – or even all four, to split the enemy's declining strength? But would the current state of supply support several thrusts? Once again, decisions were called for. There was no obvious solution, no easy answer… but some decision was needed and needed soon, or the Allied armies would be without direction.

For help in making these decisions, Eisenhower could look at the studies provided by SHAEF before D-Day. Having rejected the Flanders plain route (too many rivers and canals) and the Ardennes route (terrible terrain), the planners had reduced the choice of route to two, via Aachen or the Saar, north and south of the Ardennes, and by the end of August the latter option was already being hotly pursued by General Patton. On the other hand, there were the proposals put forward by Ike's British subordinate and Ground Force Commander – at least for a few more days – General Sir Bernard Montgomery, a man who, for all his faults, was never short of ideas. Monty's current idea was to form a battering ram and push the Germans back to the Rhine in the north, ignoring the watery problems of the Flanders plain.

On 18 August Montgomery outlined his ideas on future strategy in a letter to the Chief of the Imperial General Staff (CIGS), Field Marshal Alanbrooke. Monty suggested that after crossing the Seine, two Army Groups, Bradley's 12th and Montgomery's 21st, should: 'keep together as a solid mass of forty divisions, which would be so strong that it need fear nothing.' This force, said Monty, should advance northwards, 21st Army Group on the western flank to clear the Channel coast, the Pas de Calais, West Flanders, and secure the vital port of Antwerp and south Holland before moving across the Rhine in the north and so to the Ruhr. Meanwhile, the 12th Army Group would form the eastern flank of this manoeuvre and move with their right flank on the Ardennes – being directed via the Aachen Gap towards Cologne and the Rhine. Such a move would lead to a pincer-like thrust on the Ruhr, the industrial centre of the German Reich.

On the previous day, 17 August, Montgomery had discussed this plan at a private meeting with his American colleague, General Omar Bradley, and come away with the impression that, as he told Alanbrooke, 'Bradley agrees entirely with the above project', and would support this scheme when they presented it jointly to General Eisenhower.

Monty could not have been more wrong. Bradley had already been working on another scheme with his Third Army commander, Lieutenant General George Patton, to whom Bradley deferred too often, and Bradley had no intention whatsoever of following any plan proposed by Bernard Montgomery. It might have been more honest if Bradley had said so at their meeting, for Bradley and Patton proposed a 'predominantly American plan for emphasis on a thrust to the Reich straight through the middle of France to the Saar and beyond the Saar to the Rhine in the vicinity of Frankfurt... both the First and Third US Armies would be required for this main effort.'[1]

As any possibility of a joint approach to the Supreme Commander by the two Army Group commanders fell apart, the matter of future strategy became an ongoing debate that occupied higher minds at SHAEF during the latter days of August. The outcome could only be settled by General Eisenhower.

Therefore, on 20 August Eisenhower called a meeting at his HQ in Normandy. This was attended by the SHAEF staff and General Bradley, with

Major-General Freddie de Guingand, 21st Army Group's Chief of Staff, representing Montgomery. It appears to have been a committee meeting rather than an Orders Group, one to discuss options rather than issue instructions, but two decisions were reached. First, confirmation that Ike would take direct command of the Army Groups on 1 September. Second, that Bradley's 12th Army Group was to advance towards Metz and the Saar and link up with Devers' Army Group – currently called the Dragoon Force – as it came up the Rhône valley. This decision shifted the weight of Allied strategy to the east and left the 21st Army Group with no clear strategic role, other than to clear the Channel ports, eliminate German rocket and flying bomb sites in the Pas de Calais, and capture the port of Antwerp.

The SHAEF staff was about to issue orders for this move when de Guingand suggested they should wait until Montgomery could be consulted. De Guingand then briefed Montgomery on what had been decided and Monty sent him back to Eisenhower with a page of notes on future strategy.

Readers may wonder why Montgomery did not attend the 20 August meeting in person, or fly at once to Eisenhower's HQ to state his case, rather than use the mediation of his Chief of Staff on both occasions. As we shall see, Monty rarely attended SHAEF meetings, citing pressure of business or – more discreetly – admitting that since he was vastly unpopular at SHAEF and with his American colleagues, 21st Army Group's case would be better put by the well-liked Freddie de Guingand. Whatever the true reason for non-attendance, Montgomery's absence from these meetings was a serious mistake.

Montgomery's note to Eisenhower was both brief and blunt:

1 The quickest way to win this war is for the great mass of the Allied Armies to advance northwards, clear the coast as far as Antwerp, establish a powerful air force in Belgium and advance into the Ruhr.

2 This force must operate as one whole, with great cohesion, and be so strong it can do the job quickly.

3 Single control and direction of the land operations is vital for success. This is a WHOLE-TIME JOB for one man.

4 The great victory in N.W. France has been won by personal command; only

in this way will future victories be won. If staff control of operations is allowed to creep in, then quick success becomes endangered.

5 To change the system of command now, after having won a good victory, would be to prolong the war.

This statement might profit from a little analysis. It covers two linked but separate issues, command and strategy, and represents the opening shots in a battle that would continue throughout the Rhine campaign. The strategy issue arises in Point 1 and the command issue in Points 4 and 5.

There is little to quibble about in Point 1. Germany had – and still has – two major industrial areas, the Ruhr and the Saar. Of these two, the Ruhr basin is by far the larger and most productive. If Germany lost the Ruhr it would no longer be able to prosecute the war. There is no need to debate this point for no one has ever denied it, at the time or in the decades since; Eisenhower was as eager to get to the Ruhr as Montgomery and equally aware of its importance. In addition, this strong thrust to the north by the Allied armies would clear the Channel coast, remove the V-1 and V-2 threat to London, and open the port of Antwerp, a port large enough to supply all the Allied armies for the subsequent advance into Germany, so solving the looming logistical problem. All in all, it is hard to fault Montgomery's memorandum on matters of strategy. The problem was that it flew in the face of Eisenhower's decision of 20 August and departed from reality over the command issue, in what was seen as a clear bid to retain his role of Ground Force Commander.

As we shall see, Montgomery was to harp on about the issues of strategy and command for the next several months and linking the two issues was a fundamental mistake. He might have carried the strategic argument, but he lost it by linking strategy to the question of command. Eisenhower was open to argument over strategy, perhaps because he never really grasped what strategy meant, but he knew all about the question of command and the desirability of keeping it in US hands. Ike was determined to hang onto the field command of the Allied armies in Europe and was backed in this resolve by his superior in Washington, the US Chief of Staff, and Chairman of the Allied Combined Chiefs of Staff Committee, General George C. Marshall.

The question of command in war is always crucial and never more so than in this Allied pursuit phase after the Normandy campaign. Roosevelt and Marshall wanted a US general in command of the Allied armies in Europe. Marshall had wanted the command himself and only gave up that ambition at the request of President Roosevelt, who needed him in Washington. However, if Marshall could not have the European command, the man he wanted for the job was his surrogate, Dwight D. Eisenhower.

There were three main reasons for this decision. Firstly, military demographics. The bulk of the troops in the European Theatre of Operations (ETO) were American and the US percentage could only increase as Britain and Canada had run out of manpower: it was therefore both logical and inevitable that a US general should command the Allied armies. Secondly, or so Marshall alleged, the US press and public would no longer tolerate American troops serving under British command. Finally, or so it was said, the US generals detested Montgomery, and would not serve under him.

These views require analysis, and to understand the issues it is necessary to go back to the command arrangements established for the D-Day landings and the Normandy campaign. As already described, Montgomery had prepared the strategic plan for the Battle of Normandy and had been entrusted with the conduct of the campaign as the Allied Ground Force Commander for the invasion phase. The duration of the invasion phase had never been spelled out, but it was tacitly accepted to cover the period up to the Normandy breakout. After that, Eisenhower intended to take on the role of Ground Force Commander in addition to that of Allied Supreme Commander.

This had always been the command set-up but now the moment for the changeover was at hand, Montgomery demurred. He believed the command set-up that had delivered victory in Normandy should be continued. The Americans disagreed and their first point, military demographics, appears perfectly valid; the US had more troops 'in theatre' and it seemed only right that the senior command posts should go to American commanders.

However, this point ignores two details: that the Allied Supreme Commander – the most senior command of all – was an American, and that US troops had served under British tactical command in Normandy and were currently serving under British command in Italy, without significant complaint from anywhere outside the ranks of the generals and certain politicians. The first point also begs the question: if national command was judged so vital to national morale, why should it be supposed that the million-plus British and Canadian troops in Europe would be content to serve under US commanders?

On the matter of US press and public opinion, where is the evidence of widespread discontent in the USA? Television was not widely available at this time and unlike Britain the USA does not have national newspapers like *The Daily Telegraph* and *The Sun*. The archives of such major US newspapers as *The New York Herald Tribune* do indeed reveal leaders and feature articles from US correspondents at SHAEF, complaining about Montgomery's 'slowness' and 'caution' during the Normandy battle, and the widespread British influence at Allied HQ, but fail to mention that the senior British officers at SHAEF, Tedder, Coningham and Morgan, were all Eisenhower loyalists and devoted enemies of Montgomery. While any military contingent – American, British, Canadian – would probably feel happier serving under its own national commanders, there is scant evidence that the US public at home or the US soldiers in the ETO were up in arms over the command issue.

The US newspapers of 1944 contain few references to any soldiers in the European theatre other than US troops, who as 'Yanks', 'Eisenhower's men' or 'Patton's Army' are depicted as 'storming', 'surging' or 'advancing' in all directions at this time. An American civilian in 1944 – or indeed today – would be hard pressed to realise that British, Canadian, French or Polish troops were serving in Western Europe *at all,* either in Normandy or the subsequent campaign. (In the course of taking four American groups to the Normandy beaches in 2004, over 200 people in all, the author did not find one who was even remotely aware of the full extent of the British/Canadian participation on D-Day. One visitor, making his third visit to the D-Day beaches, had never previously been east of Omaha beach.)

However, Marshall and the US generals alleged the US public were exercised over this issue and that US public opinion was vitally important to winning the war. 'Public opinion wins wars', Eisenhower told Montgomery – to which Montgomery replied bluntly: 'Victories win wars; give the public victory and they won't care who won it.'

Remove the US generals' chronic craving for publicity and this seems to be correct. Back home in Canada or Britain or the USA, the families wanted their men back in one piece and as quickly as possible. Provided that happened, questions of national prestige were irrelevant. The truth is that the US generals raised the public opinion issue because it seemed a better reason to advance than the real one, military demographics: 'we have more troops here and we intend to run the show.'

The final reason – attitudes to General Montgomery at SHAEF – has rather more validity. Montgomery was indeed vastly unpopular with some US generals; their post-war memoirs – especially those of General Bradley and the US parachute commanders – are laced with sneers at Montgomery and snide remarks about the British. However, it has to be said that Montgomery was also detested by many of the senior British officers at SHAEF, notably Air Marshal Tedder, Eisenhower's Deputy, Air Chief Marshal Coningham, commander of the 2nd Tactical Air Force, and Lieutenant General Sir Frederick Morgan, the originator of the pre-invasion Cossac Plan and now Deputy Chief of Staff at SHAEF to General Bedell Smith – people in an ideal position to drip poison about Montgomery into the ears of Eisenhower and the US newspaper and radio correspondents accredited to the ETO.

Montgomery was detested because, in many ways, he was indeed detestable. He was vain, dictatorial, obsessive, a sore trial to his peers and superiors and not above tinkering with the truth, though he was not alone in any of this. On the other hand, Montgomery was beloved by his soldiers, affable with his subordinates, capable of admitting mistakes and supportive of his Allies – and the most experienced and professional Allied general in Western Europe.

The reasons for this ongoing American antipathy to Montgomery, which still exists, sixty years after the end of the war, are very hard to comprehend, but should be considered, for they affected the command arrangements and the conduct of the 1944 campaign. Montgomery was actually in command of US forces for some ninety days in Normandy; ninety days during six years of war – or three and a half years of war for the Americans – and then at a distance, for Omar Bradley commanded the US armies in the Normandy campaign.

During six years of war Monty commanded British, Canadian, Australian, New Zealand, Indian, Polish French, Greek and Italian troops in battle and on campaign. None of these national contingents complain about General Montgomery,[2] but from the USA we have had nothing but a sixty-year-long whine about Monty's various transgressions, his professional failings, and how impossible he was to work with – coupled with those aforementioned sneers at the 'slowness' and 'caution' of the British Army. It should be noted that these whines usually come from US generals and their sycophantic historians – very few complaints about Monty or the British will be heard from American front line fighting men.

Other Allied generals – Canadian, Australian, New Zealand – may not have always seen eye to eye with Montgomery, but they got along with him perfectly well, and many US generals seemed quite content with his methods and manner. Writing on the Normandy campaign after the war Bradley wrote that he: 'could not have wished for a more considerate commander.' On 22 June 1944, just two weeks into the Normandy campaign, General Walter Bedell Smith, a man not noted for flattery and no fan of Monty, wrote to Montgomery stating that he had heard from an unimpeachable source that the American troops: 'talked about General Montgomery with actual hero-worship.' What appealed to them, said Bedell Smith, beyond Monty's friendliness, genuineness and lack of pomp, was that the general: 'visited every one of the outfits going over and told us he was more anxious than any of us to get this thing over and get home.' Bedell Smith added that: 'Having spent my life with American soldiers, and knowing only too well their innate distrust of anything foreign, I can appreciate far better than you what a triumph of leadership you accomplished in inspiring such feeling and confidence.'

Montgomery's faults were personal, not professional, but the first affected peoples' attitudes to the latter. Even so, the fact that Monty was difficult to handle should not be allowed to obscure the fact that he was a professional soldier to his fingertips, a general who took good care of his men, knew what he was doing, and had a very clear idea of how the post-Normandy campaign should be fought; that is, to a clear, logical, progressive *strategic plan*, not to an ad hoc series of arrangements, altered day by day.

Command in war is not a popularity contest. The only reason for introducing this matter here is that Montgomery's unpopularity with certain US generals appears constantly in the histories of the period and was, apparently, a factor in the conduct of the campaign and questions of command.

It is therefore important to separate the character of Montgomery from his professional expertise: it is more than probable the former aroused American hostility and the latter aroused American jealousy. Montgomery had seen more service than all the US generals put together, and he did not trouble to conceal the fact that he regarded some of them – but by no means all of them – as amateurs.

The hard fact remains that from 1 September 1944, Montgomery's role as Allied Ground Force Commander was over. Monty should have accepted that fact, and he probably would have done, had he any reason to believe that Eisenhower knew what he was doing and was taking steps to formulate a sound strategic plan – and see it implemented.

On the question of strategy Montgomery was on firmer ground, but when de Guingand presented Monty's suggestions for a northern thrust to Eisenhower on 22 August, the Supreme Commander was not convinced and rejected the proposals. Montgomery then asked Eisenhower to meet him for lunch at his Tactical HQ on 23 August. During the morning of the 23rd Montgomery flew to meet Bradley at Laval, and only then did he find 'to my amazement' that Bradley had 'changed his mind' about their supposed agreement of 17 August. Bradley was now 'a whole-hearted advocate of the main effort of his Army Group being directed on Metz and the Saar.'[3]

Montgomery then flew back to meet Eisenhower, to press the merits of his plan on the Supreme Commander yet again, but – above all – to urge that Eisenhower make a prompt decision on *some* plan, one that took into account the chronic and growing problem of supply. 'We do not have the resources to maintain both Army Groups at full pressure,' Montgomery stated. 'The only policy is to halt the right and strike with the left, or halt the left and strike with the right. We must decide on one thrust and put all the maintenance to support that; if we split the maintenance and advance on a broad front we shall be so weak everywhere that we will have no chance of success.'

This was true but the command issue again intervened. Monty also urged Eisenhower to remain as Supreme Commander and not 'descend into the land battle and become the ground C-in-C'[4] but let someone else run the land battle for him. Monty also pressed the matter of a strong thrust to the north, adding that he needed US support if he was to make it, as 21st Army Group did not have the men to carry out all the tasks assigned to it, half of it – the Canadian First Army – already being employed clearing the Channel coast.

For a while it seemed as if this part of the discussion was going Montgomery's way, but a soon-familiar pattern began to emerge. On 20 August, Eisenhower had directed that the main effort would be made by the *entire* US

12th Army Group on Metz and the Saar. Now, on 23 August, Ike agreed that a push up to Antwerp was important and that the left wing of the US First Army, far from heading for Aachen, must cover Dempsey's flank. On the other hand, he declined to stop Patton's thrust to the east and switch all necessary supplies to the northern front. The military principle known as concentration of force did not appeal to him: the fact that the available supplies of fuel were inadequate to fully support two thrusts all the way to the Rhine was simply ignored.

The advance across the Seine would therefore be on a broad front. The 12th Army Group would push east towards the Saar with its right flank – Third Army – supported by the right flank of First Army, while the left flank of the First Army covered Dempsey's thrust towards the Somme, the Belgian frontier and Antwerp. One effect of this decision was to thin out the First Army divisions over many miles of front – a front that would grow wider as the British moved north and Patton moved east. This did not seem a problem at the time and it fell in with Eisenhower's broad front concept – basically that all the Allied armies should push forward all the time, on their respective fronts.

At this point it should be made clear that the broad front policy made sense *while the Allied armies were advancing*. By advancing on a broad front the armies avoided congestion on the roads and could make better time than by trailing along one behind the other. The problem arose when the enemy was encountered: then the advancing armies needed to concentrate their force to overwhelm the opposition at some point and so keep moving.

Once across the Seine, said Eisenhower in his memoirs,[5] he always intended to 'pursue on a broad front with two Army Groups, emphasising the left to gain the necessary ports and reach the boundaries of the Reich and threaten the Ruhr.' On the right, 'we would link up with the forces that were to invade France from the South,' that is Devers' Dragoon force, later the 6th Army Group. He would also 'build up a new base along the western border with Germany by securing ports in Belgium and in Brittany, as well as in the Mediterranean and while building up our forces for the final battles, keep up an unrelenting offensive to the extent of our means, both to wear down the enemy and gain advantages for the final fighting.'

This post-war explanation of Eisenhower's post-Normandy strategy is not in accordance with the facts at the time. Far from 'emphasising the left to gain the necessary ports and reach the boundaries of the Reich and Ruhr' – the policy advocated by Montgomery – he was emphasising the right and supporting Patton's push to the Saar and the link-up with Devers, dragging the main weight of his armies away to the south and east. The problem was that the execution of either strategy depended on solving or correctly estimating the problems and demands of supply.

During the Normandy battle the Allied armies had been supplied via Cherbourg, some of the smaller Norman ports, through the Mulberry harbour at Arromanches, or over open beaches. This proved adequate until the start of August because the Allied armies had not moved far from the coast. To supply the Allied armies as they moved north, the logistical planners also hoped to use the cross-Channel ferry ports – Le Havre, Dieppe, Boulogne, Calais, Ostend – small though they were, damaged though they would be. The real problem in the autumn of 1944 was not supply but *transport* – finding a sufficient number of trains and trucks to shift supplies from the depots to the front line units.

This problem could be handled for a while, but no one doubted that the major asset, the port that had to be acquired and opened for business as soon as possible as the armies surged north, was the Belgian city of Antwerp, sixty miles from the sea up the River Scheldt and one of the largest cargo terminals in Europe. However, at the end of August 1944 Antwerp still had to be taken and the Scheldt estuary had to be cleared. While all that was happening, the advancing Allied armies still had to be supplied.

This raised another series of difficult questions. What operations could the existing supply situation sustain? Could it support a thrust to the north, or a thrust to the east? Could it support both? What was the best option given the supply situation: Montgomery's narrow front proposal or Eisenhower's broad front policy? Finally, how *far* could the Allied armies go with the present state of supply – to the Rhine, to the Ruhr, to Berlin? If it could not support all of these, which of them could it support – or was it better to admit that all these plans for rapid pursuit were risky and the best and safest decision was to halt the Allied armies until Antwerp had been cleared and the supply problem solved?

Reaching the right decision would not be easy and was compounded by another unexpected factor – the sudden collapse of the German armies in Normandy at the end of August and the need to keep up the pursuit as they fled across the Seine. This rapid defeat had not been anticipated. The Allied planners had visualised a gradual withdrawal of enemy forces to the Dives and the Seine; there would then be a major delay, or at least a prolonged pause, probably in September, due to expected German resistance on the river line: a pause that would allow the Allied armies to move up their supplies. But the defeat of the German armies in Normandy had changed all that and a hot pursuit was on.

The principle of pursuit is quite simple and is worth repeating: once you have the enemy on the run, you keep him on the run, denying him the opportunity to regroup or counter-attack, always aiming to turn his retreat into a rout. Like many other military principles, however, this one is simple, but not easy. As he falls back, the enemy may reach previously prepared defensive positions, or find a line, often a river line, that he can defend. The essence of the matter is *time*: give the enemy time to regroup and he will find the means to mount a defence.

At this point it might also be as well to consider the competing merits of the narrow front and broad front policies. When Montgomery put forward his plan for a powerful attack due north across the Flanders plain he was still the Allied Ground Force Commander. Preparing a plan for the next phase of the war in Western Europe was his duty – he was not intruding on Eisenhower's prerogative at this time, and he would have to submit this plan for Eisenhower's approval anyway. Although Montgomery was fully aware that changes in the command set-up were pending, he clearly hoped the success achieved in Normandy would justify his bid to stay in post as Ground Force Commander; that set-up had delivered victory in Normandy and he saw no reason to break up a winning team now – a faint hope in the circumstances, but an understandable one.

Eisenhower's broad front policy reflected the man and his view on the strategic conduct of campaigns. It also reflected the policy he had been attempting to impose on Montgomery throughout the Normandy campaign – that all the armies, corps and divisions should attack the enemy everywhere, all the time. Bedell Smith has compared Eisenhower's actions in Normandy with those of 'a US football coach, racing up and down the touchline, urging everyone into play.' Attacking everywhere, all the time, was Eisenhower's policy in Normandy, so when he became Ground Force Commander this was the policy he was bound to pursue – and there was now no Montgomery to get in the way.

In his excellent biography of Eisenhower,[6] Carlo d'Este states that Eisenhower's broad front strategy was drawn from one of Ike's boyhood heroes,

Hannibal, and his double envelopment of the Roman Army at Cannae in 216 BC. Ike intended a similar double envelopment of the Ruhr, north and south of the Ardennes – a strategy that, says d' Este, 'bears more than a passing likeness to the plan of another general Eisenhower had studied at length, Ulysses S. Grant and his 1864 strategy for defeating the Confederacy.' The essence of Grant's 1864 strategy was that all the Union armies should be in action all the time, so that the Confederates could not switch their forces from one front to another and would therefore be overwhelmed by sheer numbers – and battles of attrition. One can see certain similarities with Eisenhower's broad front policy in 1944 – just eighty years after the US Civil War.

The problem lies in the terrain. The European front in 1944 was far wider than the territory Grant's armies had to span south of the Virginia Wilderness in 1864. To implement such a broad front policy in 1944, Ike required either far more troops or a thinning-out of the front line divisions. The former increased the logistical problem, for more troops must be supplied; the latter meant that the US armies were not strong enough anywhere to force a decisive breach in the German line when they turned to fight... and the Germans were turning to fight, as Patrick Hennessey of the 13th/18th Hussars can confirm:

> The fighting was becoming more difficult with the Germans putting up a more determined defence as we neared German soil; we had a number of sharp encounters and in one instance we learned a very sombre lesson. It was laid down in standing orders that when we had to abandon a Sherman tank the gun must be pointed forward directly over the front of the tank. If this was not done the gun mantle would prevent the driver from opening his hatch and escaping. On the occasion we were obliged to witness, a tank was hit and immediately burst into flames. The turret crew evacuated leaving the gun pointed at 11 o'clock, directly over the driver's hatch. We could see him trying to open the hatch but it was fouled by the turret; there was a floor hatch but he did not even try to use it, the tank became an inferno and the driver perished.[7]

Montgomery came from a country with smaller military resources and a completely different military philosophy to that of the US generals. Montgomery believed in a balanced army, one that never over-reaches itself or spreads its assets too wide. He also believed in the importance of logistics – 'bringing up the administrative tail' as he called it – before pressing home his attacks. Another Montgomery principle – indeed a basic military principle common to all armies and most generals – was concentration of force.

This need for concentration was influenced by the relatively small size of Britain's forces. These were never large enough to be strong everywhere, so it was necessary for British commanders to concentrate their assets in order to be sufficiently strong at the point of attack, strong enough to win the battle and carry the day. To achieve this, Monty believed in stretching the enemy line, weakening the opposition with a series of wide-ranging attacks – but then striking hard with the greatest possible force where the enemy was weakest. This type of strategy calls for great skill, but it had carried Montgomery's armies to victory in North Africa and Normandy, and that was the strategy he hoped to use in North-West Europe – given the chance.

Montgomery would not get that chance. Eisenhower did not accept or perhaps even understand this philosophy. Like many of his subordinates, Ike regarded the business of probing for weak spots as too slow and too cautious. Like many at SHAEF he regarded Montgomery as a timid commander, excellent perhaps in the set piece battle but fairly useless in mobile warfare.

This cautious label has stuck to Montgomery over the decades, and there is some truth in it. It can be fairly said that Montgomery was not a reckless commander. On the other hand he was a versatile and very experienced commander – not a one-note general like George Patton, who only understood attack and pursuit – but one familiar with every aspect of war. Professionally, Montgomery is a hard act for any objective observer to fault and his grasp of strategy, of how campaigns can be fought and won, should have proved a major asset in the Allied struggle.

The tragedy is that Montgomery never succeeded in building up a truly strong personal or professional relationship with his superior officer, General Eisenhower. The fault here is largely Montgomery's: Eisenhower displayed vast amounts of tolerance towards him and (usually) supported Monty when he came under attack from his numerous enemies at SHAEF. It is a tragedy because, between them, the two men had all the necessary assets for the successful prosecution of an Allied campaign: vision, a lack of chauvinism, a sound knowledge of logistics and administration, the tact to handle politicians and wide, practical front line experience of modern war. The combination could have been formidable but it never developed: the two men fundamentally disagreed on two basic aspects of war – strategy and command.

This being so, it could be that Eisenhower's tolerance of Montgomery's foibles was a mistake. He was the Supreme Commander and should have taken command. Montgomery was a commander who gripped his subordinates tightly – he gave them clear orders and expected them to be obeyed to the letter – but like all men with grip, he needed to be gripped himself.

Montgomery was well aware of this. Writing of his relationship with the Chief of the Imperial General Staff (CIGS) Field Marshal Alanbrooke, Monty states: 'He saved me from getting into trouble on several occasions before the war ended and always backed me when others tried to down me. At times he would get angry and I received quite a few backhanders from him; but I would take anything from him and I have no doubt I deserved all I got.'[8] Monty's numerous critics should note these comments. Monty was well aware of his faults and he could take correction and criticism without resentment.

Alanbrooke knew that Monty needed gripping and told Eisenhower as much. During the Normandy campaign he even offered to grip Monty on Eisenhower's behalf, if Ike did not fancy the task personally. The offer was declined and gradually the Eisenhower-Montgomery relationship deteriorated.

Regarding Montgomery as a cautious general, Eisenhower doubted if he had the talents to execute the plan he was now urging on the Supreme Commander – a plan Eisenhower came to describe as a 'knife-like' or 'pencil-like' thrust. Without descending into detail at this juncture it is necessary to point out that Montgomery's proposed strategy was no 'pencil' or 'knife-like' thrust – he was talking of an advance by forty divisions, a force 'so strong that it need fear nothing'.

However, a more likely explanation for confining Montgomery to 21st Army Group is the understandable desire of the US commanders at SHAEF and in the US Army Groups to take control of this campaign and run their own show. Bradley certainly felt this. He had served as a corps commander under Patton in Sicily and as an army commander under Montgomery in Normandy: now he had his own Army Group and was responsible to no one but the Supreme Commander, his old friend Ike. Bradley was naturally eager to show what he could do.

Nor was Monty's idea of a Ground Force Commander on Normandy lines really feasible. At the end in Normandy, two Army Groups composed of four armies were operating in the same tight area. From now on there would be three Army Groups, composed of seven armies, spread across the Continent from the North Sea to the Swiss frontier, a distance of some 600 miles – four of those armies would be American, one British, one Canadian and one French. Even if an intermediate commander should have been interposed between the Army Group commanders and the Supreme Commander, he would most probably be an American – a fact Montgomery recognised at that meeting with Eisenhower on 23 August when, in an attempt to retain the post of Ground Force Commander in the Allied command set-up, he offered to serve under Bradley.

Eisenhower's command strategy called for the creation of two Army Groups – the Army Group of the North (Montgomery's 21st Army Group) and the Army Group of the Centre (Bradley's 12th Army Group), each under its own commander-in-chief, acting directly under the orders of the Supreme Commander – Dever's Army Group of the South being added later. The reality of the situation was that no subsidiary commander would be appointed because Eisenhower wanted the field command for himself during this last campaign. Put bluntly, the Allied armies in Western Europe were now George Marshall and Dwight Eisenhower's 'train set', and no one else was going to play with it – certainly not Bernard Law Montgomery.

Eisenhower's plan was quite clear – the Allied armies of all three groups would advance towards the German frontier on a broad front – but a plan is not a strategy: a strategy is the way of working out the plan, taking into account the multiplicity of factors that help or inhibit success. Just telling every commander to push ahead hardly amounts to a strategy. There is a touch of Mr Micawber in Eisenhower's plan, the notion that with all the armies pushing north and east towards the Rhine, something would turn up to give them victory. Indeed, Monty expressed doubts that Eisenhower even had a plan. 'The trouble is', he says in his *Memoirs*, '*We had no fundamental plan which treated the theatre as an entity. Our strategy was now to become unstitched.*'[9]

Even allowing for Montgomery's pique, Eisenhower's plan contained some basic flaws and one major error. He had made no arrangements for handling the problems of field command. The duties of a Supreme Headquarters and a Field Headquarters are very different and SHAEF was not equipped to handle the job. Ike's Headquarters was hundreds of miles from the front and his communications were poor: the facilities to exercise the command function quickly, in response to changing situations on the ground, simply did not exist.

Eisenhower also lacked one basic command skill: the ability to issue orders that were unequivocal, and could not be either re-interpreted or regarded by his subordinates as the basis for debate. In short, for most of the time, Ike lacked grip. There are few absolutes in war or in generals – Monty was not always detestable and Ike was not always reasonable and, if provoked, Eisenhower could display grip – but he did not do so consistently or nearly often enough.

Eisenhower's major error was that the broad front policy depended on finding a solution to the logistical problem. At the end of August the Allied Armies were still being supplied via Cherbourg, the British Mulberry harbour at Arromanches, and the open beaches in the bay of the Seine. Thanks to the sterling efforts of the supply echelons this had proved adequate when the front line was close at hand, but as the armies moved north towards Belgium and Holland their supply lines lengthened and the problem of supply was increasingly compounded by a shortage of transportation.

The most effective way to ship fuel and heavy stores up to the leading divisions was by rail, but the French railway system had been comprehensively destroyed in the pre-D-Day bombing offensive and could not be quickly repaired. Moreover, the Allied armies – or at least the US proportion – were growing in size. Every man landing needed food and guns, every truck and tank needed fuel, and fighting vehicles all needed ammunition. Unless these assets could be supplied in growing quantities, the Allied advance would grind to a halt.

The logistical problem is so deeply entrenched and so crucial to the understanding of this campaign that an entire chapter has been devoted to it later in this book, but even at this early stage in the story the logistical problem has to be taken on board. Both strategies – Eisenhower's and Montgomery's – depended on an appreciation of the logistical situation. Montgomery, anxious to follow up the defeated enemy, recommended halting part of the Allied armies and throwing all necessary supplies of fuel and ammunition behind one strong thrust. To Marshall and Eisenhower this meant halting George Patton, who was currently gaining ground in Eastern France along with large headlines in the USA. Stopping Patton in mid-career at this time was politically impossible – especially if it meant switching supplies to the detested Montgomery.

At this point it would be as well to stress the matter of Antwerp. If Cherbourg was the essential port for the Normandy campaign, Antwerp was necessary for the successful prosecution of the advance into Germany, if not for the maintenance of the Allied armies even before that advance was attempted. One of the great arguments over the post-Normandy battle concerns the significance of Antwerp and why its importance did not lead to the rapid clearance of the Scheldt estuary after the port itself was captured in early September.

The answer, yet again, is complicated. The Scheldt estuary lay astride the path of the First Canadian Army and that Army was tasked with clearing it. The snag was that the Canadian Army was small, with only two corps, and had been obliged to divert much of its strength to the investment of the Channel ports long before the Scheldt estuary was reached. Therefore the Canadians needed help from the British Second Army… but the British Second Army was intent on pushing back the Germans and heading for the Rhine and the Ruhr – if it diverted strength from its left flank to help the Canadians on the Scheldt, it would need help from the US First Army on its right flank, which Bradley was most reluctant to provide. Again, someone had to make a decision here – Antwerp or the Rhine – for the British and Canadians could not do both. The only person who could make that decision was Eisenhower.

Eisenhower's plan recognized the logistical problem and the importance of Antwerp, but he had originally intended to shelve it until Antwerp was taken by bringing supplies forward while the Allied forces were halted on the Seine. The snag was that the Allied armies did not halt on the Seine. The advance continued and so, said Monty, at the end of August, 'We all got ready to cross the Seine and go our separate ways.'[10]

Some indication of the problem appears in the US Official History, which states:

> In essence, the decision emerging from the 23rd August meeting resulted in
> a temporary shift of the main effort from the Maubeuge – Liège – Aachen axis
> to the plain of Flanders, a route that pre-invasion planners had blackballed as
> a primary axis into Germany. Yet the shift was more tactical than strategic,
> in that it was made for the purpose of gaining intermediate objectives vital to
> a final offensive along the lines of the original strategic concept. It could be
> argued that it required no real shift of any kind because of the broad
> interpretation that had come to be put on the route 'north of the Ardennes'.[11]

The first steps towards gaining an understanding of the situation on the ground are to study the map and refer to the pre-invasion SHAEF plan issued on 3 May 1944.[12] This plan declared that Allied strategy looked towards the capture of Berlin. But – it added – on the way there the Allies wanted some economic objective, the loss of which 'would rapidly starve Germany of the means to continue the war.' This objective was the Ruhr industrial basin, the loss of which would deprive Germany of 56 per cent of her coal and 65 per cent of her steel. So let the objective of Allied strategy be determined: the Ruhr and Berlin, the industrial and political hearts of the Reich, should be the main objectives of the next campaign... and the first step on the road would be the crossing of the Rhine.

On 1 September 1944, Montgomery's role as Ground Force Commander ended and Eisenhower became both Supreme Commander and Field Commander. He could now do exactly what he wanted. If he got it wrong he was on his own: so the next point to consider is whether what Eisenhower wanted was the right thing to do.

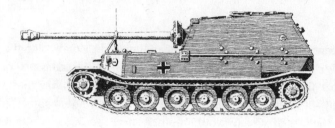

2 · EISENHOWER TAKES COMMAND
1 SEPTEMBER – 4 SEPTEMBER 1944

The proper tactics now are for strong armoured or mobile columns to by-pass enemy centres of resistance and to push boldly ahead.

INSTRUCTIONS TO BRITISH SECOND ARMY *29 AUGUST 1944*

On 1 September General Eisenhower took direct command of the Allied Army Groups. As a consolation prize, General Montgomery was promoted to the rank of Field Marshal by King George VI and duly received a warm letter of congratulations from the Supreme Commander. By now all the Allied armies were well across the Seine but the events of the next few days, the rapid advances made on every front and the clearing of Antwerp, were to colour the campaign for some time to come.

At various meetings with his commanders in August, Eisenhower had first decreed that the 12th Army Group – Hodges' First Army and Patton's Third – would direct its efforts east, towards Metz and the Saar. That order had then been modified: a revised order stated that the main thrust should be in the north towards the Ruhr, but that a secondary thrust should be made towards the Saar, not least to link up with the Dragoon Force – later Devers' US 6th Army Group – coming up the Rhône valley towards Alsace and the Vosges.

The one consistent thread of Eisenhower's policy at this time was for a move towards the Rhine, north and south of the Ardennes. This requirement was in line with his broad front strategy but the rapid advance of the Allied armies north of the Seine was now putting that strategy under the microscope. Another option was becoming apparent – the chance to defeat the enemy again quickly and drive him back, pell-mell, to or beyond the frontiers of the Reich.

From 1 September, says the British Official History, 'the pace of 21st Army Group's advance quickened.'[1] The Canadians were moving west, to invest Le Havre and clear the Channel ports, while Second Army was advancing on Brussels with XXX Corps on the right and XII Corps on the left – VIII Corps having been grounded south of the Seine so that its transport could supply the front line units of the other two corps as they rolled rapidly into Belgium. This pursuit of the retreating German armies soon took on the attributes of a celebration, as Trooper David Taylor of the Lothian and Border Horse recalls:

> On again, and this time we passed through the town of Elbeuf and crossed the River Seine near a place called Boos close to Rouen, on Bailey bridges built by the Royal Engineers. We could see many other blown bridges dipping into the river as we looked towards Rouen. We then passed through a heavily built-up area, driving our Flail tanks through cheering crowds, all waving flags and going wild with excitement. The roar of our tracks seemed to shake the very foundations of the buildings.
>
> We felt as if we were taking part in a huge Victory Parade; everyone turned out to cheer us, we threw sweets and cigarettes to the people and in the background Rouen cathedral stood magnificently close to the river. In the countryside French peasants turned out in their hundreds to greet us and many an old farmer came near to being shot as they burst through the undergrowth in their excitement to get a look at us, the first British soldiers they had seen since 1940.[2]

The spearhead of this British advance to Brussels and Antwerp was Lieutenant General Sir Brian Horrocks' XXX Corps. Following Montgomery's orders 'to press on boldly', on 29 August Horrocks' units went surging north towards the Somme. By noon on August 30, XXX Corps was halfway to the river and meeting only light opposition. Horrocks therefore ordered the leading formation, 'Pip' Robert's 11th Armoured Division, not to stop at dusk but to press on and 'bounce the Germans out of Amiens', preferably before they could destroy the Somme bridges.

Thus urged, XXX Corps pressed on, a seemingly endless column of tanks, armoured cars and lorried infantry, forging with dimmed lights through the darkness and sudden squalls of rain. There was a certain amount of opposition, from company-strong groups of German infantry, sometimes supported by a couple of tanks – a kampfgruppe – but the armoured brigades bustled on and by 2359hrs that night XXX Corps had covered much ground and taken over 1,000 prisoners.

As Trooper Taylor has related, news of their advance preceded them. Villagers appeared in the streets to cheer the soldiers as they roared past and in the grey light of dawn on 31 August the leading armoured cars drove into Amiens. On the way they passed close to the HQ of the German Seventh Army, where General Sepp Dietrich was about to hand over command to SS General Hans Eberbach. Though surprised by the sudden appearance of the British, Dietrich managed to get away but Eberbach's staff car was shot up by an 11th Armoured Division scout car and the general and his map case fell into British hands, the maps revealing the full extent of the chaos currently prevailing in the German command set-up.

The British did not stay long in Amiens. General Sir Miles Dempsey now 'had his tail up' and Horrocks needed no urging to press on. A brigade of the 50th Division arrived to take over Amiens and mop up any remaining opposition, while 11th Armoured Division prepared to press on yet again. With the line of the Somme broken at Amiens, the Guards Armoured Division came up on the flank of 11th Armoured and by midday on 2 September, British armoured cars had crossed into Belgium, south-east of Lille. Later that day two US armoured divisions of the VII Corps of First Army, on the left of Second Army, reached the Lille to Mons road.

Three Allied Corps – Horrocks' XXX , the XII Corps and Collins' VII US Corps – were now across the Belgian frontier, but Patton's Third Army, further east, had been brought to a halt by a shortage of petrol – and by the remains of the German Fifth Panzer Army gradually reassembling on their front. This development illustrates two points: the Allied logistical problem was starting to bite, and the Germans were starting to reform.

This rapid advance still had a dire effect on the already desperate German position. The German Fifteenth Army was being pressed against the Channel coast by the Canadian First Army and was about to be outflanked by the British Second Army, while the German Seventh Army had been levered away to the east of Soissons by this Anglo-American thrust. A wide gap was now developing in the German front and as the Second Army was pushing into it the Germans had no option but to fall back in disarray.

Apparently nothing could now stop the Allied advance. On Sunday 3 September, the leading elements of the British Second Army crossed the Belgian frontier, the Guards Armoured Division heading for Brussels, 11th Armoured heading for Antwerp. The Guards were in Brussels, seventy miles from the border by late afternoon, by which time their tanks were covered with flowers, girls and cheering civilians, the somewhat embarrassed tank crews deluged with fruit, bottles of wine, cakes, chocolate and kisses.

A day later, 4 September, the 11th Armoured Division entered Antwerp. Ignoring the lure of Brussels and waving aside the crowds that blocked their path, Pip Robert's division entered the port against light opposition to find it virtually undamaged. This itself was a minor miracle and some indication of the state of German morale at this time, for Antwerp was a modern port, with electrically-operated lock gates and sluices, very easy to destroy.

Unfortunately, Roberts did not press on a few miles north of Antwerp to cross the Albert Canal. Had he done so, the German Fifteenth Army would have been denied easy access to the Beveland Peninsula, which formed the north bank of the Scheldt and was a useful defence line along the Albert Canal itself. This wide canal was the next major physical obstacle on the road north and Horrocks later wrote that 'If I had ordered Roberts not to liberate Antwerp but to by-pass the town and advance only 15 miles north-west towards Woensdrecht, we should have blocked the Beveland isthmus.'

As it was, the Germans were able to ferry troops from Fifteenth Army across the Scheldt and proceeded to turn the Albert Canal line into a strong defensive position – and by ordering his armies to stop on this line for three days Montgomery gave them time to do so. The reason for this delay was understandable – to bring up supplies and stay balanced – but XII Corps had enough fuel to press on beyond the Albert Canal and should have done so.

The capture of Antwerp, welcome as it was, presented the Supreme Commander with the need for another decision. Second Army had advanced 250 miles to the north in less than a week, carrying all before it and capturing the two most important cities of Belgium, one of them a major port the Allies needed to supply their advance into Germany. The snag was that Antwerp lay sixty-five miles from the sea, up the winding estuary of the Scheldt – and the banks of the Scheldt, and the fortified island of Walcheren at the seaward end, were still occupied by the German Army. Clearing the Scheldt would take time and resources that many felt should currently be devoted to chasing the Germans back to Germany. On the other hand, once the banks of the River Scheldt had been cleared and Antwerp opened for business, all the Allied armies could be supplied and Eisenhower's looming logistical nightmare would be over. The problem was that clearing the Scheldt and simultaneously moving on the Rhine and the Ruhr were beyond the resources of 21st Army Group.

For Field Marshal Montgomery there was further dilemma. With this whirlwind advance into Belgium Monty had demonstrated that he was not merely a master of the set piece battle. He was clearly perfectly capable of handling a hot pursuit: the much-vaunted Patton could not have gone faster in the advance to Brussels and Antwerp. Monty could now either devote the full strength of his Army Group to the task of opening Antwerp, or press on to the north in pursuit of the enemy. General Eisenhower currently wanted both of these objectives, but which one had priority?

Here came the first miscalculation, that the Canadian Army was capable of clearing the Channel coast and the Scheldt on its own, while Dempsey and the Second Army, hopefully with the assistance of elements of Hodges' First Army, surged on to the Rhine.

There is, however, a small but significant caveat to this hopeful appraisal: speed was not everything. Any rapid advance against the German Army usually depended on the enemy's capacity to resist. Patton had made great advances since Normandy and gained a great deal of personal publicity since the St Lô breakout in July because his Third Army had not faced any significant resistance – at least until it reached Metz, when matters changed somewhat. The British advance from the Seine after the breakout benefited from the same situation and they taken full advantage of it: but if the enemy were given the chance to regroup, matters would not go so well or the Allied advance be so rapid.

The other issue was the need for a strategic decision. A month later, on 4 October, after attending a post-Market Garden meeting at Versailles, Field Marshal Alanbrooke wrote in his diary: 'I feel that Monty's strategy for once is at fault. Instead of carrying out the advance on Arnhem, he ought to have made certain of Antwerp in the first place... Ike nobly took all the blame on himself, as he had approved Monty's suggestion to operate on Arnhem.'

This diary entry displays the benefits of hindsight. Since Eisenhower – the Supreme Commander and Ground Force Commander – approved the Arnhem operation rather than a push to clear the Scheldt, then surely he was right, as well as noble, to accept the responsibility and any resulting blame? The choice in early September was the Rhine or Antwerp: to continue the pursuit or secure the necessary facilities to solve the logistical problem? The decision was made to go for the Rhine, and that decision was Eisenhower's.

On 4 September, as Antwerp was about to fall, Montgomery and Dempsey met Bradley and Hodges to discuss what to do next in order to expedite Eisenhower's bid for the Rhine. According to the latest intelligence reports they had two German armies to their front: the Fifteenth, which the Canadians were driving north along the coast, and the shattered Seventh, which was attempting to break away to the east, towards the West Wall or Siegfried Line. As his contribution to the broad front strategy, Montgomery elected to push Second Army into the gap between these two German armies and then use British and Polish airborne forces to seize the Rhine bridges between Arnhem and Wesel. The Airborne would then hold these bridges until Second Army arrived. This airborne operation was codenamed Comet.

Bradley's choice was more difficult. His First Army was well placed to head east and follow the traditional invasion route into Germany via the Aachen Gap, and Eisenhower had indeed ordered Bradley to keep the First Army advancing deep into Belgium, through Liège on the River Meuse and so north of the Ardennes towards Aachen. Bradley, however, preferred to support Patton's thrust towards Metz and the Saar and, again, there was not enough maintenance available to keep both US armies advancing. This being so, Patton got the bulk of anything that was going – plus the V Corps of First Army to guard his flank. The net result of all this was that by mid-September, the eight divisions of Hodges' First Army were deployed on a 150-mile front, covering the ground between Patton thrusting for the Saar and Dempsey heading for Arnhem: this did not leave anything to spare for a First Army push east towards the Aachen Gap.

On the Channel coast, Crerar's First Canadian Army was well in the hunt and heading north but here too a snag was revealing itself. The Channel ports had been prepared for defence and as the Canadians came up, the German garrisons occupied these defences and prepared to resist eviction. General Crerar's force of six divisions, which was not large to begin with, therefore began to shed strength besieging the small ports of Boulogne, Calais and Dunkirk.

At most of the Channel ports the German garrison dug-in and hung on – Dunkirk held on for months, while taking Le Havre proved a tough proposition for Crocker's British 1st Corps. Set at the mouth of the River Seine, Le Havre was an obvious objective for the Allied armies. It was a useful supply port with a daily unloading capacity of 20,000 tons, and the enemy were anxious to deny it to the Allies for as long as possible. The town had been well fortified and was garrisoned by some 11,000 men of the German Fifteenth Army, supported by artillery. General Crocker elected for a set piece attack, Operation Astonia, which began on 5 September when the port was bombed by the RAF and shelled by the 15-inch guns of the battleship HMS *Warspite* and the monitor HMS *Erebus*. The battle for Le Havre lasted a full week before the garrison surrendered, during which time the port had been comprehensively wrecked. While Crocker's Corps was thus occupied, Lieutenant General Guy Simonds' II (Canadian) Corps was pushing up the coast to Boulogne and Calais, but resistance from the German Fifteenth Army was stiffening all the time.

On 4 September, Generalfeldmarschall Gerd von Rundstedt, who had been dismissed by Hitler in July, having advised OKW that after the Normandy landings their only choice was to 'Make peace, you damned fools', was reappointed to the command of OB-West and became responsible for shoring up the German position on the Western Front.

A quick survey of the German Order of Battle at this time would have made gloomy reading. It gave von Rundstedt a force theoretically consisting of forty-eight infantry divisions and fifteen panzer divisions, plus several panzer brigades.

This sounds a significant force but – unlike the Führer – von Rundstedt was well aware that some of these divisions existed only on paper and all of them were severely worn down and short of everything needed to sustain the fight, from men and guns to tanks and ammunition. A more realistic calculation was that von Rundstedt's force amounted to about twenty-five divisions of various types, most of them manned by exhausted men. With these assets he had to oppose the forty-nine Allied divisions which, logistics permitting, Eisenhower could employ in the west, without taking into account the vast resources of the Allied air forces and the ample reinforcements en route from the USA.

However, von Rundsted was a resourceful commander. Like Montgomery, he saw what had to be done during this crucial period and fully realised that the current need was not for tanks, guns and men, but time. If he could gain enough time, fresh assets could be provided, his men could be rested, and the strong defences on the German frontier, the West Wall (or as the Allies tended to call it, the Siegfried Line) could be re-equipped and manned. Not everyone shared this view. On 4 September, Field Marshal Model told OKW that if he was to hold the West Wall or the Army Group B front, which ran from Antwerp to the Luxembourg border, he would need at least twenty-five fresh infantry divisions and five or six fully-equipped panzer divisions.[3] As Chester Wilmot remarks, Model 'might as well have asked for the moon.'[4]

Nevertheless, the Germans *were* finding men. Every man in the German Army was a fighting man. His service career, be it as cook, driver, anti-aircraft gunner, sapper or clerk, began with a thorough grounding in weapon handling, field craft and infantry tactics and when time permitted, these skills were revised and rehearsed. A comb-out of rear echelon units quickly produced around 150,000 soldiers to repair and man the West Wall fortifications. These may not have been first-class troops but they were German soldiers and when manning defensive positions they would prove more than adequate in stemming the Allied advance.

And there was more. On 4 September, Field Marshal Goering, the head of the Luftwaffe, informed the staff at OKW that he had some 20,000 men available, fully trained and equipped, in six parachute regiments. (German parachute regiments were part of the Luftwaffe, not the Wehrmacht.) To this, Goering could commit another 10,000 men – aircrew and ground staff for whom the Luftwaffe no longer had a use. This was a real bonus: within hours these regiments had been formed into the core of what became the First Parachute Army, a force commanded by General Kurt Student, who had founded the German parachute arm and led it during the invasion of Crete in 1941.

Hitler also ordered that three other parachute units, the 3rd, 5th and 6th Parachute Regiments, currently refitting in Germany after Normandy, plus the 719th and 347th Infantry Divisions and training units of the Waffen SS, plus men from anti-aircraft units, should also be sent to this new Parachute Army. Gathering up other forces, including all the German troops on the Dutch mainland east of the Scheldt, Student took his army into the line and occupied a sixty-mile front between Antwerp and Maastricht. He was also tasked to hold that new defence line north of Antwerp, the one confronting the British along the Albert Canal and then along the Meuse to the Upper Moselle.

The advent of the First Parachute Army was not a massive reinforcement but it was a very useful one. Von Rundstedt charged Student with gaining time until the West Wall could be put in a sound defensive state, and in particular to make a strong front along the Albert Canal. Von Rundstedt also pointed out to OKW that to get the West Wall defensible would take around six weeks; if the Allies made a strong push anywhere during that time, he could not hold them. On the other hand, if the Allies continued to advance on a broad front from the Saar to the Channel, he could probably muster enough defensive strength to hold them or slow them down. It therefore appears that in September 1944 what von Runstedt could do depended very largely on what Eisenhower did.[5]

As related, on 3 September Montgomery and Dempsey met Bradley and Hodges and Montgomery proposed pushing the Second Army into the gap between the two German armies on their joint front. Provided Bradley would protect its left flank, Second Army would then push on towards the Rhine, hitting the river somewhere between Arnhem and Wesel and join the airborne troops of Operation Comet. The push would begin on 6 September and this three-day delay proved a mistake: during that time units of Student's First Parachute Army were able to occupy positions along the Albert canal.

Elsewhere, the Allies were still advancing and pushing the Germans back. To the east of Second Army, the VII Corps of Hodges' First US Army had pushed across the Belgian frontier near Mons, where they rounded up some 30,000 prisoners from the Seventh Army. By 4 September the XIX and VII Corps of First Army were on the River Meuse at Namur and were pushing east into the southern edge of the Ardennes towards the Aachen Gap, but slowing down as they gradually ran out of fuel.

Further south still, Patton's Third Army had crossed the Meuse at Verdun and seemed set to push east towards Metz, Lorraine and the West Wall, hoping to overrun the latter before the Germans could occupy it. Logistics permitting, that hot pursuit, which the sudden collapse of the German armies dictated, was currently going very well.

Unfortunately, the logistics did not permit. Between 1 and 4 September,

Patton's Army was grounded by a shortage of fuel. By the time he was able to resume the offensive on 5 September, the German resistance on his front had stiffened. On the whole though, and with the exception of the First Canadian Army, which had a much harder task advancing against the German Fifteenth Army on the Channel coast, every Allied army was taking ground to its front, the speed of its advance depending on available fuel and German resistance.

By 4 September, with Montgomery in Brussels and Antwerp, Bradley with Patton on the Meuse south of the Ardennes, and Hodges on the Meuse north of it, the strategic options open to Eisenhower suggest not two possible axes of advance into Germany but three: a thrust north by 21st Army Group towards the German frontier and the north of the Ruhr; an advance by most of the US First Army, north of the Ardennes on the Liège – Aachen axis towards the southern end of the Ruhr; and a thrust east, south of the Ardennes towards Metz and the Saar by Patton's Third Army.

This was probably one axis of advance too many, but there was a further complication – and the complication was caused by Eisenhower. Each primary task appeared to involve an equally important subsidiary task. Pushing north towards the Rhine from Antwerp and Brussels was not the only task facing 21st Army Group. Montgomery was also tasked with opening Antwerp, which would involve clearing the Scheldt. The urgency of that task was brought home to Montgomery by a signal sent to Eisenhower from the Naval Commander-in-Chief, Admiral Sir Bertram Ramsey, on 3 September: This stated:

> It is essential that if Antwerp and Rotterdam are to be opened quickly the enemy must be prevented from:
>
> Carrying out demolitions and blocking the ports.
>
> Mining and blocking the Scheldt and the new waterway between Rotterdam and the Hook.
>
> Both Antwerp and Rotterdam are highly vulnerable to mining and blocking. If the enemy succeeds in these operations the time it will take to open these ports cannot be estimated.
>
> It will be necessary for coastal batteries to be captured before approach channels to the river routes can be established.

These coastal batteries were on the island of Walcheren at the mouth of the Scheldt so, according to Ramsey, Walcheren must be captured and the German Fifteenth Army cleared away from both banks of the estuary, and all that done quickly before the Antwerp approaches were mined. This task had been given to the First Canadian Army, which was currently employed clearing the Channel ports, and it was highly debatable if Crerar's Army had the strength to complete this task *and* clear the Scheldt estuary without a considerable amount of help from Second Army, which was currently contemplating a strong push north for the Rhine. So, again, what was the *primary* task – the Rhine or the Scheldt?

Bradley's Group was also affected by a multiplicity of tasks. This included the pursuit of two main objectives for the US First Army: apart from moving east towards the Rhine on the axis Liège–Aachen, it had also been directed to support the right flank of the British Second Army – which certainly needed such support – in its push north to the Rhine. The other half of the 12th Army Group, Patton's Third Army, apart from moving on Metz and the Saar, was also tasked to link up with Patch's Seventh Army in Dever's 6th Army Group – the Dragoon Force – currently coming up the Rhône Valley from the South of France. One result of this variety of tasks was to stretch Bradley's forces considerably.

Bradley's group was also badly affected by the logistical situation. In spite of the sterling efforts of the 'Red Ball Express' – a dedicated truck convoy, working round the clock to ferry supplies up from the Normandy bases on pre-marked, one-way routes – Bradley was receiving no more than 7,000 tons of supplies every day, less than two-thirds of what he needed to keep both his armies moving.

Since Eisenhower had decreed that the northern thrust must have priority, in early September Bradley was sending a daily allocation of 5,000 tons to Hodges' First Army and 2,000 tons to Patton's Third. This allocation produced predictable results. Patton was furious and, aided and abetted by Bradley, was soon finding ways to get round this restriction, so undermining Eisenhower's strategic plan. Instead of insisting that his orders were obeyed, on 2 September Eisenhower called yet another meeting, this time with only Bradley and Patton attending. Patton claimed that if he was only given the fuel, his army could quickly take the Saar, punch through the West Wall defences and reach the Rhine in a matter of days. Bradley supported this proposal and urged that First Army should abandon the northern thrust – and protecting 21st Army Group's flank – and turn east to the Aachen Gap. Inevitably, the result was a compromise. Ike agreed that the V Corps of First Army and the Third Army could go east and attack the West Wall and the Saar, and Patton was authorised to secure crossings over the Moselle as soon as the necessary fuel was available. Eisenhower's plan of attack had been changed for the third time in two weeks.

Then, on 4 September, Eisenhower issued a fresh directive. This ordered the forces north-west of the Ardennes – 21st Army Group and two corps of the US First Army – to secure Antwerp (which had in fact been secured that day) and 'reach the sector of the Rhine covering the Ruhr and then seize the Ruhr.' This part of the directive seems to overlook the rather tricky matter of crossing the Rhine: the Ruhr lies on the east bank of the river. The directive then continues: 'The forces south of the Ardennes, Third Army and the V Corps of First Army shall occupy the sector of the Siegfried Line (West Wall) covering the Saar and then seize Frankfurt.' Here again, Ike's geography seems to have been at fault; Frankfurt lies on the River Main, some distance *east* of the Rhine.

These geographical confusions can be set aside for the moment. The directive stated that: 'This operation should start as soon as possible but the troops of the Central Group of Armies, (Bradley's group) operating against the Ruhr, north-west of the Ardennes, must first be adequately supported.' This part of the directive seems more than a little unclear. Were the two corps of First Army north-west of the Ardennes to move to the Aachen Gap or cover Monty's thrust for the Rhine north of the Ruhr? In fact, from what follows, it appears that the idea was to continue pushing towards the Saar, Aachen and the Rhine north of Antwerp. The 'broad front' policy was still in good shape.

While extracting this concession from Eisenhower, Patton concealed the fact that Third Army had just captured 110,000 gallons of fuel from the Germans at Sens, more than enough to carry his tanks to the Moselle and even beyond it. This may seem praiseworthy initiative, and so it was, but the general effect was to drag the US effort away to the east when it should have been devoted to progress in the north, either directly north to the Rhine or east to the Rhine via the Aachen gap. An attack on the Saar, while looking good on maps and in newspapers, actually did very little to advance the Allied cause. If Ike wanted to leave Antwerp for a while and go for the Ruhr, his choice was via Aachen or via Arnhem.

There were thus two snags with Patton's latest advance. First of all, it undermined Eisenhower's recently issued plan, which clearly called for advances towards the Ruhr, the main strategic target. Secondly, in spite of his assurances that, given the necessary maintenance, Third Army could 'get through the West Wall like grass though a goose', Patton's Army was coming to a halt. Unfortunately for his extravagant claim, Patton was about to make the surprising discovery that the laws of war against the Germans applied as much to him as to anyone else. The day after Patton got the go-ahead from Eisenhower and Bradley, Hitler ordered Field Marshal Walter Model, commander of Army Group B, to assemble panzer forces on the Moselle and smite Patton's army when it came within reach.

On 4 September, two questions needed to be addressed. First, what exactly was the current strategic plan – the one that promised the best way of prosecuting the war and defeating Germany? Second, which of these various advances should be the main offensive(s) and which the subsidiary or supporting ones – or did they all have equal importance?

As a result of the hot pursuit since crossing the Seine, there were now, in effect, three major offensives in progress. Second Army was heading towards the north – the Rhine and the Ruhr. So too was First Army, north of the Ardennes, heading via the Aachen Gap to the Rhine, Cologne and the Ruhr. Finally, to the east of Paris and south of the Ardennes, Patton was heading for the Rhine via Metz and the Saar.

All these offensives were some making ground, the press was delighted and it all looked very good on the maps back at SHAEF, but this continuing, three-pronged offensive to the Rhine ignores the dire and chronic logistical situation, which to maintain all three thrusts clearly required the opening of Antwerp. With Patton obliged to stop his advance in early September through lack of fuel and Dempsey obliged to ground an entire Corps for lack of transport, it was becoming increasingly obvious that the current logistical set-up could not support every forward movement for much longer. Sooner or later, someone would have to decide who would advance and who would halt.

That apart, this diversion of effort along the entire Allied front from the Scheldt to the Vosges was spreading the Allied effort very thin: the well-established military principle requiring a concentration of force at some point was being ignored in favour of a general push all along the line. This may not always be a bad thing; textbook rules are not always suited to every situation. When conducting a pursuit, an advance on a broad front is good strategy, for it brings the pursuers' total force into play. But a concentration of force is usually wise when the pursuer is about to assault the enemy in prepared positions as, for example, along the West Wall, which was now looming up along the First and Third Army fronts and being hurriedly manned and re-equipped by the enemy.

The counter-argument to concentration says that dispersing the effort along the front obliges the enemy to thin out his defending forces. The Allies had done just that during the recent Normandy campaign, when the feint, or spoof Operation Fortitude had kept most of the Fifteenth Army north of the Seine throughout the battle while OKW anticipated another Allied invasion in the Pas de Calais. The difference is that Fortitude was a feint and dispersed *enemy* strength, not Allied strength – unlike the current broad front policy, which would soon spread the Allied armies out on a 600-mile front from the Swiss frontier to the North Sea.

There are few absolutes in military matters and this wide deployment might not have mattered had the Allies been able to assemble a strong reserve for some decisive push. This reserve could have been used to back up the advancing units at some point and so achieve concentration of force, but apart from the Allied Airborne Army back in England, no reserve existed. Eisenhower's broad front policy required every division in the line.

That busy day, 4 September 1944, was not complete without another unfortunate signal from Montgomery to Eisenhower. Flushed with the capture of Antwerp, Montgomery stated that:

1 I consider we have now reached a stage where one really powerfu and full-blooded thrust towards Berlin is likely to get there and so end the German war.

2 We have not enough maintenance resources for two major thrusts.

3 The selected thrust must have all the maintenance resources it needs. without any qualification whatsoever, and any other operation must do the best it can with what is left over.

4 There are only two possible thrusts; one via the Ruhr and one via the Saar.

5 In my opinion the one most likely to give the best and quickest results is the northern one via the Ruhr.

6 Time is vital and the decision regarding the selected thrust must be made at once and Para 3 will then apply.

7 If we attempt a compromise solution and split our maintenance resources so that neither thrust is full blooded, we will prolong the war.

8 I consider the problem viewed as above is very simple and clear cut

9 The matter is of such vital importance that I feel sure you will agree that a decision on the above lines is required at once.

At least on this occasion Montgomery managed to propose a strategy without raising the command issue. This missive did little good, though the exchange does serve to illustrate another current problem: communications. Montgomery sent this signal on 4 September. Ike received it on 5 September and replied at 1945hrs that day. The reply did not reach Montgomery's HQ until 0900hrs on 7 September – and then only the last two paragraphs arrived. The *first* two paragraphs of Ike's message did not reach Monty until 1015hrs on 9 September – it was taking four full days for two senior commanders to exchange messages, a fact which gave little encouragement to the one urging prompt decisions and quick action.

Nor was the reply encouraging. Eisenhower agreed with the concept of a powerful and full-blooded thrust towards Berlin, 'but did not agree that it should be initiated at this moment to the exclusion of all other manoeuvres.' Eisenhower stated that since the bulk of the German Army in the west had not been destroyed, the Allies must immediately exploit their present success by promptly breaching the West Wall, crossing the Rhine on a wide front, and seizing the Ruhr *and the Saar* before the Germans could regroup. Ike then continued:

This I intend to do with all possible speed. It will give us a stranglehold on two of Germany's main industrial areas and largely destroy his capacity to wage war, whatever course events may take. It will assist in cutting off forces now retiring from South West France. Moreover, it will give us freedom of action to strike in any direction and will force the enemy to disperse over a wide area such forces as he may be able to muster for the defence of the West.

While we are advancing we will be opening the ports of Le Havre and

Antwerp, which are essential to maintain a powerful thrust deep into Germany. *No relocation of our present resources would be adequate to sustain a thrust to Berlin.* [Author's italics]

My intention is initially to occupy the Saar and the Ruhr and by the time we have done this Havre and Antwerp should both be available to maintain one or both of the thrusts you mention. In this connection I have always given priority to the Ruhr – rpt Ruhr – and the northern route of advance, as indicated in my directive of yesterday, which crossed your telegram. Locomotives and rolling stock are today being allocated on the basis of priority to maintain the momentum of your advance and those of Bradley, north-west of the Ardennes. Please let me know at once your further maintenance requirements.

The reference to a 'directive of yesterday' refers to Eisenhower's 4 September directive – which Monty had not yet seen.

This missive is exasperating. Even the British Official History, usually noted for its tact, refers delicately to the somewhat indefinite phrasing of the Supreme Commander's objectives.'[6] What exactly does Eisenhower want? Now, apparently, the 21st Army Group (does he mean all of it or just Second Army?) and two-thirds of First Army were to cross the Rhine and take the Ruhr... and Eisenhower seemed to believe that it was possible to open Antwerp and take the Ruhr and the Saar at the same time!

Antwerp had already fallen – though Eisenhower may not yet have known this – but in any event, taking Antwerp and clearing the Scheldt were quite different tasks. But Ike may not have appreciated this either. This directive makes no reference whatsoever to the use of Antwerp or the need to seal off the escape of Fifteenth Army. Indeed, with the Rhine dominating their thoughts, none of the Allied commanders seem to have considered either clearing the Scheldt or eliminating the Fifteenth Army as their next priority.

This directive appears to send the entire 21st Army Group to the Rhine and dismembers Hodges' command, leaving the First Army commander without troops – his other corps, the V Corps, is currently supporting Patton Patton, who is still on the Meuse, has to cross the West Wall and the Saar and the Rhine and take Frankfurt, a city well inside Germany, but is not to attempt any of this until the forces north of the Ardennes have been 'adequately supported'. Who by? Or does this refer only to logistical support? Events were to overtake the orders in this directive but it hardly reveals a clear grasp of the current front line situation at SHAEF.

Just to add further complications, Bradley and Patton were already undermining this directive. On 4 September, the day this directive went out, Bradley reached the conclusion that the situation in the north had already been stabilised and Patton could be turned loose again – though in fact he had never stopped. Bradley authorised Patton to 'cross the Moselle and force the Siegfried Line' – allocating half of 12th Army Group's supplies to Patton for this purpose. In addition, apart from the detaching of V Corps from First Army to cover Patton's left flank, Bradley also allocated the 2nd French Armoured Division and the 79th Infantry Division, formerly with Hodges' XIX Corps, to Patton, forming them into the XV Corps, which would operate on Patton's southern flank.

If Eisenhower really intended to give priority to the northern thrust, this intention seems to have eluded Bradley and Patton. Hodges' army now had to extend its right to cover Patton instead of using its left to support the drive for the Ruhr. Patton resumed his advance on 5 September and by the 10th had two small bridgeheads over the Moselle south of Metz, where his advance stalled as Model's units came up to contest the Moselle position. However, on 10 September, the French 2nd Armoured Division made contact with the 1st French Infantry Division of Devers' group near Dijon, so linking the Dragoon and Overlord forces. Two days later Devers' 6th Army Group was activated as part of Eisenhower's ever-expanding responsibilities.

Eisenhower's reply of 5 September to Montgomery deserves analysis, not least the part that concerns logistics. The interesting point is that Eisenhower apparently believes that it is possible to cross the Rhine and take both the Ruhr and the Saar – and open the Scheldt – using the existing logistical resources. If this is so – and Eisenhower was the Supreme Commander and the Ground Force Commander and who else was in a better position to know – it is hard to see why concentrating all the resources on 'one powerful, full-blooded thrust', would not carry the 'Northern Group of Armies' across the Rhine and 'towards Berlin'.

It might have been better if Montgomery had refrained from mentioning Berlin at all and concentrated on efforts to cross the Rhine and take the Ruhr. As we shall see, none of these objectives, not the Rhine, not the Saar, not the Ruhr

– certainly not Berlin – were crossed or captured in 1944. Mentioning Berlin simply provided his numerous enemies with a whip to beat him with, both at the time and since, a lesson Montgomery should have learned after the Caen arguments in Normandy. However, the sum total of this exchange reveals that taking any of these objectives is little more than wishful thinking because there was no viable strategic plan, no detailed orders from SHAEF, telling the field commanders what to do next.

On 6 September, Second Army resumed its advance from east of Antwerp towards the Rhine with XXX Corps moving on two roads, the one through Eindhoven to Grave and Nijmegen, and the other through Tilburg and Zalt-bommel. If all went well, both routes would end up on the Lower Rhine – the Neder Rijn – at Arnhem.

All did not go well. In the days since the fall of Antwerp, the Germans had strengthened their positions along the Albert Canal and in the industrial suburbs north of the port: the attack of the 11th Armoured Division, employing only its infantry brigade, was therefore quickly held. On the following day, 7 September, Horrocks ordered the 50th Division to establish a bridgehead over the canal, but again only one infantry brigade, the 69th, was available. This brigade attacked on 8 September, got across the canal and established a small bridgehead, being joined there on the 9th by the 151st Infantry Brigade and some tanks. This proved enough to hold off strong German counter-attacks and the bridgehead was gradually extended to include the town of Gheel, two miles from the canal, before more counter-attacks forced a withdrawal to positions between the canal and the town. That was as far as they could go. On 12 September, XII Corps took over this bridgehead to free XXX Corp for the Market Garden operation.

On 10 September, while this engagement was in progress, Eisenhower flew to Brussels for a meeting with his British subordinate. As usual, it was Eisenhower who had to make the trip and this was not easy, for Ike had injured his knee and was unable to leave the aircraft. The meeting took place on board and, also as usual, Montgomery tried to insist that he and Eisenhower discussed matters in private, with no staff officers present. In this instance the demand was not met: Air Marshal Sir Arthur Tedder, the Deputy Allied Supreme Commander and a strong opponent of Montgomery, stayed in the aircraft.

The meeting did not go well. Montgomery produced the various signals that he had received in recent days – signals that would have tried the patience of a more placid man than Monty – and proceeded to attack Eisenhower's proposals and directives, piece by piece and root and branch, throwing in his far-from-high opinion of the Supreme Commander's strategy and stating bluntly where these policies would lead. Eisenhower displayed his usual patience for a while and then, placing his hand on Montgomery's knee, said 'Steady on, Monty. You cannot talk to me like that. I'm your boss.'

This stopped Montgomery in full flow and he apologised. (It is interesting that no mention of this exchange appears in Montgomery's *Memoirs*, where the meeting is covered on page 275.) Although the rest of the meeting passed off amicably, no changes were made to Eisenhower's last directive: the broad front policy would be pursued. Even so, Montgomery was urged to press on with his plan to use the Allied Airborne Army in one powerful, full-blooded thrust to the Lower Rhine at Arnhem – a thrust that just a week later would become Operation Market Garden.

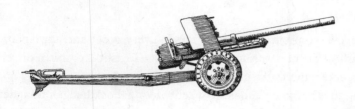

3 · THE MATTER OF LOGISTICS
AUGUST – SEPTEMBER, 1944

*Seldom a subject for news headlines, logistic considerations nevertheless exert a
strong influence not only on strategic planning but also on the conduct
of operations once the battle has begun.*

ROLAND G. RUPPENTHAL *LOGISTICS AND THE BROAD FRONT STRATEGY,* 1944

At this point in the story, and before moving on to Market Garden, it seems
necessary to take a close look at the question of logistics, that arcane area of
the military art concerned with the problems of supply. Roland Ruppenthal
subtitles his contribution on the US supply situation *The Tyranny of Logistics,* a
very accurate description for the problems supply was to cause the Allied commanders in the post-Normandy period.

As Ruppenthal points out, logistical problems rarely make the headlines,
perhaps because they are too complicated, perhaps because they are considered a distraction from the fascinations of combat and command. As for the
commanders at SHAEF, they were most anxious to keep their supply problems
out of the headlines, for the US supply organisation in the ETO – an organisation usually known as COMZ – was a total shambles.

Logistics are inseparable from combat and command: neither function can
be carried out for long unless the relevant logistical concerns have been
addressed. This being so, at least a basic understanding of logistics is necessary
in order to understand the difficulties facing General Eisenhower and his subordinates in the autumn of 1944. During this period, the problem of logistics

was on everyone's mind and appears in every order and appreciation but, curiously, very little was done to address the logistical problem directly until some weeks into the campaign.

Logistics had been a major concern among the Allied commanders since long before D-Day. Indeed, the extension of the Cossack plan of 1943, which originally called for a limited, four-division assault in the centre of the bay of the Seine, to the fifty-mile wide landing that actually took place on 6 June 1944, was largely inspired by the need to extend the landing areas into the Cotentin peninsula and so rapidly secure Cherbourg as a supply port, capable of landing many tons of supplies every day, whatever the weather or conditions at sea.

Until Cherbourg was captured and cleared, which was not until the end of June, the Allied armies were forced to rely on the Mulberry harbour at Arromanches, or landing stores over open beaches like Utah, or the limited facilities of the smaller Norman ports around the bay of the Seine – Isigny, Port-en-Bessin, Courseulles – as ways of supplying the armies in the field. Since the armies did not move very much until the end of July, these facilities proved adequate. Cherbourg proved its worth during the August fighting but as the armies raced away to the Seine and beyond, after the Normandy breakout, the use of Cherbourg as a supply port gradually declined.

The problem now was not one of availability or storage, or port facilities – the Allies had plenty of supplies. The problem after the breakout was *transportation*, the sheer difficulty of shifting tons of military stores, particularly petrol and ammunition, from the vast dumps established in Normandy to the Allied armies now advancing across Belgium and eastern France.

The situation was compounded by two factors: the armies were advancing much faster and further than anticipated and there were more divisions in the field than the planners had allowed for. The Allied armies had reached the Seine eleven days ahead of schedule, which was not in itself a problem, but they had not then paused on the river line to regroup, as the planners had anticipated, because the enemy was in full retreat. The Allied divisions had forged after him in hot pursuit, and to take the US armies as an example, by 1 September, Bradley had *sixteen* US divisions beyond the Seine. That was four more divisions – a 25 per cent larger force – than SHAEF had anticipated having to handle at this time, and all sixteen were 150 miles ahead of their planned position.

The British and Canadians were also forging ahead, far beyond anything anticipated before the breakout, but since their armies were smaller and could be supplied by the Channel ports, Montgomery's logistical problems were somewhat smaller than those confronting Bradley. On 30 August, when Hodges and Patton ran low on fuel, Dempsey could report to SHAEF that 'his supply situation was satisfactory.' This happy situation did not last and 21st Army Group's supply problems were soon to rival those of the American armies – though the organisation for handling them was far superior.

Supply problems did not greatly affect the Dragoon Force – Devers' 6th Army Group – which drew adequate supplies through Marseilles and Toulon. The supply problem mainly affected Bradley's 12th Army Group, but the chronic problems of supply had a knock-on effect with 21st Army Group and the entire Allied operation north of the Seine. As the armies advanced the supply lines grew ever more stretched and the distribution of the available stores was neither equitable nor in line with Eisenhower's strategic concept.

Given the complaints freely voiced at SHAEF about 'stalemate' and slow progress before the Normandy breakout, the Supreme Commander might have welcomed this progress, but it caused problems, and the facilities to cope with the situation were limited. Months of bombing before the invasion, and many weeks of shelling, tactical bombing and sabotage by the French Resistance after it, had reduced the French road and rail network to ruins: track destroyed, bridges and tunnels blown-up, marshalling yards wrecked and the majority of French locomotive and rolling stock crippled.

Road transport was the obvious alternative, but weeks of use with little time for maintenance during the Normandy battle meant that a significant proportion of the army trucks available were constantly breaking down or out of action through a lack of spare parts. Some help was provided by transport aircraft flying supplies to the front, but air supply could never deliver the necessary tonnage – and the aircraft were also needed for airborne operations.

The best way to ship supplies from the base depots to the front was by rail, but weeks were to go by before the French and Belgian rail networks were in any state to handle a viable quantity of traffic. That placed the SHAEF transportation problem back in the hands of the army transport companies. They had to truck the necessary stores to units at the front, using large quantities of precious fuel and wearing out the trucks still further in the process. The situation was not helped by the discovery in September that no fewer than 1,500 three-ton lorries supplied to the British Second Army to tackle the transportation problem had faulty pistons and could not be used at all.

A further problem arose over the transportation of petrol. The Allied armies took no fewer than 22 million jerry cans to France in June, yet by August about half of these had disappeared, either sold to French farmers or stolen. The result, says Martin van Creveld, was that 'the loss of this humble item limited the entire POL (Petrol, Oil and Lubricants) supply system.'[2]

An understanding of the total picture must embrace the fact that the two national armies, British/Canadian and American, had different supply requirements. Many items – ammunition, weapons, wireless and vehicle parts, even rations – were not interchangeable. Two separate supply organisations were set up to cater for these differing needs, the British electing to establish their main supply dumps around Bayeux during the course of the Normandy battle, the US supply organisation, the Lines of Communications Zone, or COMZ, moving its headquarters from Britain to the Cotentin in July, and then into Paris shortly after the city was liberated in August.

Since the COMZ operation had a very direct effect on the operations of the rapidly expanding US armies, it can be covered first – a step which will quickly reveal that the US supply problems were by no means confined to transportation. The COMZ move into Paris took place between the end of August and the middle of September, at a time when the US armies were driving hard for the German frontier, and this move added administrative headaches to the usual round of supply problems. Many of the chronic US supply problems were rooted in the US army command system, whereby the logistical services were largely outside the control of the General Staff at SHAEF and had a separate chain of command leading back to Washington.

COMZ was a vast organisation, commanded by Lieutenant General J. C. H. Lee – a lay preacher – nicknamed, without much affection, 'Jesus Christ Himself' Lee, who reported directly to Lieutenant General Brehon Somerville, General Marshall's logistical adviser and head of the Supply Services in Washington, rather than to Eisenhower, the Supreme Allied Commander in Europe. This alone infuriated Eisenhower's Chief of Staff, Walter Bedell Smith, who had no say in matters of supply, rightly regarded Lee as a stuffed shirt and, equally rightly, felt that the Supply Services in the ETO should be responsible to, and take orders from, the Allied Supreme Commander.

But, as Graham and Bidwell put it, 'In the ETO, Lee was to be a commander outside the control of SHAEF and Chief of General Staff, Bedell Smith.'[3] Essentially, the US Supply Services, which supplied the armies with the means to fight, were completely independent of Eisenhower's staff.

Had push come to shove, it is possible that Eisenhower could have sacked Lee, but not without provoking an almighty row in Washington where Lee had powerful friends and Marshall had encouraged Somerville to act independently. Besides, the ever-reasonable Eisenhower thought that any conflict over administrative matters could be settled in round-table discussion between men of goodwill. Eisenhower disliked rows and resisted all pressure from Bedell Smith to put Lee firmly in his place – only to find that goodwill was in very short supply between SHAEF and the Supply Services.

It was Lee who decided what the armies in the field should have. This was bound to create problems because the armies' requirements changed according to their situation. When they were advancing, they needed fuel; when they were about to attack they needed ammunition; when they were moving over to the defensive they needed mines, wire and trench stores. When the weather turned cold, the soldiers needed winter clothing; and there was a constant demand for food, medical supplies, radio batteries and basic stores.

None of this impacted on General Lee and his minions. They went by the book and if goods were not in the book they could not be issued at all. Moreover, items were issued to scale, or a pre-calculated requirement – and if the troops were using fuel or food or ammunition in excess of scale, no extra supplies would be forthcoming from COMZ: 'If an item was not on the authorised scale of equipment it could not be issued. If a unit's demands exceeded its authorised scale its operations should be modified since obviously the scale could not be changed.'[4]

Needless to say, through sheer necessity, the troops in the field found ways round this bureaucratic insanity. Foraging parties went back to the base depots and took what they wanted or bribed the storemen to supply their needs; petrol trucks destined for one army, corps or division, were hi-jacked by men from units in greater need. This last behaviour was particularly common in Third Army, where Patton, who was fully aware of what was going on, described it as 'not war, but magnificent'.

The fact that combat units were reduced to such expedients should have been a cause for shame and some drastic action, but nothing was done.

In practice, COMZ amounted to General Lee's private army. Strange tales were soon in circulation at SHAEF about what COMZ got up to – for example, that an aircraft was despatched to Morocco every week and returned loaded with citrus fruits so that General Lee and his favoured few could enjoy freshly squeezed orange juice for breakfast and sliced lemon in their gin and tonics. COMZ was also deeply involved in the thriving Parisian black market, where scarce items like cigarettes and petrol were more valuable than gold.

Ralph Teeters, a 66mm mortar man in the 22nd Infantry Regiment, 4th Infantry Division, describes how this attitude impacted on the line infantry:

> We had been living on 'K' and 'C' rations for what seemed like months because our field kitchens had been left behind in Paris, to save fuel I guess. Anyway, when they finally caught up with us, the Company Commander urged the mess sergeant to cook us a hot meal... and the cooks had nothing, but nothing, to cook.
>
> They had given away everything in exchange for the good life in Paris – the booze and the women. I can't say I blamed them but the Company Commander *chewed* on the Mess Sergeant for a good fifteen minutes; you could hear him all over the Company area... and when those cooks finally found something to feed us they could hardly look us in the eye.[5]

COMZ was vast. When it moved to France in 1944 the COMZ HQ near Valognes in the Cotentin contained no fewer than 11,000 administrative staff and occupied more than half a million square feet of office space – not counting the huge area covered by the supply dumps or the thousands of men engaged in actually picking out the stores and loading the trains and trucks. No sooner had this base been established in Western France than General Lee decided that the COMZ operation should be moved to Paris – a move that infuriated General Eisenhower, who rightly suspected that the main attraction was the Paris fleshpots rather than administrative efficiency.

Paris had been designated as a leave centre for US combat troops but COMZ personnel quickly occupied no fewer than 296 city centre hotels, some 90 per cent of the available accommodation. COMZ people were also accused – with considerable factual basis – of being more interested in the Paris nightlife than in supporting the troops in the field. COMZ staff soon became involved in the thriving black market, where filtering off PX stores or comforts intended for the front line troops were a way of obtaining the good things of life – girls, fine food, liquor.

Reports that COMZ staff and a growing number of Army deserters were dabbling in the black market reached Eisenhower's ears and he was soon complaining to Lee that the dress, conduct and discipline of US troops in Paris was 'little short of disgraceful'.

That was putting the situation mildly. Rival gangs, many containing American deserters, were soon hijacking trains, stealing truckloads of fuel and engaging in gunfights in the Bois de Boulogne. By mid-September there were around 15,000 American deserters in the Paris area, all supporting themselves on the Black Market by raiding the Supply Services. By the autumn of 1944, Paris was a wide-open town, as Ralph Teeters recalls:

> Leave came round to the longest serving man in the Company that had not had any. First we went back to Regiment and got cleaned up and a wise old sergeant told us that money was useless in Paris – the currency was American cigarettes and he piled my arms with cartons of Chesterfields, like piling up logs.
>
> He was right, the rate of exchange was around three or four packs of cigarettes for one Parisian whore and maybe a carton for a bottle of brandy; women were cheaper. I did not know how long I would be in the war or how long I would survive so I did not go up the Eiffel Tower or see the Louvre – I don't even know if it was open. I went to 'Pig-Alley' as we called Pigalle and wore myself out in forty-eight hours on drink and sex... and then we got back in the trucks and went back to the war.[6]

Had COMZ been efficient none of this might have mattered much – some corruption is common in the rear area of all war zones – but COMZ was overstaffed, badly commanded by Lee and totally ignorant of, and less than interested in, the problems of the troops in the field. Far from being one of the solutions, COMZ became one of the problems, and inevitably these problems extended to those of command. Bedell Smith and Lee were always at each other's throats but, secure in his support from Washington, Lee felt able to ignore Bedell Smith and Bradley and, if he so wished, engage directly over their heads with Hodges and Patton. Meanwhile, Patton was not slow to butter Lee up: when Lee visited the Third Army in the autumn of 1944, Patton welcomed him with an Honor Guard and a band.

Lee could do this because in the US army, group and corps commanders were concerned solely with operational matters and not with the details of supply. How operational matters could be organised *without* control of supply was yet another problem that Eisenhower failed to tackle, thereby increasing his own problems as the Allied armies headed for Germany.

Montgomery's 21st Army Group had a very different and somewhat easier supply set-up, not least because the British and Canadian supply services were totally subordinate to Montgomery and had far fewer divisions to maintain. British maintenance was organised around a Rear Maintenance Area at Bayeux and an Advanced Base in the Brussels area, which began to form in early September. Montgomery's divisions were not flush with supplies but they had enough to keep moving – and could have gone further had their transport situation been improved. Transport was the key: it all depended on improving the rail network or finding more trucks.

As more and more divisions landed and the battle front moved north and east, the supply situation became more acute and would remain acute until a major port, close to the area of operations, became available. Other Channel ports did slowly come on stream – Le Havre, Dieppe, Ostend – but none were big enough or close enough to the front to put a serious dent in the logistical problem. There was, in fact, only one realistic answer to the chronic logistical problem, not merely of supply, but of transportation – Antwerp.

Antwerp lies at the root of the dilemma facing the Allied commanders and the question of why it was not opened to shipping immediately after the port itself was taken remains one of the on-going arguments surrounding the post-Normandy campaign.

At this point we have to tackle the problem of ends and means. As the previous chapters have shown, at the end of August and in early September the Allies were thinking of three 'ends', or objectives: the Rhine, the Ruhr and Berlin. The question that has to be answered is whether the existing means were sufficient for all or any of those ends. Or would it be necessary to abandon all hope of advancing even to the Rhine until the Allies improved their logistical situation by abandoning the pursuit – so giving the Germans time to regroup – and opening the port of Antwerp?

The evidence from the two previous chapters seems to suggest that, *provided the right strategy was employed*, getting to the Rhine by the end of 1944 was probable, seizing the Ruhr was possible – but taking Berlin was a pipe-dream, even if the Allies had opened Antwerp by, say, the end of September.

The Allied failure to grasp the need for Antwerp baffles this historian. This is not to say that the need to open Antwerp was not realised, either at SHAEF, or by Eisenhower and Montgomery, by tacticians and logisticians at the time, and by every historian who has written about this campaign since 1944. Eisenhower's directives and the correspondence with his commanders usually refer to Antwerp and the desirability of bringing it into use. Historians now agree, if only with the inestimable benefit of hindsight, that opening Antwerp should have been the prime objective for the Allied armies after the Seine crossing.

The difficulty lies in finding out why, given the importance of Antwerp, clearing the Scheldt was not the major priority and orders – not directives or suggestions or requests – but *orders*, firm unequivocal orders for the opening of Antwerp were not given to the relevant Army Group commander, in this case Field Marshal Montgomery, by Eisenhower, and the 21st Army Group barred from any other task until this one had been completed. As Supreme Commander and Ground Force Commander, Eisenhower should have given Montgomery a direct order to clear the Scheldt early in September. However, on the day Antwerp fell, Eisenhower's new directive ordered 'the forces north-west of the Ardennes' – 21st Army Group and two corps of the US First Army – 'to secure Antwerp, reach the sector of the Rhine covering the Ruhr and then seize the Ruhr.' In other words, not one priority task, but *three*.

Antwerp was already secure but the task given to 'the forces north-west of the Ardennes' was formidable enough and would absorb every division Montgomery had or could borrow. This left him with nothing to spare to assist the Canadians in the clearing of the Scheldt – and that task was not specified in Eisenhower's orders at all.

One argument, popular in the United States, is that the need to open Antwerp was so evident that Montgomery did not need a direct order from Eisenhower. He should have cleared the Scheldt anyway, they declare, employing whatever forces were necessary from 21st Army Group to complete the job quickly. There is some merit in this argument. Had Montgomery decided to divert Second

Army away from the northern thrust and direct it towards the South Beveland peninsula, the destruction of the Fifteenth Army and the opening of the Scheldt, it is hard to imagine that anyone would have stopped him. Although Eisenhower declared that the northern thrust was his main priority, that did not stop Patton charging off to the east and Eisenhower did little or nothing to stop him. Had Montgomery elected to act in a similar fashion and send Second Army west, no doubt he would have been allowed the same latitude.

However, Montgomery's attention was also fixed in the north, his aim a crossing of the Rhine between Arnhem and Wesel. He entrusted the task of opening the Channel ports and clearing the Scheldt to the First Canadian Army, but his hopes here may have been conditioned by some other factors. Clearly, taking Antwerp was a leap in the right direction, but without clearing the sixty-five-mile estuary of the Scheldt, Antwerp could not be used.

The choices open to Montgomery on 4 September were either to assist the Canadians clear the Scheldt – which offered the bonus of destroying the German Fifteenth Army – or, hopefully with the assistance of a corps or two of Bradley's Army Group, pursuing the more attractive course of pushing on to the Rhine, perhaps even to the Ruhr, with all the attendant glory that might bring. In his *Memoirs* Montgomery states: 'I thought that the Canadian Army could clear the Scheldt while Second Army took the Ruhr and I was wrong.'

Divisions of the British Second Army should and could have been diverted to the Scheldt or used to seal off the South Beveland peninsula after the fall of Antwerp. This was not done because, like everyone else at this time, Montgomery's eyes were fixed on the Rhine: he was busy urging Dempsey's army north in pursuit of the German armies and, from mid-September, he was busy with Operation Market Garden.

It should also be remembered that Montgomery was no longer the Allied Ground Force Commander, directly concerned with the implementation of strategy. He was concerned with the progress of events in 21st Army Group. The man responsible for strategy, for the selection of tasks in order of priority, was Dwight Eisenhower. It would not do to pass the buck for strategic decisions to one of his Army Group commanders.

However, Eisenhower was currently obsessed with the various moves necessary to implement his broad front policy – and so, for all these reasons, Antwerp slipped down the scale of priority at SHAEF and 21st Army Group.

Therefore nobody gripped the chronic problem of supply, which continued until Antwerp was finally opened at the end of November. So, given that Eisenhower decided *not* to give priority to opening Antwerp, what could his armies achieve *with their existing resources*?

It would be as well to examine the two strategic proposals on the table at this time – Eisenhower's broad front policy and Montgomery's end of August proposal to Bradley for a powerful thrust to the Rhine or even into Germany by forty divisions – '*a force so strong it need fear nothing*' – which later became known as the narrow thrust policy.

The first question is where these forty divisions would come from. At the end of August 1944, there were just forty-seven Allied divisions on the Continent. If forty were formed up for Montgomery's powerful thrust, would seven divisions suffice to stem any German counter-attack or continue the pursuit elsewhere? In the event, reality soon took over and the narrow thrust was reduced to the Second Army and two US corps, the XIX and VII of Hodges' First Army, a total of around eighteen Allied divisions, nine from Second Army, nine from Hodges' First Army. With the addition of several independent tank brigades from Second Army, the total force for the proposed narrow thrust would amount to some twenty divisions, a more realistic but very powerful force.

The choice of strategy was Eisenhower's, but quite apart from the need to choose a workable strategy soon and get on with implementing it, the success or failure of either strategy depended almost entirely on logistics. Since the calculations are smaller – and it was never actually tried – the proposed narrow thrust strategy can be considered first. Here arises the first query – could an Anglo-American force of, say, twenty divisions, be supported while it advanced rapidly towards the Rhine in the north? Putting aside the fact that an army pursuing a beaten foe has different logistical requirements from an army mounting an offensive, and sticking solely to global tonnage, however composed, what daily supply tonnage would such a force require?

Inevitably, estimates vary. In his essay on logistics and the broad front strategy, Roland G. Ruppenthal gives 650 tons per division, per day, as the basic requirement for the US First Army.[7] This figure is accepted as a working average for both British and US armies by another authority, Martin Van Creveld.[8] If this is correct, a twenty-division force would require 13,000 tons of supply every day. On the other hand, van Creveld adds that 650 tons per division is 'generous to a fault'[9] and other estimates – usually British – range from 300 to 400 tons per division per day.[10]

However, accepting that 650 tons per division, per day, is indeed necessary to sustain a strong advance, did the Allies have such a quantity available and could it be transported to the advancing units? Montgomery obviously thought it could. When evaluating this opinion it should be borne in mind that from his desert days Montgomery always insisted on commanding a balanced force – one where the fighting units were supported by the supply services – and was particularly insistent on 'drawing up his administrative tail': halting his forces if need be to bring up supplies, an insistence that had infuriated the Americans on many occasions and underpinned many of their accusations of slowness and caution.

From 1942 to 1943 Montgomery had conducted a 1,500-mile pursuit of Rommel in North Africa in the months after Alamein – and North Africa had long been regarded as 'a tactician's paradise and a quartermaster's hell.' If any commander could evaluate the possibilities of this proposed advance in North-West Europe, that commander was Bernard Law Montgomery. However, the matter of supply is not an easy one to evaluate, since the supply situation varied from army to army and was subject to further variations caused by the weather – which was starting to deteriorate as the summer ended.

Even so, again according to van Creveld, in the second week of August COMZ was shipping 17,000 tons of supplies per day to the First and Third US Armies and, as already related, on 30 August, Dempsey reported that the Second Army supply situation was 'very favourable'[11] with his service units capable of unloading 17,000 tons of supplies a day. This gives the four Allied armies in the North – Canadian First, British Second, US First and Third – the notional quantity of 34,000 tons of supplies per day (Dever's 6th Army Group, currently forging up the Rhône valley, is left out of this calculation as it was being adequately supplied via Marseilles and Toulon, and the Allied forces in Normandy and Brittany – the first divisions of Lieutenant General William Simpson's Ninth Army – were close to the supply dumps and had few transportation problems).

However, assuming that Second Army and attached units took 13,000 tons, that still left 21,000 tons for the rest of the US First Army and the Third Army and, according to Chester Wilmot, in early September Bradley's 12th Army

Group needed only 10,000 tons per day and was rubbing along with 7,000 tons per day, of which 5,000 were destined for Hodges and 2,000 for Patton.[12] Even allowing for error, the gap between the amount needed to keep the armies moving and the amounts that, allegedly, could have been supplied, lead one to suppose that the Rhine or the Ruhr could have been reached on the existing logistical resources – provided these supplies could reach the front.

It will be appreciated that this is a rough calculation with no margin for error and no spare capacity anywhere for the build-up of a logistical reserve. Besides, although these figures are as accurate as calculations based on official information can be – i.e. not very – they refer to supplies landed at the ports and beaches, not to supplies at the front. Did the Royal Army Service Corps (RASC) and the US trucking companies, with a certain amount of help from railways and aircraft, have the capacity to move these stores forward? There were, inevitably, a number of snags here. In the recent busy weeks time for vehicle maintenance had been much reduced, putting many vehicles out for repair, while hundreds of trucks had been lost to mines or damaged in crashes. The US armies, if richer in transport than the British or Canadian, still had none to spare, and were employing every available truck on the Red Ball Express to supply First Army. The airlift of supplies to the front never exceeded 1,000 tons per day – barely a drop in the bucket – and was highly weather dependent.

This puts the responsibility for supply squarely on the US and British transport companies. There were never enough of these and the US History calculates that Montgomery's thrust, by three British and two US Corps, would require the attention of no fewer than 489 truck companies and only 347 were available – a shortage of 137.[13] It was then calculated that this could be partly made up by transporting 2,000 tons of supplies every day by air – the equivalent of sixty truck companies. The balance, and a surplus for emergencies, would be supplied by grounding up to ten Allied divisions and taking over their organic truck companies for the supply role, so creating another 181 extra truck companies. Van Creveld's conclusion is that there were adequate transport facilities to carry the narrow thrust to the Ruhr;[14] it therefore appears that a sufficiency of stores and transport existed to support this narrow thrust to the Rhine and Ruhr – if only just.[15]

At this point it should be remembered that in early August Montgomery scaled down his 'powerful thrust' considerably, from forty divisions to eighteen

– nine from Hodges' First Army, nine from Dempsey's Second Army, the former using the Maastricht –Liège position as their Start Line, the latter jumping off from the Meuse–Escaut canal east of Antwerp. Keeping to the same logistical calculation as before, this combined force would need 11,700 tons of stores per day – a more achievable figure.

Therefore, on this very rough calculation, it appears that Montgomery's narrow thrust to the Rhine and the Ruhr was logistically possible. There was of course another cost in political terms: if Patton's Third Army was stopped to let Montgomery and Hodges forge ahead, the US press and public would, at least according to Marshall and Eisenhower, be infuriated.

However, pressure on the enemy could still be maintained by Patton, albeit at a slower pace. From the logistical point of view therefore, reaching the Rhine in the north would be possible using a twenty-division Anglo-American force – *provided* such a force could penetrate the German positions north of the West Wall, which petered out south of Arnhem.

Yet with such a large number of 'ifs' in play, Montgomery's narrow thrust must still be regarded as a gamble. This plan was proposed during the time when hot pursuit was the dominating priority in the Allied armies. The need to press on after the enemy was fuelled by the need to deny him the time to rest, regroup, occupy defensive positions and reinforce the battered units of the retreating German armies.

It will be recalled that Montgomery proposed this 'powerful and full blooded thrust' to Eisenhower on 4 September, the day the Second Army entered Antwerp, stressing that there was not enough maintenance for two thrusts and that the one in the north, via the Ruhr, would be the most decisive – a fact which few have disputed and we can accept. But this single course of action did not appeal to Eisenhower – or rather, while agreeing with the benefits of 'a powerful and full blooded thrust towards Berlin', he was equally sure that this need not mean the abandonment of all other operations by Bradley and Patton. In fact, according to that message sent to Montgomery on 5 September, Ike thought it was perfectly possible to capture the Ruhr *and* the Saar – but not Berlin – move the armies up to the West Wall and cross the Rhine on a wide front, before the enemy could muster an adequate defence and, while all this was going on, open the ports of Antwerp and Le Havre and thereby ensure sufficient maintenance to sustain an all-out drive into the heart of Germany.

This is baffling. If the Allied armies could actually do all this, then there was no logistical problem – though everyone said there was. Then, having come out in favour of a broad front strategy, Eisenhower said that he still intended to give priority to the northern route – though with his resources so widely dispersed it is hard to see how he could do so.

Patton's actions also deserve study, not least for the effect they had on the supply situation. In the original, post-Normandy plan, any southern thrust into Germany by the Third Army, via Rheims, Verdun and Metz, was regarded as a secondary operation: the main target was the Ruhr, either via Arnhem–Wesel or through the Aachen Gap. The tasks of Third Army were to move on the West Wall, link the northern armies with Devers' forces coming up the Rhône valley, form a broad front, and prevent the Germans shifting more troops north to oppose the main Allied thrust. Patton's rapid, headline-grabbing advances to the east had moved this secondary plan into a more central role.

However much the overall strategy and the logistical situation dictated a halt, Patton fully intended to forge ahead regardless, and Bradley elected to support him, in spite of any effect this might have on his other force, the First Army. Eisenhower lacked sufficient grip to override their joint demands and prevent the undermining of his policy, besides being understandably pleased that an American army was making the ground and the headlines at this time. Stopping Patton in mid-career to Metz was not an option Eisenhower was eager to consider.

With all the Allied commanders believing victory was just around the corner, the US commanders clearly hoped that if Third Army could get across the Rhine, that alone might precipitate a German collapse. The arguments for supporting Patton were similar to those advanced by Montgomery for his narrow thrust in the north: if Third Army's ten or twelve divisions could have all the available logistical support, the Rhine could probably be crossed in the south and, perhaps, the US troops could even enter Frankfurt, one of the major German cities.

'This entire proposal', states Ruppenthal, 'was predicated on the conviction that the enemy could be frightened into instant capitulation.'[16]

He adds that: 'Such a result was by no means assured at this time', and concludes: 'Should the enemy refuse to be shocked into immediate surrender, the operation, in the view of the logistic planners, would bring the Allied forces to the brink of administrative disaster.'[17]

If the arguments for the narrow thrust are typically Montgomery, the notion that everything he wanted could be still be achieved without the need for painful decisions is typically Eisenhower. He had now heard from both his Army Group commanders – or Commanders-in-Chief as they were currently called – and reached the conclusion that they were both right; that it was possible to achieve everything, even with lengthening supply lines and without Antwerp. In thinking this Ike was wrong. It might be as well to point out that the Rhine was not crossed by the Allied armies for another six months, until March 1945, and the Ruhr was not occupied until early April, barely a month before the European war ended.

This raises the next question; *why* did Eisenhower believe the broad front strategy was valid without Antwerp? He was a staff officer of vast experience; his administrative skills were one of the reasons he had been chosen for Supreme Command, and if anyone was capable of taking a balanced view of the Allied situation, that man was Dwight D. Eisenhower.

There is no clear answer to this question. Writing to Marshall on 4 September, he noted: 'We have advanced so rapidly that further movement on large parts of the front, even against very weak opposition, is almost impossible.'[18] This indicates that Ike had now seen the downside of his broad front strategy. Two weeks previously, on 15 August, he had 'violently castigated those who think they can measure the end of the war in a matter of weeks.'[19] But then, says d'Este, 'he too fell victim to the prevailing optimism' and on 15 September, 'he issued a circular to his commanders, based on the assumption that the Allied armies were about to close on the Rhine' and stating 'it was time to plan the final offensive' to capture Berlin. Yet when Montgomery proposed a thrust in the direction of Berlin, Eisenhower was quick to dismiss it as impossible.

Eisenhower was not alone in the virulent optimism of September 1944. In early September Patton declared that if he were only given sufficient petrol, he would 'be in Germany in two days'. In the event it took Patton six months and a great number of lives to get into Germany. Only Winston Churchill, brooding over his maps and Ultra decrypts in London, was more pessimistic: 'It is at least as likely that Hitler will be fighting on 1st January, as that he will collapse before then', he noted. 'If he does collapse the reasons will be political rather than purely military.'[20]

The euphoria gripping SHAEF had Eisenhower in its power but he was also the Ground Force commander and if these hopes were to be fulfilled he needed to take a very close interest in events at the front as they developed. That was not currently possible: the old command bugbear, communications, prevented such attention to detail.

When Eisenhower shifted SHAEF to the Continent he established it in the town of Granville on the Atlantic coast of Normandy, some 400 miles behind the current front line. Communications between Granville and the Army Group commanders were poor – as indicated by that signal from Eisenhower to Montgomery on 5 September which took two days to arrive and arrived in two parts, the second part first. Chester Wilmot records that it was taking twenty-four hours for situation reports to reach SHAEF and another twenty-four hours for Eisenhower's response to get back, an impossible situation when the armies were advancing rapidly and the situation was fluid.[21] There were no telephone links between either Army Group HQ and SHAEF: inevitably, Eisenhower's appreciation of the battles his field commanders were conducting was less up to date than it should have been

On 10 September, the day Ike and Monty met at Brussels airport, these issues had yet to be resolved. Eisenhower was still devoted to his broad front policy but had agreed to 21st Army Group making a drive up to the Rhine at Arnhem, supported by three divisions of the Allied Airborne Army. And so, while the Canadians push for the Scheldt and Patton strives to reach Metz, the attention turns to the northern front and Operation Market Garden.

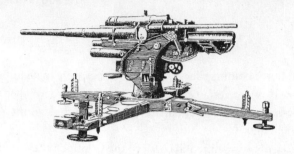

4 · THE ROAD TO ARNHEM
10–23 SEPTEMBER 1944

Market Garden was not a matter of A Bridge Too Far, *but of a road too few.*

LIEUTENANT SYDNEY JARY,
4TH BATTALION, THE SOMERSET LIGHT INFANTRY

The Allied land and airborne operation of September 1944, codenamed Market Garden, is better known to the British public as the Battle of Arnhem. To concentrate on events at Arnhem is actually taking the narrow view, for the great stand of the British 1st Airborne Division north of the Arnhem bridge was only one battle in a series of engagements on the sixty-four mile road from the Meuse–Escaut Canal to the Neder Rijn.

The codename arises from the fact that the Allied planners saw this operation in two parts: Market, the parachute and glider assault by three airborne divisions to seize the bridges over the intervening rivers and canals; and Garden, the advance to Arnhem and beyond by the armoured and infantry divisions of Lieutenant General Sir Brian Horrocks' XXX Corps, spearheading the advance of Second Army.

Horrocks' orders to XXX Corps for Garden were quite specific:

> XXX Corps will break out of the existing bridgehead on 17 September and pass through the airborne carpet which has been laid down in front of us, in order to seize the area Nunspeet–Arnhem and exploit north to the Zuider Zee… the Corps will advance and be supplied down one road – the only major road available – 20,000 vehicles will be involved.

> Tough opposition must be expected at the break out and the country is
> very difficult. Speed is absolutely vital as we must reach the lightly equipped
> 1st Airborne Division, if possible in forty-eight hours.

The story of Market Garden is complicated and readers must approach this chapter with an open mind, ignoring any previous impressions, ingrained beliefs and media myths. This may be difficult. Over the decades since 1944, Market Garden has become shrouded in a large number of myths, many of them either media inspired or the product of cinematic imagination, all of them tending to fog the true situation: a countless number of veterans have urged me to ignore most of the story told in the film *A Bridge Too Far*.

As an example of these myths, many people believe that a traitor in the Dutch Resistance betrayed the Arnhem operation to the Germans. Though the Gestapo had penetrated the Dutch Resistance early in 1944, there is no firm evidence to support this belief. Others believe that Market Garden failed because it was 'a bridge too far' – that in going for the Arnhem bridge the planners were biting off more than their troops could chew. There is little evidence to support this theory either; without the Arnhem bridge, Market Garden was pointless.

The real reasons for the failure of Market Garden are more mundane than imaginary spies and an over-ambitious plan. It is arguable that had better plans been laid, some basic mistakes avoided, and more drive been applied at every level during the operation itself Market Garden would have succeeded in establishing a bridgehead across the Neder Rijn, but the true story of the Arnhem operation is still obscured by three persistent myths.

The first myth is that the British XXX Corps was too slow in moving up to Nijmegen. The second is that the British 1st Airborne Division deliberately chose to land too far from the Arnhem bridges. The final myth is that the Guards Armoured Division failed to exploit the American success at the Nijmegen bridge on the evening of D plus 3 by immediately pushing on to Arnhem. As with most myths, there is some truth in these allegations though, again like many popular myths, they have served a useful role in concealing more painful truths.

In the event, hardly anyone but the front line fighting soldiers in XXX Corps and the Allied Airborne divisions emerges from Market Garden with much credit. To quote Major Dover, OC of 'C' Company, 2nd Parachute Battalion at Arnhem: 'Market Garden was a grand military cock-up.'[1]

This seems to be true: as we shall see, there were cock-ups at every level, from Allied Supreme Headquarters to Corps and Divisional command, and on down to the lowest infantry section. The cumulative total of these cock-ups caused Maket Garden to fail.

To deconstruct the myths of Market Garden two points have to be grasped. The first is that the sole purpose of the airborne operation – Market – was to take the bridges over the various rivers and canals crossed by the road to Arnhem and so lay out an airborne carpet for XXX Corps. Secondly, as the orders of the Airborne Army commander, Lieutenant General Brereton specify, these bridges were to be taken 'with thunderclap surprise'. That meant on D-Day, 17 September, for after D-Day the vital element of surprise would be lost. The bridges must be taken on D-Day – not when the various airborne divisional commanders got around to it.

There has been a tendency to concentrate on the airborne part of Market Garden and play down the difficulties confronting the ground forces. One Guards officer described the Garden operation as 'like threading seven needles with one piece of cotton and only having to miss one to be in trouble' – and all this had to be done in forty-eight hours. Whether the ground forces would be able to thread those needles and keep to their timings would largely depend on the actions of the airborne units.

Another point to remember is that the prime objective of Market was never achieved. The vital airborne carpet, over which XXX Corps was to drive, unhindered and at speed up to Arnhem, was not fully laid on D-Day. That fact, various avoidable errors, plus the rapid response and tenacity of the German army, prevented XXX Corps getting a fast run up to the Lower Rhine and led to the catastrophe of Arnhem.

Market and Garden were not discrete operations. Market Garden has to be regarded as a whole, though in the interests of clarity the story told here has been split into several parts. The next two chapters tell how the Market Garden plan was formulated and describe the actions of the 101st and 82nd US Airborne Divisions at Eindhoven and Nijmegen and the advance of the XXX Corps units from the Meuse–Escaut canal up to Nijmegen. The great fight of the 1st Airborne Division at Arnhem and Oosterbeek will be told in the subsequent chapter.

The story of Market Garden begins with the existence in the UK of SHAEF's only major reserve, the First Allied Airborne Army, a formation which General

Marshall, the Chairman of the CCS and General Hap Arnold, chief of the USAAF, were very eager to use for a major strategic deployment. This crack formation consisted of two British and two (later three) US airborne divisions, commanded in September 1944 by Lieutenant General Lewis H. Brereton, a general of the United States Army Air Force.

The British contingent of this army in September 1944 was the 1st Airborne Division (The Red Devils: the division was given the name by their German opponents, who referred to them as 'roten teufel' – Red Devils), of North Africa fame. The second British division, 6th Airborne, was resting and refitting after Normandy. The 'British' element in the Airborne Army also included the 1st Polish Independent Parachute Brigade, commanded by Major-General Stanislaw Sosabowski and the 52nd Lowland Division (Airportable), a formation which could be flown in to airfields seized by the parachute or glider troops.

The two US Airborne Divisions, the 82nd (All American) and the 101st (Screaming Eagles) had three parachute infantry regiments and a glider infantry regiment, a US regiment being the equivalent of a British brigade. It should be noted that US airborne divisions were 25 per cent larger than British units. 1st Airborne consisted of two parachute brigades, the 1st and 4th, each of three battalions, and an Air Landing (glider) Brigade, also of three battalions. These three divisions formed Lieutenant General Sir Frederick (Boy) Browning's 1st Airborne Corps, which, with Sosabowski's Polish brigade, was the unit tasked with Operation Market.

The 1st Airborne Division had not been employed since it returned from Italy in 1943, and by September 1944 these airborne soldiers were in urgent need of action. Between 6 June and early September no fewer than seventeen operations had been planned for the 1st Airborne Division and all had been cancelled; four when the troops had already emplaned, one when they were actually in the air. These constant cancellations were causing great frustration in 1st Airborne: crack troops need action and the men of 1st Airborne – who were starting to call their unit 'The Stillborn Division' – wanted to get back into the war.

According to the US Military History, by early September 1944 the Allied Airborne Army was an asset 'burning holes in SHAEF's pocket'.[2] Back in Washington, General Marshall and General 'Hap' Arnold were urging Eisenhower to use the Airborne Army and Eisenhower was willing to oblige them. After the Normandy breakout he had offered the airborne divisions to both Bradley and

Montgomery but the rapid advance of the ground forces had overrun a number of possible objectives before the airborne could be sent in – and Bradley anyway preferred to use the transport aircraft for hauling fuel to Patton rather than dropping paratroops. Therefore, since Bradley declined to use them, Eisenhower offered the airborne units to Monty, 'for operations with the Northern Group of Armies up to and including the crossing of the Rhine.'

In early September Montgomery had a plan ready for employing airborne forces – Operation Comet – and some details of Comet should be noted here. Comet called for the 1st Airborne Division and Sosabowski's 1st Polish Parachute Brigade to seize the Grave, Nijmegen and Arnhem bridges, using gliders for *coup de main* attacks, landing close to the bridges, rather as Pegasus Bridge at Benouville had been taken by the 6th Airborne Division on D-Day. Once the bridges had been taken the parachute brigades would land on nearby DZs (drop-zones) and join up with the glider parties to hold the bridges until the ground forces arrived.

In the Comet plan, Brigadier 'Shan' Hackett's 4th Parachute Brigade was tasked to take the road bridge over the Maas at Grave, landing on a DZ just 1,000 yards from the north end of the bridge – which, hopefully, had just been taken by a force from the 1st Air Landing Brigade in four gliders landing at the south end of the bridge. Operation Comet was planned for 10 September; then it was called off and replaced one week later by Market Garden.

The Comet plan stuck to the basic airborne rule – land as close to the objective as possible – and to the basic rule for capturing any bridge – take both ends at once. In view of the subsequent arguments over the deployment of 1st Airborne at Arnhem, one cannot but wonder why the Comet plans for taking the bridges with one reinforced British division, using glider *coup de main* tactics, were regarded as far too risky for an airborne assault by three Allied airborne divisions just one week later?

It has to be clearly understood that taking the bridges on the road to Arnhem was only a means to an end. The final aim was to establish Second Army just west of the Rhine, north of Arnhem, and just south of the Ijsselmeer (or Zuider Zee). Once there, having outflanked the West Wall, which petered out some distance to the south, Second Army could either turn south-east to outflank the Ruhr, or head due east towards Berlin. Any decision on its final destination would rest with General Eisenhower.

Having elected to use the Airborne Army, Montgomery had first to decide where to cross the Rhine. His own preference was for a crossing east of Arnhem, close to the town of Wesel, and Wesel was also the choice of Dempsey in Second Army. Wesel lay just south of the Ruhr and was the better option for Garden, with fewer canals and an easier approach to the river. However, Wesel lay within the Ruhr anti-aircraft gun flak belt and the airborne planners stated that low-flying and slow-moving glider-tugs and parachute aircraft would suffer severe losses if Wesel were chosen (readers should note that Wesel was chosen for the last airborne operation of the war, the Rhine crossing in March 1945, when the US 17th and British 6th Airborne Divisions were dropped around the town).

Therefore, since the air planners – specifically Brereton and Major-General Paul L. Williams of the IX US Troop Carrier Command – had the casting vote over the air element in Market, the decision was made for Arnhem, the target town for a thrust north from the narrow bridgehead over the Meuse–Escaut canal east of Antwerp, a route that would require the crossing of some wide rivers or canals: the Wilhelmina Canal at Zon, the Willems canal at Veghel, the River Maas at Grave, the Maas–Waal canal, the River Waal at Nijmegen and the Lower Rhine (Neder Rijn) at Arnhem (the Waal is the southern arm of the Rhine, which divides in two to form the Waal and Neder Rijn, some distance upstream of Arnhem). There were, in addition, any number of minor streams and canals restricting movement off the main north-south axis.

The point to note here is the destruction of the first Arnhem myth. The choice of drop zones was in the gift of the US Air Force commanders, *not* the airborne commanders – and the factor that governed the Air Force command-ers' choice of parachute drop zones (DZs) or glider landing zones (LZs) was the presence, actual or feared, of anti-aircraft batteries around the bridges. Since the US Air Force commanders considered that these bridges would be sur-rounded by flak guns, they selected landing zones that were, in the main, well away from the bridges.

This decision had some dire effects. The obvious one is that it gave some airborne units – most notably 1st Airborne – a long way to go through enemy territory before they even got to their prime objective. If that were all it would have been bad enough, but there was more. It also deprived the airborne soldiers of that other airborne asset, surprise. Once on the ground, airborne units lack mobility: instead of swooping from the sky onto their objectives in a matter of minutes, the men of 1st Airborne had to march there from distant DZs, and this took hours. Long before they reached the bridges over the Neder Rijn the enemy were fully alert.

In addition, one of the other prime assets of an airborne division is that it can leap over obstacles that would hinder a ground force by landing on both sides of a river bridge at once, which the 82nd Airborne did at the Grave bridge, but not at the Nijmegen bridge. At Arnhem both these assets were lost by the Air Force commanders choice of DZs, but the choice of the Arnhem drop and landing zones was *not* made by Major-General Roy Urquhart, commander of the British 1st Airborne Division.

Nor was this the only error committed by the air planners. Another was their decision that ground-attack fighters were not to be sent over the battle-field while escort fighters were in the air protecting supply drops. This decision denied the airborne units the vital assistance that these ground-attack aircraft had been giving to the troops in Normandy just a month before, and a lack of air support exacerbated the problems of the airborne units. Among other tasks, these ground-attack aircraft could have taken on the flak positions around the bridges, those anti-aircraft guns the air planners were so wary of.

But the truly dire effect was, as Julian Thompson relates: 'that the 1st Airborne Division was denied the use of a weapon the Germans, after their Normandy experience, dreaded. The enemy was able to bring reinforcements into Arnhem in broad daylight, with impunity, a move which would have been fraught with risk in Normandy a few weeks earlier.'[3]

Here we must return to the Airborne Army's command structure and the plan for Operation Market. As related, the Airborne Army commander was Lieutenant General Brereton. His force consisted of two corps, the XXIII US Airborne Corps commanded by Lieutenant General Matthew Ridgeway, who had commanded the 82nd Airborne Division in Normandy, and the 1st British Airborne Corps, commanded by Lieutenant General Browning.

However, General Browning was not only the commander of the British Corps. Following the then-popular pattern of mixing up US and British com-manders, he was also Deputy Commander of the Allied Airborne Army under Brereton. In this role he intended to command the airborne forces for Market – although, since two US divisions were involved to only one British division, that role might more readily have gone to Matthew Ridgeway, a very fine

American commander, much respected by the British. This is on the debatable assumption that another corps commander was necessary at all, for the airborne divisions would come under XXX Corps command as soon as the link-up with the ground forces was made.

At this stage some personal points intrude. 'Boy' Browning was one of the pioneers of British airborne operations and the 'Father of the Airborne Forces.' (The Parachute Regiment depot is in Browning Barracks.) He was also the husband of the novelist Daphne du Maurier – author of *Rebecca* and *Jamaica Inn* – and, allegedly, the originator of the claim that in going for Arnhem, the Airborne Army was going 'a bridge too far', though there is no evidence that Browning ever made such a comment.

An officer of that illustrious regiment the Grenadier Guards, Browning had seen plenty of front-line service. He had been decorated in the First World War and had commanded a battalion of the Grenadier Guards during the 1940 campaign that ended at Dunkirk. A fighting soldier to his fingertips, Browning was very anxious to command a full-scale airborne operation before the war ended and Market Garden looked like being his last opportunity.

Inevitably, the Americans did not like him. Indeed, it appears that no one at Allied Airborne Army HQ had much time for anyone else and mutual detestation was rife. Julian Thompson has remarked that: 'To the Americans Browning appeared too dapper and Brereton did not trust him; neither did Gavin. Browning in turn detested Brereton, who was disliked by many of his fellow-countrymen.'[4]

Browning's decision to take his Corps Headquarters on Market created several problems. Flying in Browning's Corps HQ on D-Day employed thirty-eight transport aircraft and gliders that could, and should, have been used to put more men and guns into Arnhem. Browning elected to take these tugs and gliders from General Urquhart's force, which would not be fully on the ground for four days. Browning also elected to establish his Corps HQ on the Groesbeek heights, a 100m-high wooded ridge south of Nijmegen and just east of the Eindhoven road. This decision was to have dire effects on the 82nd Airborne's operations in Nijmegen and is a point we shall return to.

Those high-level animosities did not help resolve some of the other problems facing the airborne planners: a shortage of aircraft, a dispersion of Allied HQs which prevented the holding of joint command conferences with XXX Corps and Second Army before D-Day to iron out some of the potential difficulties and – above all – a shortage of time to resolve some of these problems. The airborne divisions tasked for Overlord in June had months to plan their attack: the airborne commanders in September had less than three days to plan Operation Market, and they needed to co-ordinate their plans with those of XXX Corps and Second Army for Garden – and these commanders were in Belgium.

Some other points about the Market operation should be taken on board now. Ideally, an airborne force, be it battalion, brigade, division or corps, should be landed in one lift. For Market it was judged impossible to fly in all the Allied airborne units in one lift as there were not enough aircraft available. In fact, it was judged impossible to land any of the Allied Airborne divisions intact on the first day.

This difficulty was put down to a shortage of transport aircraft and glider tugs, but the problem actually went further than that. The British transport commander, Air Vice Marshal Leslie Hollinghurst of No. 38 Group, RAF Transport Command, wanted to solve the aircraft shortage by flying-in two lifts on D-Day. His colleague of the US IX Troop Carrier Command, Major-General Paul L. Williams, did not agree, believing that time was needed to service the aircraft and rest the crews – and this view prevailed at Allied Airborne HQ where Brereton supported it. Since the principal asset of an airborne operation is surprise, the two- to three-day deployment – an attack by instalments – was throwing this vital asset away. This decision would have some profound effects on the ground, most notably on Urquhart's 1st Airborne Division at Arnhem.

And so to the plan. On the afternoon of D-Day, Sunday, 17 September, the Allied ground forces for Market Garden, Lieutenant General Sir Brian Horrocks' XXX Corps, spearheaded by the Guards Armoured Division, were to break out of the small bridgehead they had established over the Meuse–Escaut canal at Neerpelt, east of Antwerp, and head north. Rolling down one single, narrow road, over the airborne carpet laid by the US 101st and 82nd Airborne, Horrocks hoped to be up with 1st Airborne in two days. For their part, 1st Airborne were prepared to hold on for four days. Whether either time could be kept depended very largely on the actions of the US Airborne divisions – and the enemy.

The US 101st Airborne Division, commanded by Major-General Maxwell Taylor, would drop north of Eindhoven, a town thirteen miles from the

Meuse–Escaut Canal. The 101st was charged with taking the Eindhoven bridge, the bridges over the Wilhelmina Canal at Son, the bridges at Best and Oedenrode, and those over the Willems Canal and the Aa river at Veghel. That apart, the 101st were to keep the enemy away from the fifteen-mile long stretch of road north of Eindhoven, XXX Corps' axis of advance to Grave – a stretch of tarmac the 101st troopers soon came to call 'The Hell's Highway'. Anticipating that XXX Corps would be up to join them in a matter of hours, the 101st dropped without their artillery, but at least the bulk of the division – the three parachute infantry regiments – would be landed in one lift on the first day, with the last component, a regiment of glider infantry, landing on the second day.

North of the 101st Division, Brigadier General James Gavin's 82nd Airborne Division (Gavin was promoted Major-General during the Nijmegen battle) would land by parachute and glider to take the bridge over the River Maas at Grave, the bridges over the Maas–Waal Canal at Malden and Hatert and the two bridges – one road, one railway – over the 400-metre wide, fast-flowing River Waal at Nijmegen. In addition to this, the 82nd Airborne were also to take the wooded Groesbeek 'heights' south of Nijmegen – and for some reason this last task became their first priority.

The Groesbeek task had been pressed on Gavin by his Deputy Army Commander, Browning, who wanted these heights for his Corps Headquarters. For these varied tasks, on the first day, 17 September, Gavin had the three parachute infantry regiments – nine battalions – and an artillery battalion landing by glider. A further glider infantry regiment – three battalions of the 325th Glider Infantry Regiment – would be flown in on the second day.

Before moving on to cover the actions of the two US divisions at Eindhoven and Nijmegen in detail, it is necessary to consider two further points: the allocation of aircraft lift, and the enemy. On the matter of lift, the British 1st Airborne Division, which had the furthest to go and the longest to wait for relief, had the smallest allocation of aircraft and could only land the 1st Parachute Brigade and the 1st Air Landing Brigade on the first day. Both US divisions got the bulk of their troops in on the first day. Urquhart was also obliged to compound the problem by employing his strongest formation, the 1st Air Landing Brigade, to protect the DZ for the 4th Parachute Brigade, landing on D plus 1.

A review of the enemy situation along the Market Garden route reveals another failure, one of intelligence about enemy strengths, dispositions and unit formations. As related,in early September SHAEF had estimated that the Germans in the West could muster no more than forty-eight divisions; many of these were paper formations of little consequence on the battlefield. In terms of fighting strength the Germans could probably count on the equivalent of twenty infantry and four armoured divisions.[5] A more relevant point was where these units were, and in what strength just a week later, on 17 September?

Shortly before Market Garden, two intelligence reports, one from Second Army on 12 September [6] and one from XXX Corps on 15 September,[7] were guardedly optimistic about the current state of the opposition. Second Army believed that 'the recent cost to the enemy in killed and wounded had been very heavy,' but added that 'fresh forces were gradually coming into play.' Ultra intelligence produced by Enigma would have been useful, but the situation was too fluid for any information to be accurate for more than a couple of days. A revised SHAEF estimate held that the enemy force available to defend the entire West Wall was no more than eleven infantry divisions and four armoured divisions at full strength, adding that 'the West Wall cannot be held with this amount.'[8]

The information available to Second Army was too vague to be of much help but the XXX Corps survey was rather more specific, stating that the reinforcements coming into the line from Germany and elsewhere were not adequate to stem a determined thrust, and probably consisted of one weak division from Fifteenth Army plus scratch forces composed of former anti-aircraft units, garrison formations of second line or unfit troops or, at worst, about six assorted battalions deployed along the XXX Corps axis of advance, supported by some tanks and 88mm guns.

Finally, on 13 September – four days before D-Day for this operation – 1st Airborne Corps calculated that the Germans in 'the Netherlands and vicinity' could muster no more than 'a few infantry units and between fifty and 100 tanks', though it also reported 'a recent concentration of some 10,000 troops reforming south-west of Zwolle.' Zwolle is near the Zuider Zee, some distance north of Arnhem. This Airborne Corps estimate of enemy tanks in Holland, which would have been circulated to the divisional commanders, should be borne in mind when we come to consider the 82nd Airborne's actions at Nijmegen just four days later.

German forces were reforming rapidly all along the northern front; these various surveys and calculations left out the crucial factor of which formations were coming into line. Barring the path of XXX Corps to Eindhoven and Nijmegen, and in position just north of the Meuse–Escaut Canal, was General Student's First Parachute Army of four divisions: the 176th Division, the Parachute Training Division, the 85th and 719th Division. The British Official History[9] comments that the XXX Corps advance would split General Student's forces in two. Well, perhaps. Student's divisions were not up to strength in men or equipment, but they would certainly make a fight of it when the British headed north.

All German units north of the Meuse–Escaut canal were under the command of Field Marshal Model of Army Group B who had his headquarters in the town of Oosterbeek, two miles west of Arnhem. North-east of Arnhem were the remnants of two crack divisions, 9 SS Panzer and 10 SS Panzer, both of SS Obergruppenfuhrer Bittrich's II SS Panzer Corps. These units had been badly mauled in the Normandy fighting and were currently at only skeleton strength, but they had a good commander and enough tough, experienced troops on hand to give battle should the need arise.

Neither of these SS divisions was in Arnhem. Ninth SS Panzer was at Zutphen, twenty miles to the north, and currently consisted of an SS Panzer-Grenadier regiment, an artillery battalion, two assault-gun batteries and various other units, including an armoured company equipped with Mark V Panther tanks. Tenth SS Panzer was in and around Ruurlo, thirty miles north of Arnhem, and had only a Panzer-Grenadier regiment with very little transport: two artillery batteries, an engineer battalion, a battalion of anti-aircraft guns, and a reconnaissance battalion. Thus, 10 SS Panzer was weaker than 9 SS Panzer and was due to return to Germany for a rest and major refit. However, there were some German tanks and half-tracks in and around the Arnhem–Oosterbeek area, enough to give 1st Airborne trouble and gain time for more SS troops and armour to come down from Zutphen and Ruurlo, be ferried across the Lower Rhine and challenge the 82nd Airborne and XXX Corps at Nijmegen.

Nor was this all. In and around the villages and hamlets between the Meuse–Escaut Canal and the Neder Rijn were other German forces, digging in, resting, re-equipping. They varied in strength from fortress battalions composed of second line troops who had been manning positions along the

Atlantic Wall, to small units – kampfgruppe – of the Seventh Army, Fifteenth Army or Fifth Panzer Army, deployed by Model to delay any Allied advance.

This deployment was very typical of the German army at this time, one that often gave the Allied commanders an unpleasant surprise. 'Time and time again,' says Brigadier Shan Hackett of 1st Airborne, 'however empty of Germans and peaceful the scene appeared to be, if you touched an area important to them, the German reaction was swift and violent.' Although the German forces north of the Meuse–Escaut Canal were few in number, those units present were composed of good troops, enough of them to give battle to the lightly-armed airborne formations and contest XXX Corps' advance to Arnhem. And so to Operation Market.

The 101st Airborne Division began to land in Holland at 1300hrs on Sunday 17 September 1944 – H-Hour for the entire Market Garden operation – and came to earth astride a fifteen-mile section of the Grave road north of Eindhoven. The task of the 506th Parachute Infantry Regiment was to take the bridge over the Wilhelmina Canal at Zon, then move south on Eindhoven. North of the 506th, the 502nd PIR were to guard both DZs for later use as glider LZs and take the road bridge over the River Dommel at St Oedenrode. Finally, just in case matters went awry on the main road, the 502nd were to take the bridges over the Wilhelmina Canal, south of the road at Best, four miles from Zon. The 101st's last regiment, the 501st PIR, were to take the rail and road bridges over the Willems Canal and the River Aa at Veghel.

With only some minor exceptions, the 101st's drops and landings were accurate and flak negligible. Very few aircraft were lost. The bridges over the Aa and the Willens Canal were taken within an hour and within three hours the 501st had taken all its D-Day objectives. The 502nd secured the bridges at St Oedenrode and sent a company to secure the bridges at Best, besides sending patrols to link up with the 501st. Meanwhile, the 506th PIR had assembled near Zon and within forty-five minutes was advancing towards the Wilhelmina Canal bridge – but soon ran into opposition from enemy infantry backed by 88mm guns. Clearing Zon took longer than expected and here the 101st experienced its first set-back; when the leading battalion were only fifty metres from the canal bridge it blew up in their faces. Thirty Corps' airborne carpet had a hole in it, just three hours after the operation began.

In addition to this there were two other problems. An American officer in a glider shot down near General Student's headquarters had been carrying a copy of the Allied operational orders for Market; by 1500hrs those orders were on General Student's desk. Finally, one of the gliders that failed to arrive in Holland carried the British signals contingent tasked to maintain a radio link with XXX Corps. The communications problems that were to plague Market Garden began to appear in the first few hours.

The other task of the 506th was to advance south and take Eindhoven, but bearing in mind that Eindhoven was a secondary mission, strongly held by the enemy, and a place XXX Corps might not reach until D plus 1, the 506th halted in Zon at dusk. They were still six miles from Eindhoven, but the 101st had done very well. Their primary task, *to take the bridges,* had been undertaken swiftly and although the main bridge at Zon had been destroyed, the division had captured some alternative bridges and was in position to beat off enemy attacks on the road. The big question in the airborne troopers' minds as dusk fell on D-Day was '*Where is XXX Corps?*'

XXX Corps was not yet rolling quickly forward over an airborne carpet. Indeed, it would not even step onto the airborne carpet until Eindhoven, and that town lay thirteen miles from their start line on the Meuse–Escaut Canal – another fact that is frequently forgotten. The Guards Armoured Division, spearheading the advance, began to roll forward at 1400hrs, one hour after the airborne landings, an artillery barrage extending to 1,000 yards on either side of the narrow road ahead. After half an hour of this and preceded by a creeping barrage, the leading tank squadrons of the Guards Armoured, supported by the 2nd Battalion The Devonshire Regiment, moved forward from the bridgehead.

This advance was supported by a cab-rank of Typhoon fighter-bombers from 83 Group, 2nd TAF but half an hour after starting, the Guards' tanks came under heavy fire from the woods on either side of the road. After the Battle of Normandy, the Guards Armoured Division had been reorganised into four regimental groups, the Irish, Grenadier, Welsh and Coldstream Groups, each consisting of one armoured regiment and one infantry battalion drawn from the same Guards regiment: the advance from the Escaut Canal was led by the Irish Guards Group. All went well for about ten minutes, after which, according to one account:

> All hell broke loose, the tank ahead of mine and the one in front of that
> went up in flames, the crews jumping out and the infantry diving into ditches
> on either side of the road. Looking though the smoke and flame I could see that
> several other tanks had been hit and it eventually turned out that the last three
> tanks in No. 3 Squadron and my two leading troops of 3 tanks each had all
> been wiped out in less than two minutes.

Nine of the leading Irish Guards' tanks were on fire and only after the infantry
had been deployed into the woods and RAF Typhoons called in to deal with
some 88mm anti-tank guns was the advance resumed. Resistance continued all
day and was identified as coming from five German battalions, including two SS
units: XXX Corps intelligence had detected none of these. General Horrocks had
hoped to be in Eindhoven that evening but dusk fell as the Guards reached their
declared D-Day objective, the village of Valkenswaard, six miles south of
Eindhoven, and decided to stop there for the night.

Early on 18 September, D plus 1, the 506th PIR pushed into Eindhoven,
beating off some scattered units of German infantry and knocking out a battery
of 88mm guns on the way in. Reports that the enemy were occupying Eindhoven
in strength turned out to be unfounded: only about a company were flushed
from the houses. However, resistance was stiffening in other parts of the 101st
area, with a strong counter-attack on the bridge at Best by elements of the
German 59th Division. By the end of D plus 1, 18 September, Best and the
bridges over the Wilhelmina Canal were back in German hands.

In Eindhoven the 506th had pushed on to the southern edge of the town,
besieged by hundreds of excited Dutch civilians on the way and anticipating
the early arrival of the Guards Armoured Division with its tanks and guns. The
leading armoured cars of the Household Cavalry duly appeared at 1230 hrs
but the main tank column did not arrive until 1900hrs that evening – D plus 1.
XXX Corps had taken thirty-six hours to cover thirteen miles but there was no
delay now: the Guards pushed straight through the town towards the destroyed
bridge at Zon, closely followed by sappers of the Royal Engineers bridge-building
teams who promptly set to work installing a Bailey bridge over the Wilhelmina
Canal.

The first thirty-six hours of Operation Garden saw XXX Corps cover barely
seventeen miles to Zon but that Bailey bridge was flung across the river by

0645hrs on D plus 2 (19 September) and the XXX Corps advance was resumed. Time was getting tight: if the Guards were to get up to Arnhem that day, in line with Horrocks' plan, they would have to press on quickly… as they did.

As Guards Armoured passed through the American lines, the second lift of the 101st arrived from the UK, bringing in a further 2,500 men, including two battalions of the 327th Glider infantry and some transport, including jeeps and a bulldozer. The next task of the 101st Airborne, now supported by British tanks, artillery and infantry from the two other British Corps of Second Army, the VIII and XII, was to keep the main road open in the face of strong counter-attacks from German forces to the east and west and, if possible, widen the Allied thrust. General Maxwell Taylor later described this time as: 'Like the situation in the early American West where small garrisons had to fend off Indian attacks along great stretches of road.'[10] Holding the road open would keep the 101st Airborne fully occupied until well after the end of Market Garden and cost the division many more casualties than their initial task of taking the bridges.

Having crossed the Bailey bridge at Zon, the Guards were in Veghal by 0730hrs. By 0820hrs, the Guards Armoured Division had covered another fourteen miles of road to the north, made contact with the 82nd Airborne Division at Grave, and crossed the Maas to the outskirts of Nijmegen, forty-two hours after crossing their start line.

This fact disproves the second Arnhem myth: that XXX Corps were too slow during the advance north. They had been delayed, certainly, but had now made up much of the time lost at Zon and covered more ground in two hours on the morning of D plus 2 (19 September) than they had on the two previous days. Horrocks had promised to be at Arnhem on D plus 2: XXX Corps were now in Nijmegen, just eight miles from Arnhem with the rest of D plus 2 to get up to Lieutenant Colonel John Frost's positions at the Neder Rijn bridge. They should arrive there well within the time Horrocks had forecast.

This happy situation did not endure. As the leading tanks of the Grenadier Guards Group, leading the Guards Division, passed over the bridge at Heumen and entered the outskirts of Nijmegen, they learned that the road and rail bridges over the Waal were still firmly in German hands: unlike all the other bridges on the road to Arnhem, the Nijmegen bridge had not been taken on D-Day. It was still firmly in German hands and fighting was raging within the town. Something had clearly gone wrong.

5 · NIJMEGEN
17–20 SEPTEMBER

The big Nijmegen bridge posed a serious problem. Seizing it with
overwhelming strength at the outset would have been meaningless if I did not
get at least two other bridges; the big one at Grave and at least one bridge over the
canal. Further, even if I captured it, if I had lost all the high ground that
covered the entire sector ... I would be in a serious predicament.

MAJOR-GENERAL JAMES GAVIN, *ON TO BERLIN*

Brigadier General Gavin of the 82nd Airborne Division faced a formidable array of tasks on Market Garden, and his problems were not eased by faulty intelligence and the close presence of his Deputy Army Commander, Lieutenant General Browning. The 82nd was to take the bridges at Grave and Nijmegen and the high ground, the so-called Groesbeek heights, that lie just south of Nijmegen overlooking the country between the Eindhoven-Nijmegen road and the vast forest of the Reichswald, which lies to the east, just across the German frontier.

Given that the sole aim of *all* the airborne divisions committed to Market Garden was to take the river and canal bridges on the road to Arnhem, it is curious that Generals Gavin and Browning became so obsessed with the capture and retention of the Groesbeek Ridge and regarded that as their first priority, rather than the Nijmegen bridges. According to the US Official History, General Gavin claimed in July 1945 that possession of the Groesbeek Ridge represented the key to success or failure at Nijmegen: 'With it in German hands, physical possession of the bridges would be absolutely worthless, since it completely dominated the bridges and all the terrain around it.'[1] The US Official History seems doubtful on this point: 'Whether the prospects of difficulty in holding the high ground in the 82nd Airborne Division's sector justified delay in renewing the attack on the Nijmegen bridge. . . must be a matter of conjecture.'[2] Indeed it must, and General Gavin's claim should therefore be analysed.

Gavin elected to take all his objectives on D-Day: the bridges over the Maas at Grave and over the Maas–Waal Canal at Honinghutje, the villages of Hartert, Malden and Heumen, close to Nijmegen, the road bridge over the Waal at Nijmegen – and the Groesbeek Ridge. For some reason no force was allocated to the railway bridge over the Waal at Nijmegen. The main divisional priority was the Groesbeek Ridge, not the bridges.

This was the prime mistake. Unless the parachute divisions took and held the bridges, Market Garden would fail. That was true at Eindhoven, Zon, Grave and Arnhem – and was no less true at Nijmegen. General Brereton's orders were quite specific on this point: the airborne divisions were to take the bridges *'with thunderclap surprise'*. In neglecting to do so Gavin not only departed from his orders, he also forgot one of the basic principles of war – the selection and maintenance of the aim. Why Gavin, urged on and abetted by Browning, elected to ignore this prime requirement and substitute the Groesbeek heights as the 82nd's prime objective – and why Brereton let them get away with it – remains a mystery.

Nor do Gavin's subsequent explanations hold water. According to Gavin, the problem at Nijmegen and the need to take and hold the Groesbeek Ridge arose from intelligence reports claiming that large German armoured forces were building up in the Reichswald. Should these forces surge west to cut the Eindhoven–Nijmegen road, only the Groesbeek Ridge provided ground where they could be resisted. According to Gavin, to defend the road and the Nijmegen bridges against an attack from the Reichswald, it was essential to take and hold the Groesbeek Ridge.

Well, perhaps. The questions arise, where did this intelligence about German forces in the Reichswald come from, and was it accurate? Gavin attributes it to the British and claims in his memoirs that:

> The British were greatly preoccupied with the Reichswald, a very heavily-wooded area of approximately 24 square miles, just inside the German border. It provided excellent cover and the British were convinced that considerable German armour was in the forest.[3]

This author has been unable to find any evidence that the British were concerned about the Reichswald at this time or had reported the presence there of 'considerable German armour'. Indeed, one can refer to the Airborne Corps reports mentioned above which state the Germans only had between fifty and 100 tanks in all Holland. It also has to be said that the objectivity of Gavin's claim is somewhat undermined by the sad fact that his memoirs are studded with disparaging references to the British, claiming, for example, that 'the RAF were reluctant to fly close to the heavy flak concentrations near the Arnhem bridge',[4] which is simply not true. It is also hard to see why the British should be concerned with the Reichswald at this time anyway, since it fell in the US zone of operations and was many miles from the British front.

Nor is Gavin's allegation substantiated by US accounts. The US Official History attributes this faulty Reichswald intelligence to the 82nd Airborne Division's G-2, Lieutenant Colonel Walter F. Winton Jr.[5] Winton believed that the Groesbeek Ridge 'represented the only real barrier to counter-attack should the Germans strike from the east from the direction of the Reichswald', and predicted (that this last) 'might constitute a major reaction to the landings.'

Anticipating problems is an intelligence officer's job, but where is the evidence that there were substantial German forces in the Reichwald? The various Allied intelligence reports fail to mention them and soon after landing, says the US Official History, the 505th PIR, having sent a patrol into the Reichswald, reported that 'no tanks could be seen'.[6] This report confirmed other information, obtained from Dutch civilians, that 'the report about the 1,000 tanks in the Reichswald was false.'

This last comment alone should have raised eyebrows —*1,000 tanks in the Reichswald?* The US Official History attributes this claim to an After-Action Report (AAR) of the 505th PIR, after the unit had become particularly concerned about reports that the Reichswald was 'a nest of German armour.'[7] The 505th were understandably anxious to check this out – but 1,000 tanks in the

Reichswald? In mid-September 1944? After the German losses at Falaise in Normandy a month before and the recent rapid advances against minimal opposition? Where is the evidence for this sudden and massive accumulation of German armour in the Reichswald?

There is no such evidence and Gavin's account is frequently contradicted in the US Official History. On page 169, for example, the History records Gavin's recollection that 'a Dutch underground chief told him during the morning of 18 September (D plus 1) that the Germans were in strength with armour and infantry in the Reichswald area.' However, on the previous page the same History records Dutch civilians telling the 505th PIR that 'the Germans had no armour in the Reichswald.' The same page also records that patrols from the 505th found no armour and found the high ground in the Reichswald unoccupied: *'towers are empty, woods are tank obstacles – too thick.'* The 82nd's G-2 had also changed his mind, estimating that the enemy had, probably, 'two battalions of mixed, line-of-communications troops in the Reichswald.' So what had happened to those 1,000 German tanks?

They did not exist. It is extremely doubtful if the Germans had half that number of tanks fit for action across their entire Western Front from the Swiss frontier to the North Sea. Caution is often useful but any intelligence officer with two brain cells to rub together would have quickly dismissed this report of 1,000 tanks or strong German forces in the Reichswald as an hallucination.

The British Official History makes no reference to German armour in the Reichswald at this time. The first such reference comes a week after the end of Market Garden, when the British Official History mentions that two German armoured divisions – mustering perhaps 150 tanks in all – were beginning to arrive on the Nijmegen corridor from the Aachen front.[8] The first major move by German forces from the Reichswald – some 2,000 men, amounting to a weak brigade – did not come until D plus 4. As we shall see, the main threat to the 82nd's position in Nijmegen came from the north, down the road from Arnhem – a threat that would have been greatly reduced had Gavin taken the Nijmegen bridge on D-Day.

There is one further point that makes all these claims about the need to hold the Groesbeek ridge very strange indeed. It will be recalled that Browning elected to fly in his Corps Headquarters on D-Day, taking up thirty-eight sorely needed transport aircraft and glider tugs from the 1st Airborne Division for this purpose.

Once on the ground, Browning established his headquarters on the Groesbeek Ridge. It is, to put it mildly, most unusual for a Corps commander to establish his headquarters on what he allegedly believes will shortly be the front line. A great deal of time and space could be spent picking over this point but given that the prime task of the 82nd Airborne – as of the other two airborne divisions – was to take and hold the Nijmegen bridges and lay out the airborne carpet up to Arnhem, this preoccupation with the Groesbeek Ridge was most unfortunate, and a clear failure of command.

It is worth repeating that the first and most important duty of a commander in battle is *the selection and maintenance of the aim* or, to put it in layman's terms, to answer the prime question: *what are we trying to do here?* What the airborne divisions were trying to do was to lay an airborne carpet from the Meuse–Escaut Canal to the north bank of the Neder Rijn, and that aim had to be achieved – or maintained – whatever difficulties arose on the Groesbeek heights or anywhere else. Major-General Maxwell Taylor of the US 101st Airborne also had trouble, a great deal of trouble, with strong German attacks along Hell's Highway, but he handled those – and took the bridges first, on D-Day.

It appears that at Nijmegen Gavin and Browning either forgot or elected to ignore one of the principles of war. Their *prime task* was to take the bridges, including the Nijmegen road bridge, as quickly as possible and hold it until XXX Corps arrived and advanced across it. This they failed to do and the effect on the entire operation was disastrous, creating a delay of some thirty-six hours *after* the Guards Armoured Division arrived in Nijmegen, a mere eight miles from Arnhem, on the morning of D plus 2.

This failure to maintain the aim has been largely covered up by the relentless and skilful propagation of those myths mentioned above, myths which place the blame for the failure of Market Garden squarely on XXX Corps, General Urquhart and the Guards Armoured Division. For some reason, although a number of accounts do mention the failure to take the Nijmegen bridge, no one has analysed the reasons advanced for that failure, reasons which fail to provide even the shadow of an adequate excuse.

Browning and Gavin were experienced and competent commanders, so why did they fail to concentrate on their priority target, the Nijmegen bridges? The only reason that makes any kind of sense is that General Browning wanted the Groesbeek Ridge for command and communications purposes. This was the only high ground between Eindhoven and Nijmegen and Browning hoped that with his headquarters up there he would be able to get in radio contact with every airborne division, with XXX Corps HQ and with the UK, and so play a full part in the operation before Horrocks arrived and took command.

This would have appeared as a very self-serving reason later if the result was to delay the taking of the vital Nijmegen bridges and the subsequent destruction of the 1st Airborne Division. How much better to put forward the notion of forming a defensive front against the strong possibility of a counter-attack from the east, even when there was no evidence of such a threat, and when – again – *the prime task of every airborne division was to take the bridges?*

As for Gavin, his actions seem to have been motivated by a desire to avoid the situation inflicted on Urquhart by the air commanders' choice of drop zones. Like Urquhart's, Gavin's DZs were set several miles from the bridges and a large town stood in the way. Urquhart elected to follow his orders and go for the Arnhem bridge on D-Day: Gavin decided to hang on to his DZs and only go for the bridges when the DZs were secure – a laudable aim except for the fact that it undermined the entire Market Garden plan.

Given the points raised above, it will come as no surprise that the first weight of the airborne assault fell near Groesbeek. The DZ of the 508th PIR was on the high ground north of Groesbeek – with one battalion of this regiment assigned to make a grab for the Nijmegen road bridge. The 508th was also charged with taking the Groesbeek Ridge line and blocking any enemy movements south from Nijmegen – and assist in taking the bridges over the Maas–Waal Canal at Hartert and Honinghutje. Finally, the regiment was to take ground suitable for glider LZs on the eastern slopes of the Groesbeek Ridge.

Now comes another curious lapse. In his memoirs, Gavin records that after the division was sealed in its camp before take-off, he summoned his battalion commanders and briefed them carefully, advising them that the only way to take bridges was *'both ends at once'*.[9] His advice came a little late. This requirement needed factoring into Gavin's basic plan, for if he landed his force on only one side of the bridge – as he did at Nijmegen – how were his battalion commanders to take both ends at once? It will be recalled that the 101st glider-lift stores included a bulldozer; if Gavin did not elect to take both ends of the Nijmegen bridge by a parachute assault, how did he intend to get to the north bank and why did his glider stores not include boats? Without boats to cross the river, how was a direct, frontal assault from the south side of the road bridge to be avoided?

Gavin's plan called for the 505th PIR to drop south of the Groesbeek Ridge and then take the village of Groesbeek – the site for Browning's HQ – the high ground round about and the village of Reithhorst. The regiment was also to send out patrols to assist in taking the Maas–Waal bridges. The last regiment, the 504th PIR, was to take the 1,800-ft wide span of the bridge over the River Maas at Grave and, in keeping with the well-tested theory recently restated by Gavin that 'bridges are best taken both ends at once', one company of this regiment was to land south of the bridge and the rest north of it. If this 'both ends' deployment was necessary at Grave, why was it not equally necessary at Nijmegen?

The 82nd's landings on 17 September went well and achieved total surprise – '*Landed against almost no opposition*', reported the Division's G-2, and losses were indeed very slight. The entire 505th PIR – over 3,000 men – lost sixty-three men killed, wounded and missing on D-Day, while the battalion of the 508th PIR at Hatert had just seven men wounded. Landing on both sides, the 504th had firm control of the Grave bridge in under three hours. After that the regiment established a block across the road leading south to Veghel and sent a party into Grave to investigate strange noises coming from the town hall: these, it transpired, came from the Dutch citizenry, celebrating their liberation by singing *It's a Long Way to Tipperary* – in Dutch. The 504th quickly mopped up any German opposition in their immediate area and took the bridge at Heuman, though the Germans were able to demolish the bridge at Hatert before the 508th PIR could get there.

The 505th PIR had assembled quickly on landing, cleared Groesbeek and occupied the high ground, besides sending a company-sized patrol east into the Reichswald to check out the existence of those supposed enemy tanks. As related, this patrol returned that night having failed to find any sign of them. Meanwhile, the last regiment, the 508th PIR, had completed a number of tasks, blocking the road at Mook to prevent any attack from Nijmegen into the division's perimeter and moving on the bridges at Hatert and Honinghutje.

The 508th also had a vital task – 'a special destiny', says the US Official History.[10] The 1st Battalion, 508th Parachute Infantry Regiment, commanded by Lieutenant Colonel Shields Warren, was charged with taking the road bridge over the Waal at Nijmegen: a prime task of Operation Market was being entrusted here to just one battalion from an entire division.

According to the US Official History, there was some dispute over exactly when the 1st Battalion should go for the bridge.[11] General Gavin was to claim later that the battalion was to 'go for the bridge without delay'. However, Colonel Lindquist, the 508th Regimental commander, understood that Warren's battalion was not to go for the bridge until the other regimental objectives – securing the Groesbeek Ridge and the nearby glider LZs, had been achieved: General Gavin's operational orders confirm Warren's version. Warren's initial objective was ground near De Ploeg, a suburb of Nijmegen, which he was to take and organise for defence: only then was he to 'prepare to go into Nijmegen later'[12] and these initial tasks took Lieutenant Colonel Warren most of the day. It was not until 1830hrs that he was able to send a force into Nijmegen. This force was somewhat small, just one rifle platoon and an intelligence section with a radio – say forty men. They were to check on Dutch reports that there were only nineteen Germans at the bridge and, if this was so, grab the south end of the bridge and report back. Unfortunately – but such is the fortune of war – the platoon radio failed and no word came back that night.

Meanwhile, General Gavin was clearly having second thoughts about leaving the Nijmegen road bridge untaken. At dusk on D-Day he ordered Colonel Lindquist 'to delay not a second longer and get the bridge as quickly as possible with Warren's battalion.'

In fact, Warren already had this task in hand. He had found a Dutch civilian who agreed to lead the battalion to the bridge and contacted the Dutch Resistance in Nijmegen for up-to-date – and hopefully accurate – reports on the German position there. Two rifle companies, 'A' and 'B', were to rendezvous south of Nijmegen from where a Dutch guide would lead them to the bridge. Unfortunately, Company 'B' got lost on its way to the rendezvous so only Company 'A' moved on the bridge – the efforts of an entire airborne division were now reduced to just one company. It was now around 2000hrs on D-Day, H-Hour plus seven.

Company 'A' entered Nijmegen – a city of some 100,000 people in 1944 – and moved cautiously up the main road, the Groesbeekscheweg. After two hours they reached a traffic island near the centre of the town and immediately came under automatic fire from directly ahead. As they went to ground and deployed, a German convoy arrived in one of the side streets on their flank and they heard the clatter of boots and kit as enemy soldiers leapt from their trucks. Company 'A' was just a few minutes too late: the Germans were moving troops into Nijmegen from the north and the fight for the road bridge was on.

The US Official History mourns this fact, pointing out that 'the time for the easy, speedy capture of Nijmegen had passed', which was all the more lamentable because during the afternoon, when the division had been engaged on other tasks, the Germans had 'nothing in the town but mostly low quality troops'[13]– and not many of those.

This situation was now changing rapidly. The troops arriving in Nijmegen were the advance guard of the 9th SS Panzer Division's Reconnaissance Battalion, sent south from Arnhem.[14] SS General Bittrich had also directed the entire 10th SS Panzer Division – or such of it as presently existed – to move on Nijmegen and hold XXX Corps there while the British 1st Airborne Division was cut to pieces at Arnhem. Browning and Gavin had totally misjudged the direction of the German threat: it would come from Arnhem in the north, not from the Reichswald to the east. The troops now arriving in Nijmegen, coming across the road bridge, were an infantry battalion and an engineer company from either the 9th or 10th SS Panzer Divisions: more would follow.

Company 'A' had a fight on its hands against this SS battalion and matters might have gone badly had not Company 'B' emerged out of the night to reinforce it. It is worth adding at this point that the 1st Battalion of the 508th Parachute Infantry Regiment was a very fine battalion. While this fight was going on, the Company 'A' commander, Captain Jonathan Adams, received word from a Dutch civilian that the firing mechanisms for the demolition charges on the road bridge were kept in the nearby post office. Captain Adams promptly took a platoon to the post office, shot the German guards, and destroyed what he took to be the firing mechanisms. More Germans then came up and joined the fight; Captain Adams, his platoon and some Dutch civilians were besieged in the post office for the next two days until tanks of the Guards Armoured arrived to get them out.

Lieutenant Colonel Warren and his battalion battered away at the bridge approaches until dawn but could make very little progess against increasingly tough opposition. At first light General Gavin ordered the battalion 'to withdraw from close proximity to the bridge and re-organise.'[15]

On the following day, D plus 1, Company 'G' of the 3rd Battalion, 508th PIR was ordered to take the bridge. The US Official History remarks that General Gavin was 'considering how to take the bridge with the limited forces available',[16] but Gavin's forces were in fact not all that limited. He could surely have spared more than a company for taking a bridge he was now very anxious to take – not least because soon after midday on 18 September, the 82nd's next lift arrived from the UK, 450 gliders bringing in three fresh battalions, one parachute and two glider, and a quantity of artillery.[17]

There was now some slight enemy activity from the Reichswald. Again according to the US Official History, soon after daylight on D plus 1, 'two understrength German battalions began to infiltrate from the Reichswald towards the glider LZs',[18] presumably the ones mentioned by the division's G-2. This attack was not serious: the infiltrators were chased away at the cost of just eleven US casualties before the 82nd's gliders arrived. Some 150 of the enemy had been killed so far and the 82nd had taken 885 prisoners.[19] The division had not, however, taken the Nijmegen road bridge, nor made any attempt to get across the rail bridge.

During D plus 1, Gavin was in consultation with Browning over a plan to attack the road bridge that night, using a full battalion of the 504th supported by a battalion of the 508th. Browning at first approved of this plan but then decided that holding the high ground south of Nijmegen – those Groesbeek heights again – was of more importance and Gavin concurred, 'issuing orders for the defence of the position.'

The US History points out that there was 'no incentive for urgency over taking the Nijmegen bridge as XXX Corps were not yet in Eindhoven' and it might be some time before they arrived at the Nijmegen bridge. In fact, XXX Corps had already passed Eindhoven and were waiting to cross the Bailey bridge at Zon. The US Official Historian Charles B. MacDonald, dismisses this casual approach to the question of taking the Nijmegen bridge, stating that: 'According to this theory, General Gavin had another full day to tackle the Germans at Nijmegen.' This theory also assumes that one day would be sufficient for Gavin to take the bridge – from one side only – having already sacrificed the advantage of surprise and with German strength increasing.

By now the Reichswald had been shelled by the 82nd's newly arrived artillery and bombed and strafed by Spitfires and Mustangs of the 2nd TAF, without provoking resistance or counter-battery fire, but Browning and Gavin remained convinced that the Reichswald was a threat. Gavin believed he had at least another day to take the Nijmegen bridges before XXX Corps arrived, although Horrocks had said he would be at Arnhem on D plus 2, and XXX Corps was now approaching rapidly from Zon.

Gavin was gambling. He could not know how long he would need to take the Nijmegen bridges. He had already been trying for two days but made very little progress, and there was no guarantee that his next attacks would be any more successful. If they failed this could be a problem. Whenever XXX Corps arrived they would need to press on through Nijmegen and up to Arnhem with the utmost despatch – just as they had pressed through the 101st Division's positions at Eindhoven. The Guards Armoured Division spearheading the XXX Corps advance did not need to get involved in local fighting; as the US History remarks, 'the early arrival of the ground column (at Arnhem) depended on (the 82nd) getting a bridge at Nijmegen.'[20]

Some other flaws in Gavin's thinking should be ventilated at this time. First of all, the basic query raised above, how was he to take the Nijmegen bridge? In accordance with well-established airborne practice, he should have landed a parachute or glider force on the north side of the Nijmegen bridges, in order to take the bridges from both ends on D-Day, as he had done at Grave. Not having done so, he was now faced with the grim prospect of frontal assaults on the bridge through the town – and the Germans might blow the bridges if such a direct assault looked like succeeding. Even if the post office mechanisms had been the main means of destroying the bridges, the enemy was still using the bridges and would surely have prepared them for demolition.

The only way to avoid a direct assault was to outflank the bridge defenders with a river crossing, but Gavin had no assault boats – a strange omission from the division's equipment list, given that his division would only land on the south bank of the Waal. Collapsible boats could have been brought in by glider, but there is no indication that this move was even considered. The obsession with the supposed attack from the Reichswald seems to have dominated Gavin's thinking from the start and continued to do so, even though it was increasingly clear that the main threat to his position in Nijmegen came down the road from Arnhem – and over the road bridge.

Quite apart from the fact that taking the bridges was the prime aim of the entire Market operation, taking the Nijmegen bridge was essential to the security of the 82nd's position. SS General Bittrich of the II SS Panzer Corps at Arnhem had already realised that the crux of the entire battle was at Nijmegen: if he could stop the Allies on the Waal, 1st Airborne at Arnhem could be destroyed at leisure. Elements of his two SS divisions had been ferried over the Neder Rijn and sent to Nijmegen and when the remnants of John Frost's gallant 2nd Parachute Battalion had been driven away from the Arnhem bridge, formed units of the 9th and 10th SS Panzer divisions would come swarming down the road to Nijmegen. Self-interest alone should have dictated that Gavin took the Nijmegen bridge as quickly as possible, but the bridge and much of the town was still in German hands when the Guards Armoured arrived on the morning of 19 September – D plus 2 – and linked up with the main body of the 82nd Airborne.

'From that point,' says the US History, 'priority of objectives shifted unquestionably in the direction of the bridge at Nijmegen. Already at least thirty-three hours behind schedule because of the earlier delays south of Eindhoven and at Zon, the ground column had to have a way to get across the Waal.'[21]

This last comment on the timing is a little curious. XXX Corps had crossed the start line at 1400hrs on 17 September. According to the US History, they linked up with the 82nd at 0830hrs on 19 September, so the Guards Armoured had then been travelling for forty-two and a half hours. If they were, as this comment alleges, 'thirty-three hours behind schedule', they should have arrived in Nijmegen nine and a half hours after crossing their start line – good going indeed for over sixty miles and against stiff opposition, but was this correct?

It will be recalled that 1st Airborne had been asked to hold at Arnhem for two days until XXX Corps arrived. They said they could hold for four. It was now D plus 2 and XXX Corps was just eight miles from Arnhem and still had six hours in hand; XXX Corps was back on schedule. Those earlier delays had been made up, but the Nijmegen bridge had not been taken and heavy fighting was going on in the town.

At this point we must return to the Grenadiers Group of the Guards Armoured Division, the unit spearheading the XXX Corps advance. According to Captain Lord Carrington, Second in Command of No. 1 Squadron, 2nd Battalion, Grenadier Guards:

There was no significant opposition that morning until we got to Nijmegen. There may have been the odd skirmish on the way but nothing slowed us down until we got to Nijmegen and found ourselves in the middle of a battle. That brought the column to a halt and I remember meeting Chester Wilmot, the war correspondent, who helped drink my last bottle of liberated champagne.

Here is the first significant point: the advance of the Guards Armoured to Arnhem had come to a halt and the traffic behind them, some 20,000 vehicles – tanks, trucks, armoured cars, Bren-gun carriers, fighting vehicles and supply lorries, a convoy reaching all the way back to Zon and beyond – promptly began to pile up along that single narrow highway. Captain George Thorne of the Guards 1st Motor Battalion recalls another meeting that morning:

We were in scout cars and the first person I can recall seeing is General Boy Browning, striding across the field to meet us, looking immaculate as always. Then General Gavin appeared and detailed a couple of platoons of US infantry, paratroopers, to accompany us as we went for the post office where those demolition mechanisms for the bridges were supposed to be kept. There was a battle going on, a lot of mortaring, plenty of opposition in the town and buildings on fire. We came to one street where all the buildings were on fire, intense heat, and I had a shot at some Germans outlined beyond the fire and hit a couple of them.

Another incident was the arrival of General Horrocks, with a few Bren gun carriers. He was speaking on his rear link to the division behind us, the 43rd Division, and ordering them to come up. Apparently they were complaining that the traffic congestion was terrible and they could not get forward but Horrock would have none of it. I heard him say, 'Nonsense – I have come up the centre line with three carriers and if you don't get moving in ten minutes I will come back and move you myself.'

This comment is typical of Horrocks, a hard-driving commander anxious to press on to Arnhem, but there was severe traffic congestion on the road from Eindhoven and two divisions with all their transport is a different proposition from three Bren gun carriers. Nevertheless, this exchange indicates that Horrocks was fully determined to drive up to Arnhem with the utmost despatch – once the Nijmegen bridge had been taken.

The problem was that the 82nd was engaged in a street battle even to reach the bridge. On arrival in Nijmegen, the Guards Armoured Division had to be deployed to help them win it, and their prime task, getting up to Arnhem, had to give way to this present emergency. The US History records that: 'The British provided a company of infantry and a battalion of tanks of the Guards Armoured, to assist the 2nd Battalion, 505th PIR, in another attack on the south end of the bridge.'[22] This took place a few hours after the Guards Armoured arrived in Nijmegen and from then on the US History records a series of actions where the Guards and the US Airborne were fighting together.

On page 178, the US History records General Gavin 'sending for help to the Guards Armoured Division's Coldstream Guards Group, *which had been designated as a reserve for the airborne division'* (author's italics). On page 179 the History recounts how 'two squadrons of British tanks' were to support the 504th PIR in their bid for the bridge. In other words, from the morning of September 19, D plus 2, the Guards Armoured Division was actively engaged in assisting the US 82nd Airborne in the fight for the Nijmegen bridges, instead of proceeding with their prime task, forcing a passage to Arnhem.

The arrival of XXX Corps with its tanks and artillery greatly eased General Gavin's mind and brought him valuable reinforcements. Fighting in the town went on throughout the day, several Guards' tanks being knocked out in the process. This integration of Guards and US Airborne continued, with Guards' tanks and artillery deployed to assist the 505th PIR in another attack on the south end of the bridge, and British tanks supporting a bid for the rail bridge.[23] Two of the Guards Armoured Groups were now deployed with the 82nd, the Coldstream Guards Group serving as the 82nd's only reserve and the Grenadier Guards Group coming forward to back up the Airborne troopers fighting in the town.

Gavin had meanwhile adjusted his positions, putting one battalion of the 504th into divisional reserve and ordering the former reserve battalion, the 2nd Battalion, 505th PIR, which had been in the woods west of Groesbeek, to join the drive for the Nijmegen bridge. Gavin then met with Horrocks, the XXX Corps commander, and told him that he intended to send the 2nd/505th against the south side of the bridge and, *'as quickly as possible'* send another force in boats across the Waal to take the north side. The snag was that he had no boats and must get them from the British – and that would take time.

In his memoirs Gavin comments: 'In the American Army a Corps acting in an independent role would have had an engineer battalion or regiment attached to it and that would include a company of boats.' He adds that when he asked Horrocks about this, 'he (Horrocks) said he thought they had some boats well down the road, in the train somewhere.'[24]

Gavin's comment implies that the British XXX Corps was not as well-equipped as a US Corps, but this is not correct. The Guards Armoured History confirms that: 'Plans had been made for the situation where the enemy might demolish one or more of the vital bridges along the axis. This possibility alone meant including in the column no fewer than 9,000 sappers with 5,000 vehicles full of bridging equipment.' It seems highly unlikely that General Horrocks was either unaware of this engineer support or vague on the matter of boats.

Fortunately for Gavin, the XXX Corps sappers had some canvas assault boats, thirty-three in all, part of the standard equipment for the Bailey bridge teams of the Royal Engineers. Naturally these boats were not front-line stores – Sherman tanks led the Guards advance – and it would take some time before the boats could be brought forward to Nijmegen up that narrow and congested road. In the meantime, Gavin intended to open his new attack against the south side of the road bridge and sent the 2nd/505th forward, supported by a company of Guards infantry, some Guards Armoured tanks and the artillery of the 82nd and Guards Armoured Division.

In all this we see yet another departure from the original plan, but it is pleasant to record that the British Guards and the American troopers of the 82nd Airborne fought side by side to take the Nijmegen bridge, in true comradeship and without the slightest problem – other than the enemy.

One joint force, paratroopers mounted on tanks, went off to the post office to relieve the US troops and Dutch civilians trapped there since D-Day. Company D of the 505th, commanded by First Lieutenant Oliver Banks, climbed onto five British tanks and some other vehicles and set off for the rail bridge: they were halted by an 88mm gun at the road junction and heavy machine-gun and rifle fire about 1,000 yards from the railroad. The Guards and the Airborne spent the rest of the day battering at this position but could make no progress.

A similar attack against the south side of the road bridge was equally unsuccessful and the G-2 of the 82nd had to revise his estimates of German troops in the town, arriving at a new figure of some 500 SS soldiers from the 9th SS

Panzer division, plus tanks and 88mm guns and other infantry. Elsewhere, adds the US History, it was 'a quieter day',[25] the enemy in the Reichswald, perhaps 500 men, causing no trouble – though what trouble 500 men could have caused two Allied divisions, one of them armoured, is another matter for conjecture.

During the night of September 19–20, Gavin briefed Colonel Tucker and the 504th PIR to make the assault crossing of the Waal when the boats arrived next day. The attack was set for 1400hrs on 20 September – D plus 3 – and that morning elements of the 504th, supported by Guards' tanks, set out to clear the south bank of the river close to the road bridge.

Things were now hotting-up on the Reichswald front. This suddenly came to life with the arrival of the first units of the German II Parachute Corps, seven under-strength infantry battalions, amounting to some 2,000 men in all. These put in a strong attack on the Allied line around Mook and Riethorst, their assault supported by 88s, mortars and multi-barrelled nebelwerfers. This attack made some progress until the early afternoon, when it was halted and driven back by the Coldstream Guards Group which, as related, had now been detached from XXX Corps to form part of the 82nd's divisional reserve.

As this attack petered out on the evening of D plus 3, the 3rd Battalion, 504th PIR put in a gallant assault across the Waal, an action the US History rightly describes as 'one of the most daring and heroic in all the Market Garden fighting.'[26] This assault, across 400 yards of fast-flowing river, was supported by fire from two squadrons of British tanks, part of another 504th battalion and around 100 American and British guns.

The flimsy assault boats did not arrive until twenty minutes before H–Hour, and according to Gavin there were only twenty-six of them, not the expected thirty-three. Undaunted, the first wave of paratroopers scrambled aboard, picked up the paddles or deployed their rifle butts, and set out for the north bank. Under fire all the way, the water lashed with machine-gun fire and mortar bombs, the first wave got across – or rather about half of them did. Those who landed scrambled up the bank and dashed for the shelter of a bank some distance away, while the sappers who had crossed with the US paratroopers paddled the boats back for the next lift. In all, these boats – the eleven that survived the first two crossings – made six crossings of the river that afternoon, taking across the 3rd and 1st battalions of the 504th PIR in the face of enemy fire. It was a superb example of what well-trained, aggressive infantry can do. Once on the north bank the 504th proceeded to attack the enemy positions defending the road and rail bridges.

It might be mentioned that, contrary to most popular accounts, this assault was not an exclusively US affair. The paratroopers were accompanied by British sappers of the 615 Field Squadron and 11th Field Company, Royal Engineers, who made five river crossings in all, taking heavy equipment and ammunition across before a small bridgehead was established on the north bank.[27]

Nor was the 504th the only Allied unit attacking the Nijmegen bridge. On the 'both ends at once' principle, tanks of the Grenadier Guards Group were mounting an assault on the south end of the bridge, where Colonel Vandervoort's battalion of the 505th PIR, supported by Guards' tanks and infantry, was wearing down the resistance in the town. By 1700hrs British tanks and American infantry had driven the Germans back to the bridge, but the bridge was a bastion. When it fell, it was discovered that thirty-four machine guns, an 88mm gun and two 20mm cannon were mounted on the bridge, with plenty of snipers and machine-gunners deployed on the girders. As the enemy were pushed out of Nijmegen, they were able to cross the bridge and reinforce the SS troops fighting with the 504th paratroopers on the north bank, who now stood in urgent need of tank support.

This was a difficult moment, but cometh the hour, cometh the man. With a good chance that the bridge would be blown at any time, a troop of Guards' tanks, led by Sergeant Robinson of the Grenadier Guards, crossed the Nijmegen bridge under fire, arriving at the far end just as three troopers of the 504th PIR ran to meet them. And so, at 1910hrs on D plus 3, the US 82nd Airborne – and the Guards Armoured Division – took the Nijmegen bridge.

Sergeant Peter Robinson gives his account of the crossing at Nijmegen bridge:

> The Nijmegen bridge wasn't taken, which was our objective. We reached the far end of the bridge and immediately there was a roadblock. So the troop sergeant covered me through and then I got to the other side and covered the rest of the troop through. We were still being engaged; there was a gun in front of the church three or four hundred yards in front of us. We knocked him out. We got down the road to the railway bridge; we cruised round there very steady. We were being engaged all the time. Just as I got round the corner and

turned right I saw these helmets duck in a ditch and run, and gave them a burst of machine gun. I suddenly realised they were Americans. They had already thrown a gammon grenade at me so dust and dirt and smoke was flying everywhere. They jumped out of the ditch; they kissed the tank; they kissed the guns because they'd lost a lot of men. They had had a very bad crossing.

Well, my orders were to collect the American colonel who was in a house a little way back, and the first thing he said to me was: 'I have to surrender'.

Well, I said, 'I'm sorry. My orders are to hold this bridge. I've only got two tanks but if you'd like to give me ground support for a little while until we get some more orders then we can do it.' He said he couldn't do it, so I said that he had better come back to my wireless and talk to General Horrocks because before I started the job I had freedom of the air. Everybody was off the air except myself because they wanted a running commentary about what was going on. So he came over and had a pow-wow with Horrocks. The colonel said 'Oh very well' and I told him where I wanted the men, but of course you can't consolidate a Yank and they hadn't been there ten minutes before they were on their way again.

Lord Carrington joined us about two or three hours after because he had been sitting on the north end of the [road] bridge protecting that.

The first British officer across the bridge was Captain Lord Carrington, then second-in-command of a tank squadron, later to become Foreign Secretary in Margaret Thatcher's 1980s Government:

During the day – D plus 3 – I had been told that my task was to rush the road bridge and we spent most of the day waiting to be ordered forward; the waiting in a park just south of the bridge went on for hours. When the order came the first tank across was commanded by Sergeant Robinson followed by three others, and off they went. This was in the early evening, just before dark and I went after them; mine was the fifth tank across the bridge and there were still Germans in the superstructure.

When I got across there was no sign of Sergeant Robinson or indeed anyone else, so I halted my tank at the north end of the bridge and wirelessed back that the bridge was open. I was there for a short while, about ten minutes, and then more tanks started coming across and I went forward to find Sergeant Robinson. He was stopped about a mile up the road, talking to some US paratroopers, who were very pleased to see us.[28]

Andrew Gibson-Watt was with the Welsh Guards:

> My own complaint is the acceptance of the thesis (which has been propounded by other historians) that Guards Armoured Division should have gone on to Arnhem on the night they captured the Nijmegen bridge. The Division, 'off-balance' and still heavily embroiled in Nijmegen town, could not have done so. There was nothing to go on with: the main preoccupation was now to defend the bridge against the expected counter-attack. Any element which had gone on would have found it very hard to get over the Arnhem bridge, which was not (and never had been) held by John Frost's gallant force; and if it had got over it would have been met by the greatly superior German forces in that part of Arnhem. An advance that night was 'not on' and general military historians have erred greatly in assuming that it would have been possible and should have been done.
>
> We have always been fed the story about fired-up American paratroopers railing at the British tankers for not going straight on; but Sergeant Peter Robinson's memoir tells a very different tale.
>
> It is time for this accusation, which does not stand up to detailed examination, to be finally refuted.

The credit for this joint Allied operation in taking the Nijmegen bridge has gone to the troopers of the 504th Parachute Infantry Regiment whose courage and tenacity in pressing their river assault home is beyond all praise. Nevertheless, there is a question here.

Why was a parachute unit, expensively trained to cross obstacles like river bridges by air on D-Day, reduced to making a frontal assault in borrowed boats three days later? This is not to question the gallantry and professional skill of the 504th PIR – far from it – but it remains a valid question and one that reflects on General Gavin. Had the 82nd landed a parachute force north of the bridge on D-Day or moved at once to take the bridge from the south, this costly river assault would not have been necessary… and the Guards Armoured could have pushed on to Arnhem on D plus 2.

The answers to that question have been obscured by myth and on the evening of D plus 3 the myths were joined by controversy – and some very unpleasant and unjustified accusations. As related, the first four tanks across the Nijmegen bridge were quickly joined by the 1st Squadron Second-in-command, Captain Lord Carrington.

Carrington recalls meeting 'a perfectly civil American officer who was very pleased to see us.' If so, this pleasure did not last. This American officer was later to castigate the Guards as 'yellow-bellied cowards' and alleged that he felt 'betrayed' when these five Guards tanks did not immediately set out down the road to Arnhem to relieve the beleaguered 1st Airborne Division. He was told that there were German anti-tank guns and armour up ahead to which he replied, again allegedly, that his men would mount the tanks, come with the Guards and clear the guns out of the way.

Lord Carrington again:

> My recollection of this meeting is different. I certainly met an American officer but he was perfectly affable and agreeable. As I said, the Airborne were all very glad to see us and get some support; no one suggested we should press on to Arnhem. This whole allegation is bizarre; just to begin with I was a captain and second-in-command of my squadron so I was in no position either to take orders from another captain or depart from my own orders which were to take my tanks across the bridge, join up with the US Airborne and form a bridgehead. This story is simply lunacy and this alleged exchange did not take place.

Gavin's memoirs tend to confirm Lord Carrington's point:

> The tanks of the Grenadier Guards engaged two 88mms dug in on the northern shore, destroyed them and continued across the bridge. The first people to greet them were the paratroopers of the 504th. So enthusiastic were they that one of them actually kissed the leading British tank.[29]

This alleged incident between Peter Carrington and an American officer, widely reported and probably exaggerated, still leaves a bad taste. The first allegation is unfair: 'yellow-bellied cowards' do not cross a river bridge in tanks, knowing that it might blow up beneath them at any moment. Nor does a mere captain – even a captain of His Majesty's Foot Guards – take it on himself to rush off into enemy territory, especially when his current task is to aid the American forces on the north bank hold their bridgehead in the face of counter-attacks.

Gavin is far from blameless in this matter. In his memoirs, published in 1978, he records a meeting on the following morning with Colonel Tucker of the 504th, who, says Gavin, was 'livid... I had never seen him so angry.'[30] Tucker 'had expected that when he had seized his end of the bridge the British armour would race on to Arnhem and link up with Urquhart'. Tucker then asks Gavin: 'What the hell are they doing? Why in the hell don't they get to Arnhem?' 'I did not have an answer for him,' says Gavin.[31]

This lack of an answer is curious. The Guards Armoured Division had been helping Gavin's division for the last two days and it seems surprising that Gavin did not know this. In recent hours the Coldstream Guards Group were helping to beat off a belated attack on the Groesbeek position, the Irish Guards Group had gone back down the road to Eindhoven to deal with another enemy incursion and the Grenadier Guards Group had just taken part in the river crossing at the bridge – yet Gavin claims he did not know what the Guards Division was doing. Very curious.

Let us therefore provide an answer to Colonel Tucker's question. The Guards Armoured Division were not ready to advance up the road to Arnhem on the evening of D plus 3 because for the last two days they had been scattered all over Nijmegen and the south bank of the Waal, an area of some twenty-five square miles, assisting the 82nd Airborne Division carry out a task General Gavin had neglected to complete on D-Day.

Only five Guards' tanks – part of Carrington's squadron – were north of the bridge and they were engaged supporting Tucker's men: it is surprising that Colonel Tucker did not know this. The bridge fell to the Guards at around 1900hrs, when dusk was falling. Before pressing on to Arnhem the Guards Division tanks must be collected overnight, reformed, rearmed, refuelled and their crews briefed for the next phase of the advance – always assuming they could be spared from the fighting that was still going on south of the river, and defending the narrow Allied bridgehead on the north bank.

Let us be frank. The 82nd should have taken the Nijmegen bridge on D-Day, September 17. By failing to do so Gavin made a major contribution to the failure of the entire Arnhem operation and it will not do to pass the blame for that failure on to the British or to Captain Lord Carrington. Colonel Tucker bitterly complains about a delay of twelve hours but Gavin never provided the slightest explanation for the delay of thirty-six hours his failure to take the Nijmegen bridge imposed on the entire Market garden operation.

Gavin never expressed one word of apology for not taking the Nijmegen bridge on D-Day or the slightest acknowledgement of the help given to his division by the sappers of XXX Corps and the tank crews of the Guards Armoured Division. All the credit was down to him, any blame went to the British:

> In my opinion, the capture of the bridges intact, like the other bridges in this area, was the result of careful study and planning on the part of the parachutists of the 82nd Airborne Division and the careful carrying out of those plans by everyone, regardless of his rank or position, who was associated with the task.[32]

It seems a pity that this 'careful study and planning' did not extend to how the 82nd were to avoid a frontal assault on the Nijmegen bridge and when they were to carry it out. A more perceptive analysis comes from Major-General John Frost, commander of the 2nd Parachute Battalion at the Arnhem bridge:

> The worst mistake of the Arnhem plan was the failure to give priority to capturing the Nijmegen bridge. The capture would have been a walkover on D-Day, yet the 82nd Division could spare only one battalion as they must at all costs secure the Groesbeek heights where the Corps HQ was to be sited.[33]

These numerous attempts to divert attention from this failure, and pass the blame to a captain in the Guards Armoured Division, have been shameful... and highly successful. The myths surrounding the Nijmegen bridge have persisted and been engraved on the public mind by the media and the cinema. Given the US commanders' chronic tendency to pass the buck and blame their British allies at every opportunity, it certainly might have been better if some effort had been made to get elements of the Guards Division on the move to Arnhem that night. That, however, is the romantic view, bolstered by hindsight. In practical terms it takes time to assemble an entire armoured division from a battlefield in the dark streets of a town, issue fresh orders and prepare it for another advance.

Another problem seems to have been an abundance of chiefs in Nijmegen. By the evening of D plus 3 Nijmegen contained the XXX Corps commander,

Lieutenant General Horrocks, the Airborne Corps commander, Lieutenant General Browning, the Guards Armoured commander, Major-General Adair, and the 82nd Airborne Commander, Major-General Gavin, all debating what to do – mop up in the town, secure the bridgehead north of the Waal, beat off attacks now threatening Groesbeek and down the road from Eindhoven, and whether to bring up the infantry of the 43rd Division for the push to Arnhem.

The senior commander was General Horrocks, so the finger of decision points at him, but someone could have rounded up some tanks and guns, loaded a battalion or two of that enthusiastic US infantry into trucks and sent them up the road to Arnhem. How far they would have got is a matter of speculation – not very far in this author's opinion – but it would have given evidence of effort and spiked an unpleasant and unjust controversy that has rumbled on from that day to this.

It is not hard to understand the immediate reaction of that US officer who allegedly spoke to Lord Carrington, or of Colonel Tucker to Gavin: their unit had just pulled off a great feat-of-arms and they wanted to see this success exploited by the rescue of their British brother-paratroopers at Arnhem. However, once passions have cooled, it is hard to see how this strident position could be maintained, as it still is maintained in some quarters, sixty years after the battle. The US Official History makes the point that even after the Nijmegen bridge had finally been taken:

> The Guards Armoured's Coldstream Guards Group still was needed as a reserve for the Airborne division. This left but two armoured groups to go across the Waal. Even those did not make it until next day, D plus 4, 21 September, primarily because of diehard German defenders who had to be ferreted out from the superstructure and bridge underpinnings. Once on the north bank, much of the British armour and infantry had to be used to help hold and improve the bridgehead that the two battalions of the 504th Parachute Infantry had forged. By the time the Nijmegen bridge fell on D plus 3, it was early evening and it would be dark before an armoured column could be assembled to march on Arnhem. North of Nijmegen the enemy had tanks and guns and infantry of two SS Panzer divisions, in unknown but growing strength, established in country ideal for defence.[34]

This account adds that:

> At the village of Ressen, less than three miles north of Nijmegen, the
> Germans had erected an effective screen composed of an SS battalion rein-
> forced by eleven tanks, another infantry battalion, two batteries of 38mm guns,
> 20 20mm anti-aircraft guns and survivors of earlier fighting in Nijmegen.[35]

American readers should note that the above comments come from the US
Official History, where the notion that Lord Carrington and his five tanks could
have penetrated this screen and got up to Arnhem on the night of D plus 3 –
even supposing such a move was ever suggested – is revealed as a delusion.

Besides, it was already too late to save the men holding the Arnhem bridge:
by 20 September, Colonel Frost's force had run out of everything but courage.
On the morning of D plus 3, in a radio message to General Urquhart, Colonel
Frost called for ammunition, medical supplies, food and a surgical team. Later
that day, Frost was wounded and the shrinking battalion perimeter was under
constant attack from tanks and infantry; most of the buildings around the bridge
were on fire.

The stand of the 2nd Battalion, The Parachute Regiment and other remnants of 1st Airborne at the Arnhem Bridge ended at 0900hrs on Thursday,
21 September – D plus 4. The 2nd Battalion did not surrender: with only
150 men left and many of them wounded, Frost's force was overrun by the
SS Panzer Grenadiers. Had the Guards Armoured been able to drive directly
across the Nijmegen bridge when they arrived in the town on the morning of
19 September, it might all have been very different.

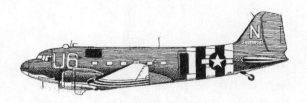

6 · THE BATTLES OF ARNHEM AND OOSTERBEEK 17–26 SEPTEMBER 1944

These men don't ask much; all they ask is something with which to fight back.

STANLEY MAXTED, CANADIAN WAR CORRESPONDENT,
BROADCAST FROM THE 1ST AIRBORNE PERIMETER, ARNHEM

On Thursday, 14 September 1944, the Airborne Division commanders for Market Garden met Lieutenant General Browning at the 1st Allied Airborne Corps HQ at Moor Park, west of London. Each divisional general was invited to outline his plans for the forthcoming operation and the last to do so was Major-General Roy Urquhart of the British 1st Airborne Division. As related, when Brigadier General Jim Gavin heard Urquhart's plan for the Arnhem drop, it caused him considerable surprise and not a little alarm: 'As he outlined his plan and told us that he had selected drop and landing zones six to eight miles west of the Arnhem bridge, I couldn't believe my ears,' said Gavin. 'I turned to my G-3, Colonel John Norton, and said, "My God, he can't mean it," and Norton replied "He does and he is going to try to do it."'[1] What Urquhart was 'going to try and do' was carry out his orders and take the Arnhem bridge.

There can be little doubt that the selection of drop and landing zones was the first error in the 1st Airborne plan for Arnhem, but the US Air Force planners selected the drop zones. The same is true for Gavin's drops for the assault at Nijmegen, so his astonishment at 1st Airborne's plan is a little difficult to understand. At both Arnhem and Nijmegen the DZs were on one side of the river, and well outside the town.

Gavin must therefore have known that Urquhart was simply making the best of a situation that had been imposed on both of them. It is also notable that no Air Force officers or staff from the First Airborne Army HQ attended this final briefing at Moor Park. This was the last chance anyone would have to query any point in the overall plan and ask for changes: yet another result of the speed with which the Market Garden operation had been mounted.

However, it should also be understood that in any military operation, things will go wrong; that *'No plan survives the first contact with the enemy'* is a well-established military maxim. No commander should be unfairly criticised for errors that occur once the battle has started, provided he has made a sound plan beforehand, preferably one based on previous experience, and takes any necessary remedial action quickly when matters go awry. On the other hand, commanders can be held to account for agreeing to plans that fly in the face of all previous experience and lack common sense. The decision of the Army Air Force officers to drop the gliders and paratroops well away from the bridges was understandable, but wrong, and this decision should have been revoked by Browning or Brereton. It will not do to blame General Urquhart for it.

Roy Urquhart was an experienced infantry soldier. He had served in the Western Desert and commanded the 231(Malta) Infantry Brigade with great success in Sicily. Granted, he had no airborne experience and may therefore have lacked the confidence to argue matters out with superiors like Brereton and Browning. He may also have had the sensible view, not uncommon among non-airborne people, that the parachute and glider landings, however exciting and glamorous, were merely another way of getting men into battle: once the men were on the ground the usual rules of war apply.

There is also the possibility that he did not appreciate that for all their high standards and superb personnel, airborne units have their limitations. Once on the ground they were immobile compared with 'heavy' infantry units with their abundance of transport. Nor was his plan without error. Though the Air Force planners chose the drop zones, Urquhart and his staff chose the lifts and it is strange that he seems to have paid little attention to the previous Comet plan, which allowed for glider *coup de main* attacks against the bridges, or made no use of the DZs south of the Arnhem road bridge until the Polish Parachute Brigade landed there on D plus 4.

Granted, the US Air Force planners might have vetoed this proposal, though the British air planners had clearly approved it for Comet. Had this southern DZ been used on the first day for a full brigade or a even battalion, it is more than possible that the bridge could have been stormed from the south before the troops dropped north of the bridge could hack their way through the town. Once again, however, the question arises: if the accepted way to take a bridge was 'from both ends at once', why were the 1st Airborne units only dropped north of the river? A lack of army-air force liaison or any common understanding of tactical requirements for airborne operations seems the only explanation.

However, another answer points the finger at Browning, who as related took thirty-eight aircraft and gliders from 1st Airborne's lift to carry his Corps Headquarters to Nijmegen and the Groesbeek heights. This left Urquhart with insufficient aircraft to get his division to their main drop zones, leaving no aircraft spare to carry the Polish Parachute Brigade to their drop zone south of Arnhem bridge on D-Day.

These questions hover over the initial airborne plan, but on matters of battlefield command Urquhart was perfectly competent and his brigade commanders at Arnhem were content with his leadership. Brigadier 'Shan' Hackett of the 4th Parachute Brigade, a man not noted for tolerating fools, said: 'Roy Urquhart was all right. He was sound, unflappable, very experienced; I could not have wished for a better battlefield commander.'[2] Urquhart encountered many problems at Arnhem but it is hard to see where his personal competence was at fault.

When matters go wrong in war they usually go wrong from the start. As with the rest of Market Garden, the Battle of Arnhem went wrong with the forming of the basic plan, but if there is a redeeming factor in the series of miscalculations and avoidable errors that led to the destruction of the 1st Airborne Division, it lies in the superb conduct of the fighting officers and men. The soldiers of the British 1st Airborne Division wrote a page in military history that will never be erased. After their first few hours on the ground it was clear that their situation was deteriorating, that the divisional plan had begun to fall apart, that the enemy had swiftly interposed himself between their drop zones and their objective. After the battle, various generals and historians would write about the 'failure' of 1st Airborne at Arnhem.

This is an unjust accusation: 1st Airborne did not fail. Matters went awry, certainly, and those matters must be examined, but the men did not fail; by their tenacity in defence, by their street fighting skills, most of all by their sheer guts, the men of 1st Airborne provided ample time for the commanders further south to come to their aid and redeem the situation.

It bears repeating that the 1st Airborne Division was asked to hold the Arnhem position for two days. They said they could hold for four days – and they held it for nine. Nine days for Second Army to get through, nine days for the Tactical Air Forces to occupy the skies over Arnhem, suppress the enemy anti-aircraft guns and destroy the enemy armour, nine days for fresh troops to come in, nine days for Horrocks or Dempsey or Browning to retrieve the situation. If one single, lightly equipped, airborne division could hold out more than four times longer than it was asked to do, surely some other element south of the Neder Rijn could have done *something*? But, as it was, a chapter of mistakes and those miscalculations by Gavin and Browning south of the Neder Rijn left the 1st Airborne Division to fight it out alone.

The battle at Arnhem began early on the morning of Sunday September 17 when the men of 1st Airborne filed on board their gliders and transport aircraft at various airfields in England. Here arose the second error, a forced decision that again was not Urquhart's fault. Having lost thirty-eight aircraft to lift Browning's HQ, Urquhart decided to take the divisional artillery in on the first lift, which would also consist of Brigadier Gerald Lathbury's 1st Parachute Brigade, Brigadier Philip Hicks' 1st Air Landing Brigade, less two companies, the Divisional HQ, the artillery, 21 Recce Squadron, the divisional reconnaissance force, and the divisional medical and engineer units.

Urquhart's decision to take the guns was sound: landing far from XXX Corps, it might be days before his infantry units were supported by tanks and field artillery and they might well need their own divisional artillery long before then; Urquhart was not to know that 2nd TAF's ground-attack aircraft, so useful in Normandy, would be less than helpful here. However, taking the guns meant leaving the 4th Parachute Brigade in England for the next lift on D plus 1, and that meant leaving the 1st Air Landing Brigade on the DZs to hold them for the first twenty-four hours of the operation. In short, due to a shortage of aircraft, Urquhart's initial thrust for the Arnhem bridge was reduced from a full division to a single brigade – and worse was to follow.

Urquhart was well aware that the Arnhem bridge was his major priority and his Operational Orders from Corps confirm this fact:

1 Primary Task. Your primary task is to capture the Arnhem bridges or a bridge.

2 Secondary Task. Your secondary task is to establish a sufficient bridgehead to enable the follow up forces of 30 Corps to deploy NORTH of the Neder Rijn.

3 Third Task. During your operations immediately after the landing of the first lift, you will do all in your power to destroy the flak in the area of your DZs, LZs and Arnhem, to ensure the passage of your subsequent lifts.[3]

The task of grabbing the road bridge was given to a *coup de main* force from 21 Recce Squadron, which would race to the bridge in jeeps equipped with Vickers 'K' guns, followed at best speed by the infantry battalions of Lathbury's 1st Parachute Brigade. Hicks' Air Landing Brigade would, as related, protect the various LZs and DZs west of the city until Hackett's 4th Parachute Brigade arrived on D plus I. Finally, Major-General Sosabowski's 1st Polish Parachute Brigade would land *south of the river* and close to the road bridge on D plus 2 – though as we shall see, Sosabowski's men arrived south of the river on D plus 4. As at Nijmegen, there is little evidence this plan reflected Brereton's prime demand: that the airborne divisions should '*grab the bridges with thunderclap surprise*' – the air planners' choice of DZs and LZs saw to that.

The largest airborne armada the world will ever see – 1,545 transport aircraft and 478 gliders, supported by over 1,000 fighter aircraft and preceded by bombers, set off for Holland on the morning of Sunday 17 September. Losing height as they crossed the Dutch coast, the parachute aircraft and glider tugs roared low over the Hartenstein Hotel in Oosterbeek, just as the commander of Army Group B, Field Marshal Model, who had established his HQ in that comfortable hotel, was about to go in to lunch. Leaving the meal on the table, Model and his staff left Oosterbeek immediately, driving off at speed to locate SS General Bittrich and the HQ of the SS Panzer Corps II and organise some rapid resistance to the airborne invasion. Bittrich and the other SS commanders in the area were already on the move, assembling whatever men, guns and armoured vehicles they could find, and taking on any airborne soldiers that came within reach. By 1500hrs, about the time the British started to move off their landing and drop zones, General Bittrich had already assembled a blocking force west of Arnhem.

The leading wave of aircraft carried the 21st (Independent) Parachute Company, the pathfinders for the 1st Airborne Division, the men who marked the drop zones. The pathfinders went out the door at precisely 1200 hrs, the battalions and gliders followed within twenty minutes, the gliders swept in and by 1500hrs the 1st Parachute Brigade and the 1st Air Landing Brigade had assembled on the ground and the 1st Brigade was preparing to march on Arnhem... by which time another snag had appeared.

Not all the gliders carrying the jeeps of 21 Reconnaissance Squadron had arrived. The men of the Recce Squadron landed safely but among the thirty-nine gliders – some 10 per cent of the glider force – that failed to make the LZ were twenty-two carrying the Recce Squadron's armed jeeps. This destroyed the first element in Urquhart's plan, that rapid *coup de main* in jeeps to seize the road bridge.

The task of taking the bridge now devolved on Brigadier Gerald Lathbury's 1st Parachute Brigade, which must march some eight miles to reach the bridge – and the road bridge was not their only objective. The Neder Rijn was also crossed by a railway bridge, a pontoon bridge, and a car and foot ferry, the latter running across the Neder Rijn from Heveadorp near Oosterbeek to the little town of Driel on the south bank all these crossing points must also be secured.

In an effort to speed up their advance, Brigadier Lathbury had given each of his three battalions a different route into Arnhem, so avoiding the need to proceed in one long brigade column. Lieutenant Colonel John Frost's 2nd Parachute Battalion was to move along the north bank of the Neder Rijn – the Lion Route – and take the railway bridge and the pontoon bridge before making for the road bridge. The 3rd Battalion (Lieutenant Colonel John Fitch) was to take the main road into the town – the Tiger Route – and head directly for the road bridge. The 1st Battalion (Lieutenant Colonel David Dobie) was to take the most northerly road – the Leopard Route – and occupy the high ground north of the town to form a protective flank. This, at least, was Lathbury's pre-landing plan and it was flexible: if his troops encountered stiff resistance on one route, he would switch the axis of advance to one less opposed. The important thing was to get to the bridges *quickly*.

The main thrust of this advance fell on John Frost's 2nd Battalion on the

Lion Route. Frost detailed 'A' Company for the road bridge and 'B' Company to seize the pontoon bridge, while 'C' Company took the railway bridge, crossed the river, and then moved along the south bank to seize the far end of the road bridge, so 'taking both ends at once'. The 2nd Battalion had got to Oosterbeek before they encountered any opposition from more than snipers, but when 'C' Company attempted to cross the railway bridge the leading platoon had barely moved onto the track when the bridge blew up in their faces. The enemy was clearly fully alert and starting to fight back – hard.

By then, Major-General Urquhart had discovered yet another problem: his radios did not work. This news will not surprise any old soldier. It is one of the fundamental rules of warfare that as soon as the first shot is fired, the radios go on the blink and radios were – and still are – particularly prone to not working in built-up or well-wooded areas. This communications problem continued throughout the Arnhem battle at all levels from corps down. It is hard to identify what radio links were working at any one time but generally, during Market Garden, communications at every level were at best intermittent.

Major Anthony Deane-Drummond of the Divisional Signals, an officer who entertained the deepest doubts about the entire Arnhem operation, had anticipated the possibility of the radios not working in the urban Arnhem area before the assault. Deane-Drummond had indented for more powerful signal sets weeks before but his request had been refused. He had applied again, and again been refused, on the grounds that 1st Airborne would usually operate in such a small area that their present sets would be perfectly adequate. In the event this was not so, and communications problems, within the division and with XXX Corps and Airborne Corps HQ at Nijmegen, and with the UK, were added to Urquhart's growing list of problems.

Roy Urquhart was too big and heavy for parachuting. He came in by glider and while his jeep was being unloaded he went to watch the drop of the 1st Parachute Brigade on DZ X, a few hundred yards to the east. When he came back he found that his tactical headquarters (Tac-HQ) had been set up, but his signals officer was already very anxious. There was no contact with the Recce Squadron, no contact with the battalions of the 1st Parachute Brigade, no contact with the UK or with Browning at Groesbeek. Urquhart had not been on the ground for half an hour and he was already completely isolated from the bulk of his command and from his base.

However, this situation was not unusual in war and Urquhart was a very experienced soldier. He got into his jeep and set off to tour the position and assess the situation as he found it. He soon caught up with the rear elements of Frost's 2nd Battalion, marching towards Oosterbeek and Arnhem and already meeting opposition from mortar fire, snipers and isolated German platoons. This opposition was not heavy, but it had to be dealt with and it all caused delay, not least because it was proving difficult to deploy off the road and outflank the enemy through the houses and gardens.

Leaving Frost to press along to the river, Urquhart went off to find Brigadier Lathbury of the 1st Parachute Brigade while his signallers made continual efforts to raise the other battalions and the Recce Squadron. Urquhart found Lathbury on the Arnhem to Utrecht highway, urging on the 3rd Battalion and inspecting a shot-up German staff car and the body of Major-General Friedrich Kussin, the commandant of Arnhem. Men of the 3rd Battalion had deployed into the cover of the surrounding woods and Lathbury and Urquhart were soon busy rousting the sections and platoons out of the trees, urging them on towards Arnhem.

This process indicated another problem that was just starting to appear. The airborne soldiers of the 1st Brigade were not pushing on as fast as they might have done towards the bridges. Where there was no sign of the enemy the troops were being greeted – and fêted – by the Dutch civilians, who came out to talk to them, offer food and drink, and greet their liberators. The soldiers were naturally delighted with this warm reception, but it slowed them down.

So too did the growing enemy resistance, and this was not being handled too well either, the airborne soldiers displaying an understandable tendency to go to ground, or deploying to mount local counter-attacks, though most of the German resistance was small scale and could have been ignored or brushed aside. The main task, indeed the only task of the 1st Parachute Brigade at this time, was to get to the river and seize the bridges – especially the road bridge – *and do so as quickly as possible*. One is forced to the conclusion that there was a certain lack of grip among the battalion officers and NCOs, who should have been ordering their men to press on, at the double where possible, ignoring all events – friendly or hostile – that stopped the soldiers getting to their objective. As it was, the advance into Arnhem was simply not fast enough and by early evening Dobie's 1st Battalion had been brought to a halt by rapidly mustered German opposition west of the town.

All these delays, major and minor, played into the hands of the opposition. The German commanders, Field Marshal Model, General Bittrich and their SS subordinates, were showing no such hesitation in responding to the airborne assault. They had seen the aircraft arrive and the British gliders and parachutes come down west of Arnhem. There could be no doubt that the bridges were the objective of this assault and the German commanders were summoning men, ordering up whatever tanks and armour they had available, getting mortar and artillery fire down on the airborne positions and sending strong patrols and small kampfgruppe out to the west of Arnhem to delay the airborne advance and drive directly into the airborne formations. With every minute that passed the strength of the German opposition was mounting.

SS General Bittrich had fought British soldiers before and had a shrewd idea of their strength and weaknesses. 'We must remember', he told his officers, 'that the British soldier will not act on his own initiative when he is fighting in the town and it is difficult for the officers to exercise control. The British soldier is incredible in defence but we need not be afraid of his offensive capabilities.'

With German opposition increasing on the two northern routes, the thrust for the bridges was devolving on Frost's 2nd Battalion. 'C' Company, thwarted at the railway bridge, had returned to the north bank and pressed on into Arnhem, where it was quickly involved in the street fighting: with German armour now in the town it never rejoined the main battalion. 'B' Company discovered that the pontoon bridge had already been dismantled and therefore pressed on to take part in the fighting for the high ground just north of Arnhem.

It was not until 2000hrs, some seven hours after the landing, that Frost got his first sight of the Arnhem road bridge. A whole parachute brigade had been despatched into Arnhem from DZ X but when Frost totalled up the number of men under command at the north end of the road bridge that evening, he had just over 700, from a variety of units, including 'A' Company, the HQ Company and two platoons of 'B' Company from his own 2nd Battalion, but no 'C' Company – though forty-five men from 'C' Company of the 3rd Battalion, some sappers from the 9th Parachute Field Squadron and seventeen glider pilots also turned up in his lines, as did two jeeps of the Recce Squadron.

Frost made two attempts to get across the bridge that evening. Both attacks were beaten back by heavy fire from a German pillbox in the centre and an armoured car at the southern end. Four German trucks that attempted to cross the bridge were set on fire and this fire thwarted any German attempt to cross the bridge under cover of darkness. Frost therefore deployed his men in houses at the north end of the bridge, distributed the available supplies of food and ammunition and prepared to hang on and await events: his signallers could not raise either Brigade HQ or Urquhart's Tac-HQ.

Both the other parachute battalions were in trouble. The 1st Battalion had been held and the 3rd Battalion, having moved off down the Utrecht road, first killed Major-General Kussin and was then heavily mortared at the nearby crossroads – crossroads being places easily targeted off the map by mortar teams. Pushing on, the battalion was stopped yet again on the outskirts of Oosterbeek by German infantry, backed by self-propelled (SP) guns and then by Kampfgruppe Kraft, a company-sized force supported by the first elements of 9 SS Panzer to arrive in the town. One German half-track, mounting an 88mm gun, was especially well handled: the crew knocked out a British 6-pdr anti-tank gun before it could open fire and then rolled down the road into the centre of the 3rd Battalion position, spraying the hedges on either side of the road with its heavy machine gun. Attempts to knock out this SP gun were thwarted when the Germans picked up the wounded from the anti-tank gun and laid them across the front of their vehicle. As night fell, most of the 3rd Battalion stayed in position outside Oosterbeek, but 'C' Company, sent round the southern edge of the German road block, lost contact with the battalion and eventually pressed on to join Frost at the road bridge.

The 1st Battalion, moving on the northern Leopard Route, made good time until it ran into German tanks and infantry half-tracks north of Wolfhezen, a village astride the railway line, north-west of Oosterbeek. The paratroopers had only their PIATS (Projectile Infantry, Anti-Tank) and Gammon bombs, a form of grenade, to deal with the enemy armour, and the fight here quickly became confused, the Germans pressing forward with tank support, the airborne soldiers repelling the German infantry with bayonet charges. This was a one-sided fight against infantry and armour, and when Dobie's signallers, frantically switching channels in an attempt to make contact with Brigade, picked up a signal from the 2nd Battalion asking for assistance, Dobie decided to hang on where he was, abandon the original task of taking the high ground north of the town, and move as quickly as possible towards the bridge.

The presence of German armour, tanks, half-tracks and armoured cars, came as a great shock to the airborne soldiers, who had not been informed that elements of two SS Panzer divisions were anywhere near Arnhem. This failure has been traced to Airborne Corps HQ, where a Major Brian Urquhart – no relation of the general – had concluded from air photographs that there was at least a small quantity of German armour in the Oosterbeek–Arnhem area, quite enough to disrupt the airborne landing. This intelligence was confirmed by Enigma decrypts, but when Major Urquhart attempted to bring it to the attention of his superiors at Allied Airborne HQ, Browning rejected his evidence. When Major Urquhart pressed the matter he was sent on compulsory sick leave, allegedly suffering from a nervous breakdown.[4] Why General Browning wished to conceal this information from his troops remains a mystery.

In spite of growing German opposition, other airborne units, recalling their briefing on the basic strategy for Market Garden, were pushing for the Arnhem road bridge. During the night of 17–18 September, Frost was joined by most of Brigade HQ – without Brigadier Lathbury – and, most usefully, by an RASC section driving a captured German truck which they had loaded with ammunition from the DZ. All this was to the good, but the situation in Arnhem was already grave, just eight hours after the landing. Only one company of the 3rd Battalion got through to the bridge that night; both the 1st and 3rd Battalions should have used the hours of darkness to press on.

The division had become fragmented, communications had broken down, and the enemy had reacted with speed and aggression. On the other hand, the 2nd Battalion had got a foothold on the Arnhem bridge. If they could be supported and some order restored, all might yet go well – but by the time it grew dark on 17 September, SS infantry held the south side of the bridge in some strength and German tanks were entering Arnhem from the north.

The first day's fighting had also been costly. Two days later the divisional medical officer, Lieutenant Colonel Warrack, drove back down the route into Arnhem used by the 1st Battalion and reported that it was the scene of 'a hell of a battle; wrecked trucks and tanks, overturned guns, bodies, smashed houses – the road for over two miles looked as it it had been hit by a tornado.' Nor was this all: sometime during the first day the 1st Airborne Division lost contact with its commander.

Urquhart had spent most of that day with Brigadier Lathbury, urging units into the town and attempting to get in touch with the Air Landing Brigade back on the LZ, whatever had arrived of the missing Recce Squadron, and the other parachute battalions. Radio contact was at best intermittent and this task became even more difficult when a mortar bomb struck Urquhart's jeep, wounding his signaller and damaging the set; Brigadier Lathbury's radio was not functioning at all.

Urquhart was now faced with an unsolvable dilemma. He had left his Tac-HQ because he had no radio contact with his units and needed to discover the situation on the ground; this was difficult and the information limited to those units he could find. He therefore realised that he must return to his Tac-HQ at the LZ and pick up a working radio, only to discover that German troops had cut the road between the landing zones and the town – another dilemma.

He decided that matters must be left in the hands of his subordinates, since they had been carefully briefed and he had no means of influencing events. He would stay with 1st Parachute Brigade and press on into the town. The Air Landing Brigade would hang onto the dropping zones. Tomorrow Hackett's 4th Parachute Brigade would arrive and radio communications might somehow be restored. If everyone did their best to follow the main plan, as they surely would, all might yet be well.

Urquhart and Lathbury therefore stayed with the 3rd Battalion, whose RSM, a formidable grenadier called Lord, appointed himself the general's bodyguard. Urquhart and Lathbury set up a joint HQ on the outskirts of Oosterbeek and sent a signal to Frost that the other battalions would attempt to reach the bridge after daylight on Monday – D plus 1.

Though it is hard to see why they waited until dawn before moving, it is not hard to imagine the mental agonies Urquhart must have been enduring at this time. In his book on the battle he comments that:

> I have many times gone over in my mind the reasons for the battle of Arnhem going the way it did, the mistakes and misjudgements and inadequacies... on the first night, as a Divisional Commander mixed up in a battalion encounter and personally situated in the middle of the column at that, I was in the worst possible situation to intervene too much but all the time I was conscious of precious seconds being wasted.[5]

When daylight came on D plus 1, Lathbury's men pushed on again, anxious to secure the town by the time Hackett's 4th Parachute Brigade arrived, but

Hackett's force had been delayed in the UK by bad weather and did not arrive until the afternoon. Once it arrived, the 4th Brigade and the Air Landing Brigade could hasten to join the troops by the bridge. Urquhart might then hope to have a division under command again, though at this time he still did not know Frost actually had the bridge. Meanwhile, in the face of continued German pressure, the 3rd Battalion split up into companies, the companies into platoons and sections. Fighting became fierce and at close quarters, with German tanks now rumbling through the streets, firing their heavy guns into the houses, and raking the airborne positions with their machine guns. A number of the tanks were equipped with flamethrowing equipment that set the houses on fire.

Nor was this all they were doing. Early on 18 September – D plus I – Bitterich had gone into the town and told his commanders that the key to this battle lay at Nijmegen – *Der Schwerpunkt ist süd* – and ordered them to round up men and tanks and, with Frost controlling the north side of the road bridge, ferry these men and tanks over the Heveadorp ferry and get them south to oppose the 82nd at Nijmegen. While this was going on, a fresh misfortune overtook 1st Airborne.

Urquhart and Lathbury, dodging about among the bullets while heading towards the bridge, were obliged to take shelter in a house. Unfortunately, by the time they had run upstairs to get a better view of the situation, a German tank had rumbled to a stop outside and German infantry were already in the garden. The two officers were trapped in this house for several hours, engaging any passing enemy with their personal weapons, Brigadier Lathbury doing especially good work with a rifle. In the early afternoon the two men made a break for it, sprinting down the street under machine-gun fire until a bullet hit Lathbury in the back, chipping his spine and causing temporary paralysis. Urquhart and a couple of young officers dragged the brigadier into a house and as they laid Lathbury down in the front room Urquhart looked up and saw a German soldier staring at them through the window. Urquhart shot the soldier dead with his .45 pistol.

After checking Lathbury's wounds they deposited the brigadier in the basement and left again, only to be driven into yet another house by the approach of German infantry and a self-propelled gun. With Germans swarming outside, the three officers decided to wait until dusk and then attempt to get away under cover of darkness.

So much for the senior commanders on the second day of the battle: Major-General Urquhart was in hiding, Brigadier Lathbury was wounded, Brigadier

Hicks was confined to the landing zones and out of communication range and Brigadier Hackett was waiting impatiently in the UK. That Brigadiers and Major-Generals were engaging the enemy with pistols and rifles is more eloquent of the situation than many longer accounts might be. All over Arnhem, just a few hours after the landing, individual soldiers, sections, platoons and companies of the various parachute battalions were fighting private battles. The radio net needed to co-ordinate their actions was virtually non-existent, but from commanding general to private soldier the 1st Airborne Division was putting up one hell of a fight.

Clearly, matters had not gone according to plan but the British had the bridge, or one end of it anyway. Fortunately, Lieutenant Colonel Frost was a very experienced officer who had reduced the Arnhem problem to the simplest terms: *hang onto the bridge*. He knew that if his men had orders to hold the north end of the bridge, and could be kept supplied with ammunition, they would not be easily dislodged. There was more to holding the bridge now than simply keeping it for XXX Corps: while Frost dominated the north end of the bridge, SS General Bittrich was prevented from sending armour over it to contest any advance from Nijmegen. Bittrich was well aware of the importance of Nijmegen and was desperate to get control of the Arnhem bridge.

German attacks on the bridge defenders therefore began soon after first light on 18 September, and continued at intervals throughout the day. Every attack was beaten off without great loss, parachute morale duly soared, and although there was no radio contact with the other units of the Brigade the 2nd Battalion signallers could at least hear radio traffic from the tanks of XXX Corps south of Nijmegen, an encouraging sign that relief was not far away. The only dark clouds in Frost's perimeter were a shortage of ammunition and the growing number of wounded in need of medical attention.

The ammunition shortage was becoming crucial. By early afternoon it was found necessary to stop the sniping and tell the men only to open fire with the Brens and mortars when an attack was actually in progress, a move which, though sensible, enabled the enemy to move about more easily and find positions from which more fire could be directed on the battalion positions. Sorties against the enemy netted the paratroopers a further bag of prisoners, many of them SS Panzer Grenadiers from 9 SS Panzer Division.

Although the bridge was being held and more men were gradually trickling into Frost's position, the overall situation of 1st Airborne Division was not improving. Urquhart and Lathbury had not reappeared at their headquarters and on the evening of 18 September, D plus 1, Brigade Major Tony Hibbert asked Frost to take command of the 1st Parachute Brigade, at least until Lathbury was found or his fate known.

Frost duly took command of the Brigade and got a message to the COs of 1 and 3 Para, telling them to hang on where they were and form a perimeter, but to send what men they could spare to the bridge. Chaos was clearly reigning, but if they could only hang on, matters must improve. Horrocks' XXX Corps was about to join General Gavin's 82nd Airborne Division at Nijmegen, just eight miles away, but they were still south of the Waal and the link-up was clearly going to take more than the allotted two days.

On D plus 1 the 1st Air Landing Brigade was fully employed hanging onto the landing zones eight miles to the west. Brigadier Hackett's 4th Parachute Brigade was already emplaned in the UK, where their take-off was delayed for four hours by the weather; and the communications problem again intervened. There was no communication – or very little, and that intermittent – between the various elements of the Airborne Corps; Urquhart or Frost at Arnhem, Browning on the Groesbeek heights, Hackett and Sosabowski in the UK, so none of this information reached Urquhart.

One obvious course of action was to order Hicks's brigade into the town at once and land Hackett's full brigade on that DZ just south of the road bridge. To send yet another brigade to the western DZs, from where they faced another contested march through the town, was clearly inadvisable, but there was no means of discussing this idea or implementing it – the communications were too bad, and not helped by the fact that Browning, perched on the Groesbeek ridge, was far away from all his subordinate units, except the 82nd Airborne. This being so, the original plan went ahead.

The flight of the 4th Parachute Brigade to Arnhem on D plus 1 was more eventful than that enjoyed by their comrades the previous day. The enemy was fully alert: a force of German fighter aircraft attempted to break through the Allied fighter screen and get at the transports. They were beaten off, but once over the German lines light flak cost the brigade at least one aircraft and twenty soldiers and when, at 1500hrs, the aircraft went in to drop on DZ-T, they were low enough to see the German gunners, hemming in the Air Landing Brigade perimeter, staring up at them and firing with everything from anti-aircraft guns to rifles. Ground attack aircraft should have been deployed to deal with these guns but they were forbidden to intervene while escort fighters were in the air. As a result, many aircraft were hit, but most of the men landed more or less in the right place, though a number were killed and a larger number wounded while still in their parachutes. Once on the ground, the 4th Brigade had to assemble under fire and, like their colleagues on the previous day, they now had some eight miles to march to their objective.

According to the original plan, the prime task of the 4th Parachute Brigade was to seize the centre of Arnhem town and support the men of 1st Parachute Brigade, who by now should have been comfortably settled at the bridge. Brigadier Hackett had already told his senior officers that the task of holding the town centre was the least of their worries and was probably impossible anyway. Any surprise gained by the previous day's drop would have long since disappeared: their most difficult task lay in covering the ground between the dropping zone and the bridge.

This proved to be the case. Hackett's brigade was in trouble from the moment they reached the ground, when Hackett discovered that Urquhart had vanished on the previous afternoon and that Brigadier Hicks had taken temporary command of the Division. Hicks' assumption of command was in accordance with Urquhart's orders for the command succession issued before the Arnhem operation started, but Hicks was junior to Hackett and Hackett did not like this demotion. He liked it even less when he was met on the DZ by a staff officer from 1 Air Landing Brigade and told that one of his battalions, Lieutenant Colonel Lea's 11th Parachute Battalion, had already left the DZ at Hicks' orders and was marching into Arnhem with the South Staffordshire Battalion of the Air Landing Brigade in an attempt to reach the 1st Parachute Battalion trapped somewhere in the town.

Given the situation at this time, Hicks was well within his rights, but Hackett sought him out and told Hicks that he, Hackett, was the senior officer here and that he would, if necessary, take command of the Division, if only to get 'some proper orders'. Brigadier Hicks, unsurprisingly, disputed this proposal. News of this disagreement swept through Divisional HQ and Urquhart's senior staff officer, Lieutenant Colonel Mackenzie, GSO 1 of the Division, was roused from some well-earned sleep and told that 'The brigadiers are having a flaming row.' A form of chaos was now reigning everywhere, but to have two of the brigadiers quarrelling over seniority while the divisional commander was absent and the Germans were swarming everywhere, seems little short of bizarre. In the event, the 4th Parachute Brigade never got into Arnhem – except for the 11th Battalion, sent there by Hicks. The other two battalions, 10th and 15th, were stopped dead outside Oosterbeek

Hackett had decided to take his brigade into Arnhem along an axis north of the railway line, aiming to take the high ground overlooking the town at Koepel, picking up another of the Air Landing battalions, the 7th Battalion, The King's Own Scottish Borderers (7th KOSB's) on the way. This was in line with the orders given to him by Urquhart before D-Day but the situation had changed and now this decision was wrong. The only feasible aim was to get as many men and guns – and as much food and ammunition – as possible into position around the Arnhem bridge, and the only way to get there was along the north bank of the river. There was one alternative route, the Driel ferry, which was still undamaged and might have been used to send the 4th Brigade or one of its battalions over the river and onto the south end of the Arnhem bridge.

The command problem inhibited such action. Hicks might have ordered Hackett to try crossing the river or use the north bank route to the bridge, but apart from their current disagreement, Brigadier Hicks was only filling-in for the missing General Urquhart. The divisional commander had not been reported dead or captured and might reappear at any moment, so abandoning the divisional plan was not an option Hicks was willing to consider. Attempts therefore continued to make the original plan work – with predictable results. The 4th Parachute Brigade's battalions pushed into the town and were duly chewed up in the streets of Arnhem.

Fortunately, on the night of 18 September, D plus 1, Urquhart was able to escape from his hiding place. He quickly met up with soldiers of the 11th Battalion of the 4th Brigade and the South Staffordshire Regiment of the Air Landing Brigade, who told him that divisional HQ had moved off the LZ, which was now in enemy hands, and was established at the Hartenstein Hotel in Oosterbeek, the former headquarters of Field Marshal Model.

Urquhart returned to his HQ at 0715hrs on the morning of 19 September, D plus 2, having been out of touch with his command for a day and a half. On that morning, just eight miles away to the south, the tanks of the Guards

Armoured Division made contact with the 82nd Airborne in Nijmegen. Operation Market Garden had been running for just over forty hours.

At Oosterbeek, Lieutenant Colonel Mackenzie, the GSO-1 of the division, was very pleased to see Urquhart and quickly put him in the picture: specifically, that Brigadier Hackett was still trying to get onto his original objective, the ridge north of the town, and was currently battering his way there via the town centre. Urquhart saw no point now in defending any area outside the road bridge perimeter and in mid-morning, having assessed the situation as desperate, he ordered Hackett to withdraw into the town. 'And now,' says Urquhart in his memoirs, 'on this fateful afternoon of Tuesday, 19 September, everything began to go awry.'

This seems rather optimistic. Matters had been going awry since the time the Air Force officers chose those distant DZs, but Urquhart's comment is a fair summation of the situation at the time – and nothing could be done about it. 1st Airborne were dispersed around Arnhem and XXX Corps were stalled at Nijmegen, where the road and rail bridges had still not been taken.

How long 1st Airborne could hold out was debatable, for supplies of food and ammunition sent by air were mostly being dropped into German hands; signals sent to England changing the dropping points were either not received at Airborne Army HQ or ignored. The Germans had also started lining up their anti-aircraft guns along the flight paths of the supply aircraft and greeted the slow-moving and low-flying transports with blasts of AA fire. As a result, most of the supplies went astray, and food, medical supplies and ammunition within the airborne perimeter began to run out. The RAF transport squadrons began to suffer heavy losses.

What did not run out – what never ran out at Arnhem – was fighting spirit and courage, in the air and on the ground. Accounts of the Arnhem battle are full of tales, sights and actions that make one want to weep. There was the C-47 Dakota, coming in low across the perimeter, every German flak gun firing on it as it dropped one load, its starboard wing already blazing; then it turned and came back to drop the rest of its cargo, the dispatchers still standing in the doors, pushing out the bales as their aircraft went down.

Urquhart writes that from their battered trenches and foxholes, hundreds of airborne soldiers watched this aircraft complete its task and crash. Only one of the crew survived and the pilot, Flight Lieutenant David Lord, was later awarded a posthumous Victoria Cross. Of the 163 transport aircraft that attempted to drop supplies to 1st Airborne on 19 September, thirteen were shot down over the drop zones and ninety-seven others were damaged by anti-aircraft fire. Undeterred, the RAF returned to the task on successive days and pressed home their sorties with great courage and at considerable cost. Eighty-four transport aircraft were shot down on 601 sorties to Arnhem, but of 1,431 tons of food and ammunition dropped only 106 tons fell to 1st Airborne: the Germans got the rest.[6]

No account of the Arnhem battle is complete without mention of Mrs Kate Ter Horst, whom Urquhart describes as 'a tall, slim Dutchwoman, with blond hair and calm, ice-blue eyes'. When her house was taken over as an emergency dressing station, Mrs Ter Horst moved her children into the basement and stayed to help comfort the wounded who soon occupied all the beds and every inch of floor space in her house. Her home was quickly knocked to pieces, the windows blown in, the walls pitted with shell fragments, but Mrs Ter Horst did not flinch. When field dressings ran out, she tore up her sheets, towels and table linen for bandages; she carried water and she fed the wounded. When men were distressed or dying, she was on hand to encourage or comfort them. At night, when German tanks rumbled past or shells and mortar bombs shook the walls, she would console her children in the cellar with a fairy story, then climb the stairs to visit the wounded by candlelight, quietly reading an appropriate verse or two from the Bible:

> Thou shall not be afraid, not of any terror by night, nor for the arrow that flieth by day. Nor for the pestilence that walketh in darkness; nor for the sickness that destroyeth in the noon day... A thousand shall fall beside thee and ten thousand on thy right hand; but death shall not come nigh thee, for Thou, Lord, are my hope and Thou hath set Thy house of defence very high.

Mrs Ter Horst and her five children remained in the house throughout the entire battle, and when it ended there were 300 wounded men sharing their home and fifty-seven dead soldiers in the garden. Kate Ter Horst was a very gallant lady and the surviving soldiers of 1st Airborne have never forgotten her. Nor will they forget the hundreds of other people of Arnhem, Oosterbeek and the surrounding villages who helped them in the battle at the risk of their own lives, both during the fighting and from subsequent German reprisals.

Five VCs were awarded at Arnhem – all but one posthumously – including that awarded to Flight Lieutenant Lord. Another went to Sergeant J. D. Baskey-field, an anti-tank gunner in the South Staffordshire Regiment, who stood off three German tanks near Oosterbeek. He knocked out a tank with his first shot and disabled another with his second shot. His own gun out of ammunition, he ran to another where the crew had been killed and brought that into action, engaging the third tank alone until he was slain.

Lieutenant John H. Grayburn of the 2nd Battalion, The Parachute Regiment, commanded a platoon at the bridge from 17 September. Though wounded several times, he and his platoon drove off repeated attacks by German tanks and infantry. Numbers fell, but he continued to command what was left of his Company until he was killed on 20 September. Another parachute officer, Captain Lionel Queripel of the 10th Battalion, although wounded several times, refused to go to a dressing station. When his battalion was ordered to retire to Oosterbeek, he remained behind to cover the withdrawal and was last seen engaging the advancing enemy with a rifle. The only VC to survive was Major Robert Cain of the Northumberland Fusiliers, attached to the South Staffordshire Regiment. He engaged enemy tanks with a PIAT, knocking out several at very close range, despite being wounded, and when he ran out of PIAT ammunition, he continued to engage the enemy with a 2-inch mortar.

The British soldier, a notoriously bloody-minded individual, always fights well in defence, and in spite of their numerous problems – most particularly a shortage of ammunition – the 1st Airborne soldiers had no intention of giving in. They were tired but they could go without sleep; they were hungry but they could manage without food. If they were defeated, they refused to admit it; and they would not run. No one has defined their state of mind better than one of their own officers in a short speech made in the church of Oosterbeek during the height of the battle. Dickie Lonsdale, second-in-command of the 11th Parachute Battalion, though wounded in the landing on D-Day, had been ordered to form an ad-hoc unit, Lonsdale Force, drawn from the remnants of the 1st and 11th Parachute Battalions, the South Staffs and some glider pilots, about 250 men in all, to defend the Oosterbeek perimeter. He assembled these remnants in the church at Oosterbeek, haggard men, many of them wounded, weary from days without sleep:'not in their Sunday best,' says Lonsdale, 'but still defiant, still unbroken'.

While they were filing in, occupying the pews and cleaning their weapons,

Lonsdale climbed into the Minister's pulpit, told them that this was a fight to the last man and the last round of ammunition and finished his address with some words the Parachute Regiment would remember:

> This is by no means the first time we have fought the Germans. We fought the cream of their army in North Africa, in Sicily and again in Italy. We defeated them in those campaigns and now we are up against them again here. They were not good enough for us then, and they are bloody well not good enough for us now. In one hour's time you will take up defensive positions on the Oosterbeek–Arnhem road. Make certain you are well dug-in. Make certain your weapons and ammunition are in good order. We are getting short of ammunition, so conserve it and when you shoot, shoot to kill ... and good luck to you all.

And so they fought on, day after day, as German tanks and guns pulled the town down about them. They used the bayonet a great deal, charging into the German lines yelling the 1st Brigade's North African battle cry, 'Waho, Mahommed', using German weapons when they could get them. For some it became a game, hunting Tiger tanks among the ruined houses with the hand-held infantry PIAT, going out in twos and threes to find food or ammunition or to snuff out snipers. Somehow, in spite of everything the enemy could throw against them, Frost and his men held the Arnhem bridge for three days and four nights.

Resistance at the bridge ended at 0900hrs on Thursday, 21 September – D plus 4 – and even at the end they did not surrender. With Frost wounded, most of the officers and NCOs dead or wounded, ammunition expended and only a few men left, the surviving defenders of Arnhem had to be blasted out of the ruins by the bridge, house by house and room by room. Frost's force was overrun by superior numbers – but they never surrendered.

Elsewhere, in the battered streets outside Oosterbeek, Hackett's 4th Parachute Brigade was being destroyed and on D plus 3 his battalions had been ordered to fight their way back to the new perimeter that Urquhart was forming around Oosterbeek, two miles to the west. Not many men made it but they all tried, fighting their way back through the streets and woods, beating off the enemy, Hackett's men even forcing a passage with the bayonet. The Oosterbeek perimeter began to form late on the afternoon of 19 September, and became an oblong position about a kilometre wide and two kilometres deep, on the north bank of the Neder Rijn, running inland around Oosterbeek.

Inside this tight area, on D plus 3 and 4, under the plunging mortar bombs and artillery shells, Urquhart assembled some 2,000 men from the Parachute Regiment, the Air Landing battalions, the Glider Pilot Regiment and the supporting units: signals, engineers, RASC. Each unit was given a section of the perimeter to defend and here they prepared to hang on while higher minds at XXX Corps, Airborne Corps HQ in Nijmegen, and in the UK decided what to do next. It was now 20 September, D plus 3, and on the following day – D plus 4 – the survivors of the battle at the bridge came in to join them. The battle for Arnhem was over; the battle for Oosterbeek had begun.

At this point we turn to Major-General Sosabowski's 1st Polish Parachute Brigade. In the original plan this brigade had been tasked to land on D plus 2 – 19 September – on DZ K, south of the Arnhem road bridge, but bad weather had put this drop back and the plan was then changed. On D plus 3, a radio message from 1st Airborne requested that the Poles should be dropped at Driel, south of the Heveadorp ferry, cross the river there and take up positions west of Oosterbeek.

Sosabowski's Brigade duly dropped at 1530hrs, landing on a DZ north of Driel. There they found that the Heveadorp ferry had been scuttled by the Dutch ferrymen on the previous night and there was no way across the river. Nor did all the Brigade drop: almost half the C-47's tasked to carry the brigade had been forced to turn back by bad weather, so only about 750 men, about half the force, arrived while some of the gliders, carrying their anti-tank guns and ammunition, had been landed north of the river on D plus 2. Accounts of this time vary: some say that the Germans captured and sank the ferry, but this seems unlikely, as they would have found it useful. Other accounts allege that Sosabowski got some 1,400 men in on D plus 4. The total given above is from Volume Two of the Official History.

The Poles made contact with 1st Airborne by sending some staff officers swimming across the river – once again the radios were on the blink. Unable to cross the river to the airborne perimeter, Sosabowski and his men dug in to hold their narrow bridgehead on the south bank as a possible launching pad for a XXX Corps crossing – when they arrived.

This was encouraging, but at midnight on 21 September, Urquhart surveyed the strength returns from his battalions within the Oosterbeek perimeter; they made grim reading. The 1st Battalion was down to 116 men, the 11th to around 150 and the South Staffordshire Regiment to 100. The 3rd Parachute Battalion was forty strong, the 10th, 250 strong and the 156 Parachute Battalion perhaps 270; ammunition was very low, PIAT ammunition was exhausted, and wounded men were everywhere. And there was still no sign of XXX Corps, four days into the fight.

On the 22nd, two of Urquhart's staff officers, including his G-1, Lieutenant Colonel Charles MacKenzie, crossed the river in a rowing boat and told Sosabowski that even a few platoons or a couple of companies could make all the difference in the airborne perimeter. This being the case, on that night Sosabowski managed to get a couple of platoons – around sixty men – over the river and into the airborne perimeter. This was not much, but contact had been made and there was now a link between the Polish bridgehead on the south bank and Oosterbeek on the north bank: if XXX Corps could come up, something might yet be salvaged.

At this point we return to XXX Corps operations at Nijmegen. As related, the first elements of XXX Corps arrived in Nijmegen at around 0820hrs – some accounts say 1100hrs – on 19 September, D plus 2. The bridges were taken by the 82nd Airborne and the Guards' Armoured tanks at around 1900hrs on 20 September, D plus 3. XXX Corps resumed its thrust for Arnhem at around 1330hrs on 21 September, D plus 4, after the ground ahead – known as 'The Island' – had been reconnoitred by armoured cars of the Household Cavalry. The cavalry encountered enemy tanks at Elst, south of the Arnhem bridge, which was now in German hands.

The British Official History describes 'The Island' as:

> Flat low-lying land, drained by innumerable ditches and waterways, which separate its fields instead of hedges. The main road to Arnhem in particular ran between deep, wide ditches, within which the advancing tanks were firmly enclosed; there was no escape on either hand.

This narrow road – a country lane set on an embankment, offering a one-tank wide advance – came to resemble a fairground shooting gallery, with the tanks in the role of ducks, easily picked off against the skyline. The Guards' advance was quickly opposed by elements of 9 and 10 SS Panzer with Panther tanks and 88mm guns. Five tanks of the leading Irish Guards

Group were quickly 'brewed-up', creating a flaming barrier across the only road.

The Guards had very few infantry and little artillery, and it was therefore decided that the Guards Armoured should be replaced as the XXX Corps spearhead by the 43rd Infantry Division, commanded by Major-General Ivo Thomas, a man known to his men – without much affection – as 'Butcher' Thomas. This decision caused delay, for the 43rd Division had to be brought through Nijmegen, up a road and through a town already jammed with tanks, troops and vehicles – a road now under attack to the south by German forces from the Fifteenth Army.

The 214th Brigade of 43rd Division duly pushed forward on 22 September, and the 5th Duke of Cornwall's Light Infantry (5 DCLI) and some tanks of the 4/7th Dragoon Guards joined up with the Poles at Driel in the early evening. It should also be mentioned that during this time, German units were attacking and sometimes cutting the road further south in the 101st Airborne sector, between Eindhoven and Nijmegen, and some Guards' Armoured tanks from Nijmegen had to be sent south to deal with them.

These alarms delayed the advance of the 43rd Division's brigades but by the evening of 23 September the 130th Brigade had also joined the Poles at Driel. That night a further 150 Poles got across the river in rubber dinghies borrowed from the Royal Engineers. The intention now was for all the Poles and part of 130 Brigade to cross the river into Oosterbeek but assault boats were in short supply – here, as at Nijmegen, no one had visualised a river crossing in boats.

On 23 September, D plus 6, the Airborne Division also got its first close-support from ground attack fighters and fighter-bombers of the Tactical Air Forces, which came in to pound the German positions and rake enemy convoys heading into Arnhem. This was useful but, like the artillery support, it came far too late. That night Urquhart sent a message to XXX Corps stating: 'Casualties heavy. Resources stretched to utmost. Relief within 24 hours vital.' This news seems to have galvanised XXX Corps, for on the following day, Sunday 24 September, a message reached Urquhart from XXX Corps, saying they were within reach of the river and hoped to put the 130th Infantry Brigade of the 43rd Division over the river that night.

This message followed a meeting on the morning of 24 September when Sosabowski went to Valburg for a conference with Horrocks, Browning and Thomas. As noted in previous chapters, relations among the Allied commanders were not always of the best and it appears that trouble was now brewing between 'Butcher' Thomas and Sosabowski. This trouble revealed itself at the conference when Thomas declared the river would be crossed that night by a battalion of the Dorset Regiment from the 43rd Division, followed by a battalion of Poles – another battalion of Poles crossing the river further east. This was news to Sosabowski, who pointed out, correctly, that feeding more troops in small amounts into the Oosterbeek perimeter was achieving very little: what was needed was a major assault across the river further downstream by the entire 43rd Division.

Sosabowski was quite right but for the moment such an attack was logistically impossible and would anyway take too long to arrange. Horrocks therefore ordered that these night crossings should proceed, adding that if Major-General Sosabowski did not like it, he would be relieved of his command – a most insulting comment to a loyal ally and a fighting soldier and indicative, perhaps, of the strain Horrocks was under at this time.

This statement seems to mark the start of rapidly deteriorating relations between Sosabowski and his British superiors. It is fair to say, but unpleasant to record, that Browning, Horrocks and to some extent Montgomery seem to have decided that Sosabowski was to be the scapegoat for any failures at Oosterbeek. In their various ways they all pressed their case – that Sosabowski was 'arrogant' and 'difficult to work with' – even, according to Montgomery, that the Polish Parachute Brigade was unwilling to fight – another foul slander – until Sosabowski, most unfairly, was indeed relieved of his command.

More boats were needed to ferry the Poles and Dorsets over the river to attack, so during 24 September five lorry-loads of assault boats were sent up to Driel. Disaster attended the entire operation: four lorry-loads of boats never arrived and the one that did brought boats without paddles. The crossing still went ahead, though there were not enough boats, none at all for 130 Brigade – which could only put a battalion of the Dorsets over – and only enough for one Polish battalion. In the event, only 300 men of the 4th Dorsets got across the river that night; most of the rest were swept away from the airborne perimeter by the current and landed directly under a German position, many being killed, wounded or captured in the subsequent fighting.

The battle in Oosterbeek over the days from 19–25 September is better imagined than described. Buildings collapse as tanks knock away their corners;

the constant rattle of machine-guns, the thump and crash of mortar fire, the ripping noise of the belt-fed German Spandau competing with the slower beat of the magazine-fed British Bren. German tanks grind freely through the rubble-strewn streets, stopping to fire their heavy guns into the parachute soldiers' positions, while their supporting infantry tackle the airborne soldiers with grenades and flamethrowers – to be thrown back time and again by grimy men in camouflaged smocks and faded berets, who come surging down upon them with the bayonet, grenades and the Sten gun.

Brigadier Shan Hackett had been wounded twice and was in a German hospital with a shell fragment in his stomach, the second of the Airborne briga-diers to be wounded in this action. With a great number of wounded men within the Oosterbeek perimeter – around 2,000 by now – and no medical supplies, on Saturday 23 September Colonel Graham Warrack, the Chief Medical Officer, made contact with SS General Bittrich, asking for a truce in which the British wounded could be evacuated to German hospitals in Arnhem. Bitterich willingly agreed and the British wounded were promptly ferried through the lines and well-treated in the hospitals of the IInd SS Panzer Corps. The remainder battled on and their losses continued to mount.

Following the failure of the crossing on the night of 24–25 September the decision was reached that the 1st Airborne Division would be withdrawn; this information was passed to Urquhart on the morning of 25 September. The remnants of 1st Airborne held their lines for the rest of the day and started to pull out at 2200hrs that night, many brought across the river in thirty-six assault boats provided by the British and Canadian engineers, the crossing covered by a heavy bombardment from the artillery of XXX Corps. Those men too badly wounded to move stayed behind to fire rifles and machine-guns and give the impression that their trenches were still held.

This deception worked and the evacuation was successful. By first light on 26 September, D plus 9, the remnants of the British 1st Airborne Division, 1,741 men – just sixteen from Frost's 2nd Parachute Battalion, thirty-two from the 3rd Battalion, 422 of the gallant Glider Pilot Regiment, that regiment of sergeants who fought as infantry after their gliders landed, men from every unit of 1st Airborne, plus seventy-two men from the 4th Dorsets and 160 Poles, all that was left from the 10,000 airborne soldiers that had flown into Arnhem in recent days, had been ferried to the south bank. Around 100 were killed making the crossing; many who could not be ferried across in boats and decided to swim were swept away and drowned. All the doctors, chaplains and medical orderlies stayed behind with the wounded and passed into captivity.

When the Division reassembled after the battle, it was discovered that 1,400 men had been killed and over 6,000, more than a third of them wounded, had been taken prisoner. On the morning of 26 September, D plus 9, the autumn mist drifted away from the river, the firing gradually ceased and the smoke of battle cleared from the battered streets of Oosterbeek and Arnhem, and the Germans too could count the cost. At least 3,000 German soldiers had been killed or wounded in the Arnhem battle; but they had the consolation of victory.

One of the last to leave the north bank was Major-General Urquhart who, having seen his men to the XXX Corps lines, made his way to Browning's HQ at Nijmegen. Deciding to 'display a little briskness' when Browning eventually appeared, Urquhart saluted and reported: 'The Division is nearly all out now, Sir. I am sorry we haven't been able to do what we set out to do.'

'Never mind,' said Browning briefly, 'I'm sure you did all you could.'

The reception accorded to the men of 1st Airborne by the infantry and tanks crews of the Guards Armoured and the 43rd Division south of Arnhem was even more chilly. '*Call that a f***ing battle?*' they yelled out to the weary paratroopers rolling past their column in trucks. 'Seven f***ing days up the sharp end and then back to Blighty?'[7] These harsh critics can be forgiven; they had been fighting for three solid months, on Hill 112 and on Goodwood in Normandy and all the way north from the Seine – they had taken heavy losses and seen a lot of war and knew that more was to follow – and they did not yet know what the 1st Airborne Division had done.

Fortunately, when it was realised what 1st Airborne had done the praise poured in, with General Eisenhower writing a eulogy to General Urquhart on 8 October:

> The proud record that your Division has established needs no embellishment from me. Pressed from every side, without relief, reinforcement or respite, they inflicted such losses on the Nazis that his infantry dared not close with them... for nine days they checked the furious assaults of the Nazis and when, on 26 September, they were ordered to withdraw across the river they came out a proud and haughty band... soldiers all.

Field Marshal Montgomery added his own congratulations:

> In the annals of the British Army there are many glorious deeds. In our
> Army we have always drawn great strength and inspiration from past
> traditions and endeavoured to live up to the high standards of those who
> have gone before. But there are few episodes more glorious than the epic
> of Arnhem and those who follow after you will find it hard to live up to the
> standards you have set. In years to come it will be a great thing for a man
> to say, 'I fought at Arnhem'.

All this is very true but the praise heaped on the fighting men of the 1st Airborne
Division and the gallant actions fought by all the units on Market Garden should
not blind us to the numerous failings of the higher command. Command failings
are often concealed by the heroism of the troops and, all too often, criticising the
command is taken as a criticism of the men, when exactly the opposite is true.

The various command failings on Market Garden, not least those at
Nijmegen, have been detailed in the last two chapters and need not be repeated
here. However, in 1951, the Army Council commissioned a book which listed
the harsh command lessons of Market Garden.[8] This critique goes on for pages,
but the main points are as follows.

An airborne division is designed to fight as a whole; if it is flown in by
degrees, its effective strength is reduced to that of a brigade, which is what
happened. The reasons for choosing DZs so far from the objectives are far from
clear, but an RAF officer claims that the overriding factor was the inability of
gliders to get down in enclosed country. Whatever the reasons, it seems that
more risks might have been justified during the initial stages of the operation, for
it would have been possible to land gliders and parachute troops closer to the
bridge. The maps available from 1944 seem to bear this out.

If the plan had included a whole brigade to be dropped near the Arnhem
bridge on D-Day – say on the south bank – the outcome of the battle might
have been very different. The intelligence information supplied to 1st Airborne
was 'sketchy and inaccurate'. The operation suffered from a lack of close air
support from the 2nd Tactical Air Force throughout. The whole question of
supply by air needed reorganising and the means to suppress enemy flak over the
supply drop zones improved. The Arnhem operation proved that high-powered
wireless sets, and more of them, were required. Throughout the battle, com-

munications were bad: there was little or no direct communication with 1 Airborne Corps (Browning) for the vital first two or three days and many of the messages that were passed went via war correspondents and the BBC in London.

Finally, Arnhem proved, yet again, that the principle of an early relief of airborne troops – usually within forty-eight hours – was essential, especially where the enemy was alert and well organised and the dropping of air supplies could not be relied on. As it was, the link-up failed and most of the supplies fell into enemy hands.

Montgomery was later to claim that Market Garden was '90 per cent successful'. Few authorities, at the time or since, have been convinced by this claim, but given the number of planning and command failures it seems fair to say that had fewer mistakes been made at every level, Market Garden *might* have succeeded in putting Allied forces across the Rhine in September 1944.

This attempt had clearly failed and attention must now be turned to other, pending tasks: the clearing of the Antwerp approaches and the struggle of Bradley's 12 Army Group in its efforts to reach the Rhine. But as we move away to other battles, remember the men of 1st Airborne, who held their position for nine days against everything the enemy could throw against them.

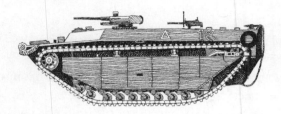

7 · THE STRUGGLE FOR THE SCHELDT
SEPTEMBER – NOVEMBER 1944

I must emphasize that I consider Antwerp of first importance to all our endeavors on entire front from Switzerland to Channel. I believe your personal attention is required in operation to clear entrance.

GENERAL DWIGHT D. EISENHOWER,
MESSAGE TO FIELD MARSHAL MONTGOMERY, 9 OCTOBER 1944

One of the great controversies of the North-West Europe campaign hinges on an assessment of the strategic merits of the Rhine – or Arnhem – versus Antwerp in September 1944. Even Montgomery's stoutest supporter, Field Marshal Alan Brooke, the CIGS, felt that the choice of Arnhem was wrong, and his previously-quoted comment is worth repeating: 'I feel that Monty's strategy for once is at fault. Instead of carrying out the advance on Arnhem he ought to have made certain of Antwerp in the first place... Ike nobly took all the blame on himself as he had approved Monty's suggestion to operate on Arnhem.'[1]

This comment rather overlooks the fact that Marshall and Arnold had been urging Eisenhower to deploy the Airborne Army for weeks. Ike therefore saw the Arnhem proposal as an excellent way of getting his Washington superiors off his back – and perhaps gaining a bridgehead over the Rhine. Nevertheless, the point remains and has to be considered: which should have had the priority, Arnhem or Antwerp? Clearly, in early September, Montgomery thought that with two armies – and some American support – he could handle two objectives, Arnhem and Antwerp, believing the First Canadian Army alone could clear both the Channel ports and the Scheldt estuary.

As Montgomery later admitted, this assessment was optimistic. Writing in his *Memoirs* he states: 'I must admit a bad mistake on my part – I underestimated the difficulties of opening up the approaches to Antwerp so that we could get free use of the port. I reckoned that the Canadian Army could do it while we were going for the Ruhr. I was wrong.'[2] Bearing in mind Montgomery's well-established reputation for arrogance, it is worth noting that he is the only Allied general who openly admits making mistakes.

The Antwerp–Arnhem argument also exposes the competing merits of those current military requirements: the need to pursue a beaten foe and keep him on the run, versus the necessity of maintaining a balanced force and not out-running the supply lines. These two arguments in turn affect any judgment on the merits of the broad front versus narrow front policy – which in turn leads back to the matter of command.

With the ending of Market Garden the narrow front policy effectively collapsed. Whatever its faults or merits, the narrow front approach – banking everything on a single, well-supported thrust towards the Rhine – had had its day and Eisenhower's broad front policy was the only option left. And that meant Antwerp.

It should be understood that this broad front policy did not mean that a solid wall of Allied tanks and soldiers, 600 miles long and stretching from the Swiss frontier to the North Sea, would now advance, shoulder to shoulder and track to track, on the German frontier and the Rhine. It simply meant that discrete but coordinated attacks would be made on their respective fronts by all the Army Groups – 21st, 12th and 6th – with the available logistical support spread out as evenly as possible. This policy was in accordance with a long-held US military doctrine, dating back to Ulysses S. Grant and the US Civil War, that every army should be in action all the time – which was also General Eisenhower's personal philosophy.

In theory there is nothing wrong with this strategy, but it depends on the current situation and the determining factor in the autumn of 1944 was logistics. Could all the Allied armies be supplied if they were all attacking, all the time? There was also the other question: was the policy of attacking everywhere, all the time, negating another military principle, that of concentration of force? By attacking everywhere, were the Allies denying themselves the possibility of being strong enough to achieve a decisive result anywhere? This last factor was of increasing importance by the end of September, when the German armies were rapidly regaining their strength and fighting with their familiar skill and tenacity.

Eisenhower believed that his broad front policy would work and achieve quick results, *provided the armies could be supplied.* This was the problem with his policy: it would not work without a strong logistical base close to the front. Ever since taking up the role of Ground Force Commander, Ike had needed a major port close to the front, but apart from periodic exhortations and reminders to Montgomery about the importance of Antwerp, he had done nothing to obtain one – such as issuing a direct order to the 21st Army Group commander to take Antwerp at all costs, with the least possible delay, and abandoning the drive for the Rhine. Eisenhower's orders were usually subject to interpretation and Patton was not the only Allied commander to take advantage of this fact.

However, by 1 October, Market Garden was over and with the acquisition of Devers' Dragoon Force, which became the 6th Army Group on 15 September, Ike now had fifty-four divisions under his command. This sounds a formidable force until one realises that under the broad front policy this amounted at best to little more than one division for every twelve miles of front. Every division created its own supply problem – and eight of these divisions were currently grounded, or stripped of their transport, either because of supply problems or because their transport was needed to supply the rest.

The only answer to this logistical nightmare was Antwerp: close to the front, it could handle up to 40,000 tons of cargo daily. It had been in Allied hands since 4 September, but as yet not a single shell had been landed nor a single Allied soldier disembarked there.

The reasons why SHAEF, Marshall, Eisenhower, Montgomery, and practically everyone else opted for a push to the Rhine in September rather than a concentration on opening Antwerp have already been explained. However, with the end of Market Garden, the opening of Antwerp became the main strategic task of the Allied Armies – and in particular of the First Canadian Army.

The task of opening up Antwerp can be divided into several phases. First of all, the Canadian Army would have to move up to the south bank of the

Scheldt, capturing or masking the German-held coastal ports on the way. Then it would be necessary to clear the north bank of the Scheldt – a task that might have been tackled by Second Army had it not been otherwise engaged on Market Garden. Finally, unless it could be taken from the landward side, the heavily fortified island of Walcheren, which much resembled a cork stuffed into the neck of the Scheldt, would have to be taken by amphibious assault, and that meant launching men and craft against some of the most powerful batteries on the North Sea coast. All these tasks were fraught with difficulty, but the main source of that difficulty was the German Fifteenth Army, still strong and fighting hard on the Channel coast.

Les Wagar took part in the long haul up the Channel coast to the Scheldt with the Queen's Own Rifles of Canada:

> Most of the time I did not know what was going on or where I was. I recall snatches of action in Boulogne and the Scheldt, fleeting moments of a stopover in Ghent, and the workaday misery of a water-filled slit trench in a rest area before moving up to Nijmegen in December; otherwise that time is a blur.
>
> Dieppe was easy but the next little port was Boulogne and that was another matter and the first problem that had to be dealt with was a well-bunkered anti-aircraft battery that the Chaudières (the French-Canadian Regiment de la Chaudière) had run afoul of yesterday and taken a beating; this had to be taken out and the job fell to 'C' Company.
>
> During the night, with no moon to betray us, we crawled to within twenty yards of the forward trenches of the battery. There was a Vickers MMG in a building some 100 yards or so to the left, lined up on the guns to prevent the gunners from manning them. At dawn the Vickers opened up and we attacked and were onto and into the battery defences almost immediately – only one 20mm managed to get a round away and by the time I got there a chain of surrendering Germans was emerging from the large bunker and nasty Canadian riflemen were rifling pockets for anything of value and liberating watches.
>
> I remember nothing of Calais, although I know we were there. As for the battles of the Scheldt, all I remember is the mud and the lack of cover. Companies did not go into battle here; this was section-job fighting, done by platoon-size groups acting alone, with widely variable mortar and artillery support, bounding or crawling from one set of farmhouses to the next, yard by

yard, dike by dike, over polders with little or no cover, day after day. Tanks could not be used here but I do recall one action that went in with Universal (Bren Gun) carriers mounting flamethrowers. We set up a firing line in the neighbouring farmyard some 200 yards to the left, just to shoot up every shape that we saw trying to get away from the flamethrowers; I don't know for sure but I think that in the Scheldt the Canadian Army lost more dead and injured than we lost in Normancy.[3]

Many of the difficulties confronting the Canadian Army on the Scheldt might have been avoided had SHAEF taken account of Antwerp and the problems of opening it up to traffic at the end of the Battle of Normandy If Eisenhower had nominated it as his prime strategic target, which it certainly was, and devoted adequate troops and supply to the task of opening it for traffic, a priority in early September, the problems of opening Antwerp later that autumn might never have arisen.

At that time, with the enemy in full retreat and few units defending this part of the coast, the Canadian Army might have reached and cleared the south bank of the Scheldt with relative ease. An amphibious landing on Walcheren could have cleared the seaward entrance, and an advance north by Second Army to the landward end of the South Beveland peninsula could have cut off the retreating Fifteenth Army and cleared the north bank of the Scheldt. Indeed, during September, when Second Army was preoccupied with Arnhem, General Crerar tried to do just that, but taking that waterlogged area was a task for infantry and Crerar's six-division force was very short of infantry – its most powerful infantry element, the British 51st (Highland) Division, was immobilised at Le Havre, lacking transport.

The crux of the matter was time, compounded by the basic Allied misconception that the retreating German armies would go on retreating. In the event, the Fifteenth Army, directed by Adolf Hitler, dropped off divisions to hold the Channel ports and the land south of the Scheldt, firming up there in an area that became known as the Breskens pocket. Second Army captured Antwerp on 4 September but the 11th Armoured Division had failed to secure the landward end of South Beveland peninsula, and the amphibious craft needed for a seaward attack on Walcheren had now been sent to the Mediterranean. The difficulties of opening the port of Antwerp were concealed by the euphoria of the rapid advance to the north and the urgency of Market Garden. Now that rapid advance had stalled and Market Garden had ended, the matter of Antwerp rose rapidly to the top of the Allied agenda.

It would take the full attention of 21st Army Group and almost two months of hard fighting to open Antwerp, and the task did not really begin until 27 September, when Montgomery ordered the First Canadian Army to obtain 'free use of the port of Antwerp', adding that 'the opening of the port (Antwerp) is absolutely essential before we can advance deep into Germany.'[4]

It is fair to say that this order represents the first real indication that the Allied commanders had finally woken up to the fact that Antwerp was – and had been for some time – the key to the success of any long-term strategic plan. It does not, however, indicate that Montgomery had as yet appreciated that the First Canadian Army could not execute this task on its own. Nor had SHAEF; the chapter head quote above shows that it was not until 9 October, more than a month after the fall of Antwerp, that General Eisenhower told Montgomery to devote his entire attention to the clearance of the Scheldt.

By that time the Canadians had cleared, or were investing, many of the Channel ports, including Dunkirk, which was to hold out until the end of the year, and closed up towards the south shore of the Scheldt estuary, where the full extent of the problem revealed itself. The key to the Scheldt was Walcheren, but the only landward approach was down the South Beveland peninsula and across a narrow causeway. The southern shore approach was difficult, for the advance was opposed by a number of canals, one of which, the Leopold Canal, formed a natural front line for the Breskens pocket, a waterlogged area of ground now occupied by the 14,000-strong 64th Division of the Fifteenth Army, a force that had fought on the Russian front: tough soldiers, not easily dismayed, well-equipped with artillery, and occupying territory that offered every advantage to the defender. Everywhere Crerar looked he saw problems.

To pick up the story of the Scheldt campaign it is necessary to go back to the start of September and look at the actions of Lieutenant General H. D. G. (Harry) Crerar's First Canadian Army. Following the Normandy breakout, this force had been charged by Field Marshal Montgomery with clearing the Channel ports, eliminating the V-1 sites, which were still bombarding London, destroying the German Fifteenth Army, and opening up the Scheldt estuary from Antwerp to the sea.

ABOVE Field Marshal Sir Bernard Law
Montgomery, Commander, 21st Army
Group – a forceful, opinionated but very
experienced commander. *(Imperial War
Museum, London, B 5336)*

LEFT General Dwight D Eisenhower,
Supreme Allied Commander in Europe
and, from 1 September 1944,Ground
Force Commander in North West
Europe. *(Author)*

ABOVE The generals, from left to right, General Omar Bradley, commander of the US 12th Army Group, Field Marshal Montgomery of the British–Canadian 21st Army Group and Lieutenant General Sir Miles Dempsey, commander of the British Second Army. *(Author)*

RIGHT Lieutenant General Harry Crerar, left, commander of the Canadian First Army. *(IWM CAN 539)*

ABOVE LEFT Lieutenant General George S. Patton of the US Third Army. Belligerent and Anglophobic, Patton's popularity with the US media was a potent factor during the NW Europe campaign; his military skills were somewhat less apparent. *(IWM EA 35720)*

ABOVE RIGHT Lieutenant General Jacob Devers, Commander, 6th US Army Group, left, presents the Distinguished Service Medal to Lieutenant General Alexander M. Patch of the US Seventh Army. *(IWM EA 58879)*

ABOVE LEFT Major General James Gavin of the US 82nd Airborne Division receives the British DSO from Field Marshal Montgomery. *(IWM B 15742)*

ABOVE RIGHT Lieutenant General Courtney H. Hodges, commander of the US First Army, being decorated by Montgomery. Hodges, an undistinguished general, was frequently outshone and outmanoeuvred by his Third Army colleague, General Patton. *(IWM B 15725)*

RIGHT Major General Roy Urquhart, DSO and bar, GOC British 1st Airborne Division, photographed outside his HQ in Oosterbeck during the Battle of Arnhem. *(IWM BU 1136)*

BELOW Left to right, Lieutenant General F.A.M. (Boy) Browning of the Airborne Corps discussing plans with Air Chief Marshal Sir Arthur Tedder, Deputy Allied Supreme Commander, and Brigadier General Floyd Parks, Chief of Staff of the Allied Airborne Army, before the start of Market Garden. *(IWM CH 13856)*

OPPOSITE TOP The logistics war. Supplies for the US Armies are collected from a field in Normandy; transportation, not supplies, was the chronic Allied problem during the battle for the Rhine in 1944. *(IWM PL 26538)*

OPPOSITE BELOW US infantry of XX Corps advance through heavily shelled country towards the Siegfried Line, or West Wall, during the battle for the Rhine. *(IWM EA 34627)*

OPPOSITE TOP Running along the German frontier, the Siegfried Line, or West Wall, proved a formidable obstacle to the US Armies advancing on the Rhine. *(Author)*

OPPOSITE Sherman tanks of the British XXX Corps set off from Normandy for the Rhine, June 1944. *(IWM B 5685)*

ABOVE Celebration! The citizens of Brussels greet the men of XXX Corps on 4 September 1944. *(IWM BU 483)*

TOP A US staff sergeant cook pours out the tea for British paratroopers of 1st Airborne before they take off for Arnhem, September 1944. *(IWM K 7589)*

ABOVE The gliders take off for Arnhem on Operation Market Garden, 17 September 1944. Gliders were essential to airborne operations, carrying guns, jeeps and artillery ammunition, as well as men. *(IWM CL 1155)*

OPPOSITE TOP Gliders, paratroops and transport aircraft above and on the DZ at Arnhem. *(IWM BU 1163)*

OPPOSITE RIGHT Men of the US 82nd Airborne extract kit from a wrecked glider at Nijmegen, 17 September 1944. *(IWM EA 38134)*

OPPOSITE TOP A British Achilles tank destroyer moves toward the Rhine. *(IWM BU 2396)*

OPPOSITE BELOW Troops of the British 1st Airborne Division march into Arnhem from their DZ, 17 September 1944. *(Author)*

ABOVE Four men of the 1st Parachute Battalion, 1st Airborne Division, engaging the enemy in Arnhem. *(IWM BU 1167)*

RIGHT A 3-inch mortar crew on 21 September, the fourth day of the Arnhem battle. *(IWM BU 1099)*

BELOW Men of the 4th Special Service (Commando) Brigade land at Flushing during the operation to clear Walcheren island at the mouth of the River Scheldt. *(IWM BU 1244)*

ABOVE An American convoy ambushed by the Germans during the early days of the Battle of the Bulge December 1944. *(IWM EA 47960)*

BELOW A German tank destroyed during the battle for Bastogne, in the Ardennes, during the Battle of the Bulge. *(IWM EA 48892)*

ABOVE   Heavily laden Canadian infantry of II Canadian Corps advancing on the Scheldt. *(IWM HU 38856)*

BELOW LEFT   Hard weather means hard times for the infantry; an American soldier stands guard in the wintery Ardennes during the battle. *(Author)*

TOP A Sherman tank moves forward during Canadian operations on
the Scheldt. *(IWM B 14923)*

ABOVE US infantry advances during the Battle of the Bulge; the second man
in the column is carrying a tank-busting rocket launcher. *(IWM EA 48296)*

LEFT Field Marshal Walter Model, commanding the German forces
defending the Rhine, 1944. *(IWM MH 12850)*

LEFT A machine-gunner of the Waffen-SS photographed during the Battle of the Bulge. *(IWM EA 48001)*

BELOW A column of American prisoners passes a German tank during the Battle of the Bulge; other US prisoners were murdered by the SS at Malmedy. *(IWM EA 47966)*

This would have been a formidable challenge for any army, but Crerar's was simply too small for such a sizeable and varied task. It consisted of just six divisions in two corps, Crocker's 1st (British) Corps and Guy Simonds' II (Canadian) Corps and – as related – one of the most powerful infantry elements, the 51st Highland Division, had to be grounded on 13 September by a direct order from Montgomery so that its transport could lift the 49th Division to Antwerp. Chester Wilmot is correct in describing the First Canadian Army as 'the Cinderella of Eisenhower's forces',[5] but in spite of a shortage of men and supplies the Canadians continued to advance. After crossing the Seine, the Canadians turned west to clear the Channel ports, starting with Le Havre, a port with an unloading capacity to rival Cherbourg, which General Eisenhower was most anxious to obtain.

Supported by strong bomber forces, I Corps attacked Le Havre on 10 September. The port was in Crocker's hands two days later but the dock facilities had been badly damaged and the port would not be usable for some weeks. Meanwhile, Simonds' II Corps had moved on Dieppe, Boulogne, Calais, overrunning the V-1 launch sites in the Pas de Calais. The Canadian Army forced its way up the coast, laying siege to these ports and shedding troops all the time, supported towards the end of their advance by British long-range artillery firing across the Channel from the coast of Kent.

The attacks on these ports were all set-piece affairs, the infantry supported by heavy bombers, plenty of artillery, tanks, and the specialised armour of Hobart's 79th Armoured Division. Like Montgomery, Crerar was concerned about his manpower situation and rightly anxious to cut his losses by the extensive use of firepower – which was sensible but took time – and, wherever possible, by sending in his infantry in Kangaroos – a turretless tank or SP gun adapted to carry infantry, a device invented by Simonds in the later stages of the Normandy campaign. Sergeant Bill Heil served in Canadian Armoured Carrier Regiment (The Kangaroos):

> The Kangaroos were so called because, like a kangaroo, they carried their charges in pouch like conditions. Each converted tank carried twelve infantrymen. The pattern of a Kangaroo attack was that we would attack at night, preferably a cloudy night. Two searchlights would be shone onto the clouds and our target would be the area between those searchlights. Our job was to put

the infantry right into that area so they could punch a hole in the German line.

We would line up in a field and the infantry would arrive and pile into the back of the tanks, crammed in pretty tight; the infantry did not like us much and called us 'rambling coffins' but once they realised how successful we were we were involved in every push, except the Scheldt which was simply too boggy. In the many attacks we were involved in we carried Canadian troops but we carried British troops as well. When we were ordered to advance we took off at speed, 30mph – the earth really shook when 50 tanks took off at full speed, directed by a captain in a scout car. I remember one attack when it was quite foggy; shells were falling and we were told one tank had broken down. We got out to take a look at it and suddenly shells were falling all around us, as the fog had lifted and we were in full view of the German gunners – we got out of there fast.[6]

By 1 October the Canadians had taken most of the small Channel ports and done so at little cost – 30,000 German prisoners had been taken for some 1,500 British or Canadian casualties. This advance took the best part of September and did little to ease the supply problem. Dunkirk still held out and all the captured ports had been thoroughly damaged by the enemy before surrender. None of this reduced the need for Antwerp and when Market Garden faded, Allied attention finally turned to the question of clearing the Scheldt.

The task of opening Antwerp was greatly affected by the question of ground and readers are therefore advised to spend a few minutes studying the map of the area. The River Scheldt flows west and north out of Antwerp – which is in Belgium – widening to a broad estuary as it crosses the frontier into Holland, which now provides both sides of the estuary before it reaches the sea – fifty miles from Antwerp. There are, in fact, two Scheldt estuaries, the whole divided by the Beveland peninsula into the West Scheldt and the East Scheldt. The Beveland peninsula is linked by a causeway to the island of Walcheren; to the north-east of Walcheren lies the island of North Beveland.

Much of the land south of the Scheldt is polder country, below sea level, created by the erection of sea-dykes and draining but still crossed by numerous wide canals, each a perfect obstacle to tanks. By 1 October, the enemy had broken the dykes and flooded much of the land north of the Belgian cities of Bruges and Ghent and south of the ferry port of Breskens on the Scheldt, so creating a highly defensible area, the Breskens pocket. By mid-September strong elements of the German Fifteenth Army were now withdrawing across the Scheldt from Breskens to the port of Flushing on Walcheren, deploying from there to the mainland, where they were able to threaten the western flank of the Second Army on its thrust towards Arnhem and the Rhine.

Clearing the South Beveland peninsula and Walcheren therefore offered not only the certainly to opening Antwerp; there was also the possibility of cutting off and destroying large parts of the Fifteenth Army – which was continuing to withdraw, virtually without loss. On 23 September, Model's HQ at Army Group B was able to report to OB-West that in the last two weeks, 82,000 men, 530 guns, 4,600 vehicles, including tanks, and 4,000 horses, all of Fifteenth Army, had been ferried across the Scheldt from Breskens to Walcheren.[7] This was a most useful addition to German strength in Holland but sufficient forces remained south of the Scheldt to offer the Canadians battle.

This, then, was the task confronting the First Canadian Army on 1 October when, having cleared the Channel ports, it stood in a tight half-circle, east to west between the North Sea and the Terneuzen canal, broadly along the line of the Leopold Canal. To clear the Scheldt and open Antwerp it must defeat the enemy in the Breskens pocket, clear South Beveland, and assault the island of Walcheren. This attack would be made under Guy Simonds, for General Crerar was ill and had been sent back to England for urgent medical treatment.

Lieutenant General Simonds was a first-class general: he had commanded the II Canadian Corps since Normandy and was one of the star corps commanders on the Allied side – and had displayed an original turn of mind by inventing the Kangaroo, a forerunner of the modern armoured personnel carrier (APC) to transport and protect his infantry during attacks. Major-General Foulkes, commander of the 2nd Canadian Infantry Division, took command of the II Canadian Corps.

General Simonds and his men faced a formidable task at Breskens. Quite apart from the canals and the flooded ground, this area had been part of Hitler's Atlantic Wall and was strongly fortified, with heavy guns in the coastal batteries of Walcheren and along the south shore between Breskens and Zeebrugge, and the powerful 64th Division, holding the Breskens pocket. Pushing into the Breskens pocket would not be easy, not least because the Germans were well aware of the importance of Antwerp and intended to deny the Allies access for as long as possible – at the very least until the oncoming winter took a hand in affairs.

That this was the German intention at this time is confirmed by an order issued on 7 October by General von Zangen, the Fifteenth Army commander:

> After overrunning the Scheldt fortifications, the English would finally be in a position to land great masses of *matériel* in a large and completely protected harbour. With this *matériel* they would be able to deliver a death blow at the North German plateau and at Berlin before the onset of winter... each day you deny the port of Antwerp to the enemy will be vital.

A similar sense of urgency is evident on the Canadian side. General Simonds was very anxious to get on with the job and estimated that taking the Breskens pocket, so paving the way for the attack on Walcheren, would take three or four days; in the event it took a full month.

The task of clearing the Scheldt estuary began while the rest of 21st Army Group was busy with Market Garden. Simonds saw that the task of opening Antwerp divided into three parts: the sealing off and clearing of the South Beveland peninsula by the 2nd Canadian Infantry Division, supported by the 1st Polish Armoured Division; the clearance of the Breskens pocket south of the Scheldt by the 3rd Canadian Infantry Division; and finally a seaborne assault on the island of Walcheren by the 4th Special Service (Commando) Brigade, which was now attached to the Canadian Army. This task began when the II Corps attacked across the Albert Canal in mid-September and sealed the eastern end of South Beveland, the 2nd Canadian Division pushing up the peninsula. The 4th Canadian Armoured Division then headed north up the shoreline of the East Scheldt towards the town of Bergen-op-Zoom, but could make no progress up that narrow axis without more support.

By 1 October, the Canadian Army was deployed as follows. The 1 (British) Corps had a bridgehead over the Turnhout Canal east of Antwerp, from which the 49th (British) Division and the 1st Polish Armoured Division were preparing to advance north on Tilburg and 's-Hertogenbosch, so severing German forces in the South Beveland peninsula from those on the mainland. Their advance would be opposed by the German LXVII Corps, which now had the equivalent of three infantry divisions in the line and orders to prevent a northern thrust by 1 Corps 'at all costs'.

Crocker's advance was strongly contested but his divisions – 49th (British), 1st (Polish) Armoured and 2nd (Canadian) Infantry pressed ahead hard, the 2nd Canadian pushing the Germans out of Merxem, a suburb of Antwerp north of the Albert Canal and moving towards the South Beveland peninsula. This move thoroughly alarmed the Germans – '*the overland connection with the island of Walcheren is in danger*' – and a kampfgruppe from the German 85th Division, including paratroopers from the elite 6th Parachute Regiment, of Normandy fame, was thrown against the Poles near Alphen.

Fighting to push north and seal the landward end of the Beveland peninsula continued until 16 October, when von Rundstedt recognised that all attempts to hold I Corps back had failed. Von Rundstedt's diary for that day records that: 'In the area of the Scheldt estuary, a recapture of the land connection with Walcheren can no longer be expected. C-in-C West therefore consents to the flooding of the area.'[8] This success had been costly: I Corps had advanced just fifteen miles in ten days but the 2nd Canadian Division alone had lost 1,500 men and the Official History records that Polish losses in tanks and men had been severe.

Clearing the south bank of the Scheldt – the Breskens pocket – was to prove equally testing. The Canadian II Corps had made two previous attempts to break into the pocket, on 22 September and 5 October, both without success against the stout resistance put up by the experienced men of the 64th Infantry Division, who possessed a quantity of artillery, some 270 guns of various calibre including twenty-three of the formidable 88mm anti-tank guns. As an additional obstacle, much of the ground in front of the pocket had been flooded.

This position was to be attacked by the 3rd Canadian Infantry Division and the 4th Canadian Armoured Division. They would make a two-pronged attack: first a frontal assault by the 3rd Division's 7th Brigade, pushing across the Leopold Canal near Maldegem, east of Bruges, and then an amphibious assault by 9th Brigade in armoured craft called Buffaloes, landing on the Scheldt coast near Hoofdplaat, east of Breskens.

This assault began with the push across the Leopold Canal on 6 October. Supported by Wasps – Bren-gun carriers modified to carry a flamethrower – and air cover provided by the fighter bombers of No. 84 Group, 2nd TAF, the Canadians crossed the canal and held their positions in the face of fierce counter-attacks before gradually pushing deeper into the pocket. This grinding battle in the flooded pocket continued over the next two days, until early on the morning of 9 October when 9 Brigade came ashore in 100 Buffaloes, each carrying 24 men, west of the Braakman inlet. The attack began at 0200hrs and by 0900hrs they had two battalions ashore. The reserve battalion was also about to land and this unit moved on the village of Hoofdplaat, which fell on 10 October.

On that day, the infantry of the 4th Canadian Armoured Division was repulsed in the attack across the Leopold Canal and it was therefore decided to switch the main attack to the 9 Brigade area around Hoofdplaat. Fighting then spread along the canal, and with an improvement in the weather, air support arrived from the fighter-bombers of No. 84 Group and RAF Bomber Command. After a week of intensive fighting much of the Breskens pocket had been overrun by the Canadians, but the Germans of the hard-fighting 64th Division were determined to hang on as long as possible and resistance continued until the end of the month.

The Breskens pocket was not finally eliminated until 2 November when the ancient fortress of Sluis fell and the German positions around Knokke and Zeebrugge were abandoned. A month of hard fighting had cost the 3rd Canadian Division alone some 3,000 casualties: total Allied casualties in this phase exceeded 7,000 men killed, wounded and missing.

By the time Breskens fell the amphibious assault on the island of Walcheren had already begun. On 16 October Montgomery had ordered that the opening of Antwerp should have: 'Complete priority over all other offensive operations in Twenty-First Army Group, without any qualifications whatsoever.' Such an unequivocal order produced results and even before Breskens fell, plans were fully advanced for the seaborne attack on Walcheren.

This operation – Infatuate – was a three-phase affair. The 2nd Canadian Division would advance down the South Beveland peninsula and attack the island from the mainland, this attack beginning on 24 October. The sea dykes protecting Walcheren had been breached on 2 October by RAF Bomber Command and most of the island was now under water. Once the enemy were fully engaged fending off this thrust from the mainland, No. 4 (Army) Commando would assault the port of Flushing on the south shore of Walcheren, and finally, the Royal Marine Commando units of Brigadier 'Jumbo' Leicester's 4th Special Service (Commando) Brigade would assault the German guns at Westkapelle on the seaward side of the island.

The 2nd Canadian Division attack began at 0430hrs on 24 October after a heavy artillery bombardment. The advance began well, but it soon became apparent that this was a task for infantry, as the tanks and armoured cars were unable to deploy off the narrow metalled track – just forty metres wide – running west from South Beveland to Walcheren. It became known as the causeway battle. It took until the early hours of the following day before the leading units reached Rilland, and that was only three miles from the start line. This opposition was somewhat unexpected since the unit charged with defending Walcheren was the 70th Infantry Division – a 'stomach' division, filled by men with gastric disorders, plus some artillery units, a total of some 8,000 men; even so, here as elsewhere, the Germans put up a fight, aided in their defence by the extensive floods.

The 2nd Division's advance continued, slowly, until dawn on 26 October when news arrived that the 52nd (Lowland) Division had landed on South Beveland in Buffaloes and were about to outflank the enemy defenders. This new assault did not seem to dismay the defenders and the battle to clear the Beveland peninsula was still under way on 1 November when the commando assaults on Flushing and Westkapelle began. Bill Powell of the Calgary Highlanders took part in this battle on the causeway:

> As I recall, after two others and I joined 12 Platoon,'B' Company, our strength was fifteen or sixteen men. A full platoon was supposed to consist of thirty-three men; full strength for the battalion was 817 men so you can see we were about half strength. There was a great shortage of reinforcements.
>
> I won't go into details of our everyday life except to say that it consisted of attacking the enemy, living in slit trenches when we came to a halt and dug-in. It was a life where the main exhaustion was fear. Total exhaustion most of the time. There were two men to a slit trench and we had 50 percent guard, which meant that all night one of us had to be awake. A week at the front seemed more like a month and so much of what I experienced has been blotted out.
>
> This account is supposed to be about the causeway battle but first I must explain a few things. The Battle of the Scheldt started on 1 October at the Albert Canal and it was not over until November, when the British invaded Walcheren from the sea. The 3rd Canadian Division got the job of clearing the Breskens pocket south of the Scheldt and had a very rough time, water

and dykes everywhere – they were known as the Water Rats. The assignment of my division, the 2nd Division, was to cut off the German escape route from Walcheren to the South Beveland peninsula, which involved several battles, of the Albert Canal, Hoogerheide and Woendrecht, to name but three.

The causeway leading to Walcheren Island was 1,200 yards long, forty yards wide and straight as a gun barrel. On it ran a two-lane road, an elevated railroad track and a cycle path. On either side were salt flats of deep mud, impossible to cross. The Germans had blown a huge crater about 500 yards up the causeway and built brick-lined slit trenches, positioned an 88mm to fire down the length of the causeway and two others north and south of the causeway; they also had light and heavy machine guns and mortars and had sighted their artillery for miles around on the causeway, there were mines and a road block – they had spent years getting this ready.

We reached the western end of the South Beveland peninsula on 31 October. The last remaining obstacle was the causeway and Walcheren Island, and the Black Watch of our 5th Brigade were ordered to advance down the causeway until they 'bumped' the enemy. They duly set off in the afternoon and managed to get about half way down the causeway under heavy fire but could go no further; casualties were heavy.

I will now give a personal account of the causeway battle, which happened a long time ago and after such a long period of time one has doubts about the accuracy of one's memories. However, anything I have been able to check is quite accurate.

It was 31 October – Halloween. We started out just before midnight as our artillery opened up. How many guns I do not know but they were 25-pounders firing close over our heads; it is impossible to describe what it was like, stuff was flying everywhere. We got about half way down the Causeway when we came to an immense crater and our whole platoon got into it for protection, just a few minutes and we went on again. There were many casualties in our platoon and the Jerries were firing rifle grenades; as we lay in the road a grenade rolled into one fellow and exploded. His last words, crying out were '*I am dying*' – I wish I could remember his name. We got up and proceeded further.

We must have been really close to the far end of the Causeway when all hell broke loose – machine guns and everything you can imagine; how many of us were left after that I can't say, but the Regimental History says 'B' Company lost most of 12 Platoon.

One thing does come back to me. Whether it was on the first night or the next I can't say for sure, but I think it was on the second day when I received a slight graze over one eye which amounted to practically nothing. The second one was more serious, a partially-spent piece of shrapnel went into my backside about half an inch and bounced out. At the RAP I was ordered to lower my pants and long underwear and the medic took one look, cut off a large piece of bandage, slapped it over the wound, gave me a big shot of rum and said 'Back you go'. So much for my hopes of getting a Blighty – a wound bad enough to get you out of the war but not bad enough to handicap you for life. I don't remember what happened after that but I presume I rejoined my company.

The battle went on for fifty-three consecutive hours and cost the 5th Brigade 135 men killed or wounded; I am surprised it was not more. These battles cost the 2nd and 3rd Divisions 355 officers and 6,012 other ranks, killed, wounded or missing. In closing, I would just like to say that I am proud to have been a member of the Calgary Highlanders.[9]

While the 2nd Canadian Division was battering its way along the Causeway, the 4th Commando Brigade was preparing to assault Walcheren Island, beginning with the port of Flushing. The historic seaport of Flushing had been turned into a fortress, with artillery and machine guns protecting the outer suburbs and the interior of the town turned into a maze of defensive positions, well supplied with wire, more machine guns and mines. These defences were softened up by artillery fire from across the Scheldt, and on the evening of 31 October by low-level attacks on Flushing's waterfront defences by RAF Mosquitoes of 2 Group, 2nd TAF. No. 4 Commando, with some thirty Dutch Commandos of No. 10 (Inter-Allied) Commando attached, sailed from Breskens harbour at around 0445hrs on 1 November and came ashore at Flushing about an hour later – achieving almost complete surprise.

Before the defenders were fully aware of what was happening, the first wave of No. 4 Commando were among their positions. Although the second wave, landing at around 0630hrs, met a stiffer reception, losses were light and the port area was quickly cleared, allowing the 4th Battalion, The King's Own Scottish

Borderers (4th KOSBs) and other units of the 52nd (Lowland) Division to come ashore and commence clearing the rest of the town.

Meanwhile, the four Commando units of the 4th Special Service Brigade – Nos. 41, 46, 47 and 48 (Royal Marine) Commandos – had commenced landing at Westkapelle, supported by the guns of the battleship HMS *Warspite*, the monitors *Erebus* and *Roberts* and the guns and rockets from the craft of the Support Squadron, which sailed in with the Commandos' assault craft and provided covering fire right up to the muzzles of the German guns. The Support Squadron of the Royal Navy pressed home their attack with great resolution: of the twenty-five craft that sailed to the assault on Walcheren, nine were sunk and eleven were badly damaged.

Royal Marine Fred Wildman of 47 Commando gives an account of this action:

> We boarded our LCT soon after midnight at Ostend and set sail for West-kappelle in the early hours. Soon after dawn our escort destoyer gave the go-ahead for the landing and the scene was impressive, to say the least. Shells from *Warspite* and the monitors were whizzing overhead and the rocket ships were tucked right up under the dunes, firing at the German batteries. The Germans were replying, and accurately it seemed to us, as boat after boat went up in flames – we heard afterwards that the Navy lost four out of every five of these rocket craft.
>
> As we approached the beach we came under fire and suddenly the whole front of the LCT seemed to go up in flames – but what had happened was that one of the Buffaloes carrying spare fuel had been hit. We had to disembark from the LCT into Buffaloes – tracked landing craft – and to my amazement I suddenly saw my Troop OC, Captain O'Connell, mouthing epithets in my direction from the deck of his Buffalo. He brought the craft alongside and, chucking my rifle down first I leapt after it – luckily there were plenty of bodies crammed there to break my fall. We went in and landed on the north side of the gap and by the evening we had only three left out of our twenty craft, and had taken around thirty casualties, including Jimmy Day who was killed outright by an 88mm.

Major Dan Flunder, of 'A' Troop, 48 Commando, took part in this action:

It isn't easy to believe in premonition but my friend Derek de Stackpoole of Y Troop hated the idea of Walcheren from the start and told me n Bruges, just before we embarked, that he had never felt like that before. Anyway, while we were training at De Haan, A Troop fired over 55,000 rounds of small arms ammunition and I think all he other Troops did the same, using anything as targets – bottles, tin cans, whatever we could find.

The plan was for us to and, on one side of the Westkapelle gap blown by the RAF, in Buffaloes launched from tank landing craft and with A and Z Troops in the second wave. When we started our run the supporting Landing Craft Guns (LCGs) were trying to keep the heat off us and paying the price. The debris looked bad but we soon heard that the leading Troops were ashore and had cleared the beach defences... and we then came under fire ourselves. A Troop had lost ten men before we even left the landing craft, and shells were falling in the gap as we went ashore.

We moved along the dunes and into the battle and then I heard that Derek de Stackpoole had already been killed, leading his Troop against the battery emplacements. I passed the rest of this operation in a vengeful mood and the Troop caught it from me – my A Troop and Derek's Y had always been chummy.

That day and the next we pressed on along the dyke, using fire and movement and Mike Aldworth's 3-inch mortars and taking some 200 prisoners. In one bunker we found the population of a village, taking shelter from the floods and the firing and I had just said 'You are now safe from the shelling of the British Navy' when a 15-inch shell from *Erebus* arrived with a noise like a train; everything shook and the air filled with dust. I heard later that the CO's language as he watched this shelling had to be heard to be believed... but it convinced the Navy to stop the shelling.

This assault began at 0815 hrs on 1 November when HMS *Warspite* and *Roberts* opened fire on the Domburg battery (No. W17). This fire was accurate but did little to quell the fire from W17; even after a dozen direct hits from the 15-inch guns of the *Warspite* the battery remained in action. The first aim of the 4th Commando Brigade was to land on either side of the gap blown in the dyke at Westkapelle by Bomber Command, some Buffaloes actually sailing through the gap to land their troops inside. From there the Marines would advance south and east along the dyke to Flushing, clearing any German positions on the way to link up with No. 4 Commando and the 52nd Division. Meanwhile, other units of the brigade went north-west, to complete the clearance of the dykes and overcome any batteries that might engage the offshore shipping.

The Support Squadron were met with a heavy fire as they sailed in, most of them being damaged before they were close enough to use their armament. Still they pressed on, three craft being sunk by enemy fire, until the rocket craft were near enough to fire their salvoes at the enemy batteries. At this point Typhoon fighter-bombers of No. 84 Group appeared over the dyke and commenced to rocket the enemy positions, a timely assistance because, according to the Official History: 'some 80 per cent of the support craft were now out of action due to enemy fire.'[10]

Many Commandos were landing from LCIs (Landing Craft Infantry) and two of the three craft charged with landing the first wave were hit on the way in. Nevertheless the Marines rapidly secured the left side of the Westkapelle gap and fanned out to attack the W15 battery, which was not taken until noon. Other craft brought ashore elements of the 79th Armoured Division – two flail tanks to clear mines, a bulldozer and two AVREs (Armoured Vehicles, Royal Engineers) – only a small percentage of the specialised armour the Commando Brigade had hoped for, but many AVREs had been lost when their landing craft were destroyed on the way in.

In spite of heavy losses and continued enemy resistance, by 1000hrs Nos. 41 and 48 (Royal Marine) Commandos were ashore, together with most of No. 10 (Inter-Allied) Commando. By this time the W13 battery had run out of artillery ammunition but its machine guns were still able to beat off No. 48 Commando, which had to put in several attacks before the battery surrendered that afternoon. The Commando Brigade continued to come ashore, with No. 47 Commando and Brigade Headquarters landing in the early afternoon. As the day ended, Captain A. F. Pugsley, RN, commanding the Support Squadron, decided that those of his craft still afloat should withdraw to Ostend. In supporting this Royal Marine assault at Walcheren the Royal Navy had lost or suffered severe damage to twenty gun or rocket craft out of the twenty-five committed and incurred casualties of 170 dead and some 200 wounded – a record of gallantry and dedication that few small units can surpass.

Major Flunder again: 'There is a postscript to all this. Forty-one years later, now aged sixty-three, I went to the CWG cemetery at Bergen-op-Zoom and stood looking at a stone: *Major D. W. R. de Stackpoole, 48 Royal Marine Commando, Aged 26 years, 1 November 1944*... and after all those years, it still hurt.'

The fight for Walcheren continued for another week. Amphibious warfare continued in the flooded centre of the island until 6 November, when Lieutenant General Wilhelm Daser, the German commander in Middelburg, surrendered to a lieutenant in the Royal Scots. General Daser had at first declined to surrender to a junior officer but the brief elevation of this Royal Scots officer to the rank of colonel solved the protocol problem: Walcheren was at last in Allied hands.

Naval operations to clear mines from the Scheldt had started even while the struggle for Walcheren continued, employing more than 100 minesweepers. This task alone took another three weeks and it was not until 28 November, almost three months after the 11th Armoured Division freed the port, that a Canadian ship, the *Fort Catarqui,* led a convoy of nineteen Liberty ships into Antwerp.

The hard fight of the First Canadian Army for the Channel Coast and the Scheldt estuary has often been overlooked in accounts of the post-Normandy, pre-Bulge fighting, yet this Canadian campaign on the Scheldt has all the hall marks of an epic. In the course of battling their way north from the Seine to the Scheldt the Canadian Army – which admittedly contained a considerable British contingent – had taken Le Havre, Dieppe, Boulogne, Calais and Ostend and then bottled up the German garrison of Dunkirk.

Pressing on up the coast, without a great deal of support from the rest of the Allied Armies, the First Canadian Army had then cleared the Scheldt estuary in appalling conditions, taking 68 000 prisoners and killing an unknown quantity of German soldiers in the process. This victory had not been achieved without cost: the First Canadian Army sustained 17,000 casualties in those dreary autumn weeks, of which 3,000 had been killed.

As the British Official History accurately reports: 'The part the Canadian Army played in the Allied actions during those months was outstanding,'[11] while the Canadian Official History pays full tribute to 'the infantry soldier, whose dogged determination carried him through mud, water and fire to dislodge the stubborn foe.'[12]

8 · THE WEST WALL

*The first thrust towards the West Wall and the Rhine devolved upon
the V and VII Corps, both widely extended, virtually devoid of hope for early
reinforcement and dangerously short of supplies. Still there was reason
to believe that the reconnaissance in force might succeed.*

CHARLES B. MACDONALD, THE SIEGFRIED LINE CAMPAIGN

The end of Market Garden and the subsequent opening of the Scheldt in
November marks the end of operations of 21st Army Group west of Antwerp:
from now on Monty would concentrate on clearing the enemy from the west
bank of the Rhine in preparation for a major attack east, through the Reichswald. While this is in hand there is time to turn our attention to the exploits
and problems of Bradley's 12th Army Group, and in particular Hodges' attempts
to gain the Rhine via Aachen.

It is therefore necessary to go back to the start of September and follow the
operations of Bradley's 12th Army Group – Eisenhower's 'Central Group of
Armies' – astride the Ardennes and against the German West Wall, a network
of fortifications west of the Rhine. These defences were generally known to the
Allies as the Siegfried Line, and that name is used in the official history of the
campaign, but the German term West Wall will be employed here.

Construction of the West Wall started in 1936, immediately after Hitler's
forces had reoccupied the Rhineland. The Wall was first intended as a narrow
defence line on a limited front, running parallel to the French Maginot Line.
In 1938, however, the Führer decided to extend the West Wall along the entire
western face of the Reich. Half a million men, a third of Germany's concrete

production, a great quantity of Reichmarks and the construction talents of Fritz Todt, builder of the autobahn, went into this defensive line, which by 1940 stretched from Cleeve, north of Aachen, south across the frontier with Eastern France to the Swiss border. While strong everywhere, a notably strong set of defences protected the Saar industrial area and a double line of defences – the Scharnhorst Line in the west and the Schill Line further east – spanned the Aachen Gap. These last two lines blocked the traditional invasion route into Germany.

The West Wall consisted of about 3,000 bunkers and pillboxes, all offering interlocking fields of fire, fronted by deep minefields and forests of concrete anti-tank obstacles, generally known as Dragons' Teeth, the whole covered by artillery and machine guns. The defences varied in depth from a few hundred yards to five miles between the Scharnhorst and Schill Lines, running between Geilenkirchen and Aachen, but they were formidable everywhere if supplied with men, artillery and ammunition.

With the outbreak of war and Germany's rapid conquest of France and the Low Countries, work on the West Wall ceased. When the war gradually turned against the Nazis in 1943, more attention was paid to the new defence line along the Western coast – the Atlantic Wall – than the straggling, overgrown and neglected fortress network east of the Rhine.

Then came D-Day and the Battle of Normandy. In August 1944, as matters went awry west of the Seine, orders came that the West Wall was to be cleaned up and equipped with everything necessary for its defence. In the circumstances described in the previous chapters, it is not surprising that reviving the West Wall in the autumn of 1944 proved far from easy. Ammunition and heavy guns were in short supply and it was soon discovered that the embrasures of 1938–40 were often too small to accommodate the big guns of 1944. There was also a great shortage of wire, mines, wireless sets and machine guns. Those deficiencies were, however, among the minor problems: the biggest problem facing the defenders of the West Wall was a shortage of troops to man it.

The Germans were, as always, resourceful, and by mid-September were feeding units of all kinds into the West Wall, especially around the Aachen Gap, including such elements as an infantry division from East Prussia, a tank brigade equipped with Mark IV and Mark V Panthers, and two armoured battlegroups (kampfgruppe), plus any other forces they could find. The Germans knew that if positioned in fixed defences, even half-trained or mediocre troops could inflict heavy casualties on an attacking force.

All this was done with Teutonic speed and efficiency. In a matter of weeks the West Wall became a formidable obstacle. It will be recalled from Chapter Four that one object of Market Garden was to outflank the defences of the Wall in the north and so offer the Second Army a clear run east into Germany. Bradley's 12th Army Group, on the other hand, intended to tackle the West Wall head-on, both at Aachen and the Saar, and batter a way east towards the Rhine.

This task was to prove difficult. The actions of Bradley's 12th Army Group – the First Army under Lieutenant General Courtney Hodges, the Third under Lieutenant General George Patton, and later the Ninth under Lieutenant General William Simpson – were closely affected by the terrain, in particular by the hills and forests of the Ardennes, a rocky and forested massif lying just west of the German border, and with a geographical extension called the Schnee Eifel to the east of it. This sprawling region of hills and forests, cut about with river valleys, presented a formidable obstacle to any troops trying to cross it to the east or west: but German troops had surged across the Ardennes in 1940 and were to do so again in mid-December 1944. However, the main effect of the Ardennes massif on the Allies in the autumn of 1944 was to split Bradley's Army Group in two – and everywhere they would be confronted by the West Wall.

As related, although the plans for reaching the Rhine were constantly changed, the original intention for the Allied advance, post-Normandy, was to abandon the obvious but difficult northern route across the Flanders plain via Arnhem and the Lower Rhine – outflanking the West Wall – and move into Germany and the Ruhr via a dual thrust further south. One thrust would go through the Aachen Gap, north of the Ardennes, and be made by the British 21st Army Group. The second would be made south of the Ardennes, via the Moselle, Metz and the Saar, by US 12th Army Group. Both thrusts would involve breaching the West Wall but, if successful, they would lead to the rapid overrunning of both the Saar and the Ruhr, Germany's main industrial areas: were these to be lost, Germany could not prosecute the war.

This strategy was in line with Eisenhower's broad front policy and according to Butcher, on 11 September:

Ike is thinking in terms of advancing on a wide front to take advantage of all existing lines of communication. He expects to go through the Aachen Gap in the north and the Metz gap in the south and bring the Southern Group of Armies (Devers' 6th Army Group) to the Rhine south of Koblenz. Then he thinks he should use his airborne forces to seize crossings over the Rhine, to be in position to thrust deep into the Ruhr and to threaten Berlin itself... Ike has decided that a northern thrust towards the Ruhr under Montgomery is not at the moment to have priority over other operations.[1]

This aperçu comes just six days before the launching of Market Garden, and makes no mention of Antwerp or how these widespread thrusts were to be maintained.

Nor was this all. The events previously described quickly altered this plan. The need for the left flank of First Army – in effect, Corlett's XIX Corps – to cover Second Army's drive to Antwerp and beyond had already pulled the left flank of First Army north of the Ardennes, and Patton's drive for the Moselle had pulled V Corps, on the right flank of First Army, away to the south and east. As a result, Bradley now had one Army on either side of the Ardennes and his front was becoming ever more stretched. By 8 September the Americans had crossed the Meuse at Liège and advanced into the Ardennes as far as Bastogne. Their advance, however, was slowing: the eight divisions of First Army were now spread across 150 miles of front between the diverging armies of Dempsey and Patton and were nowhere strong enough to push east and mount a serious attack on the West Wall at Aachen – the principle of concentration had yet again been forgotten.

Nothing was done to remedy this situation because it developed the broad front strategy, which was Eisenhower's main aim at this time: what it did towards defeating the German armies before they could regroup behind the West Wall is quite another matter. It also reveals the fundamental flaw in the broad front strategy; if the Allied armies were stretched too thinly along the front, they would not be strong enough anywhere to force a breach.

From the map on page 16 it will be seen that the Ardennes lie east of the River Meuse and much resemble a giant pear, the massif widening as it spreads east, with the Eifel hills of Germany extending the Ardennes across the German frontier, and the dense Huertgen Forest overlooking Aachen from the south – part of the West Wall, the Schill Line, runs through the Huertgen. Then comes the central Ardennes area and the towns within it, Bastogne, St Vith, Houffalize, Malmedy; all of these places would see bitter fighting in the weeks and months ahead.

In early September 1944, the left wing of Hodges' First Army surged north alongside Montgomery's 21st Army Group while – to Patton's ill-concealed fury – the Third Army was halted before the Moselle for three days due to a fuel shortage. Once this shortage eased, Bradley's plan was to send his two armies east through the West Wall to the Rhine, First Army cutting through the Aachen Gap by the city of Aachen – formerly Aix-en-Chapelle – to Cologne and the Rhine, while the Third Army surged across the Moselle and the Metz gap to the Saar and Frankfurt. Once across the Rhine, both armies would turn north to encircle the Ruhr – though the passage up the narrow Rhine valley from the Saar to the Ruhr was bound to be difficult.

Hodges' First Army had the more difficult task, facing a combination of terrain, the West Wall and a rapidly reviving enemy but, according to the US Official History, on 15 September, First Army were: 'almost sanguine over the possibility of an enemy collapse in the Rhineland and the enormous strategic opportunities of seizing the Rhine bridges intact.' [2]

Whatever the cause of this belief, it was seriously misplaced. The Germans were indeed in trouble for the moment, but their supply lines were growing shorter, more units were being formed, and more tanks and heavy guns were coming up to confront the advancing Allies. On 1 September the Führer ordered that all 88mm guns, all Tiger tanks, and all Jagdpanther mobile anti-tank guns, together with 200 Mark V Panthers, were to go to the Western front. Standing firm in prepared positions, set in terrain ideal for defence, the German forces – most notably the Seventh Army, now defending the West Wall around Aachen – were ready to make a fight of it.

The dictates of terrain – notably the need to avoid attacking across the central Ardennes – led the First Army to concentrate on penetrating the West Wall via the Aachen Gap. Unfortunately, the Aachen Gap was the most obvious place for the Allies to make a thrust towards the Rhine and therefore the most heavily defended sector on the German front. Nor was this all. First Army was being starved of supplies. Up to 4 September, of the 7,000 tons reaching 12th Army Group, 2,000 had gone to Patton and 5,000 to Hodges. Now the supplies were

to be evenly split and V Corps of First Army was directed to shift south and
cover Patton's Army as it pressed for the Saar. Thus supported, Patton renewed
his drive on 5 September only to run into heavy opposition five days later on
the Moselle.

Nor was the First Army sufficiently concentrated to force a breach. By 11 September, General Corlett's XIX Corps, which had been covering Second Army's
advance in the north, was still pushing east with the River Meuse and the
Maastricht Appendix, that part of Holland which reaches south into Belgium
and called the Dutch Panhandle in US accounts, still to be crossed. Nineteen
Corps' 2nd Armored Division was on the left, keeping in touch with the British
30th Division, and a cavalry group on the right. Corlett's corps was short of
fuel and too far away to play any part in First Army's next move, a strong thrust
through the West Wall by Collins' VII Corps and the now distant V Corps.

In early September Lieutenant General Joe Collins' VII Corps lay within
ten miles of Aachen, with the 1st Infantry Division astride the Liège to Aachen
highway, the 9th Division at Verviers, east of Liège, the 3rd Armored Division
on the Belgian border and the 4th Cavalry Group – light tanks and armoured
cars – in Malmedy, responsible for covering the twenty-five-mile gap between
Collins' corps and General Gerow's V Corps, which lay deeper in the Ardennes.
Gerow had the 4th Infantry Division in the small town of St Vith and the 28th
Infantry Division in the north of Luxembourg. South of here, the 5th Armoured
Division covered another gap of thirty miles before linking-up with the Third
Army.

These dispositions reveal another problem. Apart from being thinly stretched,
these V Corps units were widely dispersed, with vast gaps between the various
divisions. These corps also had fewer divisions than they had in Normandy. At
the St Lô breakout, back in July, Collins had six divisions in VII Corps: now
he had only three, the men in these divisions were very tired, and their next
battle was about to begin. It started at around 1800hrs on 11 September, when
armoured and infantry patrols of General L. T. Gerow's V Corps – the 4th,
29th and 5th Armored Divisions – crossed the German frontier north of the
Ardennes near Prum to begin the First Army's assault on the West Wall, a thrust
described in the US Official History as a 'reconnaissance in force'.[3]

At first all went well. These patrols met little resistance and returned to
report that the West Wall was apparently unmanned. For the moment this was

quite correct. Three days previously, on 8 September, Field Marshal Model of Army Group B had reported to von Rundstedt, who had returned to take command of OB-West on 6 September, that 'only a very thin defence line composed of seven or eight infantry battalions held the West Wall on a front of 120 kilometres [75 miles].'[4]

However, on 14 September, when stronger US forces pushed up to the West Wall near Prum, they discovered that more German troops had come up in the last few days. Although a US armoured column penetrated eight miles beyond the Wall it then encountered stiff resistance and was swiftly forced back: once again, the Germans had reacted quickly when an area vital to their security was threatened. This check came as a most unpleasant surprise to General Gerow, for V Corps intelligence had advised him that he would meet only the battered, much-written-down elements of three divisions – Panzer Lehr, 5th Parachute and 2nd Panzer, with at most two thousand men and a handful of tanks.

Other units, though scratch forces at best, were coming forward, and on 14 September, the I SS Panzer Corps – 2nd Panzer and 2nd SS Panzer (Das Reich) began to occupy the West Wall. The V Corps intelligence estimates held that their divisions might encounter some 6,000 enemy troops and the VII Corps about 7,700.

The VII Corps had meanwhile thrust deep into the defences south of Aachen, penetrating the first – Scharnhorst – line of West Wall defences quickly and to a depth of five miles, only to be checked at the Schill Line, which ran east of the city. Model was rushing up an infantry division, two kampfgruppe and a panzer brigade from East Prussia to strengthen the Wall at this point, and the task of breaking it could only get harder.

The V and VII Corps had both moved forward in force on 14 September and what followed is best explained by briefly describing the actions of the various divisions, starting with those of the V Corps. Gerow had three widely dispersed divisions – the 4th Infantry for the Schnee Eifel, the 28th Division – known as the Bloody Bucket from its divisional shoulder patch – to the south and west of the Eifel, and the 5th Armored Division on the right flank, keeping in touch with Third Army. The 28th Division was the first to come up against the West Wall but the division had only two regiments, the 109th and 110th Infantry, having detached the third infantry regiment, the 112th Infantry, to assist the 5th Armored Division on the right flank.

These two regiments moved up towards to Wall on 10 and 11 September and by the evening of 12 September were ready to put in their assault. There were, however, a few latent snags. The divisional artillery was very short of ammunition and the infantry was very short of the special equipment necessary for reducing fortified positions – man-packed flame-throwers and engineers with explosives; some of the British 79th Division's specialised armour would have been useful here. Nor was there much in the way of artillery or anti-tank support, except for some 57mm anti-tank guns and a few M-10 tank destroyers. Since it was believed that the enemy strength was much reduced no one was greatly worried about this lack of support, and the attack on the West Wall duly went in soon after dawn on 13 September, though a number of US battalions had infiltrated forward on the previous evening.

Matters started to go awry quite quickly. Each regiment committed one battalion to the attack but heavy machine-gun fire, mortars and artillery from positions on high ground brought the American advance to a halt half-a-mile from the Wall. The main opposition was from the much-reduced 2nd Panzer Division. This unit had only three tanks and eight assault guns, but panzergrenadiers and other troops had manned the West Wall pillboxes and bunkers and they brought down a heavy fire on the advancing US infantry units which, as related, lacked close armoured support.

On the following day, 14 September, both regiments went forward, each with three battalions but now supported by tanks. After heavy fighting they managed to make one or two small penetrations through the Wall before the Germans counter-attacked and drove them back. And so it went, to and fro. The 28th Division continued to batter away at the West Wall for the next two days, and the two regiments had sustained some 1,500 casualties in return for one narrow penetration before General Gerow called off this part of the offensive on 16 September.

Apart from sustaining heavy casualties for so little territorial gain, the Americans were somewhat discouraged by the knowledge that their losses and containment was not due to any overwhelming enemy opposition. The enemy were shoring-up their line with whatever men and equipment they could find, but it had proved enough to bring the 28th Division to a halt. To quote an appreciation from the 110th Infantry: 'It doesn't much matter what training a man has had when he is placed inside the protection of a pillbox. Even if he just stuck his weapons through the aperture and fired occasionally, it kept our men from moving freely ahead.'[5]

Four miles away to the north of the 28th Division, the veteran 4th Infantry Division was attacking from the east of St Vith towards the Schnee Eifel. Here again the advance began with patrols on 12 September, with the main attack going in on 14 September. The Divisional Commander, Major-General Raymond Barton, elected to advance with two regiments in line – the 12th and 22nd – and the 8th Infantry Regiment in reserve. Ralph Teeters recalls this time:

> The 4th was the first US division to march through Paris on 25 August 1945. We got a great reception from the flag-waving, champagne-drinking hysterical crowd, but we marched on through the city and out the far side and on to the war again to take part in the attempts to break the Siegfried Line. The 22nd Regiment commander was a man named Lanham, he was a friend of Ernest Hemingway, who called him Buck Lanham and once described the regiment taking some pillboxes in the Siegfried Line with the help of a tank destroyer... this was a stiff one, but nothing like the Huertgen forest we fought in later.[6]

Patrol activity had indicated very little opposition and General Barton anticipated little trouble in penetrating the West Wall. The first patrols to reach the Wall pillboxes had found them empty and by the evening of 14 September both regiments had penetrated the Wall and were digging in a mile or more on the far side.

The defending forces hereabouts came from the 2nd SS Panzer Division (Das Reich), a once-powerful unit now consisting of about 2,600 assorted German soldiers from a dozen battalions, supported by fifty-one guns of various calibre and just one Mark V Panther tank. This force hardly seemed enough to stop General Barton's advance when it began again on 15 September, the division spearheaded now by the three battalions of the 8th Infantry Regiment.

Moving forward at first light, the 8th Infantry found their path barred by roadblocks and blown bridges, and an increasing amount of artillery and mortar fire – the latter proving especially galling as the mortar bombs burst in the treetops, showering shrapnel on the troops below. Nor was this all: German infantry, in company strength, was found to be active in the Eifel woods, either putting in local counter-attacks or offering a stout defence from pillboxes and bunkers. For the 4th Infantry Division, 15 September saw hard fighting, rising casualties, and an intensifying of German resistance, and the same story applies on the two following days. The fighting was in close country and inevitably confused, the kind of situation that gave every advantage to the defender. The struggle for the Schnee Eifel ended on the night of 17 September, when General Gerow called off the V Corps attack and put the Corps on the defensive.

Before that happened, the final V Corps assault was made by the 5th Armored Division which, had it succeeded, might have altered the entire picture. The 5th Division had been charged with a number of tasks: covering the V Corps flank, protecting the city of Luxembourg, and maintaining First Army's link with Third Army. The Divisional Commander, Major-General L. E. Oliver, had therefore split his division into a number of armoured and infantry detachments called combat commands, with Combat Command R (CCR) charged with probing the West Wall and attacking towards Bitburg in the centre of the Eifel plateau. CCR patrols came back with much the same information of those of the 28th and 4th Divisions: few signs of the enemy, West Wall pillboxes empty, no apparent problem.

On the afternoon of 13 September, CCR bombarded the village of Wallendorf and failed to draw a single shell in response. This news was reported back and Oliver was therefore ordered to advance through Wallendorf and the West Wall and occupy Bitburg, twelve miles inside Germany and the centre of the Eifel road network. This advance began on 14 September with the advance of CCR across the Sauer into Germany.

At first there was indeed little or no opposition. CCR passed through Wallendorf, over several small rivers, and onto the higher ground beyond, and had made good progress to the east before German anti-tank guns and mortars began to contest their advance on the banks of the Pruem river, six miles inside Germany. The news that his armoured division was now at large behind the enemy lines was very encouraging to General Gerow. He ordered General Oliver to reach Bitburg as soon as possible and swing there to come up in rear of the forces currently opposing the 4th and 28th Divisions on the West Wall.

The Germans were now fully alert to the danger. Scratching up men to oppose this armoured thrust, more German forces soon appeared in front of Bitburg, including artillery and tanks in sufficient strength to hold CCR at the Pruem river. Nevertheless, CCR was preparing to push on when, at 2040hrs on 16 September, orders came from General Gerow for the 5th Armored to call off its offensive and consolidate its gains. Gerow's reasons for halting the V Corps attack were that its advance had only been visualised by Hodges as a reconnaissance and would only proceed if the opposition proved negligible. When German resistance proved to be considerably more than negligible, Hodges ordered Gerow to call off the attack.[7]

The results of these four days of fighting were slim indeed and very costly. Gerow's Corps had lost some 2,300 men and although the West Wall had been breached in several places, no useful penetration had been made: the Rhine was still well out of reach. A combination of factors contributed to this outcome: poor weather that grounded the air support, thick woods and difficult terrain, a shortage of artillery ammunition and stubborn, growing German resistance from the forces occupying the West Wall.

There was also that chronic failure to concentrate the divisions or combine their efforts for mutual support. Across the entire front, there was insufficient strength anywhere to overcome even the limited amount of resistance the enemy was able to offer. Gerow's advance hardly amounted to a corps attack: his three divisions had in effect been fighting separate battles.

Gerow's corps was not to be left in peace to consolidate its slender gains in the Wallendorf bridgehead. On 17 September, strong counter-attacks came in against the 112th Infantry and although they dug in and held on, they were ordered to abandon their Wallendorf positions beyond the River Prum. The fighting around Wallendorf went on for the next three days before the Wallendorf bridgehead was abandoned – and all V Corps' gains had been lost.

This brief account of V Corps' operations makes it clear that even by mid-September any window of opportunity for a swift breach of the West Wall before the Germans could man it had been closed. By now the fighting on this part of the line had spread to the front south of Aachen, where Major-General Collins' VII Corps was pushing east and quickly becoming engaged with the infantry and armour of the German Seventh Army, their old adversaries from Normandy.

'Lightning Joe' Collins was well named. His plan aimed at breaking through the West Wall in one hard rush, without pausing for rest or reinforcement until the Wall was behind him, but his forces faced some considerable problems with the ground. To begin with, although his attack was theoretically through the

Aachen Gap, the main thrust of the advance would be made south of Aachen, in a narrow gap north of the dense Huertgen Forest called the Stolberg Corridor. Avoiding the Huertgen was sensible, but part of the Gap was blocked by the industrial sprawl of the towns of Stolberg and Eschweiler, and the other towns and villages south and east of Aachen – and part of it by the soon-to-be-notorious Huertgen Forest itself, beyond which lay another possible route to the east, the Monschau Corridor.

Forests are not good places to fight battles and Collins therefore elected to make his main thrust along the Stolberg Corridor, beginning with another reconnaissance in force on 12 September by two combat commands of the 3rd Armoured Division and the 1st Infantry Division. Everywhere the same pattern emerged. Initally the Americans met little resistance but within hours the Germans had found enough troops and tanks to shore up their front, turn every village and factory site into a strongpoint, mount counter-attacks and contain or reverse the early US advances.

Collins had no intention of attacking Aachen: his target was the second, Schill Line of the West Wall, east and south-east of Aachen. If that was penetrated the city defenders would be outflanked – and totally cut off when XIX Corps came down on the north side of the city. His intelligence G-2 told him the defenders of the West Wall here probably consisted of no more than 7,000 men from the battered 105th Panzer Brigade and the 116th Panzer Division, though another 18,000 men, some of them SS, might be assembling in the rear – so all the more reason to press the attack home soon.

Collins' thrust – the battle of the Stolberg Corridor – lasted until 17 September and consisted of a strong armoured thrust by the 3rd Division, protected on either flank by the infantry. At first the attack went well, with the 3rd Armored Division making a rapid drive through the Scharnhorst Line on 13 September. On the following day the division thrust again for the Schill Line, though the 1st Infantry Division on its flank had yet to penetrate the Scharnhorst Line and heavy fighting developed between these two defence lines, notably around Geisberg, where the 16th Infantry encountered 'some of the fiercest fighting of the West Wall campaign.'[8]

Collins battered away at the defences south of Aachen for four days and got through the second line of the West Wall to the east of the city before running into even more resistance in the urban area between Aachen and the Stolberg, where his armour was held up by German infantry with anti-tank guns and panzerfausts. These units brought his advance to a halt and then began to put in counter-attacks.

By 17 September – the first day of Market Garden – it was clear that no progress would be made around Aachen until Corlett's XIX Corps came up to match Collins' attacks from the south with some equally strong attacks from the north. One result of this discovery was that there was now no chance of First Army doing anything to support Market Garden. Another realisation was that First Army was not strong enough anywhere to make any decisive penetration of the West Wall. The basic principle of concentration had yet again been mislaid in the rush to overwhelm the German defences everywhere.

German strength had little to do with this reverse at Aachen. The German defenders of the Aachen Gap consisted of three much-reduced corps of the Seventh Army – 1st SS Panzer Corps, LXXXI Corps and LXXIV Corps. These three Corps might now muster around 20,000 men with perhaps 150 tanks – roughly the equivalent of just one SS Panzer division in Normandy. Even so, this force elected to defend the Stolberg Corridor and did so with skill and considerable valour. In this task they were aided by the decision of General Collins that taking Aachen by direct assault and getting involved in heavy street fighting in the city would defeat his main purpose of breaching the West Wall and isolating the city. He therefore directed the 1st Infantry Division to take the high ground east of the city and hold it until XIX Corps arrived to encircle the city from the north. This decision perplexed the German commander in Aachen, General von Schwerin of the 116th Panzer Division, who was fully prepared to either evacuate the city or surrender it to the Americans – who did not want it – and this in spite of a direct order from Adolf Hitler that Aachen must be held to the last man and last bullet.

Collins was successful in pushing his forces down the Stolberg and Monschau Corridors south of the city, with one division, the 9th Infantry Division, making the first US penetration into the gloomy thickets of the Huertgen Forest. This advance took VII Corps up to, into, and in one or two places, through the West Wall, but nowhere was there any real breakthrough. Every advance was contested, every move expensive, but VII Corps were giving as good as they got and grinding down the opposition.

The snag was, as General Collins noted on 18 September, that the enemy kept finding and bringing forward fresh forces and 'as long as his adversary had reserves and he had none, further large-scale advances were impossible'[9] – another result of the broad front policy was an American inability to create reserves. On 26 September, the VII Corps drive through the West Wall stopped and its troops switched over to defence.

Collins later recalled that a combination of things stopped VII Corps at Aachen: 'We ran out of gas – that is to say we were not completely dry but the effect was much the same, we ran out of ammunition and we ran out of weather – the loss of our close tactical air support because of bad weather was a real blow.' Even so, Collins was not too disappointed: 'We went in thinking that if we could break it [the West Wall] then we would be just that much to the good; if we didn't, we would be none the worse.'

So the first, three-week long attack around Aachen, the First Army's first attempt to breach the West Wall, came to a halt with the enemy line all but intact and two US corps exhausted. They had tried – and tried hard – but the weather, the Wall and the enemy had defeated them. The First Army had stalled north of the Ardennes. How was George Patton's Third Army getting on to the south?

As General Collins pointed out, one of the factors affecting the progress of V and VII Corps north of the Ardennes was a shortage of supplies, especially fuel and artillery ammunition. Eisenhower had quickly realised this and on 16 September, while these battles were in progress, he ordered Bradley to halt Patton in front of Metz and divert all possible supplies to Hodges' forces at Aachen.

Bradley and Patton elected to ignore this order. Patton had no intention of stopping and had evolved a way – his 'rock soup' method of gradual commitment – to get round any direct order to halt. This was typically Patton. First he kept reconnoitring forward until the enemy was encountered and engaged, then he was naturally obliged to reinforce the reconnaissance forces, and so, gradually and quite deliberately, his entire force became involved and had to be supported. On 12 September, Bradley had told Patton about Market Garden and warned him that if it succeeded, the Third Army might be held back on the west bank of the Moselle for weeks while the detested Montgomery performed wonders in the north.

Patton therefore suggested to Bradley that he cross the Moselle and get his forces so involved beyond the river that Eisenhower would be unable to stop him and must therefore support him. This ploy proved unnecessary: Eisenhower changed his mind yet again, at least in part, telling Bradley that he might 'push his right wing [Patton's Army] only far enough for the moment so as to hold adequate bridgeheads beyond the Moselle, and thus create a constant threat.'

This was all that Patton needed to cross the river and surge ahead as far as he could, never mind the point about bridgeheads. By the evening of 14 September, the day V and VII Corps of the US First Army opened their attacks, Patton had established half a dozen crossing points over the Moselle, and was heading east, consuming great quantities of fuel and ammunition. The outcome was that Patton did not stop until brought to a halt by the German army in front of Metz. It should be noted that this move, designed by Bradley and Patton to check Montgomery, actually had a dire effect on Bradley's other contingent, the US First Army, which was starved of fuel and artillery ammunition at Aachen.

On 16 September, when Eisenhower told Bradley that logistical priority must go to First Army and Patton must stop, Patton again told Bradley that the Third Army must get involved 'at once' and asked Bradley to ignore this order and 'not to call me until after dark on the nineteenth.'[10]

On 17 September, again defying his Supreme Commander and with the backing of his Army Group commander, Patton launched an all-out attack on his two prime objectives, sending XX Corps against Metz and XII Corps in a drive for the Rhine. Success can justify such actions, but neither attack succeeded. The XX Corps was quickly halted at Metz and XII Corps was stopped by a German counter-attack at Luneville. Although he did not know it, George Patton's glory days of rapid advances against slight opposition were over: the enemy on the Third Army front was firming-up and starting to fight back, and the costly struggle for Lorraine was about to begin.

Success might have justified Bradley and Patton's cavalier treatment of Eisenhower's direct order, but the Germans stopped Eddy's XII Corps east of Nancy. Here, as at Aachen, the Germans were bringing up men and tanks and here, as elsewhere, the Americans lacked the force necessary to force a passage to the Rhine. Nor was this all: Hitler had brought General Hasso von Manteuffel over from East Prussia, placed him in command of the reconstituted Fifth Panzer Army and ordered him to smite Patton's southern flank hard.

Bradley now faced a considerable dilemma. By favouring Patton at the expense of Hodges he had ensured that neither Army could actually achieve anything – and he had undermined Eisenhower's current strategy at the same time. By 20 September, the Allied armies had to face the unpalatable fact that the days of rapid advances against a retreating foe were over. At Arnhem, Aachen and the Saar the enemy had recovered and was digging-in or occupying the West Wall, ready to make a fight of it. Three weeks after General Eisenhower took over the field command, his armies had come to a halt.

What had gone wrong? The basic problem seems to lie in a lack of clarity over the best course of action to pursue *at the time and with the current resources.* The current strategy, to pursue the enemy rather than ensure a reliable flow of supply was quite sound, provided that strategy took account of the fact that, unable to be strong everywhere, the Allies needed to be strong somewhere – and operate within their logistical restraints.

The chronic problem, that shortage of supply, is easier to understand than to solve, but it cannot be considered without taking into account the lure of fast pursuit. The real problem, however, would seem to lie in that lack of grip: an apparent inability on Eisenhower's part to make a decision and force his commanders to obey his orders – or else. The snag here is that those orders were all too often quickly modified or open to selective interpretation. If Eisenhower was frustrated at the way things were going – and he certainly should have been – the reasons, and the solution, were in his own hands.

Eisenhower realised that something had gone seriously wrong with his master plan. His answer was to call yet another meeting, this time at Versailles on 22 September. With one exception, every commander on the Western Front attended, a total of twenty-three assorted generals, air marshals and admirals. The exception was Field Marshal Montgomery, who had been wrangling with Eisenhower over strategy for the last month and saw no point in going over it all again before an audience largely composed of his enemies. To represent 21st Army Group he sent his wise and popular Chief of Staff, Major-General Freddie de Guingand.

The last week had been discouraging for the Supreme Commander. Writing to Monty and Bradley on 14 September – the day the first battle for Aachen began and three days before Market Garden started – he had predicted: 'We shall soon, I hope, have achieved all the objectives set forth in my directive of September 4 and shall then be in possession of the Ruhr, the Saar and the

Frankfurt areas.' With that much achieved, Ike added, he proposed moving on Berlin with both Army Groups and 'would like his Commanders' views on the best route – or routes'.

By 22 September, the day of the Versailles meeting, the events of the past week and the progress of the battle for Arnhem had dented this hopeful summary and Montgomery's reply to Eisenhower's missive had been depressing: time was the critical factor, there was not enough supply for more than one thrust beyond the Rhine, so the choice, as ever, was between north and south. Monty favoured the northern route – naturally – but if Ike preferred the southern one, then Bradley should have all the maintenance. No mention was made of Antwerp.

In his reply to his blunt missive, Eisenhower agreed with Montgomery's proposal for concentrating on the northern route to Berlin, but added that this could not be done until Antwerp was open. It will be noticed that the *prior need* for Antwerp had not been mentioned in Ike's letter of 14 September. With the Arnhem battle at a crucial stage, Montgomery was becoming convinced that any thrust deep into Germany was unlikely, but thought that it might still be possible to cross the Rhine and take the Ruhr if sufficient maintenance was provided and the decision was made soon. With this proposal on the table, the Versailles conference began.

Steered tactfully by de Guingand, Montgomery's proposal carried the day – or so it seemed. The conference concluded that 'the envelopment of the Ruhr by the 21st Army Group, supported by First Army, is the main effort of the present phase of operations,' but in addition, 21st Army Group was, 'as a matter of urgency', to open the port of Antwerp by clearing the Scheldt. No one seems to have debated the competing claims of a 'main effort' and a 'matter of urgency'.

Bradley was directed to turn the US Third and Ninth Armies over to a defensive role and send two First Army divisions to take over the south-eastern sector of the Second Army front, thus allowing the Second Army to concentrate north of the Maas for the drive to the Rhine and Ruhr. However, there was the inevitable caveat: in addition to this, Hodges was also to 'prepare to attack the Ruhr from the south in concert with 21st Army Group's attack from the north...' and Patton was to lose his most southern corps, which would be transferred to Patch's Seventh Army, so making Devers' US Army equal in strength to his French one.

These decisions infuriated Bradley and Patton and delighted Montgomery, but they were to have little effect on the progress of the campaign. Had these orders been issued before the launching of Market Garden – and had they been adhered to by the various parties – it might have made all the difference, for they offered a sound strategic plan for the reduction of the Ruhr from the north and south. By the day of the Versailles conference that chance had gone: the Aachen attack had failed and Market Garden was about to fail… and Patton was hell-bent on carrying the war into Lorraine.

9 · THE QUESTION OF COMMAND

*Eisenhower had jumped on a moving bus. Instead of confirming the plan
that Montgomery had already made, or giving fresh but clear orders he issued
ambiguous orders that he subsequently changed.*

GRAHAM AND BIDWELL, *COALITIONS, POLITICIANS AND GENERALS*

At this stage, halfway through this account of the battle for the Rhine and
slightly less than halfway through the period between the end of the Normandy
breakout and the start of the Battle of the Bulge, it seems necessary to take a
very close look at the question of command and its effect on strategy. This
question forms one of the two arguments that have dominated the controversy
over the post-Normandy campaign for the last sixty years and centres on
whether, had the right command structure been in place, the Allied strategy of
late 1944 would have delivered a more useful outcome.

In the event, since victory in Europe was delayed until May 1945, it might be
argued that the correct command structure was clearly not in place in late 1944.
On the other hand, it is not enough to state a case and point to the outcome as
the final evidence: it is necessary to *prove* the case by examining the opposing
arguments, and it is at least possible that no strategy or command structure
would have delivered victory sooner than it actually arrived. Nor is it enough
to consider military matters alone. Into this debate one must also throw such
topics as national attitudes and politics; for in late 1944 the question of command
in north-west Europe was largely a political issue.

Even so, by early October 1944, a month after Eisenhower took direct
command of the Army Groups, one question – or perhaps three – can be

examined: should there have been a Ground Force Commander below Eisenhower, what would have been his duties – and who could it have been?

The answer to the first question might appear simple – *Yes* – if only because Eisenhower obviously had too much on his plate, but a closer analysis reveals that these questions are hedged about with many other issues, ranging from the basic but conflicting rules of military strategy, such as the need to concentrate while pursuing an apparently beaten enemy versus the logistical situation, the need to select and maintain a strategic aim, and other points which have already been mentioned, not forgetting the views of the popular press in the United States and Great Britain and the personalities and ambitions of the various generals and politicians. As we shall see, when all the circumstances are taken into account, reaching a fair judgement on any aspect of the post-Normandy campaign is a very complicated matter.

The question of command was not only a matter for Ike or SHAEF. Over the Allied commanders in north-west Europe hangs the long shadow of General George C. Marshall, the US Chief of Staff and Chairman of the Allied Combined Chiefs-of-Staff Committee. Marshall had clout and was not afraid to use it: his aims and ambitions, not least for the reputation of the US Army, should be considered first. Marshall was no rabid Anglophobe; his close friendship with Field Marshal Sir John Dill, head of the British Mission to Washington, was one of the cornerstones of the Atlantic alliance and from 1941 Marshall defended the 'Germany First' policy against the pressures exerted by Admiral King, head of the US Navy, for a greater concentration on the Pacific. Like Eisenhower, his subordinate and protégé, Marshall believed that Anglo-American accord was the key to victory.

That said, from the moment the USA entered the war in December 1941, Marshall was fixated on the need for an Allied invasion of western Europe. He agreed to 'Germany First' at the Arcadia Conference in December 1941 on the understanding that 'Germany First' also meant 'Germany Soon'. He deplored British attempts to pursue the war in the Mediterranean, or the north of Italy, or indeed any efforts that detracted from Overlord – or were perceived in Washington as in Britain's long-term post-war interests.

Marshall's unwavering aim was to see the US army play a major part in the European war and garner the credit for the victory in which the Allied armies served under American command. Marshall therefore saw to it that the Supreme

Commander in Europe was always aware of US interests and did not waver in pressing them in the Allied councils – especially when they came under attack from the British commanders, Field Marshals Alanbrooke and Montgomery, the latter a man whom Marshall cordially detested.

Marshall's view, that the Americans should control the war in Europe, naturally had a profound affect on the command situation. Had the Ground Force Commander in Normandy been an American officer there can be little doubt he would have continued in post for the subsequent campaign. Indeed, Marshall's main argument for Eisenhower taking over the field command in September 1944 was not that the current command set-up was unsound, but that the US press and public were urging the end of British dominance in the European command structure. What Marshall wanted, Marshall got, and for all his talents, Montgomery had to go.

Monty's demotion did not always work to the benefit of the US commanders. One problem that has bedevilled any objective study of Anglo-US military history in the post-war decades is the tendency of some US commanders and many US historians to play the 'British' or 'Montgomery' card in order to conceal some glaring American blunder. Omar Bradley's disastrous failure to provide adequate armoured support for the US divisions landing on Omaha on D-Day, with the terrible losses thus caused to the infantry companies of the 1st and 29th Divisions, have been largely expunged from the public mind – at least in the United States – by constant harping about the British or 'Montgomery's' failure to take Caen on D-Day – a failure that turned out to have no strategic significance whatsoever.

Nor is Omaha the only example. As we have seen in earlier chapters, harping on about the 'slowness' of XXX Corps or the 'flawed' plan of General Urquhart at Arnhem, has successfully diverted critical minds from the cock-up in command that prevented the 82nd Division from either taking the Nijmegen bridge on the first day of the attack or avoiding a frontal attack across the Waal in borrowed boats three days later.

It appears that all that was necessary to avoid critical press comment in the USA and any unwelcome Congressional interest in the competence of any American commander, was to murmur 'the British' or – better still – 'Montgomery', and critical comment in the USA either subsided or went unvoiced. Now, post-September, with Montgomery put back in his box as an Army Group

Commander, there was no means of passing the buck to America's foremost ally. As both Supreme Commander and Ground Force Commander, all responsibility for command failures fell on General Eisenhower. To his great credit, Ike never attempted to avoid that fact or duck the responsibility inherent in these posts – if anything, he took too much of the blame on himself instead of directing it to where it really belonged, with some of his subordinate commanders, notably Bradley and Patton.

Command is not a simple function: a lance-corporal and a field marshal both exercise command, but the weight of responsibility and the talents required are vastly different. So too were the jobs that Eisenhower took on in 1944. The posts of Allied Supreme Commander and Ground Commander were separate and quite distinct functions, and necessarily so, not simply because the combined task of Supreme Commander and Ground Commander was too big for one man to handle, but because the qualities and talents needed for each job were different.

Eisenhower's supporters state, quite correctly, how difficult the job of Supreme Commander was and, equally correctly, praise the way in which Ike handled his immense and varied responsibilities at SHAEF. This being so, they cannot then seriously argue that taking on another, equally-demanding role was not greatly increasing this burden and the pressure on his available time. Eisenhower was a great man, but he was not Superman: if he took on more work than any human being could handle, something would go wrong.

There was also the matter of experience. Eisenhower had vast, wide-ranging experience as a staff officer but was almost totally lacking in field command experience. In the British and German armies – and most other armies, including that of the United States – staff appointments usually alternate with appointments to field command so that staff work can be matched with practical experience in the field. However, Eisenhower's outstanding abilities on the staff had been noted and appreciated in the pre-war years by such luminaries as Generals Fox Conner, Douglas MacArthur and George C. Marshall. All of these came to recognise Ike's administrative talents and harnessed them to their own particular plough. The downside of this was that Eisenhower, through no fault of his own, had been deprived of practical military experience at company, battalion and brigade level. (When the US entered the war in 1941 Eisenhower was a Brigadier General on the Planning Staff in Washington.)

Therefore, when confronted with the need to develop a philosophy for field command, Eisenhower naturally drew on his previous experience and the US Army's pre-war doctrine as studied at West Point and at the US Army's Command and Staff College at Leavenworth, where Ike had been an outstanding student and head of his class – unfortunately that was back in 1928, in a different world from north-west Europe 1944. The US Civil War Grant-Leavenworth doctrine was the one Ike constantly tried to apply: that the maximum force should be gathered and brought against the enemy, that every element in the army should be in action, everywhere, and all the time. His belief in this doctrine and on the lessons taught by his historical mentors, most notably Hannibal and General Ulysses S. Grant, led to the conclusion that victory rested on the application of superior force and ultimately on attrition.

Given the vast industrial capacity and the large population of the United States, this doctrine, if costly in lives, made sense – at least up to a point. The point is that a one-size-fits-all doctrine does not work in every case, and in the case of the German army in the Second World War, frequently got the US commanders into trouble.

Ike had also developed his own views on how command should be exercised. His staff experience led him to rely on consultation and committee work, for Eisenhower's true talent – his genius, even – was as a conciliator, a man with a unique ability to get on with disparate people from several nations, many with enlarged egos, and persuade them to work together as an Allied team. As Supreme Commander, Ike was the right man in the right place and no one, at the time or since, has thought of anyone who could have done that job better. The Allied armies and the people of Europe owe an immense debt to Dwight D. Eisenhower – as Supreme Commander.

Whether the same praise holds good for Eisenhower as Ground Force Commander in the north-west Europe campaign of 1944–45 is quite a different matter. Essentially, Ike was a committee man. He liked to summon his commanders to headquarters, listen to their views, and seek a solution or a consensus that offered something to everyone. Then, when he had mulled over the points raised, he would issue orders based on these discussions and his own judgement of the situation. This is a perfectly acceptable method of command, but his orders frequently differed from those just agreed, were rarely models of clarity and often contained at least one fatal flaw: they were subject to interpretation by those subordinate commanders – like Patton – who wanted to go their own way regardless of the Supreme Commander's overall strategy.

This last flaw is an unusual fault to find in a staff officer, especially one of such wide experience, for one of the first duties of a staff officer is to translate the wishes of his commander into clear, unequivocal orders for his subordinates to follow *and obey*. This flaw may indicate the truism that there is a wealth of difference between translating another's wishes into unequivocal prose, and expressing one's own in a similar fashion. The great Napoleon Bonaparte suffered a similar disadvantage and the clarity of the Emperor's orders owed much to the ability of his Chief of Staff, Marshal Berthier. After Berthier died, just before the campaign that ended at Waterloo, Bonaparte's grip on command began to slip. It could be that General Eisenhower needed a Marshal Berthier.

In fact, Eisenhower had a Berthier, his excellent, well respected Chief of Staff, Major-General Walter Bedell Smith. If we accept as a working proposition that Ike had too much on his plate and needed assistance, then Bedell Smith's talents might now be considered. Eisenhower's proposed command set-up, post-September, in which every Army Group commander acted as a commander-in-chief, reporting direct to Ike at SHAEF, was perfectly valid, *provided* those Army Group commanders and their subordinates did as they were told, carried out those orders to the letter, and reported back swiftly on any problems.

What Ike needed was someone who could keep his finger on the pulse of the battle, handle the day-to-day task of keeping the armies working to a single strategic plan – and stop any attempts at unauthorised private enterprise. Since Ike did not have time for that on top of everything else, he needed the assistance of some competent, well-respected officer; since, for political reasons, that officer must be an American, who better than Walter Bedell Smith?

Bedell Smith certainly had grip. Montgomery and Alanbrooke, who were generally unimpressed with the professional standards of the US generals, both respected Bedell Smith. Monty's Chief of Staff, Freddie de Guingand, was Bedell Smith's close friend – there would be no problems there. As for the American commanders, Bedell Smith had known them all for years and knew their strengths and weaknesses. For their part, they respected Bedell Smith and some were even a little afraid of him, for Walter Bedell Smith was not a man to trifle with. Finally, Bedell Smith enjoyed the confidence of Eisenhower and

Marshall: they would have listened to what he had to say and the command grip on the Allied armies would have greatly improved.

All this is speculation, for none of it happened. Of the two possible alternatives, a Ground Force Commander or all the Army Group Commanders acting as their own C-in-C's, the first was not tried and the second did not work. Ike was therefore obliged to soldier on alone, Bedell Smith remained at SHAEF and a yawning hole developed in the Allied command structure which no one seemed able to fill.

Eisenhower came to recognise this problem. In a letter to Marshall on January 1945, he admits that:

> I do not believe that any single individual could or should exercise a greater measure of control over this extensive front than is now being exercised. The organisation for command is, of course, not ideal, but it is the most practicable one, *considering the questions of nationality involved and the personalities available within the theatre* [author's italics].
>
> Because of the great size of the land forces now engaged in this front, it would be more convenient for me if my Deputy Supreme Commander were an experienced ground officer rather than air. In spite of my personal and official admiration for Tedder, he is not in a position to help me by visits and conferences with troop commanders. If I could find a man of fine personality, respected by all and willing to serve as my deputy and not under independent charter from my superiors, it would be most helpful... The only one I could think of myself would be Alexander and manifestly he is not available.

With Bedell Smith not apparently considered for the post, the choice lay between Bradley and Montgomery. Convinced that a Ground Force Commander was essential, Montgomery then offered to serve under the US commander but no one else considered Bradley even remotely suitable. That left the field clear for the impossible choice, Field Marshal Montgomery.

Montgomery's problem was not his ability but his character. Monty had little time for officers who slavishly followed the book – the received 'official' doctrine on the conduct of war. Monty followed the old military precept that the book was for the guidance of wise men and the obedience of fools. He believed that a general is paid to use his brains, to sum up the situation currently confronting his forces and act accordingly. Brute force and the commitment of overwhelming numbers – if you have them – may win a victory in the end but the cost is likely to be high. Britain had never enjoyed superiority in military numbers and learned the cost of attrition in the First World War, at Passchendaele and on the Somme. Far better to think your way through the problem rather than using your head as a battering ram.

Monty was a professional soldier to his finger tips and a student of the military art: the need to select and maintain the aim, to concentrate forces, to keep hard on the heels of a defeated foe, to pay attention to morale and logistics, to maintain a balanced force, were all engrained into his military make-up by years of practical experience. Above all, though, Montgomery had grip.

Monty believed in controlling the situation at every level. Ad-hoc, off-the-cuff measures were simply not Monty's style. Montgomery also possessed a strong sense of priority – an instinct not simply for what should happen, but for what should happen *next*. One of the sad features of the post-Normandy period is that, at least from time to time, this precious asset seems to have deserted him. One primary, post-Normandy aim should have been to open the port of Antwerp. The need for Antwerp never went away and when Eisenhower prevaricated on when to make that his priority, Montgomery should have acted on Ike's vague requests and made the clearing of the Scheldt the main task for 21st Army Group.

Monty's reasons for choosing to push north – following yet another of Ike's requirements – have been described and Montgomery admits in his *Memoirs* that he was wrong in thinking the Canadian army could clear the Channel coast and the Scheldt estuary on its own. He was also at fault for not gripping the planning phase of Market Garden. On the whole, though, Montgomery was a clear-sighted officer who understood strategy and saw how the campaign for the Rhine and the Ruhr should be fought. The snag is not that he was wrong but that he was British.

Very few people actually *liked* Monty as a person, but those who did liked and admired him very much. They were happy to tolerate his personal failings because of his military ability and because he repaid loyalty with loyalty – a fact the fighting soldiers appreciated. Monty was not as bad as he has been painted by his detractors – that would be impossible – and, as his *Memoirs* reveal, he was quite willing to admit his mistakes – something rarely found in the other generals' recollections.

Neither did Monty's admitted arrogance extend to duplicity. He argued at length with Eisenhower but he did it face-to-face or by direct memorandum: backstabbing of the Tedder and Coningham variety, or in the manner popular at SHAEF, was not Montgomery's style. Nor did he undermine Eisenhower's strategy, as Bradley and Patton constantly did. Even when he profoundly disagreed with Ike's strategy, he did what he was told to do, once ordered to do it. Once Ike had delivered his verdict or announced his current strategy, Montgomery obeyed orders and did his best to make the strategy work.

Indeed, a reading of Montgomery's correspondence with Eisenhower reveals that, most of the time, Monty was simply urging his Supreme Commander to make up his mind, choose a viable course of action – any viable course of action – and stick to it for more than forty-eight hours. In short, Montgomery was urging his superior to exercise command – and get a grip of his subordinates.

Like all great generals Montgomery had his own way of doing things, based on long and often bitter experience. Among his beliefs was that the battlefield was a confusing place where he must impose order by careful planning and tight control. In other words, chaos must be avoided, his armies must never be caught off balance and forced to dance to the enemy's tune, while outrunning one's supply train was simply stupid – without shells, an artillery piece is simply a heavy, awkward, piece of metal. He also believed that the lives of his soldiers, *all* his soldiers – American, British, and Canadian – were precious, and must not be wasted on fruitless campaigns or in battles of attrition. Two other factors underlined this conviction. Quite apart from the fact that attrition was not Montgomery's way, Britain could not afford heavy losses: by the autumn of 1944, British and Canadian reserves of manpower were at an end, and thanks to their policy of attrition, American reserves of manpower were also running low.

Professionally, Montgomery could have handled the Field Command appointment, and not getting it was an understandable personal disappointment. Consider his situation: Montgomery had just won a decisive battle in Normandy. The main credit for that victory had – and still has – inevitably gone to the Americans, on the *post hoc, ergo propter hoc* argument so popular with many US historians: the German front collapsed after Bradley's breakout at St Lô, therefore Bradley's breakout at St Lô caused the German collapse. This cosy connection ignores the fact that the strategy that delivered the Normandy victory had been Montgomery's from the start. Montgomery had planned the

Western breakout back in May, Joe Collins had done the work in July – and Bradley has got all the credit ever since, certainly in the USA.

Monty did not care who got the credit as long as the enemy were defeated. He had clung to his strategy tenaciously – 'maintaining the aim' in military parlance – as the Normandy battle developed and accusations of 'slowness' and 'timidity' from Washington and SHAEF gathered about him and the British army until that strategy succeeded in delivering the victory – and delivered it ahead of time.

Then, that battle won, Montgomery was immediately removed from his post as Ground Force Commander and reverted to Army Group Commander, a definite demotion. Monty felt that if the Battle of Normandy had needed a ground force commander to control day-to-day operations in the field, so too did – must – the subsequent and much larger north-west Europe campaign. He certainly hoped that the appointed field commander would be one Bernard Law Montgomery, but he also believed that a field commander was essential to a sound command structure.

And so, when the Battle of Normandy ended, Montgomery was a general with something to prove. He needed to demonstrate to his numerous critics at SHAEF and in Washington that he was not another one-note general only good at set piece battles, but could also handle mobile and pursuit warfare equally well. Monty's desire to push on to the Rhine was motivated partly by that military imperative, the need to pursue a beaten enemy and prevent him reforming, and partly by the belief that, if he was successful in that pursuit, the combined chiefs and SHAEF could not fail to restore him to his recently-lost and much-treasured appointment.

There was more to this than personal ambition. Montgomery believed that the right command structure was a prerequisite for military success and few will dispute this: it is simply common sense. He also believed – he *really* believed – that the job of directing the Allied armies on a day-to-day basis in the field was a full-time job for one man. Since one man commanded every army and every Army Group, it is hard to argue with Montgomery on this point either: directing seven armies in three Army Groups, spread across western Europe from the Swiss border to the North Sea, and, most important, seeing that their various activities contributed to a workable, common strategy, was a full-time job. It is hard to argue with this point either; dividing up a host of heavy responsibilities into bearable amounts, delegation in other words, is simple common sense. The problem, however, was not common sense, but politics. The war in Europe was becoming an American show and the American generals were determined to run it.

Differences in command style were another problem. Where Ike was a committee man Montgomery was an autocrat, a general who summoned his commanders to hear his views and get their orders. Monty's numerous critics state that he was not interested in debate and rode roughshod over anyone who attempted to argue with him, but this is only partially true. While Montgomery was certainly abrasive with his superiors, especially when he disagreed with their views, he was tolerant, patient and understanding with his subordinates, always willing to listen to their arguments and sympathetic to their difficulties.

Montgomery did not need to hold committee meetings to discuss operational plans and choose options because he knew what was going on with his forces all the time. He kept his Tactical Headquarters close to the front, employed a large number of liaison officers – including American officers – who went out every day to find out the front-line facts and report back every evening, while Monty himself spent a great deal of his time out visiting the troops and the commanders. Montgomery concentrated on keeping a feel for the battle: he was much less interested in attending brain-storming sessions at SHAEF. Since he knew what he was doing – and what he wanted – Monty's orders were direct, clear and simple, and this was good because in war simplicity works, and direct, clear orders are most easily followed.

There was nothing wrong with Montgomery's command style in his role as Ground Commander. It is perhaps unnecessary to add that it is impossible to visualise Montgomery as Supreme Commander. The fact that Monty rarely turned up for those meetings at SHAEF, sending his chief of staff, Major-General Freddie de Guingand instead, was one of the many things about Monty that irritated his American colleagues. They regarded his absence as an insult to Ike and – probably – to them as well. The real reason was that Monty did not believe in command by committee, was well aware that most of his colleagues loathed him, and that the well-liked de Guingand would be the best advocate for his views.

Monty's abrasive character brought on a no-win situation with his American colleagues. His habit of reducing his orders to simple terms inevitably produced criticism, not least from American historians, that he was patronising his US subordinates. This is not a complaint often heard from those subordinates – including, in moments of stress, subordinates like Simpson or Hodges during the Bulge – or even Bradley in Normandy. The first two generals appreciated the fact that Montgomery was a regular visitor to their headquarters and was always ready with help or advice – if needed. Neither American general has accused Monty of condescension, but it has to be accepted that one barrier to renewing the appointment of Montgomery to the post of Ground Commander was the widespread dislike he had incurred at SHAEF.

The command styles of these two generals were clearly very different, and that should not be a matter for surprise. The British and US armies had different traditions, experiences and training, and these differences should have been accommodated. The problems arose – and the arguments have continued since 1945 – because the Americans believed, and still believe, that there were only two military command styles, that of the US army, which was the right one, a one-size-fits-all doctrine suitable for every occasion, and all other doctrines which were, quite simply, not just different but wrong. The American experience in a number of post-1945 wars, including Korea and the one that concluded with that unseemly scramble into helicopters from the roof of the US embassy in Saigon, have not greatly dented this perception.

Montgomery was a hands-on commander who issued clear orders via his staff, orders based on his estimate of the situation, a commander who gripped his subordinates, kept in close touch with their actions – and expected his orders to be obeyed. Eisenhower – not least because of his wide-ranging responsibilities as Supreme Commander – had a more remote style, relying on consultation and discussion before the issuing of orders that often resembled a wish-list rather than a precise series of commands.

Viewed objectively, there is nothing essentially wrong with Ike's command style either, but this method is not always suited to field command. Command by committee, trying to balance opposing views and give something to everyone, often leads to compromise – and the situation on the battlefield is not always open to compromise. Montgomery made no secret of the fact that he regarded command by committee as ludicrous.

That apart, any commander can find it frustrating, to put it mildly, if or when one of his colleagues – say, for example, General Patton – chooses to interpret orders to suit his own ends. It will be even more frustrating if that subordinate is aided and abetted in such freelancing by his Army Group Commander, say, for example, General Bradley.

At this point it might be as well to consider the command qualities of General Omar Bradley, Ike's principal American subordinate and from mid-August 1944, Montgomery's equal in field command.

By the time Bradley took over 12th Army Group in Normandy, he had racked up a certain amount of experience as a field commander, most notably in Sicily, where he had commanded a corps in Patton's Seventh Army. During that campaign he had also quarrelled with Montgomery over the matter of road allocation, a simple dispute that seems to have laid the ground for an accumulating number of resentments against the British commander. After Patton had blotted his copybook by slapping two shell-shocked soldiers in a military hospital, Bradley was chosen to command the First Army for the Normandy invasion and then promoted to Army Group Commander with Patton serving under him as Third Army Commander.

In Normandy, Bradley and Montgomery got on well enough, Bradley writing in his post-war memoirs that 'he could not have wished for a more considerate commander', but he naturally resented Montgomery's attempts to keep him in a subordinate role after the end of the Normandy campaign and their relations, never exactly cordial, deteriorated steadily thereafter. However, of more relevance to the conduct of the post-Normandy campaign was Bradley's relationship with Patton.

Put bluntly, Bradley seems to have been in awe of, or even a little afraid of, George Patton, his senior in army rank and military experience, his former commander in Sicily – and a general with very decided views on how a military campaign should be conducted. Post-Normandy Bradley seemed unable to control Patton, who persistently flouted Eisenhower's directives and went his own way, aided and abetted by Bradley. This part of their relationship quickly revealed itself in matters of supply, where Hodges, the commander of the US First Army, was continually starved of fuel and ammunition in order to keep Patton's divisions rolling, even when Eisenhower's strategy required First Army to play the major role in 12th Army Group's activities.

The problem for Bradley, as indeed for Eisenhower – his West Point classmate – was that George Patton was a public hero, a man who gained favourable newspaper headlines in the USA and was always seen to be advancing and taking the war to the enemy. Given Patton's forceful personality and public persona, the Third Army commander was a hard man to grip even when his conduct was menacing the Supreme Commander's entire strategy. Someone – preferably Bradley – should have gripped George Patton.

Bradley's abilities as a field commander are hard to assess; try as one will, the words that constantly come to mind are undistinguished, or mediocre. Eisenhower thought highly of Bradley, finding him reliable or perhaps biddable, a merciful change from the nagging Montgomery and the volatile Patton – Eisenhower's 'two prima donnas' – but it is hard to think of anything significant that can be fully laid to Bradley's credit, with the possible exception of his handling of the German counter-attack at Mortain in early August 1944. It is not at all hard to think of incidents that reveal Bradley's limitations as a field commander – of which favouring Patton at the expense of Hodges' and Ike's overall strategy was just one.

It could be that Bradley had been over-promoted as a wartime commander and peaked at the post of army commander. Though he rose to command the US Army in the post-war world, it cannot be claimed that he shone as an Army Group commander in 1944. His successes can largely be laid at the door of his excellent corps commanders – Collins, Gerdhardt, Corlett, Middleton, all outstanding American soldiers. The US Army had a depth of talent at the corps and divisional level and this enabled them to overcome many of the flaws in the higher command.

George Patton, the last of the commanders we need consider here, was mercifully unique. No army in the Second World War produced a general like Patton, whose fame has lived on while that of other generals is long forgotten. Unlike some American generals – Mark Clark for example – Patton did not court publicity and rarely needed to: newspaper correspondents followed Patton like vultures, eager to record his latest indiscretion or amplify his latest success. Sooner or later, Patton was sure to open his mouth and jam his foot in it.

In some ways Patton was not unlike his British rival, Montgomery – the 'little Limey fart' as Patton engagingly referred to him – vain, arrogant, sure of his own abilities, contemptuous of his superiors and deeply jealous of the aforesaid little Limey fart. Patton played the role of fighting general to the hilt. While Monty went about in corduroy trousers and a pullover, Patton dressed in a glittering steel helmet, armed with an ivory-handled pistol. Patton seems to have seen himself as a warrior, on a stage with only one actor, always eager for battle, leading his armies from the front and carrying all before him.

Patton's style has many admirers, not least in the United States, where he is regarded as one of the Second World War's leading Allied exponents of armoured warfare – admittedly not an overcrowded field. Certainly few commanders were quicker to urge their subordinates on or press the need for pursuit. Where Montgomery was a leader, Patton was a driver, careless of casualties if he got results – his army nickname, 'Old Blood and Guts', drew the frequent comment 'His Guts, our Blood' from his soldiers. Even there, among the ranks of the front-line soldiers, men not given to hero-worship, many regard him as an outstanding general and an all-American hero.

Patton's detractors regard him as a ranting blowhard, a man who talked a good fight but, certainly post-Normandy, usually delivered less than he promised. He is also seen as being prodigal with the lives of his soldiers and unable or unwilling to obey an order that ran in the face of his own beliefs – notably that he was capable of winning the war on his own if given the necessary resources. It is even arguable that Patton was a positive menace to the Allied cause.

In a paper in the *British Defence Studies Journal*, Brigadier G. W. Berrigan, considering Patton's conduct in the 1944 campaign on the Moselle, concludes that he was 'an over-ambitious, egotistical commander on an economy of effort mission seeking glory at any cost, who refused to live within the available means.'[1] Given the circumstances and the outcome, it is hard to disagree with that conclusion, but the truth may lie somewhere between the two extremes of military genius and blowhard. Patton was no great commander but it is more than possible that a good soldier was trying to get past the bluster and the engrained arrogance.

George Patton loved soldiering. If Montgomery was the master of the set piece battle, as even his critics like to claim, Patton excelled in pursuit warfare, in following up a defeated foe and keeping him on the run. This was his talent, in driving men on, and only when the enemy turned at bay did Patton's numerous limitations appear.

Much of Patton's success in the later stages of the Normandy battle, and the subsequent rush of the Third Army towards Metz and the Saar, stemmed from the fact that the enemy had little on that front to oppose him. Then his troops got to Metz and Lorraine, where the German army promptly stopped Patton in his tracks. However, the main problem with Patton in the post-Normandy campaign was his reluctance to obey Ike's directives. Patton intended to push ahead to the Metz, the Saar, the West Wall and the Rhine and by one means or another kept doing so, in spite of the fact that his actions and his constant need for maintenance gravely affected Ike's strategic plan and the actions of his First Army colleague, General Hodges, a man Patton openly despised. It appears that Patton also despised Bradley and was dubious about Ike. Writing in his journal in July 1944, Patton records: 'Neither Ike or Brad has the stuff. Ike is bound hand and foot by the British and does not know it. Poor fool. We actually have no Supreme Commander... it is a very unfortunate situation to which I see no solution.'

Eisenhower, therefore, had problems with George Patton but many of these problems were his own fault. A field commander needs to give orders that are clear, unequivocal and not open to interpretation by his subordinates. Matters will go wrong anyway – 'no plan survives the first contact with the enemy' – but a commander's ability to command is hopelessly compromised if his subordinates are not precisely clear about what they must do or are given scope to amend their orders – or decline to carry those orders out.

The important point about a strategy, any strategy – apart from the basic point that it must be viable – is that it must be clearly understood by all those charged with making it work and their actions must contribute to that strategy and not undermine it. Isolated successes are useless; each achievement must contribute to the overall strategy. This is not to say that a strategy is set in stone and cannot be altered. If a strategy starts to go awry, or is unexpectedly successful, or changes appear necessary, the commander must change it – fast. But the basic rule remains: unless a strategy is clearly stated, understood and followed by everyone, it will not work.

A supreme commander is responsible for strategy; the ground force commander is responsible for making that strategy work. The ground force commander should be responsible for the detail, for allocating tasks and objectives, for giving the supreme commander objective, factual information on the progress of events – and for driving the armies forward. A supreme commander can be a nice guy; a ground commander has to be more hard-nosed – and either job is indeed more than enough for one man.

So, if this course of action – the clear division of responsibility between a supreme commander and his executive ground force commander - is so plainly beneficial, why was it not adopted or kept in place after the battle of Normandy? The short answers are national chauvinism – and Montgomery.

Standing back after six decades it seems insane that a sensible arrangement to fight battles or campaigns that might shorten the war could not be put in place because the US public at home would not put up with it – or so it was said. Evidence of public concern in the USA or anywhere else for anything other than the lives of their men is hard to find. The truth of the matter seems to be that the US public and the troops in the field were neither consulted nor greatly concerned with matters of command.

Charles B. MacDonald, one of the US Official Historians, an infantry officer in north-west Europe in 1944–45, winner of the Silver Star – and no chauvinist – makes that point for the fighting men:

> What did it matter to an American G.I. in a foxhole, fighting for his life
> in the harsh cold and snow of the Ardennes, who commanded him at the top?
> Who was this Montgomery? Who was Bradley? A front-line soldier was
> immensely well informed if he knew the name of his Company Commander.[2]

MacDonald served at the sharp end, and it shows. The notion that troops in muddy foxholes cared two pins about the higher command set-up is ludicrous; they have other things to worry about. As for the general public, very few read editorials about strategic or political issues: they read the headlines and skipped swiftly to the sports page. The real issue here was glory – glory for the US Administration in an election year, glory for the Joint Chiefs of Staff and glory for the US generals who depended on public and Congressional approval to get their wartime ranks confirmed in the post-war Army.

Post D-Day, it was clear that Germany was going to be defeated in this war and George Marshall wanted the US army to gain the glory for that victory – all the glory. The problem was that the German army was still in the field and fighting harder every day. Unless the Allies could find the right strategy to defeat the German army, victory would be delayed and losses would mount. Newspaper editors or politicians do not pay the price of glory – the soldiers in the field pay it.

The second problem was Montgomery. If Monty had the charm to match his ability much grief might have been avoided, but charm and Bernard Montgomery do not go well together. Nor would it have made any difference; even if Monty had been loaded with charm – an unlikely scenario – he could not have retained the post of ground force commander. Military demographics – the fact that there were more US troops in the field – militated against that option.

And yet, if there was to be a ground force commander in Europe, if the need for such an appointment were admitted, who else could it be but Montgomery? Who else had the experience and the proven capability? Monty's answer was Omar Bradley, but no one on the American side, least of all Eisenhower or Marshall, thought Bradley was the man for the job. Bradley's failure to grip Patton or apply a coherent strategy within his own Army Group area was making that fact plainer every day. Bradley was not up to it and no one would have Monty – so Eisenhower would have to do both jobs.

Eisenhower did not see this as a problem, at least to begin with. He wanted to command the armies in the field. So did every professional soldier in the Allied armies; it was the plum job in the ETO, if not the entire military world. Besides, like Monty, Eisenhower had something to prove: he wanted to demonstrate that he was not merely an over-promoted staff officer, simply a committee man and very nice guy. He wanted to show that he was a tough, fighting soldier, able to win battles and handle hard campaigns – and time to prove it was running out.

The advantage for Eisenhower was that as supreme commander and ground force commander he could apply his personal strategy – his own ideas for winning the European war – without any senior subordinate arguing with him or getting in the way, or so he thought. In fact Montgomery continued to argue and Patton ignored or watered down any of Ike's orders he did not like, aided and abetted by Bradley. Ike should have gripped Monty and Patton, telling them bluntly and in so many words to obey his orders or face the sack, but gripping commanders was not Ike's style, and again, there were problems in applying the ultimate sanction to either man.

Field Marshal Montgomery was the senior British general, and strongly supported by Field Marshal Alan Brooke, the CIGS, Churchill's main military adviser and the senior British officer on the CCS. Sacking Monty would cause an almighty row with Alan Brooke. As for George Patton, as long as he was forging ahead and getting lots of favourable publicity in the US press, he was untouchable. Like it or not, Eisenhower had trouble on both flanks, with Montgomery in the west and Patton in the east.

It is interesting to speculate what would have happened if these two generals had changed flanks. The truth of the matter was that during September 1944, the way to get into Germany and end the war quickly by taking the Reich's industrial heart, the Ruhr, and its political centre, Berlin, was by thrusting strongly up to the north in the 21st Army Group sector. The problem with getting to the Ruhr, let alone Berlin, was logistics, but getting to the Rhine and even over the Rhine was certainly possible, perhaps even probable, provided all necessary logistical support went to Montgomery and the First Army was ordered to assist him.

The snag was that that meant stopping Patton in his lunge towards the Saar and, for all the reasons described above, that was deemed politically impossible. On the other hand, had Patton been the Allied commander in the west, charged with getting to the Rhine and over it to the Ruhr, these political problems would never have arisen. Montgomery could have been put out to grass in the east and Patton could have stormed north to glory – or disaster – in the west, while Washington cheered him on. (The author is grateful to Major-General Julian Thompson for raising this interesting point.) The situation actually went rather further than Patton. Chester Willmot writes that:

> The political difficulty of restraining Patton, the universal optimism of the American High Command, and the desire to form a united front from Switzerland to the North Sea, a front broad enough for the ultimate employment of the 30 divisions still waiting in the United States were, it seems, the real factors behind Eisenhower's reluctance to provide Montgomery with sufficient resources to capture the Ruhr.[3]

Patton and Montgomery therefore remained on their respective fronts, but speculating on what *might* have happened does help to reveal the real snag – the trip wire – that so often thwarted Eisenhower in the execution of his strategy. Patton and Montgomery caused Eisenhower a number of problems he could well have done without and the 'Patton factor' remained a source of trouble, less talked about but no less intractable than that caused by Montgomery.

Command is about *responsibility* – for the conduct of the battles and campaigns, for gaining the eventual victory – for winning. Graham and Bidwell have suggested that Eisenhower was 'intellectually lazy' and never prepared himself for the decisions that might face him if things went wrong.[4] When Eisenhower took direct command of the Allied Armies on 1 September 1944, many commanders would have envied his situation. The enemy had just been soundly defeated and was now in full retreat, shattered and short of men, tanks and supplies. The Allied armies were large and growing larger, the Allied air forces dominated the skies and the seas were open for the shipment of men and supplies. The problem was that the opportunity to exploit this glorious situation now depended on the new commander making some critical decisions – quickly. Montgomery, the about-to-be-ex-ground force commander, already had a strategy and command structure in place: form the US First and British Second Armies into one mass and roll north to the Rhine, taking Belgium on the way, with himself in overall command. In other words, stick to the winning team and bash on regardless.

Eisenhower agreed with this strategy, but only up to a point. His gut instinct was to move all his armies up to the Rhine and attack on the broadest possible front. The problem was logistics and the answer to that problem was Antwerp. If Ike wanted his broad front policy to work he needed to clear the decks of all other tasks until he had taken Antwerp – and he failed to do that.

Many authorities seem to assume that the problem of logistics was absolute in the autumn of 1944 and the only answer was Antwerp, but that is a simplistic answer. The problem of logistics is related to the desired objectives. If it was the Allied aim to advance over the Rhine and on to Berlin on a broad front, that clearly required a vast logistical back-up and that meant Antwerp. But the evidence also suggests that certain necessary objectives on the road to Berlin, crossing the Rhine and perhaps even taking the Ruhr, were possible with the existing logistical set-up, provided the right strategy to do so was set in place. Montgomery's popular and astute Chief of Staff, Freddie de Guingand, certainly thought so:

> If Eisenhower had not taken the steps he did to link up at an early date with Anvil and had held back Patton, and had he diverted the resources so released to the north, I think it possible we might have obtained a bridgehead over the Rhine before the winter – but not more.[5]

Perhaps not more then, but that much alone would have been very useful – and much more than was actually achieved. This view was confirmed after the war in interviews with the senior surviving German commanders, von Rundstedt, Student, Blumentritt and Rommel's former chief of staff, General Speidel. They were unanimous in declaring that a full-blooded thrust from Belgium in September would have succeeded in crossing the Rhine and might have ended the war in 1944, since they had no means of stopping such a thrust reaching the Ruhr.[6] In the event, largely due to the faulty command set-up and lack of grip, even a bridgehead over the Rhine before the winter was still a dream in 1944.

The problem is circular. In Montgomery's opinion, this intermediate strategy, heading for the Rhine and hoping for the Ruhr, meant stopping Patton and devoting all the necessary logistical resources and some divisions of the US First Army to supporting the Second Army's drive for the Rhine. If, on the other hand, the decision was for a broad front approach, moving all the Allied armies up to the Rhine before attempting a crossing, then the main aim of the Allies *prior to that move* was the opening of the port of Antwerp.

The reader can appreciate how difficult and agonising this decision would be. Delaying any move on the Rhine did not only mean the opening of Antwerp – it would also give the enemy time to regroup and man the West Wall. On balance, given the situation at the time, arguably the best decision would have been to get up to the Rhine quickly and force a crossing; an early bridgehead over the Rhine would have been an asset. That done, with the great physical barrier removed, the Allies might then have paused to open Antwerp and devoted the time before attempting a major advance on the Ruhr to mopping up the German forces west of the Rhine. That would have ensured the logistical support necessary for the final push into Germany. While Antwerp was being opened, Eisenhower could have moved the other Allied Armies – Patton's Third and those of Dever's 6th Army Group – up to the Rhine, threatening the enemy with another crossing and keeping the German forces dispersed. Whatever the difficulties, this would at least have been a strategy, but it needed some decisions. So let us see what decisions were actually taken.

In his memoirs Eisenhower states that his intention after crossing the Seine was 'to push forward on a broad front with priority on the left (i.e. western) flank.'[7] The first problem is over the word 'priority' and displays Ike's usual lack of precision. Does this mean that the left flank should have all the necessary military and logistical support or only that which could be spared from the task of making a broad front advance? Or was it the other way round – that the left flank should have everything it needed to push on to some as-yet-unstated objective, while the other forces did the best they could with what was left?

The former appears more likely, for Eisenhower also declared that he planned to send his right wing – perhaps Bradley and certainly Patton – to the east with the aim of taking the Saar basin and joining up with Devers' Anvil forces coming up the Rhône valley. The linking of the whole front, Ike declares, 'was mandatory'. So here we have a situation where advancing on the left was a 'priority' and linking on the right was 'mandatory'.

The strategy here – though Eisenhower does not use the word – was 'to gain the whole length of the Rhine before launching a final attack on Germany.' The snags were time, logistics and the available Allied strength – and what about the military maxim on the need for a concentration of force – but if this was to be Eisenhower's strategy, how did he go about implementing it? Let us go back a little and review events.

Meeting Montgomery on 23 August, Ike rejected the notion of an advance to the north by the Second and First Armies and confirmed that he wanted Patton to continue pushing east: the broad front strategy was firmly in place. Twenty-First Army Group would clear the Channel coast and take Antwerp; in Bradley's Group, Hodges' First Army would reach the Rhine north and south of the Ardennes, while Patton's Third Army took the Saar and reached the Rhine at Mannheim, while Devers' Group came up and moved on the Rhine around Strasbourg.

On 4 September, the day Antwerp fell, Eisenhower issued another directive, ordering the forces north-west of the Ardennes – 21st Army Group and two corps of the US First Army – to take Antwerp, reach the Rhine and seize the Ruhr, while the rest of Bradley's 12th Army Group, Patton's Third Army and the V Corps of Hodges' First Army, occupied the sector of the Siegfried Line covering the Saar and seized Frankfurt on the east side of the Rhine.

These were considerable tasks, but there was more. The directive added that 'the Central Group of Armies [i.e. Bradley's] operating against the Ruhr, north-west of the Ardennes, must first be adequately supported.' This is somewhat confusing, since two corps of the First Army had been ordered to support 21st

Army Group and the remaining corps had been ordered to assist Patton. Moreover, this directive appears to give priority to the First Army but Ike added that 'I deem it important to get Patton moving again so that we may be fully prepared to carry out the original conception for the final stages of the campaign.'

Patton had been held up for a few days by a gasoline shortage, but on the day this directive was issued, Bradley deemed the situation in the north had been stabilised and decreed that Patton would get half the available 12th Army Group resources and could therefore 'cross the Moselle and force the Siegfried Line'. The priority, it seemed, had now switched to Patton but the Allied armies were now to go for the Saar, Aachen and Arnhem – and clear the Scheldt – all at the same time.

What happened to that strategy we have already seen: it failed. It failed for a number of reasons, but primarily it failed because the Allied armies were not strong enough anywhere to break through the amount of resistance the enemy was able to bring up. The broad front approach collided with the principle of concentration of force and was found to be seriously lacking, not least because Bradley and Patton were pulling the Allied effort off to the east. So much for the left flank thrust to the north having priority.

If a strategy does not work it must be changed. The various meetings and arguments during September have already been covered, but the next significant meeting took place on 22 September, at Versailles. By the time this conference convened, Monty and Eisenhower had been arguing over strategy for a full week, following that letter written to Bradley and Montgomery on 14 September in which Ike declared that:

> We shall soon, I hope, be in possession of the objectives set out in my directive of September 4, and shall then be in possession of the Ruhr, the Saar and the Frankfurt areas.

With these in Allied hands, Ike continued, he 'intended to move on Berlin with the forces of 21st and 12th Army Groups and while it was not possible at this stage to indicate the timing of these thrusts or their strength, I should be glad to have your views on the general questions raised in this letter'. Specifically, did the commanders think the final advance should go via Hanover or via Frankfurt – or both?

THE QUESTION OF COMMAND 215

Since Antwerp was still shut and none of these areas or objectives were remotely near capture, and Market Garden had yet to begin, it is hardly surprising that Montgomery demurred.

Returning to his theme in a letter to Eisenhower, written on 18 September, Montgomery stated – yet again – that time was of the essence, that there was not enough logistical support to sustain such a big effort, that one route, preferably the northern one, must have priority but if Ike preferred the southern route, then Bradley needed every available soldier and all the logistical support, and that either 21st Army Group would manage with what was left over or, alternatively, Second Army would be wanted for a secondary role on the left flank of the movement.[8] Montgomery's subtext here is: get a grip or make up your mind.

Eisenhower's reply to this letter on 20 September, D plus 3 on Market Garden, when all was coming unravelled, was that he completely agreed with Monty's proposal of concentrating on the northern approach to the Ruhr and Berlin: 'Generally speaking I find myself in complete agreement with your letter of 18 September', but he did not intend to do this until Antwerp was open and all his armies had moved up to the German frontier, if not to the Rhine, which lies east of the German frontier in many places.

Given the situation at Arnhem and the problems now facing Simonds and the Canadians in their battle for the Scheldt – problems that seemed to be passing Eisenhower by – Monty was now convinced that any chance of 'bouncing the Rhine' anywhere was gone. However, it might still be possible to get across in a pre-planned set piece attack, if his left hook proposals met with Eisenhower's approval. He would present plans for this hook at the conference at Versailles on 22 September. As related, it was Freddie de Guingand and not Montgomery who attended this full-blown strategy conference and de Guingand returned in triumph, declaring that Monty's proposals had been accepted.

Montgomery was still expecting to secure a bridgehead over the Rhine at Arnhem, but had also decided that 'to take advantage of the favourable situation in the Nijmegen area', it was essential that the right corps of Second Army – the VIII Corps, currently attempting to widen the corridor from Eindhoven to Arnhem – should develop a strong thrust east on the axis Gennep–Cleve –Emmerich, from where it could advance to the north-west corner of the Ruhr. To free VIII Corps for this task, said Monty, it was essential that the 12th Army Group should take over the VIII Corps sector at once – in other words, Bradley should cease battering at Aachen and free VIII Corps for a thrust east through the Reichswald beyond the northern end of the West Wall.

The conference agreed with this proposal, adding that 'the envelopment of the Ruhr from the north by 21st Army Group, supported by the United States First Army is the main effort of the present stage of operations.' Twelfth Army Group 'were to continue its thrust so far as current resources permit towards Cologne and Bonn [the current targets of the V and VII Corps attacking Aachen] and be prepared to seize any favourable opportunities of crossing the Rhine and attacking the Ruhr from the south when the maintenance situation permits.' The remainder of 12th Army Group – Patton – was 'to take no more aggressive action than is permitted by the maintenance situation after the full requirements of the main effort [Montgomery's] have been met.'

Since this is exactly what Montgomery had been proposing since the end of August, it is hardly surprising that both he and de Guingand were delighted, de Guingand signalling Montgomery that 'Ike supported your plan 100 per cent. Your thrust is main effort and gets full support.'[9] Then came the inevitable caveat; though the envelopment of the Ruhr was to be the main effort, 21st Army Group was also to 'open the port of Antwerp as a matter of urgency' – and that task would require more effort than the First Canadian Army could provide.

Even so, having got what he wanted, Montgomery was not about to quibble over words or extra tasks – besides, he knew it was now essential to open Antwerp and he followed this directive to the letter. On 27 September he ordered the Canadians to clear the Scheldt, while Second Army's main task, though still holding the Nijmegen bridgehead, was to 'operate strongly with all available strength from the general area Nijmegen–Gennep against the north-west corner of the Ruhr.' Meanwhile, the US First Army would assist by providing the 7th Armored Division to clear the VIII Corps sector west of the River Meuse. Monty's overall strategy is not unlike the one described above: to gain contact with the Ruhr, get bridgeheads over the Rhine and decide then on further action, while 'the opening of the port of Antwerp is absolutely essential before we can advance deep into Germany.'

All this was to the good but it came too late. The Allied front line now extended for some 600 miles from the Swiss frontier to the North Sea and to maintain this front took every division Eisenhower could find. With an over-extended front, the strength to breach the German line anywhere was simply not available. The slippage came in the west: to clear the Scheldt, the Canadians needed help from Second Army. To push east towards the Ruhr, Second Army needed help from the US First Army, not least because Model was now launching heavy counter-attacks on the Second Army salient at Nijmegen from both Arnhem and the Reichswald. To this end Bradley was supposed to take over part of the Second Army front but lacked the resources to do so – his front was already dangerously stretched and Eisenhower had to warn him that if the enemy chose to concentrate the 12th Army Group 'may get a nasty little Kasserine.' Eisenhower was referring to the German attack in Tunisia in 1943 when the US forces experienced a major reverse at the hands of Erwin Rommel.

In reaching this state of affairs, Eisenhower was largely the author of his own misfortunes. He had attempted to operate all along the front, unwilling to put all the available resources into one strong push. This compromise had not worked: now he had neither the Ruhr nor Antwerp and the enemy was not only defending the West Wall strongly, he was attacking such Allied forces as came within reach, and holding them.

There is no sadder phrase in military history than 'Too Late!' Eisenhower had now got a workable strategy, one that fitted the current situation: a month earlier this might have provided him with some solid successes – certainly the Rhine, possibly the Ruhr. Now the enemy had got his breath back, manned the West Wall, flung back the British at Arnhem and the Americans at Aachen and was getting stronger every day. A strategy that might have paid off in September was not going to work in October and a new strategy would be required.

10 · AACHEN AND THE RIVER ROER
OCTOBER 1944

The First Army… was preparing to put another corps through the West Wall,
seize Aachen and renew the drive towards the Ruhr.
US OFFICIAL HISTORY, *THE SIEGFRIED LINE CAMPAIGN*

With the advent of October, putting the various disappointments of September behind them, the Allied armies prepared to renew the struggle on their various fronts. In the West, the Canadian First Army was pressing on towards the Scheldt. Second Army was trying to expand their bridgehead at Nijmegen but had to retain four American divisions in the Nijmegen corridor even to hold it, following Hitler's direct order to Model that the British salient to the Neder Rijn should be eliminated. Patton was still hammering away towards the Saar, while on the far right flank of the Allied armies, Devers' 6th Army Group was pushing north towards Colmar and the Vosges. Hodges, meanwhile, was preparing for yet another thrust at Aachen. Eisenhower's wish, that all his armies should be in action all the time, was now being amply fulfilled.

This action was also revealing that basic flaw in the broad front policy – a failure to concentrate: everyone was fighting but nobody was making much progress. Even so, General Eisenhower's 22 September directive, which stated that 'the main effort on the present phase of operations' was the conquest of the Ruhr by 21st Army Group and the US First Army, was still in place and Montgomery and Bradley – or certainly Hodges – were anxious to get on with it.

If 21st Army Group had a multiplicity of tasks, none of the Allied armies faced a harder slog at this time than Hodges' First Army. Eisenhower found it necessary to move the boundary between First Army and the British Second Army and make the XIX Corps of First Army responsible for protecting the right flank of Second Army east of the Maas, between the Market Garden salient and the First Army. To support this shift to the west and shore up First Army, Bradley ordered Patton to send Hodges the US 7th Armored Division and the 29th Infantry Division, the latter coming up from the siege of Brest. These units took over responsibility for an area known as the Peel Marshes, which had been the preserve of Second Army, and was to pass to and fro between the Allied armies for the next few weeks.

The battle for this area east of Eindhoven, west of the river Maas, and north of Geilenkirchen, began on 28 September and lasted until 3 December, quickly becoming a very stiff battle indeed. After a week of hard fighting through 'extensive minefields, marshes, woods, anti-tank gun positions, nebelwerfer concentrations and artillery fire'[1] the US 7th Armored Division had halted in its tracks, having advanced barely two miles.

Therefore, on 8 October, responsibility for the Peel Marsh area was handed back to Second Army, though the US 7th Armored Division and some Belgian units were loaned to Second Army at the same time. The VIII Corps of Second Army then took up the struggle for the marshes but ran into the same kind of opposition. Venray, in the north of the Peel Marsh area, did not fall until 17 October – the day after Field Marshal Montgomery halted all offensive operations by Second Army, other than those designed to aid the clearing of the Scheldt. For the moment the west bank of the River Maas would be left to the enemy.

This sensible command pattern, concentrating the main effort on one objective, and not spreading slender resources too thinly, had now been adopted by General Hodges. On 22 September he stopped almost all offensive operations on the First Army front – other than those just mentioned above – to concentrate on his main task, the reduction of Aachen.

Before he could do that, however, some readjustments to the American front were necessary, not least the introduction of Lieutenant General William H. Simpson's Ninth Army into the line in the Ardennes – the Ninth Army taking over the front from St Vith to Etterrach, an area previously occupied by the V

Corps of First Army. This was all that Simpson could manage as the Ninth Army currently consisted of just one corps: Major-General Troy Middleton's VIII Corps, which had formerly belonged to the Third Army and mustered just two divisions.

Hodges had also grasped the need for concentration and elected to concentrate his troops on forcing the Aachen Gap.[2] Having pulled back from the Eifel, the V Corps now occupied a fifteen-mile front south of the VII Corps, while Collins' VII Corps' front shrank from thirty-five to twenty miles. In the north, Corlett's XIX Corps' front did not change but was only sixteen miles long anyway. Overall, at the end of September and in early October, the First Army front shrank from about 100 to sixty miles: this was good, but it would have been even better if this shrinkage had enabled Hodges to put some divisions into reserve. As it was, he still needed all his troops to hold the new front against growing German resistance.

Before Hodges could move east to the Rhine, several intermediate objectives had to be taken, most notably the city of Aachen and the Huertgen Forest. A look at the map on page 13 will be helpful at this point. This new thrust involved moving the XIX Corps through the West Wall north of Aachen to outflank the city. As Collins had found out in September, the way to take Aachen was by simultaneous flanking attacks through the West Wall, so moving on the city from the north and south, and this was the tactic Hodges intended to employ.

Corlett's XIX Corps began this process with an attack across the River Wurm and into the West Wall north of Aachen by the 30th Division, which had been watching the ground across the river and the enemy line between Aachen and Geilenkirchen for some weeks. General Hobbs, the 30th Division commander, used this time to give his men more training. After four months in action since Normandy, this was sorely needed, for many replacements were grieviously short of training: in one battalion only one man knew how to operate a flamethrower and infantry tactics could have done with some refurbishment.[3]

There was also the need to gather intelligence. Corlett's G-2, a Colonel Platt, estimated that south of Geilenkirchen the enemy was holding the line with just seven battalions, each mustering 450 men apiece, with a further seven battalions south of Rimburg. In support, they had a good amount of artillery of various calibres but very few tanks. On the other hand, more men were coming in and some armour would undoubtedly reach the German line before too long

– not least because the Germans were surely expecting a renewal of the attack on Aachen as soon as the weather permitted deployment of the Allied tactical air forces.

The plan called for the 30th Division to break though the enemy positions across the river, after which the 2nd Armored Division would come through and exploit the breach, hopefully as far as the river Roer, nine miles away to the east. Supported by air strikes and artillery concentrations, this attack began on 2 October and soon ran into trouble.

A speedy advance by the leading rifle companies carried them quickly across the shallow Wurm but enemy positions, in dugouts and pillboxes, which the artillery had failed to subdue – in spite of firing over 18,000 rounds in the pre-assault bombardment – soon slowed the attack down. On the first day only a narrow bridgehead was obtained beyond the Wurm and heavy fighting on the second day, notably around the castle at Rimburg, checked any further progress. The 2nd Armored Division did come forward in support, but mines, artillery fire and the boggy ground beyond the Wurm restricted them. Pillboxes were eliminated by the infantry using explosives and flamethrowers but progress was slow.

Corlett's battle to break the West Wall north of Aachen lasted until 7 October. On that day Major-General Hobbs of the 30th Division reported to Corlett that he had reached Alsdorf and was therefore only three miles from the link-up point with Collins' VII Corps. In addition, he now held a bridgehead beyond the Wurm six miles wide and four miles deep – and had obtained this at the relatively light cost of 1,800 casualties – more than 60 per cent of them from artillery and mortar fire. In the latter stages of this attack the 30th Division had begun to swing south, aiming to link up with VII Corps at Wuerselen, two miles north-east of Aachen, starting an encircling process – the Second Battle of Aachen – that was to occupy most of First Army for the next three weeks.

The link-up between the two corps was seen as an infantry task – the 30th Division of XIX Corps and the 1st Infantry Division of Collins' VII Corps. This was a big task for two reduced divisions but no more infantry divisions were available. The rest of Corlett's Corps was occupied holding the Wurm bridgehead and maintaining the link with Second Army, while the rest of Collins' corps, notably the 9th Division, was engaged in the Huertgen Forest, south of Aachen, where that fine Division was being cut to pieces, and the 3rd Armored

Division was engaging the enemy in the Stolberg corridor. Hobbs and Huebner, the two infantry division commanders encircling Aachen, were not dismayed by this lack of support and commenced their link-up drive on 8 October.

By that date the distance involved was not great – perhaps two and a half miles between the leading elements of both divisions – but, inevitably, the Germans got in the way. There were some 12,000 German troops defending Aachen and these, plus the usual German assets of terrain, mines and pillboxes, did all they could to stop the US infantry getting forward. One advantage of this joint attack was that the enemy could not spare troops to launch local counter-attacks, but on the other hand this concentration of two US divisions in such a small area provided the German artillery with plenty of targets: shell and mortar fire took its inevitable toll.

By the evening of 9 October the US forces had made some useful advances and on the following day, having captured the suburb of Haaren, Major-General Clarence Huebner of the 1st Infantry Division sent a message to the German commander in Aachen, demanding immediate surrender of the city and its garrison. Failing this, said Huebner, the US air force and artillery would reduce the city to rubble. In obedience to Hitler's standing orders, that every position should be held to the last, Colonel Leyherr of the 246th Division rejected this demand. Therefore, to underline Huebner's point, on the following day, 11 October, US infantry began to edge into the city and tactical aircraft from IX Tactical Air Command began striking targets in the city centre, supported by the guns of the VII Corps and the 1st Division.

However, the Germans were very determined to hang on to Aachen and fresh units were being fed into the city even as the US units attempting to take it began to tire – that lack of US reserves was again taking its toll, as did street fighting in the rubble-strewn blocks of the city centre. Try as they would, the two US divisions could not manage to link up and at 1000hrs on 15 October, the Germans defending Aachen – the 3rd Panzer Grenadier Division and 29th Panzer Grenadier Regiment, the latter including the Tiger tanks of the 506th Tank Battalion – struck back hard.

The weight of this attack fell on the 1st Infantry Division. There was considerable confusion for a while; the situation was saved by the divisional artillery bringing down a heavy fire on the advancing Germans and by the welcome arrival of P-47 strafing aircraft of the USAAF, which waded into the enemy with rockets and cannon fire. Fighting went on for the rest of the day but no significant ground was lost.

At dawn on 16 October, the Germans attacked again, sending in a kampf-gruppe of tanks and infantry to knock holes in the American line. More heavy fighting followed, but by nightfall the enemy had been driven back, defeated in the main by artillery fire and the stubborn resistance of the US infantry. German losses in this attack were severe: in battering at the US line the 3rd Panzer Grenadiers lost about one-third of their infantry and the US 16th Regiment of the 1st Division counted no fewer than 250 enemy dead lying in front of their positions. Losses in the US 1st Infantry Division in this recent fighting were around 800 killed, wounded and missing.

While the 1st Infantry Division were thus engaged, Hobbs' 30th Division were also pressing forward, but by 15 October, after a week of hard fighting, the gap between the two divisions still stood at over a mile: in three days the 116th Infantry Regiment of the 29th Division, which had been detached to help the 30th Division, had advanced no more than 1,000 yards. Persistence against a skilled and tenacious foe was the only answer and that persistence finally paid off. At 1615hrs on 16 October, tired soldiers of the two divisions shook hands at Wuerselen. Aachen was now surrounded and soon it must fall, not least because the delays in taking it were causing some dissension among the American com-manders, in particular between Hodges, Hobbs and Corlett.

On 15 October, Hodges told Corlett that Hobbs was 'either bragging or com-plaining and had not advanced an inch in four days'[4] and, says the Official History, both Corlett and Hobbs felt they were 'walking on eggs with the First Army commander' who, Corlett believed, had no idea of the difficulties Hobbs was facing and no apparent interest in finding out. Corlett elected to solve this problem as directly as possible, telling Hobbs to attack all along the line as 'I want to close the Aachen gap', and the gap was closed on 16 October.

By 16 October the defence of Aachen depended on the Wehrmacht's 246th Division, commanded by Colonel Gerhard Wilck, a force of some 5,000 men, mostly from his own division, with some fragments from other units. In support, Wilck had just five Mark IV tanks and thirty-three artillery pieces of various calibre, but he could hope for more artillery support from guns outside the city limits. Fighting went on until noon on 21 October, when in spite of various exhortations from the Führer, urging the garrison to fight to the last man and the last round, Colonel Wilck surrendered and went into captivity with some 2,000 of his men.

And so, after days of street fighting and weeks of campaigning around the Gap, on 21 October Aachen finally fell. The 30th Division had lost some 3,000 men in this action, and two battalions of the 1st Infantry's 26th Infantry Regiment alone had lost 498. These losses are higher than they might appear, for the dead and wounded were found mainly in the rifle companies, many of which had lost up to 80 per cent of their effectives. German losses amounted to over 11,000 men and some forty-five tanks. They had also lost Aachen, the central gateway to the Reich.

This victory did not save General Corlett, who was relieved of his command on 18 October. Bradley had never cared for Corlett: having commanded the 7th Division in the Pacific, Corlett had been sent to Bradley by General Marshall before D-Day, charged with advising Bradley on amphibious tactics. Bradley stood in sore need of such advice, but taking advice was not something Bradley was noted for. Corlett was first ignored, then given the XIX Corps – and now he had been sacked. The official reason for his dismissal was ill-health and Eisenhower, who regarded Corlett as a good commander, wanted him back as soon as he was fit.

The US History comments that during the early days of October it had become obvious that 'the halcyon days of pursuit had ended.' This had been demonstrated with the hard battle for Aachen and in the first attempt to capture the town of Schmidt, a key road junction in the Huertgen Forest, which will be described in the next chapter. The recent battering at Aachen had occupied the First Army for a full month and cost 20,000 casualties and yet at no point had Hodges got more than twelve miles into Germany.

Nor had Patton gone very far with his offensive towards the Saar. Although Eisenhower had put the Third Army on the defensive after the conference of 22 September, Patton had still managed to assemble enough fuel and artillery ammunition to press on with limited attacks around Metz, but this city continued to defy him. November would arrive before Patton got far beyond the Moselle. Logistics were less of a problem for Devers' group, which drew its supplies via Marseilles, but after crossing the upper Moselle in late September, this force too had been reduced to a crawl in the rugged country of the Vosges. It was clearly time for yet another conference.

This duly took place in Brussels on 18 October and was attended by Eisenhower, Tedder, Bradley, and, for once, by Montgomery, his presence required by a recent exchange of tart messages with the Supreme Commander.

To track the origins of this conference it is necessary to go back to 8 October, when Monty asked Bradley and Hodges to visit his HQ and discuss the proposition that: 'the operations of Second Army and US First Army are very intimately related and it is my opinion that the present system of command is most unsatisfactory.' Nothing new there perhaps, but when Bradley and Hodges turned up at Montgomery's HQ, they brought with them the formidable presence of General George C. Marshall, the US Chief of Staff and Chairman of the Combined Chiefs of Staff – heavy metal indeed. This being so, Monty took the opportunity to take Marshall aside and unburden himself over what he perceived as the current failings over strategy and command. Montgomery's *Memoirs* record that:

> I told him that since Eisenhower had taken personal command of the land battle, being also Supreme Commander of all the forces – land, sec and air – the armies had become separated nationally and not geographically. There was a lack of grip and operational direction and control was lacking. Our operations had, in fact, become ragged and disjointed and we had now got ourselves in a real mess. Marshall listened but said little. It was clear that he entirely disagreed.[5]

'Entirely disagreed' hardly covers Marshall's reaction. In his memoir Marshall remembers this meeting well. Marshall detested Montgomery anyway and says that he:

> came pretty near to blowing off out of turn. Montgomery was criticizing the fact that he had been relieved from command, from active command as he called it... and I was under a terrific urge to whittle him down. And then I thought, now this is Eisenhower's business and not mine and I had better not meddle though it was very hard for me to restrain myself because I did not think there was any logic in what he said, but overwhelming egotism.[6]

Once again Monty's manner had got in the way of his case. There can be little doubt that much of what he was saying was true – no objective observer can seriously maintain that Eisenhower's time in command had been marked by any significant success and some changes at the very least should have been considered. But there remains Monty's abrasive manner and the fact that his valid points on current strategy – or the lack of it – were undermined because he linked them to the question of command, a matter on which Marshall and Eisenhower were adamantine.

The next event is a telegram message from Ike to Monty on 9 October, in which, after pointing out that the recent gales had drastically reduced the landing of supplies at Cherbourg, Ike continues:

> This re-emphasises the supreme importance of Antwerp... I must repeat, we are now squarely up against the situation which we have anticipated for months; our intake into the Continent will not support our battle. All operations will come to a standstill unless Antwerp is producing by the middle of November. I must emphasise that I consider Antwerp of first importance of all our endeavors on entire front from Switzerland to Channel. I believe your personal attention is required in operation to clear entrance.

If Eisenhower had indeed 'anticipated this situation for months', why had he not taken steps to remedy or avoid it? Only now, six weeks after taking the field command, did he order Montgomery to take 'personal charge' of operations to clear Antwerp. As the previous chapters have illustrated, while Antwerp appears in almost all Ike's directives, not until 9 October is it given priority over everything else. Generals and historians have argued this point, alleging that Ike was always stressing the importance of Antwerp. This is quite true, but Ike was also stressing the importance of the northern front, the Ruhr, the Saar, Aachen and, in mid-September, Market Garden, to which he gave priority over Antwerp. Once again, let us be clear on this point: if Eisenhower wanted Antwerp above these other objectives, he had to say so and issue the appropriate orders.

As related, after the 22 September conference, Montgomery had taken steps to involve Second Army with the clearance of the Scheldt, so the matter of opening Antwerp was already in hand at 21st Army Group, and the difficulties of that task have been described in Chapter 6. However, on 10 October Montgomery sent a detailed memorandum, *Notes on Command in Western Europe*, to Ike's Chief of Staff, Walter Bedell Smith. These notes are extensive and largely concern points already made but, having outlined his view of command

and strategy, Montgomery proposed three alternative solutions to the field command question:

A That the Supreme Commander himself should move his HQ to the northern front and take direct command of the operations against the Ruhr. Monty adds that 'whether this is possible I do not know. But I do know that the task is a whole time job for one commander and he must keep in close touch with the tactical battle', or:

B That C-in-C, 21st Army Group should be named as commander and C-in-C 12th Army Group should be placed under his operational command, or:

C That C-in-C, 12th Army Group should be named as commander and C-in-C 21 Army Group should be under his operational command.

In the case that Eisenhower opted for Alternative C, said Monty, 'I would be proud to serve under my very great friend, Omar Bradley.' Monty concludes these notes with a short summary, a series of points that clearly restate his views on command:

14. I do not believe it is possible to conduct operations successfully in the field unless there exists a good and sound organisation for command and control.
15. I do not believe we have a good organisation for command and control.

16. It may be that political and national considerations prevent us having a sound organisation. If this is the case I would suggest that we say so. Do not let us pretend that we are all right, whereas we are very far from being all right in that respect.

In that last sentence, Montgomery puts his finger on the nub of the problem affecting the Allied command. Political and national considerations *were* affecting the command issue and there is no need to debate the fact. Back in August, General Marshall had admitted as much, pointing out to Eisenhower that the US media, public and Washington politicians were demanding Bradley be freed from British control, and that Ike take personal charge of the land battle. It was largely for this reason that the Allied team, the one that had delivered victory in Normandy, was broken up without any apparent advantage to either the successful prosecution of the war or the troops in the field.

Putting national or chauvinist considerations aside for a moment, there is a serious point here. While the generals argued over strategy and command or who ran the show and got the credit, and the US generals and politicians insisted on taking charge of the campaign for reasons of national politics, ordinary soldiers – American, British, Canadian, French and Polish – were fighting and dying in the fields of Belgium and Holland – and far away in Germany the trains were still transporting Jews to the gas chambers.

If the current strategy and command was wrong, and if the reason for maintaining that posture was largely motivated by national and political considerations – and according to no less a source than General George C. Marshall, such considerations were paramount – then men were dying and the war was being prolonged for the wrong reason. Surely in the context of such a struggle it does not matter who was British and who was American – it only matters who was right. Men's lives were at stake here.

Three days later, on 15 October, Eisenhower replied to these notes, a long and detailed reply that Pogue describes correctly as 'one of Eisenhower's most explicit letters of the war.'[7]

This was another very detailed letter, rebutting most of Montgomery's arguments, agreeing with others and proposing that while Monty cleared Antwerp, Bradley's group took on the task of capturing the Ruhr. There was also a strong hint that Ike was becoming increasingly exasperated with Monty's continual carping – or he might have had word of that meeting with Marshall on 8 October.

'I am quite well aware', Ike wrote, 'of the powers and limitations of an Allied Command, and if you, as the senior commander in this Theater of one of the great Allies, feel that my conceptions and directives are such as to endanger the success of operations, it is our duty to refer the matter to higher authority, for any action they might chose to take, however drastic.'

Drastic action did not mean that the strategy would change: it meant that one of them would have to go and neither could be in any doubt that once the CCS got involved the one to go would be Montgomery. Montgomery duly replied to this missive on 16 October, and in conciliatory terms:

> You will hear no more on the subject of command from me. I have given my views and you have given your answer. That ends the matter and I and all of us

here will weigh in one hundred per cent to do what you want and we will pull it through without a doubt. I have given Antwerp top priority in all operations of 21 Army Group and all energies will be now devoted to opening up that place. Your very devoted and loyal subordinate, Monty.

Had Monty stuck to that resolve and said no more on the subject of command, he would have been spared a great amount of subsequent grief. For a short while at least, he seems to have realised that carping about the command and strategy was a waste of time: both might be wrong, or not as good as they might have been, but the European war was now an American show. Monty had stated his case but if Ike chose to ignore his advice, then he must take responsibility for whatever followed. Meantime, Monty got on with the war.

On the same day, Monty issued a new directive to 21 Army Group, stating that the free use of the port of Antwerp was vital and that while the task was already being undertaken by the Canadian Army, 'the whole of the available offensive power of Second Army will be brought to bear also.'

Two days later, on 18 October, came that Army Group commanders' conference in Brussels, to discuss the operations of the 12th and 21st Army Groups in the immediate future. The meeting began with consideration of a novel proposition; one option was to do nothing, to hold the ground already taken until Antwerp was open, build up the supplies throughout the winter and attack in strength along the entire front in the spring of 1945.[8]

It is hard to believe that Eisenhower, his staff and commanders gave serious consideration to this proposition. The days when the campaigning season was short and armies moved into winter quarters were long over – although the autumn and the coming winter would restrict operations, not least in air support, on which the ground forces had come to rely.

The new proposal was that 21st Army Group would first open Antwerp. Then, as soon as possible, hopefully sometime between the 1st and 5th November, the 12th US Army Group would commence operations aiming at a foothold over the Rhine, south of Cologne – in other words, east of Aachen, not via the Saar. To cover the flank of First Army during this advance, Bradley would put the newly arrived Ninth Army under Lieutenant General William Simpson on the left or northern flank, but at a time to be decided by Bradley, Ninth Army would turn north to clear the country between the Meuse and the

Rhine and might be placed under Montgomery's command. As soon as Antwerp was open, Second Army would turn south-east and clear the country south of Venray, a tidying-up operation by both armies, the Second Army attack to begin on or about 10 November.

Then came the big change of plan: '12th Army Group will have charge of operations for the capture or encirclement of the Ruhr. Ninth US Army will operate north of the Ruhr and First US Army south of the Ruhr.'

This change abandoned the notion that the Ruhr would be taken by a thrust across the Lower Rhine. The main effort would now be made by two US armies, attacking through the Aachen gap, with the Third US Army protecting their right flank: 21st Army Group would no longer be responsible for the capture of the Ruhr.

But however welcome to the Americans, this change of plan presented General Bradley with certain problems. To clear the Aachen gap, one of the most obvious routes to the Rhine and one of the early objectives in the Allied plan, post-Normandy, had already taken the best part of two months and a quantity of good men. A major breach had now been torn in the West Wall and First Army could now press on to the next obstacle, the River Roer, which lay some forty miles west of the Rhine. But there was inevitably a snag, or rather two snags. To get to the Roer the US First Army must – or felt it must – first clear the dark woods of the Huertgen Forest, south of Aachen. Secondly, something must be done about the Roer river dams.

The dams stood south of Aachen and controlled the waters of the Roer and Urft rivers. Although three of these dams lay on tributaries of the Roer they were known collectively as the Roer river dams. There were seven dams in all, of which the Schwammenauel and the Urft were the largest and most important. The tactical significance of the dams was this: whoever controlled the dams could release at will a flood that would inundate the entire Roer valley. If that happened during an Allied advance over the Roer to the Rhine, the Allied armies would either be drowned or completely cut off by rising floodwater. Therefore, no advance towards the Rhine south of Aachen was possible until the dams were either breached – and so deprived of their pent-up waters – or firmly in Allied hands. This was not the only snag: the most direct route towards the dams lay through the thickets of the Huertgen Forest.

The battles in the Huertgen Forest were so terrible and so prolonged that they will be covered fully in the next chapter. It is now time to cover the exploits of the rest of First Army in their battle for the Roer river, the next stage in this continuing struggle for the Rhine.

Bradley would have three armies for this task – Simpson's Ninth, Hodges' First and Patton's Third. The Ninth and First were to attack on 5 November, the Third on 10 November, the day on which the Second Army should be turning south-east from Nijmegen to link up with Ninth Army. This last attack was delayed because Montgomery elected to clear the Peel Marshes and this attack could not begin until 14 November.

Neither was it possible to return the US 104th or 7th Armored Divisions, which had been attached to the British VIII Corps. On 27 October two German divisions, 9th Panzer and 15th Panzer Grenadier, made a surprise attack on the 7th US Armored Division at Meijel. The 7th Division counter-attacked but then ran into another German attack and the Americans were driven back some six miles before the onslaught was stemmed by the commitment of the 6th Guards Tank Brigade and the 15th (Scottish) Infantry Division. Charles Farrell was with the Scots Guards Battalion of the 6th Guards Tank Brigade in this battle:

> Later in October the Battalion was involved with the 15th (Scottish) Division in holding a German attack which had come in against the US 7th Armoured Division. US opposition was weak against the counter-attacking German troops. When we first arrived on the scene the US infantry were pulling back in some disorder. Some of them were shouting that there were 50,000 Heinies between us and the river.
>
> In fact there were none. I quote this story to illustrate the point I have made elsewhere, that there were good elements and poor elements in all the formations fighting in north-west Europe.

This battle in the north kept the 7th Armored Division with VIII Corps until 8 November, when it was returned to Bradley's group and the task of finally driving the Germans away from the Maas was then delegated to the British 53rd and 51st (Highland) Divisions. The outcome of this unavoidable delay was that the main US attack east of Aachen went back to 16 November. Unwilling to wait that long, Bradley asked Patton when he could attack and the Third Army duly advanced on 8 November – and quickly ran into heavy opposition.

The German Armies were still increasing in strength and with the fall of Aachen the German command had little doubt where the next blow would come: a thrust to the Roer river was the most obvious possibility and the Germans mustered in strength to oppose it. By now OKW had raised no fewer than fifty volksgrenadier divisions and now had around thirty divisions, some volksgrenadier, some panzer, some regular Wehrmacht, behind the Roer – and Hitler was also actively raising a completely new army, the Sixth Panzer Army – with which he intended to launch a counter-stroke against the Allied line west of the Ardennes in December.

The sector opposite the US line was held by Model's Army Group B, consisting of the Fifth Panzer Army of General von Manteuffel and the Seventh Army of General Brandenburger. The dividing line between these two armies ran through the northern edge of the Huertgen Forest, so the Fifth Panzer Army faced the US Ninth Army and part of the VII Corps of First Army, while Brandenburger's Seventh Army faced the balance of the VII Corps and the V and VIII Corps.

Since the Normandy breakout the Germans had pursued a policy of compensating for declining manpower by increasing the amount of firepower – the provision of machine guns, mortars and artillery in the greatest possible numbers. The US History gives as an example the support available to an infantry division, the 3rd Panzer Grenadier, which had thirty-seven howitzers, seven nebelwerfers – multi-barrelled mortars – two 100mm cannon, eleven 88mm anti-tank or anti-aircraft guns, thirty-five assault guns and two tanks – and this is without the support it could also expect from corps or GHQ artillery.

However, First Army was also up to strength and in good fettle. Hodges had three armoured and nine infantry divisions in his three corps, plus a quantity of GHQ units, a total ration strength amounting to no fewer than 318,422 men.

Every corps was now allocated a task for the coming offensive. The VII Corps, now positioned in the foothills west of the Roer plain, was directed to advance on the Rhine at Cologne, and the V and VIII Corps were to support this drive with thrusts at Bonn and Koblenz. In addition, the V Corps was to cover the VII Corps right flank by establishing a line on the Roer – a move which became the disastrous preliminary attack on Schmidt by the 28th Division on 2 November. The VII Corps prepared two plans for this offensive, one based on 5 November, with three divisions, one for 15 November with four divisions

– assuming the 104th Division had been returned by then. This did not happen but the VII Corps duly attacked on 16 November.

Unfortunately, the weather intervened. It began raining on 11 November and rain continued to fall for the next week, turning fields into bogs, streams into torrents and rivers into wide floods. This effectively stopped the use of tanks, which could not manceuvre in the sodden fields and made the bridging of rivers impossible. Patton attacked anyway but, as will be described in a later chapter, without great success. The rest of 12th Army Group also advanced but, thanks to the lowering skies, without their anticipated and much-needed air support.

With the battle in the Huertgen left for the next chapter, this chapter can conclude with an account of the advance of the rest of First Army to the Roer at Duren, and that of the Ninth Army to that river at Julich. For the First Army this meant battling through the villages and the industrial complex around Eschweiler, and over the commanding height of the Hamich ridge, both of these being tasks for Collins' VII Corps.

The advance in the north of the corps area was made by Heubner's veteran 1st Infantry Division, which faced a seven-mile push to the banks of the Roer – and the Hamich ridge stood in the way. The advance duly began, but resistance was tough, with any shortfall in enemy artillery fire more than compensated for by an abundance of mortar fire, all directed by observers on the commanding Hamich ridge and in Hamich. By dawn on 17 November, the 16th Regiment, which had started on the previous day with around 160 men in each company, had two companies down to sixty and seventy men and another down to 100. The bulk of these losses were attributed to artillery fire – and no progress had been made towards Hamich. The 16th Infantry battered away at Hamich for three days, and finally took it, street by street, house by house, room by room, on 18 November. That night the enemy brought up a fresh division, the 47th Volksgrenadier, which mounted a counter-attack on Hamich and a nearby feature, Hill 232, but this attack, mounted with tank support, was beaten off by daylight on 20 November.

The 26th Regiment was meanwhile engaged on the right wing of the 1st Division, clearing a portion of the Huertgen Forest and enduring all the travails that went with that territory. On the first day the leading battalion made no more than a few hundred yards, shedding men at every step, fighting from clearing to clearing, forest ride to firebreak, overcoming bunkers hidden deep among the trees. Four days of fighting cost the 26th Infantry Regiment over 1,000 battle casualties and some 400 non-battle casualties, which, says the US History, 'though high by ordinary standards was about par for four days of fighting in the Huertgen Forest.'[9]

German resistance was not confined to the dreary woods south of Aachen: every part of the First Army advance was contested. In the Stolberg corridor even the use of tanks and tank destroyers did not speed up the advance of Combat Command B of the 3rd Armored Division, through the four heavily defended villages of Werth, Koettenich, Scherpenseel and Hastenrath, west of the Hamich ridge. This attack went in on 16 November and although the objectives were all taken by 18 November the cost was high: the infantry of CCB – a brigade group in British terms – had sustained fifty per cent casualties. Of sixty-four Sherman tanks committed to the advance, forty-four had been destroyed.

Matters had gone even more awry with the newly arrived 104th Division, which was tasked to clear the Eschweiler industrial area at the eastern end of the Stolberg corridor and on the northern flank of the VII Corps, where the division was charged with advancing astride the narrow Inde river and the Don-nerberg plateau. The 104th battered away at these positions for two days and 'made hardly a dent on the enemy's hold on the Donnerberg.'[10] However, the 104th's commander, General Allen, summoned more artillery support and attacked again on 18 November when, suddenly and for no apparent reason, the German defences on the Donnerberg plateau collapsed. Having lost the high ground, the enemy had no chance of holding Eschweiler and the 104th Division prepared to push on towards the Roer. Enemy resistance stiffened yet again and it would be well into December before the sorely-tried First Army moved up to positions on the Roer opposite Duren.

Matters had gone rather better in Simpson's Ninth Army, which from 16 November was pushing east towards Julich. Here too, the enemy was fully alert because, says the Ninth Army history, 'knowing how the attack must come, (he) had only to block it head on and inflict the maximum casualties.'[11] The setting for this attack was also obvious: the ten-mile wide gap in the West Wall between Wurselen in the south, on the boundary with First Army, and Geilenkirchen in the north on the boundary with the British Second Army.

The advance of the Ninth Army towards Julich, a distance of some seven miles, was not impeded by forests or hilly terrain. The obstacles here consisted of a thick network of villages, each with a population of around 1,000, each now a strongpoint. One of the first tasks was to reduce Geilenkirchen, a task taken on by the British XXX Corps, assisted by the US 84th Division. General Simpson had two Corps, the XIX and the XIII, and barely enough frontage to employ them, a rare event in the north-west Europe campaign.

The enemy defending this gap in the West Wall consisted of two divisions, 3rd Panzer Grenadier and 246 Volksgrenadier, which together could muster around 20,000 men, supported with plenty of artillery and a number of tanks. The 9th Panzer Division was in reserve a few miles behind the front and Geilenkirchen was protected by a strong anti-tank gun screen. By any standards, the advance on Julich would be a difficult proposition.

So it proved. The Geilenkirchen salient was attacked on 18 November and the problem of co-ordinating an attack by the British XXX Corps and the US 84th Division – codenamed Operation Clipper – was solved by attaching the 84th to XXX Corps for this occasion – an Allied operation which went very well. The 84th enjoyed the support of the abundant XXX Corps artillery, which was well supplied with ammunition, as well as the specialised armour of the 79th Armoured Division – mine-clearing flail tanks, flame-throwing crocodiles, pillbox-busting petard tanks – as well as that of the US 43rd Infantry Division, which attacked Geilenkirchen from the north. As usual when united in battle, the Allied soldiers, especially the British tank crews and the US infantry, got on well together, as David Taylor of the Lothian and Border Horse can confirm:

> We learned that the Americans were preparing to attack the Siegfried Line with all its dragon's teeth, fortifications and guns and we in our flail tanks were to lead the assault team. This was to be the first large-scale assault on German soil south of Geilenkirchen and B Squadron were to support the 84th US Division, which had only recently arrived from the States; C Squadron was to support the US 43rd Division and to support us we had the tanks of the Sherwood Rangers and others of the 79th Armoured Division.
>
> Next day we had a full dress rehearsal of two breaching teams to drive a path through the German lines called Red and Blue and we were to clear Blue to the west. All the tank radios were netted in and everything was made ready and we turned in early and awakened at daylight. At 0800hrs the attack was

postponed twenty-four hours because of the weather and how those hours dragged! No one felt like writing letters or anything and we ended up having a sing-song with the Americans. They were extremely generous and showered us with cigarettes and rations.

Time to go, 0300hrs, and we awoke to the sound of the guns; the Americans were giving it all they had and the air reeked with cordite. They were pounding the German defences as well as the town of Geilenkirchen and Sherman tanks of the Sherwood Rangers went ahead to batter a path through the trees so that the boom of the flails did not snag.

We moved forward, over tacky ground, leading the whole cavalcade and commenced flailing as we reached the edge of the enemy minefields. As we moved forward a line of shells was exploding, blinding our vision and at last we halted, the barrage ceased and a deathly hush descended with only the isolated bang of a German gun. After a short halt we went on again.

Men of the 84th Division were silently moving and crawling past us, down the side of the lane and it was not long before the Germans sighted them and mortar bombs came down. We had to completely close down for a while, for fear of a missile coming inside; the Americans were very grateful to have us with them and showered us with Lucky Strike cigarettes and rations.

It was later when we heard that Sergeant Mackie's tank had bellied on a mine that exploded under the tank, killing Trooper Walker, the driver and S. J. Clark, co-driver. The remainder of the crew were all wounded and evacuated to an American dressing station. Clark said to me on more than one occasion that war was for single chaps, not for married men with a family; he seemed to have a premonition that he might be killed.[12]

In spite of counter-attacks by the 9th and 10th Panzer Divisions the reduction of the Geilenkirchen salient was accomplished in 6 days and on 23 November, the 84th Division reverted to the command of the XIX Corps.

While all this was going on, the rest of the XIX Corps, consisting of the 29th Infantry and 2nd Armored Divisions, attacked in the south. At first the advance went well in spite of heavy and accurate artillery fire – and hidden anti-tank guns that quickly knocked out seven US tanks at the village of Apweiler in the 2nd Division area. The 29th Division, a unit that had landed on Omaha beach on D-Day, sent two regiments forward, the 115th and 175th, and met 'the most intense and accurate small arms fire I have ever encountered', according to one platoon commander. The problem here was the open ground and the numerous villages and farmhouses, each of which offered the other supporting defensive fire. It was impossible to concentrate on taking one strong-point without coming under fire from another one – the American infantry needed flamethrower tanks and petard tanks but did not have them and the first day's advance was limited.

Matters grew more fraught on 17 November, when Tiger and Mark V Panther tanks of the 9th Panzer Divsion and the 506th Heavy Tank Battalion entered the fray at Immendorf. These were immediately engaged by the Shermans of the 2nd Armored Divsion and a tank and anti-tank gun battle then went on for most of the day, during which one 2nd Division unit, Combat Command B, lost eighteen Shermans and had another sixteen damaged.

So began a series of tank and infantry battles across the Roer plain that continued until 9 December. It had taken twenty-three days to cover twelve miles from the start line and reach the River Roer – not the Rhine, which had been the original objective of this advance. Still twenty-five miles away, the Rhine seemed unattainable as ever. Nor had this advance been without cost: the Ninth Army had sustained some 10,000 casualties, including 1,133 killed. German losses were estimated at around 14,000, including over 8,000 prisoners.

Once again the offensive had not lived up to General Bradley's expectations. A month of hard fighting from 16 November had carried his corps and divisions, at considerable cost, an average of eight miles further into Germany. Now they stood on the Roer, but there was still that other problem, the one that inhibited any further advance: the looming presence of the Roer river dams. Hodges wanted to capture these dams and RAF Bomber Command had already attempted to breach them. Until those dams were breached or captured, Bradley dared not send his forces over the Roer – and in the attempt to reach those dams his forces were wasting themselves away in the dark green misery of the Huertgen Forest.

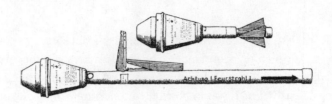

11 · THE HUERTGEN FOREST
OCTOBER – NOVEMBER, 1944

To break the winter stalemate… Bradley and Hodges flung troops into the
Huertgen Forest in a series of fruitless attacks… at a cost of thousands of casualties,
in what is often referred to as 'America's Passchendaele'.

CARLO D'ESTE, *PATTON: A GENIUS FOR WAR*

The battles for the Huertgen Forest are not much known in British military circles, largely because the Huertgen offensive was an exclusively American affair. In the US army the battles for the Huertgen Forest in 1944 count among the most notorious, difficult and bloody engagements in the entire history of the gallant and hard-fighting First Army during the European war.

In the first battle for Aachen, the Huertgen Forest, south-east of Aachen, was seen as blocking the way to the Roer river valley for the right wing – the 9th Division – of Lieutenant General Joe Collins' VII Corps. 'Lightning Joe' Collins had learned his Second World War battle craft in the jungles of Guadalcanal in the Pacific and was no stranger to fighting in close country, but that experience proved of little help in the Huertgen Forest.

Fighting in woods is always difficult. Visibility is restricted, fields of fire are narrow and short, and the advantage lies with the defender, who can remain well concealed until the attacker is almost on top of him. Shells and mortar bombs explode on contact with the branches, showering the men below with white-hot shards of jagged metal – the defenders in their bunkers and covered fox-holes are in a better position than the attackers moving in the open. Tanks have difficulty moving up in support and are often confined to narrow tracks or forest rides, which the enemy anti-tank guns and artillery will have ranged to the inch, while in the dense thickets roamed infantry equipped with machine guns and tank-busting panzerfausts.

Evacuating the wounded is difficult, communications sometimes impossible – add to this mines, pillboxes and bunkers, rugged terrain, rocks and mud, the relentless autumn rains, falling temperatures and the presence of a stubborn, tenacious enemy and it will be seen that the battle for the Huertgen Forest would be no easy affair.

This combination of evils turned the Huertgen Forest into a nightmare for the soldiers of the First Army. This attack – and a look at the map of the area south-east of Aachen – begs another question: why was the Huertgen Forest not simply ignored or pinched out? Why did First Army not surge powerfully east through the Aachen gap it had just fought so hard to clear? The short answer is that the way through the Huertgen Forest was the most direct route to the Roer River dams. Ignoring the Huertgen forest was not an option for the US First Army.

That at least is how Bradley, Hodges and Collins saw it. Besides, the open country east of Aachen between Stolberg and Dueren offered tactical problems – including many villages, farms and hamlets now turned into strongpoints – and could be flooded by opening or blowing the Roer dams. That much had been discovered in the first push through the Aachen Gap. These generals also saw the Huertgen as a threat that could not be ignored, the logical spot for the Germans to assemble strong forces and launch a counter-attack into the right flank of any US force passing through the gap.

In their eyes it was necessary to clear the Huertgen, whatever it cost. Unlike the fear of a flank attack that had inhibited Gavin and the 82nd Airborne at Nijmegen, there was some basis for believing that Germans in the Huertgen were in some strength, manning the bunkers and pillboxes of the Schill Line, that portion of the West Wall which ran through the Huertgen. Whether it was more advisable to attack with infantry rather than bomb the enemy senseless from the air is another matter.

Opting for a land battle was bound to be costly and in the end it cost a great deal; after the initial commitment of the 9th Division, four more US divisions, the 28th, 4th, 8th and 1st, suffered heavy casualties in the Huertgen and these losses fell almost exclusively among the front-line rifle companies, reducing many of them to no more than a handful of men. The Huertgen Forest ate up American divisions, starting with the 9th Infantry Division which in early October 1944 went forward to open a battle that displayed the dogged courage and tenacity of the American infantry soldier.

Various narrow, tree-lined roads ran through the Huertgen forest, most of them meeting in the hilltop village of Schmidt. Schmidt overlooked the defences in the Monschau corridor, that route south of the main Aachen line that had held up the VII Corps advance in September. With Aachen out of the way the next task was to take Schmidt and then clear the Monschau corridor, which VII Corps had worn itself out battering in October. That done, the VII Corps could then press on to the Roer and the Rhine – except for the small matter of the Roer river dams, which were still untaken and prepared for demolition. Taken all in all, the only obvious advantage of clearing the Huertgen Forest was the outflanking of the Monschau corridor: in every other respect getting involved in the Huertgen Forest would prove a costly mistake.

The prime task of taking Schmidt was given to General Craig's 9th Infantry Division. A regiment of this division, the 60th Infantry, had probed into the Huertgen in September but had got nowhere in the face of stiff opposition from the enemy – aided not a little by the thick belts of trees and the rugged terrain. Now the whole division would go forward – or rather two regiments of the division, the 60th and the 39th Infantry, would attack here. The third, the 47th Infantry Regiment, was kept back to hold a defence line further south. This was no great accretion of strength for such a task but American hopes were based on a supposed lack of German resistance and poor morale – two months of hard fighting since the Normandy breakout had as yet failed to convince the Allied commanders that the Germans would not be easily dislodged, however few their numbers, however certain their eventual defeat.

The G-2 of the 9th Division expressed this optimism. 'It is felt', he said, 'that should a major breakthrough occur, or several penetrations occur, the enemy will begin a withdrawal to the Rhine river, abandoning his Siegfried Line.' 'It was', says the US Official History, 'rather late in the West Wall fighting for this kind of thinking to persist.'[1]

This last comment understates the case. All previous experience since the breakout had shown the Germans would react quickly to any breach of their line, making local counter-attacks, or the hasty commitment of more troops – or both. Only when forced out of position by superior numbers or overwhelming firepower would they consent to withdraw, and fighting from prepared positions gave them a distinct advantage before they did so.

The man charged with defending the Huertgen Forest was General Schmidt, commander of the 275th Infantry Division and various other units, including the 353rd Division. These units were divisions in name only; though the 'ration strength' of a German infantry division was now around 9,000 men, by 3 October General Schmidt only had some 5,000 combat soldiers in the forest, but they were actively digging trenches, laying mines, stringing wire and felling trees to create strongpoints. A force reserve of around 1,000 men was constructing more fortifications further back, adding depth to the defence. The support weapons consisted of twenty artillery pieces of various calibre but as yet no tanks. However, since before Normandy the German Army had been increasing the number of machine guns and mortars at battalion level. These well trained infantry soldiers had their personal weapons for hand-to-hand fighting and the panzerfaust to cripple American tanks. Thus equipped they would put up a fierce resistance.

General Craig, the 9th Division commander, directed his two regiments to attack in line abreast, the 39th on the left, the 60th on the right. Their first task was to cut the main Monschau to Dueren road, south of the Huertgen, and get to the first major clearing in the forest on the road to Schmidt, a position just one mile from their start line. Preceded by air strikes, the advance began at 1130hrs on 5 October – and was in trouble within the first hour.

The 2nd Battalion, 60th Infantry, ran into a German outpost position, trenches and a bunker, that would take them a week to overcome and the battalion ended the first day with one company reduced to just two officers and sixty men – less than a third of its strength that morning. The 39th Infantry pushed back the first German outposts in its sector with some difficulty and the aid of man-packed flamethrowers against the bunkers, then came to a halt before the pillboxes and dugouts along the ridge above the Weiser Weh stream.

These pillboxes and well-concealed bunkers were just some of the difficulties. Keeping direction proved difficult in the thick woods, where only narrow paths led east. Any firebreaks were either blocked with felled trees or enfiladed by machine-guns. Worst of all was the constant shelling and mortaring, shells and bombs exploding in the tree tops, spraying shrapnel on the infantry below – a much smaller problem for the Germans, snug in their pillboxes and roomy dugouts and quite happy to call down fire on their own positions if the American soldiers got too close. As the day wore on the attackers' problems intensified; supplies could not get forward, grenades ran short, the wounded could not be evacuated and control of battalions, companies and platoons became more difficult. The fighting degenerated into small-scale but intense firefights between the entrenched enemy and squads, platoons and companies of these two US regiments, all too often fighting isolated battles with no means of finding or directing support.

These problems multiplied in the next few days with rising casualties, again largely among the rifle companies. 'Any numerical advantage the Americans might have possessed', says the Official History, 'lay in bug-eyed replacements, who began to arrive in small, frightened bunches.'[2]

The Huertgen battle was no place for a replacement soldier, nineteen or twenty years old, just arrived from the USA, barely out of recruit training and with no time to know his squad sergeant, the company officers, or even where he was or what was going on.

Eugene Robison describes his arrival in the front line:

> I arrived in the combat zone about noon on 16 November 1944. Fifty of us disembarked from trucks and stood about aimlessly in the yard of a house, which was battalion headquarters. An hour or so later a First Sergeant came out of the building and read off a list of names and said, 'You are in 'T' or 'K' or 'L' Company'. I was in 'L'. We climbed into the truck again and it took us to a small village. Here another First Sergeant ordered us to drop our duffle bags or packs, which we had carried since Fort Meade in Maryland. We never saw our duffle bags or packs again. That was our introduction to the war.[3]

Private Robison's experience was replicated all along the front that autumn and this rude welcome, though understandable in the conditions at the time, did these young soldiers no good. The front line is a lonely place for newcomers at the best of times; these were the worst of times and casualties duly soared.

The Germans were also receiving reinforcements and replacements, most of them battle-trained soldiers including, on 12 October, 2, 000 men of a well equipped and trained unit, Regiment Wegelein, half of them officer cadets, well able to handle the hard individual fighting in the dripping thickets of the forest. This first battle in the forest went on without pause for eleven days, until 16 October, by which time the 9th Division was both depleted and exhausted – but still fighting. No ground gained was given up but the cost was high.

In return for an advance of some 3,000 yards the 9th Division had lost 4,500 men, 90 per cent from the rifle companies. It was therefore decided that the 9th Division should be withdrawn from the forest and attached to Gerow's V Corps for rest and replenishment – itself a boon, as the normal practice at this time was to keep a unit in the line, topping it up with reinforcements – a method called 'trickle drafting', which is always expensive.

The task of reducing the Huertgen was then allocated to V Corps. Now the 28th Division, commanded by a D-Day veteran, Major General Norman D. Cota, came forward and took up the battle for Schmidt.

The US Official History draws attention to the curious fact that neither the American nor the German commanders fighting in the Huertgen paid much attention to the real objective of this battle, the Roer dams. Indeed, Colonel Carl L. Peterson of the 112 Infantry Regiment, 28th Division, the unit about to attack Schmidt, commented later that 'The Roer river dams never entered the picture.' By mid-October it appears that the current battle was to take the Huertgen, not the dams. Like some other Second World War battles, Cassino or Kohima for example, the battle in the Huertgen Forest was gathering its own momentum, becoming a private battle in a world divorced from its surroundings. Only those who fought there could know what it was like.

The battering handed out to the 9th Division encouraged General Gerow, the V Corps commander, to beef up the support offered to his 28th Division, which was reinforced with tanks and tank destroyers with Weasels – tracked vehicles – for supply and casualty evacuation. This attack would also be supported by fourteen batteries of artillery from the V and VII Corps, plus the usual air cover from fighter-bombers and medium bombers of IX Tactical Command. This was to become the theme in the story of the Huertgen – a gradual accretion of strength among the attackers, a gradual consolidation, thickening and improvement of the defences by the Germans.

There was also another problem, inherent in the orders handed to Cota by the corps commander: he was not able to deploy the whole strength of his division in one solid thrust for the objective. One regiment of the 28th Division was kept back to guard the start line and the northern flank of the proposed advance.

Another was to break into the village of Gemeter, three full miles north-west of Schmidt as the crow flies, and a good deal further on foot through the forest. That left just one regiment – three battalions – to take on the main task of the 28th Division, the capture of Schmidt village.

General Cota had by now had a look at the ground and became seriously concerned by the terrain, which the US Official History describes as 'startlingly assertive',[4] which is another way of saying 'simply terrible'. Steep slopes and sharp ridges ran everywhere and just to compound it all was the Kall trail, a deep ravine with a rushing river at the bottom, running across the divisional front and a great barrier to the passage of tanks. The Kall created a real problem, for it was becoming increasingly obvious that in spite of the difficulties inherent in using tanks in forests, the infantry in the Huertgen needed close tank support.

The second attack on Schmidt began on 2 November and lasted a full week, until 9 November. It was, at that time, the only attack being made along the entire First Army front, which now ran for 170 miles from the Maas, all the way to the junction with the Third Army near Metz. It is therefore hardly surprising that the Germans were fully aware that an attack in the Huertgen was imminent. They had a hot reception ready when Cota's men went forward.

In the north, the 109th Infantry launched their attack at 0900hrs on 3 November and immediately ran into minefields and strong opposition from enemy units that even appeared in the rear of their advance. After an advance of only 300 yards, a wide and totally unexpected minefield, closely sewn with anti-personnel mines, stopped the leading battalion and there they stuck, pinned and pounded by shells and mortar fire. On the following day the 109th attacked again, and again their advance was met with strong resistance and local counter-attacks. After a day of heavy fighting, attempting to get around the minefield, the regiment could do no more. After two days of hard fighting it had gained about a mile. During the next few days the 109th dug-in to hold what they had taken, enduring a steady stream of casualties from tree-bursting shells and mortar bombs.

Faced with this situation, Cota brought the rest of his division forward and put it into the drive for Schmidt. South of the 109th, the 112th Infantry Regiment was tasked with taking the town of Vossenack and part of the Vossenack ridge. The 2nd Battalion, 112th Infantry took Vossenack on 2 November and even got established on the ridge but on the following day, when the regiment attempted to cross the Kall trail and press on towards Schmidt, it was greeted with a storm of machine-gun and mortar fire and brought to a sudden halt. The last regiment, the 110th Infantry, was tasked to clear the woods alongside the River Kall, take the village of Simonskall and open a supply route for the advance on Schmidt.

The 110th Infantry had a terrible time, encountering the full range of Huertgen problems: mines, pillboxes, bunkers, air and tree bursts and, when they got to close quarters with the enemy, showers of German 'potato-masher' hand grenades and raking bursts of automatic fire. This account of the 110th's travails in the US Official History speaks for all the infantry units in the Huertgen at this time:

> No sooner had they risen from their foxholes than a rain of machine-gun and mortar fire brought them to earth. After several hours of costly infiltration, one battalion reached the triple concertina wire surrounding the bunker but the enemy gave no sign of weakening. Platoons got lost. Direct shell hits blew up satchel charges and killed the men who were carrying them. All communications failed. The chatter of machine guns and the crash of artillery kept frightened, forest-bound infantrymen close to the earth. In late afternoon the depleted units slid back to the line of departure.

This effort was also made without tactical air support: for the first three days of the seven-day battle for Schmidt, bad weather kept the Allied fighter-bombers on the ground. In spite of the intense opposition, by the early afternoon of 3 November the 112th Infantry had taken Schmidt, passing two battalions through Vossenack and up the Kall valley. Now they had to hang onto it when the inevitable counter-attacks came in – and clear the Kall trail as their supply route. Until they could do that, they were hanging onto Schmidt by their fingertips, with little chance to bring forward reinforcements or supplies, or evacuate the wounded.

That the Germans would counter-attack was inevitable. With the capture of Schmidt, the 28th Division had cut the German supply route to their positions in the Monschau corridor, and a strong reaction was not long in coming, led by tanks of the 116th Panzer Division and an infantry regiment of the 89th Division. The German attack was set for dawn on 4 November and to have any hope of beating it off it was essential that the 112th Infantry got some tanks into Schmidt. Unfortunately, wrecked tanks blocked the Kall trail and when the German counter-attack came in at 0730hrs it carried all before it: by mid-morning the

Germans were back in Schmidt. General Cota ordered an immediate counter-attack to retake the town but this proved impossible – it was all the 112th could do to hold their positions in the forest while preparing to attack again.

Close and heavy fighting went on outside Schmidt for the next two days. On 6 November, the 28th Division was reinforced by the 12th Infantry Regiment of the 4th Division, but this fresh unit did not arrive in time to prevent a near disaster on that same day at Vossenack, where the sorely-tried 2nd Battalion, 112th Infantry disintegrated, their fate giving a stark indication of what the Huertgen fighting could do to brave men. The US Official History records that:

> In this battalion, the company commanders reported that their men's nerves were shattered by the constant shelling and mortaring, that they refused to come out of their foxholes or eat – and that nobody was doing anything about it. The battalion commander was sitting in his command post, his head in his hands.[5]

When the German attack came in that morning, the 2nd Battalion fell apart, the men abandoning their positions and fleeing back to Vossenack. Fortunately, a platoon (troop) of US tanks and another of M-10 tank destroyers appeared at Vossenack and, with the assistance of the many 2nd Battalion soldiers who held their ground and two companies of the 146th Engineers – hastily converted into infantrymen – quickly stabilised the position.

The fighting for Schmidt went on until 10 November, when General Hodges moved the corps boundary yet again, shifting responsibility for the Huertgen from V Corps back to Collins' VII Corps. Another division, the veteran 4th Infantry, which had landed on Utah beach on D-Day, moved up and into the forest to add its blood and bones to the slaughter.

The US Official History describes this second battle for Schmidt as 'one of the most costly US division actions in the whole of World War II', and the casualty figures bear this out. In five days the 12th Infantry Regiment lost over 500 men – about 100 of these through frostbite and trench foot, a form of frostbite, for the weather was now adding to the travails of the infantry. The 112th Regiment lost 1,449 men killed, wounded or missing in seven days plus 544 'non-battle' casualties – also to frostbite and trench foot.

In total, the second attack on Schmidt cost the 28th Division 6,184 casualties. To put this in perspective, the two US divisions, the 1st and 29th, which landed on Omaha on D-Day lost over 4,000 men – and that was rightly considered a disaster. The 28th Division also lost sixteen out of twenty-four M-10 tank destroyers and thirty-one out of fifty Sherman tanks; German casualties in this period were assessed at 2,913. The tragic part is that the battle for the Huertgen Forest had hardly begun.

The next phase of the battle for the Huertgen began on 16 November and involved General Raymond Earton's newly committed 4th Infantry Division, another D-Day formation. The 4th Division had already committed one of its regiments, the 12th Infantry, to help the 28th Division and was tasked now with clearing that part of the Huertgen Forest between Schevenheutte and Huertgen and taking the town of Huertgen itself. That done, the division was then to advance to the Roer south of Duren – an optimistic forecast in the light of recent experience.

This task was part of a major VII Corps effort, involving the 1st, 4th and 104th Infantry Divisions and Combat Command 'R' (CCR) of the 5th Armored Division, an attack which aimed at reaching the open plain west of the Roer. This attack would be supported by 300 tanks, no fewer than thirty-two battalions of field artillery and, weather permitting, the largest number of ground-attack aircraft that Bradley could assemble.

The forces facing this attack, mostly from the German LXXXI (81st) Corps, were not numerous. This Corps had three divisions, none up to strength – Allied intelligence estimated that the Americans enjoyed a manpower superiority of five to one. The corps sector in the Huertgen was held by the 275th Division, and when the 4th Division attacked, this formation amounted to some 6,500 men, supported by 150 guns of various kinds and calibre. All these and the available infantry were well dug-in and ready for battle when the attack began on 16 November, the day that the exhausted 28th Division were pulled out of the line further south. This attack by the VII Corps was the main and latest effort of First Army in its continuing struggle for the Rhine, but most of that attack will be covered elsewhere: this chapter is concerned with the 4th Division's battle in the Huertgen, which will now be followed to its conclusion.

Let a front line soldier, Ralph Teeters of the 22nd Infantry Regiment, 4th Division, tell his story of the Huertgen battle:

> Our battle in the Forest began on 16 November. The Huertgen battle was marked by long evacuation routes and *tremendous* casualties. In our 22nd Regiment, the 2nd battalion once had three commanding officers in one day.

The Germans knew our routes and had the forest well mapped. Maybe our mistake was to follow the trails and firebreaks but a lot of times the casualties going back down the trail from Company HQ were more severe than those on the fighting line… the Germans had machine guns and mortars zero'd in on everything.

We faced more heavy and light machine guns, all the usual infantry weapons, but the worst was the tree bursts from mortar and artillery fire. The Huertgen was hell… it really was hell! The first day there our 3rd Platoon was sent forward to take a fire trail 200 yards ahead. All hell broke loose as soon as they got up to make the attack. We had been assigned as a mortar squad, at the time I was a mortar gunner, to back up the 3rd Platoon but the platoon leader had no use for our mortars – we could not set them up because we were under the trees and you need some clearing to fire. It was almost impossible to get food or rations up and I don't remember that we ever fired our mortars. It was a matter of hanging on, staying alive and all the time we kept getting replacements. They would come in at night and sometimes they would not last the day. That was when I realised that you did learn from some of this as the older guys seemed to survive better than the young ones.

So, anyway, by the end of the first afternoon we were stretcher-bearers, taking out the wounded. There were only five members of the 3rd Platoon left and it went in at full strength. Well, we thought, now we will be relieved, we were so decimated but instead fresh recruits were fed in and it didn't end until all this was over for us on 29 November 1944. There were a lot of people my age there but I aged very rapidly then. What I remember about that afternoon was not that I expected to be hit but when I would be hit and how badly I would be hurt. It didn't seem that anyone could live through that day.

We had about 2,500 replacements join the 22nd Regiment in the Huertgen in a regiment that probably had only 2,500 men in it at the start, so you can see how it was. When we got back to Luxembourg City we slept in beds, in houses, for the first time since Normandy and all those that had been in the Huertgen developed trench foot, which was very painful… but after a week or so, feet or not, we had to get going again, because of the Bulge.[6]

General Barton suffered his first reverse before his attack began when his 12th Infantry Regiment was taken away and sent to shore up the flank of the

28th Division. As described above, during that time the 12th Infantry had a very bad time, lost a considerable number of men, and did not return to the 4th Division until 10 November. On its return the 12th Infantry was immediately involved in a German counter-attack. Two companies were quickly surrounded and when two more companies broke through the German lines in an attempt to extricate them, the Germans let them through and closed in again: now four companies of the 12th Regiment were surrounded. These four companies could not be extricated from German encirclement for another three days.

Jack Capell was in the Forest with the 4th Division:

> There was a far better way to get the Roer dams than through the woods; had we stayed in open country there would have been no prolonged battle and yet we chose the tough way to do it. The only excuse I can think of is the notion that had we bypassed the Huertgen the Germans could have kept an army concealed there and hit us in the rear, but it was a disaster. The weather was terrible, the shelling was coming in and bursting in the trees and throwing shrapnel on anyone who was unlucky enough to be in its path and Germans could conceal themselves just a few feet away in the trees and you would not know they were there. I consider the decision to go into the Huertgen one of the major blunders of our army.

Losses continued to mount. When the Regimental commander of the 12th Regiment, Colonel James S. Luckett, counted his forces on 15 November he discovered that the last nine days had cost his regiment 1,000 men – about a third of its strength – and the main 4th Division battle had not even begun. By 20 November, Colonel Luckett had lost a further 600 men and on that day, for some reason – for no man could have done better – he was relieved of his command. It is pleasant to record that this fine officer was immediately given a regimental command in another division.

These losses in the 12th Regiment effectively left General Barton with two regiments – the 8th and 22nd – to complete the divisional task: to clear the forest on a four-mile front, make an advance of some three and a half miles to the edge of the forest and then press on a further three and a half miles to the bank of the Roer. This would have been a difficult task in any circumstances but Barton compounded the problem by electing to attack in what were, in effect, two regimental columns. The 8th Infantry would move on the left, hugging the boundary with the 26th Regiment of the 1st Division and heading in the general direction of Dueren. The 22nd Regiment was to push through the three-mile gap in the divisional centre, between the 8th and 12th Regiments, exit the forest and also head for Dueren. The US History records that this tactic had already been tried by the 9th and 28th Divisions; they had discovered that 'to send widely-separated columns through the forest was to invite disaster.'[8]

The History also records that General Barton did not like this tactic either and criticised the way his commanders carried it out: 'They are going about the attack in the wrong way, running down roads instead of advancing through the woods, buttoned up, yard by yard.' This may have been so, but the regimental commanders had little choice: they had been given wide fronts – three miles of 'jungle' for the 22nd Regiment alone – and either had to cover those fronts or have their flanks exposed to enemy infiltration, which took place all the time anyway. In fact, one of the nightmares of the Huertgen fighting was that there was no front – the enemy could appear from any direction, at any time.

The 4th Infantry Division duly attacked on 16 November and – with Ralph Teeters' account as a particular example – what happened can be quickly told, a repetition of all the previous experience. The 8th Infantry attempted to break through its first obstacle, the steep, wooded ground around the Weh creek, but found it strewn with schu mines, the undergrowth laced with barbed wire thickets ten feet high, and the whole area under incessant mortar and machine-gun fire. The leading battalion assaulted the German positions on the Weh creek three times that day and lost 200 men in the first two hours.

Several miles away and deeper in the forest, the 22nd Regiment battered away at the enemy positions along the Raven's hedge. By nightfall they had not managed to take this position largely because the task involved crossing several wide firebreaks, all heavily mined, covered by machine guns and pinpointed by artillery and mortar fire. In the first three days of this attack, the 22nd Regiment lost 300 men – including all three battalion commanders, half the company commanders and an excessive number of company officers and NCOs. The close-quarter nature of the fighting and the need for company officers and even battalion commanders to work well forward, simply to retain some measure of control, contributed to this figure. There was a further problem: all three regiments had open flanks, ideal for infiltration, an opportunity the enemy did not fail to take.

By 18 November it was obvious that no matter how difficult providing it might be, the infantry needed tank support. The engineers came up to blast paths though the trees, the forest rides became tank routes, for only when accompanied by tanks blasting away at the undergrowth with their machine guns and main armament was any significant penetration achieved – and that at some cost and not for long: enemy counter-attacks continued. There were now other problems: getting supplies up to the leading companies, evacuating the wounded, and the arrival of enemy reinforcements. To ease the first two, the advance halted for twenty-four hours on 19 November but also on that day German reinforcements arrived in the 275th Division area. These came from the 344th and 353rd Divisions and their arrival was quickly felt. Resistance stiffened and American casualties mounted, particularly in the 22nd Regiment.

By nightfall on 20 November it was clear to all that the 4th Infantry Division had shot its bolt but could not yet be relieved. So far, in return for an advance of less than a mile and a half, the division had lost 1,500 battle casualties and several hundred more to trench foot, exhaustion and battle fatigue. These losses had been made up with a stream of replacements but, as already noted, the Huertgen battle was no place for raw troops – especially in such numbers. In November alone the 4th Infantry Division received no fewer than 170 replacement officers and 4,754 men. Integrating these new arrivals into the existing platoons and squads was far from easy.

'When I get new men in the heat of battle,' records one infantry sergeant, 'all I have time to do is impress them with their platoon number and tell them to get into the nearest hole and move when the rest of us move.' The inevitable result of this was that men were coming into the line, being wounded and evacuated, sometimes within hours and often without knowing what battalion they had joined or where they had been fighting. 'Green' troops tend to stick together in close groups for mutual comfort and support – this is never a good thing to do, but was especially dangerous under the plunging artillery and mortar fire in the Huertgen.

After two weeks in the Huertgen Forest the 4th Division had advanced a little over three miles and sustained no fewer than 4,053 battle casualties – of which 432 had been killed – and some 2,000 non-battle casualties, caused by trench foot, frostbite or sheer exhaustion.

First Army Headquarters therefore decided that responsibility for clearing the forest should be passed back to V Corps, which took over the Huertgen battle by committing the 8th Infantry Division to the assault in the area of the Weisser Weh valley, tasked to beat a path towards the town of Huertgen. So yet another US division took up the pitiless struggle in the forest, opening their battle at 0900hrs on 21 November when the now-familiar pattern of events soon reappeared.

The attack of their leading regiment, the 121st Infantry, was preceded by a strong artillery bombardment, but when the infantry went forward they ran into mines, mortar and artillery fire, bunkers and barbed wire. On the first day the only company to make any progress advanced just 500 yards. The 121st kept plugging away for the next three days and never recorded a daily advance of more than 600 yards, even with the assistance of tanks – and the weather, always poor, continued to deteriorate, with freezing night-time temperatures and snow flurries.

The 121st Infantry continued to batter its way towards Huertgen town, assisted by tanks of the 10th Tank Battalion, but their progress was not quick enough to prevent the Regimental Colonel, John R. Jeter, being relieved of his command – having himself recently relieved one of his battalion commanders and two company commanders. In 1944, the US army was very quick, perhaps too quick, to replace commanders perceived as failing, whatever the situation. Fortunately, Colonel Jeter, a perfectly competent officer, was soon given another regimental command.

The town of Huertgen fell to the 121st Infantry on 26 November, but the struggle promptly shifted on to Kleinhau, a village one mile further north. So the slogging battle continued until 8 December, by which time casualties in the 8th Division had exceeded 4,000 men... and still the battle continued.

The fight for the Huertgen Forest ended, or rather petered out, in early December, after the 1st Infantry Division had come in to take up the contest and effect the final push of the First Army across the Roer plain towards Dueren. This involved more stiff fighting in those dense and dripping thickets and a final struggle for the village of Merode, on the eastern edge of the Huertgen, a place defended by a small force of German parachute troops and the scene of yet another American tragedy.

Merode was attacked by a battalion of the 26th Infantry, 1st Division, but the two companies which got into the village were promptly engulfed in a German counter-attack. Their fate was picked up on the battalion radios:

There is a Tiger tank coming down the street now, firing his 88mm into every house. He is three houses away now... here he comes.

From the two companies in Merode that day only twelve men under a sergeant made their way back to the regimental lines.

The men of the 4th Infantry Division were taken out of the forest and sent to recuperate in Luxembourg arriving there just in time to get piled into trucks and sent up to the Ardennes battle, which began on 16 December – but all those who survived recall the Huertgen as the worst fighting in their considerable experience. In all, five American infantry divisions and dozens of attached units – tanks, artillery and engineers – had been engaged in the Huertgen Forest since the 9th Division first went into the trees in mid-September. Total losses, killed and wounded, exceeded 30,000 men, an average of 6,000 per division.

Later on, many questions would be asked about this terrible three-month-long struggle. Why was it undertaken? Was this the only way to reach the Roer and the Rhine? Did not the cost outweigh any possible advantage and, above all, what was the Huertgen Forest battle *for*? The US Official History is especially critical of this battle. Even after assessing the alleged benefits, that the First Army had conquered a formidable barrier by frontal assault and destroyed a number of German divisions including some destined for the forthcoming offensive in the Ardennes, the Official History concludes:

> Beyond these the fight had achieved very little. The basic truth was that the fight for the Huertgen Forest was predicated on the purely negative reason of denying the Germans use of the forest as a base for thwarting an American drive to the Rhine.[9]

When the losses were added up, the Official Historian calculated that 120,000 men were committed to the Huertgen fighting, plus an unknown number of replacements. More than 24,000 became casualties and no fewer than 9,000 fell victim to exhaustion, frostbite or trench foot – a total of 33,000 men, most of them from the rifle companies. That same historian, Charles B. MacDonald, a man who fought in the Huertgen as an infantry officer, winning the Silver Star, wrote later that the Huertgen fight was 'a misconceived and basically fruitless battle that should have been avoided.'[10]

12 · PATTON AND PATCH
NOVEMBER 1944

*Although he would not hear of it, Patton was not the victim of Eisenhower
or Montgomery, but of the broad front strategy and a logistics system that was
simply incapable of keeping pace with rapid mobile war.*

CARLO D' ESTE, *PATTON: A GENIUS FOR WAR*

Before proceeding to the final act of this five-month battle for the Rhine – the
German counter-offensive in the Ardennes – it is necessary to take a closer look
at the actions and activities of General Patton's Third Army and briefly discuss
the two armies, one French, one American, in Devers' 6th Army Group. The
latter units and their generals have not figured largely in this narrative because,
being supplied via the Mediterranean ports, they were not hampered by the
chronic logistical problems affecting the 21st and 12th Army Groups, and Devers
wisely played little part in the other autumn campaign – the bitter war of
argument between the generals.

Not so George Patton. Patton was a constant presence during this time, his
actions and demands cropping up for attention in the highest circles. It should
be remembered that Patton was an *Army* commander, in theory no more
important in the Allied command set-up than the other Army commanders like
Hodges or Dempsey, Simpson or Patch… or so it might seem. What makes
Patton a major player in both campaigns, the actual fighting and the on-going
arguments over strategy and command, relate more to his reputation than to
his actions, less to what he did than what he was, as much to his public persona

as his exploits in the field. This being so, another look at Patton is required.

Patton was the media man's dream just as he was, with his in-built gift for the occasional indiscretion. Inevitably, the press loved him and recorded his doings and sayings with glee. His peers or superiors did not always share this delight, but it made the Third Army commander a major player in the European theatre. Everyone had heard of George Patton.

Patton had an equally high profile in the USA. To most of the American public in 1944, apart from Ike, George Patton was the only general racing across Europe, carrying all before him. This was also Patton's opinion. Since the Normandy breakout he had been convinced, and had been trying to convince others, that if only he was given the supplies, he would breach the West Wall, cross the Rhine and win the war. The snag, at least according to George Patton, was that Eisenhower – 'the best general the British have' – and Field Marshal Montgomery kept getting in the way.

When considering his military ability, the fact that Patton was an Anglophobic racist who consistently undermined his superiors' intentions has to be put on one side. Patton was a soldier, and if his reputation has been somewhat inflated by his numerous admirers, it cannot be denied that he had the soldier's first requirement – he was always ready for a fight.

Unlike Montgomery, Patton was neither universally popular nor widely respected by his troops. The *Stars and Stripes* cartoonist, Sergeant Bill Mauldin, regarded Patton as a figure of fun and guyed him constantly in his cartoons – which Patton did not find funny. Jack Capell, of the 4th Infantry Division, who served briefly in Patton's army after serving in Bradley's First Army, remarks:

> We had heard this rumour that General Patton had swum across the Saar river to get at the Germans, but I never met anyone who saw this feat so it was probably the invention of his fertile publicity team. We in the 4th Division were not admirers of General Patton. He was an accomplished battlefield commander but more reckless with the lives of his men than other commanders we had served with.[1]

Another dissenting voice comes from John Price of Astoria, Oregon:

> During the war I was personnel adjutant of the 33rd Armored Regiment, of the 3rd Armored Division of 1st Army. The 3rd Armored Division was the

spearhead of the 1st Army, commanded by General Courtney Hodges. General Hodges has yielded all the headlines to General Patton, whose 3rd Army was in a secondary role.

You will be doing a great service if you can correct the public and media perception that General Patton won the war in Europe… and that if Patton had only been given the go-ahead and the gasoline he would have been in Germany with the spring flowers.

It is hard to avoid the conclusion that Patton was a disloyal subordinate and an indifferent colleague, but the real argument here rests on whether he was right in his belief that, if properly supplied and supported, Third Army could have played the decisive part in the current campaign for the Rhine. The evidence is against him. Patton had been promising wonderful things since the Normandy breakout, but in the event proved no more successful than anyone else in the four-month battle for the Rhine.

Patton's army made ground. That made headlines and those advances showed up as great, sweeping arrows on newspaper maps. The reasons for that rapid taking of ground – while other commanders seemed bogged down in stalemate – were not often discussed. Few people queried if Patton's advances east of Paris were not merely irrelevant but, in the context of Eisenhower's somewhat evasive strategy, actually counter-productive.

The previous chapters have illustrated some of the effects of Patton's actions: now it is necessary to see whether he was successful in his own terms, whether he ever did all the things he claimed he would do. To do that it is necessary to go back to the Normandy breakout, at the end of August 1944, and study Patton's actions in some detail.

During that breakout Patton's Third Army moved east, just north of the River Loire, at some speed, capturing Orleans on 17 August, then crossing the Beauce to Troyes and pushing on via Chalons, St-Dizier and Chaumont towards Lorraine and the southern gateway to the Reich, the Saar. By the end of the month he was heading for Metz, the fortress city on the Franco-German frontier.

These fortress cities of the First and Second World Wars were not like medieval strongholds – they were the centrepiece of a network of fortifications covering many miles and acted as a bulwark before the main West Wall defences. The point is that Patton was heading east, while the bulk of the Allied forces were pursuing the enemy to the north – and the glittering prize of this campaign, a Rhine crossing and the capture of the Ruhr, lay in the north. By any objective standard, Patton's task in the Saar was a secondary objective.

Patton's rapid advance was largely due to the fact that the German forces in front of him were few in number and in full retreat. Against such scant opposition, any general would have done equally well – but it looked very good in the newspapers. Patton was advancing so Patton should be allowed to go on advancing – even in the wrong direction.

The problem with Patton's advance was that even if he succeeded in reaching the Rhine – which was the aim of every army commander at this time – the next objective was the Ruhr. To get there Patton would have to turn north and head up the narrow and highly defensible Rhine valley to Bonn and Cologne, with his flanks fully exposed all the way. While taking the Saar would be useful, taking the Ruhr was essential, and if taking the Saar inhibited steps towards taking the Ruhr, the Saar operation must be stopped.

In early September, as related, Patton was stopped and remained stopped for several days by a shortage of fuel. At this time Patton had three corps under command but only two, Walker's XX Corps and Eddy's XI Corps, were in the east: the VIII Corps, commanded by Lieutenant General Troy Middleton, was still in Brittany and would soon become part of Simpson's Ninth Army, to Patton's understandable annoyance. The problem was not a shortage of troops – in September Patton commanded some 315,000 men. The problem was logistics. To keep going at this recent rate Patton's divisions needed 350,000 gallons of fuel every day but they were only getting around 200,000 gallons a day,[2] and a single armoured division could use 100,000 gallons a day in cross-country fighting.[3] When the fuel ran out, the advance stopped.

Needless to say, Patton blamed Montgomery for this shortfall, but the real reason lay in Eisenhower's broad front strategy and the need to supply the other armies north of the Ardennes. Before his gas ran out, Patton had envisaged bouncing the West Wall and stated that he saw his army crossing the Rhine in mid-September.[4] Indeed, at a meeting with Eisenhower, Bradley and Hodges at Verdun on 2 September, he claimed – incorrectly – that Third Army already had patrols at Metz and on the Moselle.

Nancy fell in mid-September but Metz, heavily fortified before the First World War, proved a far tougher nut to crack, especially after the Germans occupied the Metz defences in strength. Metz finally fell on 22 November, nearly three months after Patton first invested the defences, but the surrounding forts were not completely subdued until 13 December, three days before the start of the German counter-offensive in the Ardennes.

The Third Army had captured Verdun on 1 September. Patton then stood just thirty-five miles from Metz and seventy miles from the West Wall; both of these positions were currently short of troops. Had Patton had the fuel to continue this advance his claim to Bradley – 'Just give me the fuel and I will put you inside Germany in two days' – may have had some validity. But the logistical situation affected all the Allied commanders, not just Patton, and the decision on which army got what was Eisenhower's. In the event, Patton's army was grounded until 5 September. On that day General Walker returned to XX Corps headquarters and told his troops that Patton's new orders 'will take us all the way to the Rhine.' The XX Corps' first target was the River Saar, some thirty miles to the east, bypassing the fortress of Metz, after which it would proceed to the Rhine at the city of Mainz.

Bradley wrote later that the failure of his armies to speed into Germany in mid-September was due to the fact that his fuel supplies had been cut off when aircraft bringing up fuel were diverted to Market Garden – in other words it was Montgomery's fault.[5] The US historian, Charles B. MacDonald, feels that this claim is 'matter of conjecture':

> The halt of both the First and Third Armies in mid-September cannot be attributed specifically to the lack of everyday supplies an airlift might have provided. The halts were due more to a combination of many causes, among them the rugged terrain along the German frontier, the presence of the West Wall, the exhaustion of American combat units, the worn out condition of their equipment, the rebirth of German strength and, it has been argued, the thinly spread formation in which American troops approached the German frontier.[6]

Once on the move again, Patton's Lorraine campaign experienced mixed fortunes. Here as elsewhere the Germans had regrouped and by mid-September were fully back in the fight with a rebuilt formation, the Fifth Panzer Army of Normandy fame. This consisted of three Panzer Grenadier divisions and four Panzer brigades – this latter amounting to slightly more than a division. The Fifth Panzer Army commander, Hasso von Manteuffel, had been ordered by

Hitler to attack 'regardless of loss, deep into the American east flank, attacking in a north-western direction from the Epinal area':[7] in other words, into the right flank of Patton's army thrusting for the city of Nancy, the capital of Lorraine, in order to roll it up.

Mantueffel tried. His armour advanced in strength on 17 September but was driven off by the aggressive tactics of Eddy's XII Corps and in particular by the magnificent performance of Wood's 4th Armored Division which, in four days of heavy fighting at Arracourt, inflicted heavy losses on the German forces, destroying a large number of Manteuffel's precious tanks.

Patton had gained a bridgehead or two over the Moselle south of Metz, but for the first time his forces were now running into fierce opposition. This resistance had its inevitable consequence – the Third Army advance stalled, not through any particular shortage of supply but because the enemy on its front had stopped retreating. Patton himself records that the fighting around Luneville was 'as bitter and protracted fighting as I have ever encountered', and matters were not to get any better in the weeks ahead.

After their defeat at Arracourt, the Fifth Panzer Army returned to the fray on 25 September, putting in strong attacks that were not driven off until the end of the month. These attacks had not given the Germans their expected victory, but they had halted Patton's sweeping advance.

German resistance was not the only problem: the weather was increasingly vile and a combination of these two elements meant that progress was slow. It took Patton a full month of hard fighting to cover those thirty miles to the Saar river – not the couple of days he had promised Eisenhower – and the defences of the West Wall then stopped the Third Army in its tracks.

Nor were matters going any better at Metz, which Patton had hoped to capture in ten days. Metz was the centre of a wide defensive ring of fortifications, embracing some thirty-five entrenched forts, first created by the Germans after the Franco-Prussian War, expanded during the First World War and still a formidable obstacle in 1944, even for XX Corps and every spare gun and round of ammunition that Patton could find. It is at least arguable that reducing the Metz fortifications was a task for the entire Third Army and not a single corps, but Patton could not accept that. The delay at Metz did not play well with Patton. Unable to accept that the conditions of war applied to him as much as to anyone else, he blamed Montgomery, Bradley, Eisenhower and

COM-Z general, J. C. H. Lee, for his present travails and their lack of support.

By the time of the 18 October conference in Brussels, little progress had been made in Lorraine. Patton's army was still battling for the Saar and Metz and the Lorraine campaign was turning into a costly waste of resources. That conference decided Montgomery and Bradley were to attack at Nijmegen and Aachen in early November, but no date was set for Patton's advance, which, said Eisenhower in his directive of 28 October, would be resumed 'when logistics permit', adding that Patton's advance would be 'subsidiary to and so timed as to best assist the main effort in the north.'

Patton did not care for either restriction, and events played into his hands. The offensive in the north was to have started on 10 November but, as related, on 27 October the Germans launched a surprise attack east of Eindhoven, on the positions of the US 7th Armored Division, which was still attached to Second Army. This attack delayed the opening of Montgomery's offensive to clear the area south of the Maas, and Monty could not return two US First Army divisions that had been attached to Second Army to assist in this move. Without their return, Bradley felt unable to launch his attack east of Aachen on 10 November, so his attack was put back to 16 November.

Patton's Army was ready to move so, on 2 November, Bradley authorised an advance by Third Army, 'as soon as the weather improved'. Patton was delighted to be let off the leash, assuring Bradley that this time he would take the Saar and breach the West Wall 'in three days'. Patton certainly had the strength to do so: his force consisted of six infantry and three armoured divisions plus other attached units, a total of over 250,000 men. Opposed to this was the German First Army with some 86,000 men covering a front of some eighty-five miles, and the only German reserve was the 11th Panzer Division with sixty-nine tanks.

Patton's plan called for Eddy's XII Corps to open the attack with an advance from Nancy towards the Saar, his advance supported by a massive air strike by 1,300 heavy bombers. A day later, Walker's XX Corps would strike out for Metz, capture the city and its surrounding fortifications, and so clear the way for an advance to the West Wall, north of the Saar. If all went well, Patton, as he promised Bradley, fully expected to reach the Rhine in a matter of days. This was a window of opportunity for Patton, a chance to forge ahead and get fully involved before Hodges' or Dempsey's forces crossed their start lines.

The problem was the weather. Patton had decided to open his attack on 8 November, but the rains came on 5 November and fell in torrents, turning fields into swamps and rivers into impassable floods. On 7 November, Eddy suggested to Patton that his attack be delayed, at least until the rains stopped, but Patton dared not wait. Eddy was promptly told to either attack... or name his successor.

Eddy attacked next morning, though the promised air support was grounded by the weather until late in the afternoon. Eddy sent in his three infantry divisions, which made slow progress through the mud and flooded fields, while the supporting tanks could not move off the road. As a result the attack stalled, and though Eddy pressed his attack for the next two days he was unable to achieve much in the existing conditions. Meanwhile, his troops suffered severely from trench foot and exposure, from an abundance of mines, from mortar fire and artillery, and the usual, dogged, skilful German resistance. In eight days of constant battle General Eddy advanced exactly eight miles.

This failure had a number of causes, some of which have been listed above. The biggest was Patton's failure to concentrate on one objective; instead he opted for a widespread attack on both Metz and the Saar, attacks that the enemy, aided by the weather and the ground, was easily able to blunt.

The need to concentrate their forces was a lesson Patton and Bradley should have learned in Normandy. Now, four months later in Lorraine, Patton made the same fundamental mistake, distributing his forces too widely, thereby enabling inferior numbers of German troops to fend off his advances and inflict heavy casualties at the same time.

Nor was this the only problem confronting the Third Army during this damp November. It was also short of artillery ammunition and, amazingly, of manpower, largely because Patton had been prodigal with both assets in recent weeks. Patton's Lorraine offensive was using up the available stocks of artillery ammunition faster than they could be replaced, and in November Eisenhower was obliged to make a special broadcast to munitions workers in the USA, urging them to increase production.

The shortage of artillery ammunition is an indication of how much the north-west Europe campaign had changed. In September, when the armies were advancing, the cry had been for fuel and more fuel. Now the Allied armies were being held everywhere, and the requirement was for artillery ammunition to beat down the German defences, to match the German advantage in automatic infantry weapons with an abundance of shellfire.

The simultaneous manpower shortage was the result of the tactic adopted by the US commanders, their conviction that the best way to win a war was to attack the enemy everywhere and all the time, accepting heavy losses in the short term in the belief that this would end the war quickly and so save lives in the long run. By the close of 1944, the American experience in Europe should have led to a reassessment of this theory. The inevitable result of this tactic was that casualties mounted swiftly and steeply, while the replacements for these losses were not well integrated with their new units or adequately trained on arrival. Losses therefore rose yet again, reaching 90 per cent or more among the ranks and even higher among the officers. This was unsustainable even to a well-populated nation like the USA.

The need to find infantry soldiers led to the introduction of black American soldiers into US combat units for the first time since the Civil War. Unlike many of their white comrades, these black soldiers volunteered in considerable numbers for combat duty and did very well in the field. It is also pleasant to record that Patton, a man fully equipped with racial prejudice, welcomed these Afro-American soldiers, declaring that 'he did not care what colour a man was, provided he could soldier.'

The shortages of men and ammunition did not help Patton with his Lorraine offensive or Bradley with his attacks east of Aachen. By the time the First and Ninth Armies opened their attack towards the Roer river on 16 November, Patton's attack, from which so much had been expected – and been promised – had already stalled. Since the end of August Patton had been promising that he would have Metz, the Saar, the West Wall, and probably the Rhine in a matter of days. Two and a half months later none of these objectives had been taken or were in any danger of being taken.

The reasons for this failure are much the same as those given for the failure of other parts of Eisenhower's broad front strategy: Eisenhower's constant vacillation; logistics; the weather; failure to concentrate; the enemy's resistance; the lack of a strategic plan. The point here is that, in spite of all his bluster, Patton had done no better than anyone else – and weakened Eisenhower's strategy in the process.

This is not chauvinism. The Lorraine campaign is widely regarded as a disaster, even among US historians. Patton's biographer, Carlo d' Este, writes that Patton:

> ... had failed to concentrate his forces for a decisive attack that might have taken Metz, then refused to accept that he had anything to do with that setback. A series of piecemeal attacks were nothing more than a return to the penny-packet warfare that had fared so badly in North Africa. In short, instead of the hoped for triumph, Lorraine became Patton's bloodiest and least successful campaign.

Nor were the Germans any more charitable. When Metz finally fell on 22 November, after heavy fighting in the streets of the town and the tunnels of the fortifications, the commander of the defenders, Lieutenant General Hermann Balck of Army Group G declared that the German success in defending the city for so many weeks was due to 'the bad and timid leadership of the Americans', a comment that would have cut Patton to the bone. There was also the cost; the three-month Lorraine campaign cost the Third Army no fewer than 50,000 casualties, about one third of all the casualties Third Army sustained in the entire European war.

A fair conclusion from all this is that Patton's efforts from August to December 1944 made no great contribution to the Allied cause and we would be right in that conclusion: his campaign for the Saar and the Rhine was longer on sound and fury than on useful results.

A summation of the Allied position at this time is not complete without reference to the other Army Group currently engaged in this Rhine campaign, Lieutenant General Jacob Devers' 6th Army Group, now battling in Alsace and the Vosges, on the southern wing of Patton's army. The 6th Army Group, then known as the Dragoon Force, had landed in the south of France on 15 August. Its task was to open the ports of Toulon and Marseilles and then advance up the Rhône valley to join up with the eastern flank of the Overlord forces – Patton's Third Army. Among these soldiers was Bill Everett, an officer in the 36th Infantry Division:

> My unit landed on Blue Beach, the only really hot beach on 15 August, the Southern France invasion. We fought our way north to cut Jerry off at Montelimar and were in constant contact with Jerry until October in the Vosges

mountains. From 15 August until October I had no clothes change and we were short of everything, including sleep, until I was hospitalised after we crossed the Moselle.

The French landed after the beaches were secured and went west towards Marseilles and we raced for the Belfort gap in the north. As we passed the Jura mountains we were turned east to cut off the German Nineteenth Army, led by the 11th Panzer Division, and our battalion was ordered to cut the escape route at La Coucorde, with my company leading the assault.

I was in command, having commanded the company from Blue Beach on, but a few hours before this attack we received a new commander, a captain; he was killed before noon and I was in command again. We suffered heavy casualties and the only officer left who had landed with me on Blue Beach was also killed. The 11th Panzer Division did not even change gears; they ran right over us. *C'est la guerre.*[8]

Dever's advance was rapid: two weeks after coming ashore the 6th Army Group, assisted by tens of thousands of the FFI – the Forces Françaises de l' Interior, the Maquis, or Resistance – were in Lyon, halfway up the Rhône valley, driving the German Nineteenth Army before them.

The 6th Army Group consisted of the US Seventh Army under Lieutenant General Alexander Patch and the French Army B, commanded by General Jean de Lattre de Tassigny. At the start of September this Army Group, which came under Eisenhower's control on 15 September, was tasked to pursue the enemy into Burgundy on the line Autun–Dijon–Langres, and thence into Alsace and the Vosges, heading for a link-up with Patton's forces which would meanwhile have taken Lorraine, the next province to the north. When that junction was complete the Allied front would stretch from the Swiss frontier to the Channel and the broad front would be a reality.

Devers' group continued to advance quickly across Burgundy until mid-October when, on entering Alsace, it encountered stiff resistance in the Vosges, that long, wooded and hilly spine that guards France, just west of the Rhine. By now, the US Seventh Army had nine divisions and the French 1st Army seven. Both armies had plenty of supplies, reaching no less than 14,000 tons a day by mid-November, and were proceeding efficiently with their designated task, to sweep north and clear the west bank of the Rhine in Alsace and Lorraine.

The problem was the terrain and the weather. The high ground in the St Die area was taken with nearly 6,000 German prisoners put in the bag, but the deteriorating weather stopped any further advance towards the key town of Colmar and the increasing cold proved very hard indeed on the Colonial troops – mostly from France's North African colonies – in the French First Army. The Germans managed to hang onto the line of the Vosges until 19 November when the French Army, which had attacked on 13 November, broke through their lines at Belfort and reached the west bank of the Rhine at Mulhouse after a lightning advance that took them forward twenty-five miles in one day.

This French advance weakened the German position in the Vosges, already under heavy pressure from Patch's Seventh Army further north. From then on the German position crumbled. On 22 November the Americans forced a passage through the Saverne gap and the following day the French 2nd Armoured Division took Strasbourg.

But this success by the French and US Armies was not without cost. Between 13 November and 16 December, 6th Army Group sustained some 28,000 casualties. Nor had it completed the task of clearing the entire German army from west of the Rhine. The German Nineteenth Army still occupied an area on the left bank of the Rhine known as the Colmar pocket – and the wooded heights of the Vosges south of St Die. Even so, 6th Army Group had done what no other group had done: it had moved up to the west bank of the Rhine.

In this part of France, the Rhine marked the frontier with Germany. Running from the Swiss frontier to the junction with the River Saar at Lauterbourg, the West Wall ran on the east bank of the Rhine and had therefore not barred the advance of Devers' group. This meant that the Rhine plain east of the river was open to attack, provided the river could be crossed and the West Wall breached – and after the Colmar pocket on the west bank was cleared. This fact was also obvious to Adolf Hitler, who ordered that the Colmar pocket must be held at all costs.

On 24 November, while on his way to a conference with Devers, Eisenhower stopped at Patton's HQ. Eisenhower's plan was that Devers should devote both his armies to the reduction of the Colmar pocket but during this meeting Patton convinced the Supreme Commander that the French Army alone could reduce the Colmar pocket. Therefore, Patton suggested, the two corps of Patch's Seventh Army should be sent into Lorraine and there help the Third Army clear their front to the Rhine by breaching the West Wall. When consulted on this proposal, Devers agreed that the French could indeed clear the pocket, as the Nineteenth Army had 'ceased to exist as a tactical force'. Eisenhower therefore abandoned the first plan and let the Seventh Army turn into Lorraine.

This change of mind, so typical of General Eisenhower, had the most unfortunate effect. The Germans in the Colmar pocket now faced an attack from only one direction – the south – and were able to beat the French back with loss and retain their useful bridgehead west of the Rhine. The full effect of this decision was not apparent at the time, but would reveal itself during the Ardennes battles in mid-December and cause a major row between Eisenhower and the prickly French leader, Charles de Gaulle.

By the end of November it was becoming clear to all that the latest offensive, the one planned at the end of October, had completely stalled. Some advances had been made: the Allied armies had tidied-up their front east of the Maas and moved their front line to the Roer, opposite Venlo, Julich and Deuren, though all these places, being east of the river, were still in German hands. But the Roer river dams were still untaken and north of the as yet uncrossed Saar a great plain lay between the Allies on the Roer and their long-desired objective, the Rhine. Nowhere had the Allied armies achieved their stated objectives, casualties had been high, particularly in the First and Third Armies, and with deteriorating weather and the onset of winter, yet another stalemate was on hand.

On 4 December Eisenhower admitted in a letter to Marshall that: 'The enemy should be able to maintain a strong defensive front for some time assisted by weather, floods and muddy ground,' adding that: 'Our problem is to continue our attacks as long as the results achieved are so much in our favor, while at the same time preparing for an all-out heavy offensive when weather conditions become favorable.'

Both these latter statements are debatable. It is hard to see where the recent attacks had been in the Allies' favour or when the weather would again be suitable for an all-out offensive. That apart, Eisenhower had just tried an all-out offensive and the results had been – to put it mildly – inconclusive and extremely costly. Where was the guarantee that if the process were repeated, the results would not be the same?

Montgomery, who had clearly abandoned his recent intention to 'say no more' on matters affecting strategy or command, had already picked up this point and, most unwisely, elected to direct attention to it. On 28 November, Eisenhower visited Montgomery in his Command Post at Zonhoven and stayed the night. It cannot have been a pleasant evening for the Supreme Commander, for Montgomery 'expressed his disappointment with the failure of operations', during the past month, to realise Eisenhower's directive.

Montgomery attributed this failure to succeed with 'the main effort in the north' – rubbing in the fact that, as directed, it was Bradley's Ninth and First Armies who had made this effort, not the British 21st Army Group – and to the efforts expended in support of Third Army's attack in the Saar, which had proved equally unavailing. Eisenhower pointed out that some gains had been made but the Field Marshal was unconvinced and repeated his arguments in a letter to the Supreme Commander on 30 November:

> We have definitely failed to implement the plan contained in the SHAEF directive of 28 October, as amended on later dates. That directive ordered the main effort to be made in the north, to defeat decisively the enemy west of the Rhine, to gain bridgeheads over the Rhine and Ijssel rivers and deploy in strength east of the Rhine preparatory to seizing the Ruhr. We have achieved none of this and have no hope of doing so; we have suffered a major strategic reverse.

One of the most irritating things about the Field Marshal – and especially irritating to his critics – is that what he said was often true. So it was here; the 28 October offensive had failed in all its stated objectives and Eisenhower had indeed suffered a major strategic reverse. Even more irritating to the American commanders was the fact that this failure could not be laid at Montgomery's door – the 'main effort in the north' this time had been ordered by Eisenhower and executed by Bradley, Patton, Hodges and Simpson. The British and Canadians had been engaged in their own affairs further north, efforts which, though limited, had been somewhat more effective and pinched out the Venlo pocket.

The aim of Eisenhower's strategy had been to gain the line of the Rhine or, should that prove impossible, to bring the German armies, plus any reserves, into battle west of the Rhine and destroy them there before thrusting into Germany. None of this had been achieved: the Allied armies were still miles from the Rhine and the German armies were, if anything, stronger than ever.

Once again the finger points at the broad front policy. Attacking on a 600-mile front from the Vosges to Nijmegen, the Allies were not strong enough anywhere to achieve a breakthrough.

While this much was undeniable, Montgomery then – yet again – spoiled his case by reverting to his old arguments: that the offensive in the north was a 'full time job for one man', that a land force commander was needed, that Bradley should come under Montgomery's command... and so on. By now everyone – including Alanbrooke, who could usually talk sense into Monty – had told the Field Marshal that this was a dead issue: he would never again be given command of the US armies and he would be well advised to accept the fact and shut up about it.

This, alas, Montgomery seemed unable to do, suggesting another meeting at Maastricht in early December, at which Bradley and the various Army Chiefs of Staff should be present – but the latter 'must not speak'.

Meanwhile, he reported his dissatisfaction with Eisenhower's strategy to Alanbrooke, who discussed the matter with Churchill. The prime minister conveyed their joint concerns in a cable to Roosevelt on 6 December but got no satisfaction either, Roosevelt declaring that 'our agreed broad strategy is developing according to plan' – though without producing any evidence to support that contention.

However, on 7 December the Allied generals met for that meeting at Maastricht, where orders were issued for the next phase of the advance towards Germany. The Lower Rhine would be cleared by joint offensives from the Americans in the Roer and the British in the Reichswald as soon as Bradley had captured the Roer dams. The target date for this offensive was 12 January 1945, and although Montgomery suggested the Allies might husband their forces until that time – not least to build up stocks of artillery ammunition – Eisenhower authorised Patton to try yet again for the Saar before the end of December – another, typically Eisenhower, diversion from the main effort.

On 12 December, Eisenhower and Tedder came to London to discuss SHAEF policy with the British Chiefs of Staff, who were somewhat dismayed when Eisenhower stated that he did not now intend crossing the Rhine before May 1945! Neither were the British Chiefs of Staff convinced that Eisenhower's latest plan – to keep up the pressure throughout the winter and if possible drive the enemy back to the Rhine and then conduct a double envelopment of the

Ruhr, 21st Army Group to the north, 12th Army Group to the south – but that the 'main attack should be north of the Ruhr' – was anything but a reheated version of a plan that had failed before – and would probably not be adhered to anyway.

To the British Commanders in Chief this sounded very much like the same old story – a 'main attack' in the north with one of those so-called 'subsidiary attacks' in the south by Patton that somehow either developed in to a major attack or drew off vital supplies and effort from the 'main offensive'. However, before these arguments could be aired yet again, the Germans entered the contest with a devastating attack through the Ardennes on 16 December, an attack that subsequently became known as the Battle of the Bulge.

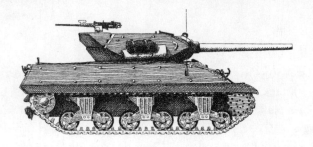

13 · HITLER STRIKES BACK
DECEMBER 1944

The bruited drive on Antwerp… is just not within his (Rundstedt's) potentiality.

21ST ARMY GROUP INTELLIGENCE SURVEY, 3 DECEMBER 1944

On 6 December, driving through the Western Ardennes for that meeting with his Army Group commanders at Maastricht, Eisenhower had noticed how few US troops were holding the Ardennes sector of the Allied line. By December Bradley, with twenty-nine divisions, had by far the largest of the three Army Groups, with nineteen divisions in Montgomery's group and seventeen in Devers' 6th Army Group. Even so, Bradley's forces were barely adequate for the tasks in hand, which included another thrust at the Roer dams by First Army and a possible renewal of the Saar drive by Patton before Christmas – and that left precious few units for the Ardennes front.

That the Supreme Commander was previously unaware the Ardennes line was thinly held is not surprising, but after the Maastricht conference Eisenhower raised the matter with Bradley. Then he learned that only four US divisions of Middleton's VIII Corps were holding the Ardennes front and that these were dispersed over a distance of at least seventy-five miles – an average of eighteen miles of front per division, and with no reserves available. In spite of Eisenhower's concern, nothing was done to remedy this situation.

One of the most surprising factors in the US Army Order of Battle during this time was an absence of reserves. As a rule, force commanders are most anxious to keep a reserve of troops on hand, to deal with any emergency, to exploit any success, or to rest or reinforce units that have been under heavy pressure in the line. When the chance presents itself, wise commanders will move some troops into reserve.

This was not happening to any extent in the US armies of 1944 partly due to the broad front strategy, which required every division in the line simply to hold the front, and partly to the fact that US divisions were constantly arriving from the USA and could be held as constituting a reserve, without pulling divisions out of the line. A small reserve also usually existed from units that were, for one reason or another, currently out of the line, resting or re-equipping. In December 1944 there were just two of these available to 12th Army Group, the 82nd and 101st Airborne Divisions, which had recently come out of the Nijmegen corridor where they had been fighting alongside the British since Market Garden back in September.

Bradley justified his dispersion on the Ardennes front by pointing out that the hilly, forested terrain was difficult to penetrate, adding that if the Germans did launch an attack there it could promptly be counter-attacked from either flank. If the enemy wanted to fight here, 'Let 'em come', said Bradley. The fact that the Germans had stormed through the Ardennes as recently as May 1940, when they had shattered the armies of three countries within two weeks, had not figured in this calculation.

Given their Normandy experience, the Allies might have anticipated some form of German reaction, something not unlike the Mortain counter-attack in early August, that attempt by the enemy to split the American forces in two by a thrust west to Avranches on the Atlantic coast. Hitler was notorious for a reluctance to let his army commanders give up ground. He was also known to favour strong counter-attacks when his position was closely threatened and in December there was no lack of Allied intelligence indicating that some form of German activity was pending.

Besides, the usual answer to an attack is a counter-attack. With the failure of the Allied attacks and SHAEF strategy all along the line in November, some German reaction in December should have been anticipated. There is no sign of such anticipation: one day before the Germans launched the Ardennes offensive, Montgomery averred that the enemy's equipment and manpower situation was such that 'he cannot stage major offensive operations.' Those German forces that had been identified were clearly mustering to defend the western frontiers of the Reich against the forthcoming Allied attacks in the Reichswald, the Roer valley and the Saar.

Hitler had, in fact, been planning a major counter-attack in the west since mid-September, and had gradually assembled a strong force of panzer divisions to carry it out. This attack was based on strategic considerations and a certain amount of delusion. The strategic consideration was that he lacked the forces and the fuel to do anything decisive against the Russian armies in the East. Therefore, any blow struck must be against their allies in the West, splitting their forces in two, inflicting heavy losses and capturing their main supply base, the port of Antwerp.

Knowing that the British were running out of manpower, believing that the Americans were less tenacious in defence than the British and less tough than the Russians, convinced that any democratic–totalitarian, East–West alliance could not hold, the Führer hoped that a major defeat in the west would impel the Allies to the conference table. 'Such a defeat', says Chester Willmot, 'would disrupt the Allied coalition, cripple the Western powers and compel them to realise the futility of trying to crush Nazi Germany... or so Hitler supposed.'[1]

Even if the attack faltered, Hitler considered that it might gain Germany some useful time. Time to produce more jet-fighters to curb the bomber offensive, time to get more schnorkel-equipped U-boats to sea and renew the attack on the Allied convoys, time to use the V-weapons against British cities and those Continental ports now in Allied hands.

The delusion in such thinking was two-fold. The first delusion was that any of the above was true, or that these new technical developments, useful as they were, would have any effect on the outcome of the war. The USA was as fully committed to this European war as her allies and would continue the fight in spite of any temporary reverse. Germany had lost the war when the Allies landed in Normandy and opened the Second Front. Caught between Allied forces in the West and the Soviets in the East, Germany's defeat was now only a matter of time and most of the German commanders were well aware of this fact.

The second delusion was that this counter-attack was either achievable or advisable, and the Führer grossly underestimated the dogged fighting ability of the American soldier. The generals at OKW, and especially the two Field Marshals, von Rundstedt and Model, thought this plan for a thrust on Antwerp was ill-advised and too ambitious. They would have preferred either a limited offensive up to the Meuse, or to husband Germany's strength for a defensive battle for the Reich along the West Wall. On the other hand, arguing with the Führer was rarely productive and indeed somewhat dangerous after the assassination plot of 20 July had made him suspicious of the generals and unwilling to heed their advice.

Besides, Hitler's plan was not without merit and took account of some hard-learned recent lessons. One was that this counter-attack should wait until the German front had been stabilised and the onset of winter reduced the level of support the Allied armies would get from their tactical air forces; in the interim, strong panzer forces could be assembled and trained and large supplies of fuel and ammunition accumulated.

With his firm intention to attack on the table, Hitler delegated the details to Field Marshal Jodl and on 8 October Jodl came back with an outline plan. By early December, he declared, the German armies in the west could assemble no fewer than thirty-two divisions; twelve of these would be panzer or panzer grenadier and highly mobile; two would be crack parachute formations and eighteen would be infantry, formed from the new Volksgrenadier forces now being mustered in the Reich.

In the event, on 16 December the Germans managed to throw eight panzer divisions, twenty infantry divisions and two mechanised brigades into the Bulge battle, a total of some 200,000 men, initially supported by 500 tanks and 1,900 guns and mortars,[2] deployed on a front of some sixty miles between Monschau, just south of the Huertgen forest, and Echternach, a front straddling the Ardennes and the Eifel. The Bulge has often been seen as a massive tank battle, since it employed around 1,800 German tanks, but quality rather than quantity was the main German armoured asset. The Germans now had three main battle tanks, the well-established and reliable 30-ton Mark IV, mounting a 75mm gun, the 50-ton Mark V or Panther, mounting a high-velocity gun, which outgunned the standard American Sherman, and the powerful Mark VI Tiger, which weighed much the same as the Panther but had thicker armour and mounted the formidable 88mm gun.

The problem with the Tiger was reliability. A Tiger contained no fewer than 26,000 separate parts and many Tigers spent half their time in the workshops or under local repair. Later US estimates hold that only about 250 Tigers took part in the Ardennes battle, the rest being either Mark IVs or Panthers.[3] There was an even more formidable machine, the King Tiger, and although very few of these reached the front, many Allied action reports remark that any tank encountered was a King Tiger.

Such a large quantity of armour was a problem to fuel. Germany was growing increasingly short of fuel and although large stocks were assembled, any continuance of the German offensive would depend on the panzer commanders capturing American fuel dumps during their advance – and these had yet to be located.

The German Commander in the West, Gerd von Rundstedt, and the commander of Army Group B, Field Marshal Model, were informed of the Führer's plans on 22 October. These called for a major offensive from the Eifel and across the Ardennes by three re-equipped armies: Sixth SS Panzer under Sepp Dietrich, Fifth Panzer under von Manteuffel, and General Brandenberger's Seventh Army, the whole supported by some 1,400 aircraft.

Each of these armies had a definite task. In the north, Dietrich's SS Panzer Army was to capture Monschau and Butgenbach, and pass three infantry divisions through to hold the northern flank of the attack east of Liège. That done, 1st and 12th SS would thrust west for Malmedy and Stavelot, while an advanced striking force commanded by SS Colonel Otto Skorzeny, dressed in American uniforms and driving captured American tanks and jeeps, would rush west and seize the Meuse bridges. To guard against any disruption, II SS Panzer Corps, consisting of 2nd Panzer and 9th SS Panzer, would be held in reserve. And this was just in the north.

In the centre, Hasso von Manteuffel's Fifth Panzer Army would thrust for the key road junctions at St Vith and Bastogne, cross the River Our and drive on for the Meuse, striking the river between Namur and Dinant. Finally, to protect these moves, Brandenberger's Seventh Army was to provide a firm flank guard from Arlon to Luxembourg.

The German armies would assemble in great secrecy behind the Ardennes, and to prevent intelligence leaks all the planning for the attack would be carried out in Hitler's HQ. No wireless signals were to be employed when mustering these divisions, and to give the impression that any forces detected by the Allies were being mustered for defensive purposes only, the plan was given the codename 'Wacht am Rhein', later changed to Herbstnebel – Autumn Smoke.

The development of this plan and the mustering of these forces proceeded throughout November without any noticeable effect on the German capacity to resist or the need to commit the Wacht am Rhein forces to the current battles. Even Manteuffel's abortive strike against Patton's advance into Lorraine did not prevent the gradual increase in the size and power of the Fifth Panzer Army. Nor did rumours of an impending attack reach the Allies, either via Enigma or by the usual routines of signals intelligence or prisoner interrogations. When Eisenhower and his commanders met at Maastricht on 7 December, nine days before the start of the Ardennes offensive, no one there even considered the possibility of a German offensive.

This confidence may have been due to a failure to correctly interpret the intelligence that was coming in. SHAEF had been informed that a Sixth SS Panzer Army of four divisions had been formed, but did not know where it was. SHAEF were also aware that at least another four panzer divisions had been pulled back into Germany and were currently re-equipping, but the supposition was that these divisions would be used to counter an Allied attack in the spring.

However, there are some indications that not everyone in Eisenhower's armies was unaware of these German intentions. On 3 December Montgomery's Chief Intelligence Officer, Brigadier E. T. Williams, had prepared a summary on German intentions, which contains some interesting comments. The general thrust of Williams' report confirmed the general SHAEF impression 'that von Rundstedt was unlikely to risk his strategic reserve until the Allies advance over the Roer' and needed adequate fuel stocks and more infantry.

That much was true, but Williams' summary also refers to 'the bruited drive on Antwerp – a dash for the wire as of old'. Here Williams is referring to Rommel's dash for the Libyan frontier during the Crusader battles in North Africa in 1942. Williams also comments that von Rundstedt might attack 'should the Allies offer the enemy opportunity to take them off-balance so that an abrupt counter-stroke could put paid to future Allied prospects for the winter.'

One would like to hear more about this 'bruited drive on Antwerp', not least on who was bruiting it about – given the broad Allied conclusion that the enemy would stay on the defensive – and on what the prospects were that the enemy might launch some form of pre-emptive strike, if given a chance to do so. Historians of the Second World War, fascinated by the possibilities of Enigma and the Ultra intelligence it produced, sometimes forget the Germans also had sources of intelligence: if they knew about the thinly-held Allied line across the Ardennes, this would present them with exactly the kind of opportunity for an abrupt counter-attack that Hitler had envisioned for Wacht am Rhein.

Whether or not the Germans were aware of how few US divisions held this part of the Allied line, it is one of the great ironies of war that the place the Germans had marked out, months before, for their counter-attack was also the most thinly-held part of the Allied front when that attack came in. On 16 December, this part of the front was held by 83,000 men with 242 Sherman medium tanks, 182 M-10 tank destroyers and 394 guns of various calibre.

This may sound an adequate force but it had a long front to cover and the essence of defence is depth; a full calculation of the winding nature of the Ardennes front gives a total length of no fewer than 104 miles, rather further than the estimated seventy-five miles as the crow flies. When the German attack came in, the 28th Division alone held a front of some thirty miles. Nor was the wide front the only problem; the 4th and 28th Divisions had recently lost some 9,000 men in the Huertgen fighting and the survivors were exhausted, the 106th Division had only been in the ETO for four days and the 9th Armored Division lacked battle experience... yet these were the units that would bear the brunt of the first German attack.

Brigadier Williams may have based his allegation about a 'bruited attack' on the various rumours that were floating about intelligence circles, based on scraps of information – that five German divisions had left the Second Army front in Holland bound no man knew where, that Hitler had ordered the formation of a 'Special Unit' for tasks on the Western Front and that volunteers must speak English and be fully trained in single combat.[4] Another Enigma intercept ordered German units to send any captured American kit or uniforms to their Divisional HQs.

All this, plus Enigma reports of a steady drift of German units to the west, tended to confirm the vague impression that something was brewing beyond the Rhine – or it might have done, if anyone had put these scraps of information together. No one did so, and the overall impression remained the one held at the Maastricht conference on 7 December – that the enemy was husbanding his strength until the Allied armies crossed the River Roer.

This would have been the preferred option for von Rundstedt and Model. When they first saw the Ardennes plan their initial reaction was that their forces and supplies were not sufficient for a major offensive designed to split the Allied armies and reach Antwerp. From then on von Rundstedt took little or no interest in the Führer's scheme, even declining to attend OKW briefings. The decision on this offensive was not in the gift of the generals: the Führer had decreed an all-out attack in the west targeted on Antwerp and the generals were to get on with it, without arguing and with despatch – and to the Führer's plan.

The attack would smash through the US First Army in the Southern Ardennes and hook north-west towards Antwerp, crossing the Meuse between Liège and Namur – from the very start of this operation, both sides realised the importance of the Meuse. Getting over the Meuse quickly was essential, so seizing the necessary bridges was a task delegated to the SS officer Otto Skorzeny, best known to the Allies as the man who had recently rescued the Italian dictator Mussolini from his prison in the Gran Sasso mountains.

Skorzeny's requirements had produced those interesting Enigma decrypts calling for men with English language and close-quarter combat skills. Speaking English – preferably with American accents – driving US vehicles and dressed and armed as American soldiers, Skorzeny's force, split into some forty separate detachments, would move ahead of the main advance, seize the bridges, destroy communications centres, kill senior American officers and in general spread alarm and despondency among the Allied troops. In this task they succeeded all too well, even obliging General Eisenhower, much to his annoyance, to stay in his well-guarded Headquarters at Versailles for much of the battle. The final element in the battle would be the Fifteenth Army in the north, which would assume command of those Sixth SS Panzer Army units holding the right flank of the German advance after it crossed the Meuse.

By the day of the Maastricht conference, Hitler had assembled no fewer than twenty-eight divisions for the Ardennes offensive, supported by over 1,300 new or repaired tanks delivered in November, with 1,000 more due to arrive within the next few weeks. The Luftwaffe was standing by to make a major contribution to the attack and, with a little luck and the advantage of surprise, the Führer was convinced the Allied line could be broken, Antwerp recaptured and the strategic situation restored.

On 12 December, the plan for the Ardennes offensive was presented to the army commanders. The generals were called to von Rundstedt's headquarters, searched and deprived of their side arms by SS guards, loaded into sealed trucks and driven about the countryside for some time until they arrived at what turned out to be the Führer's forward headquarters near Frankfurt. There they were conducted to an underground room where, with an SS guard standing behind each chair, they were briefed on the coming attack by Hitler, Keitel and Jodl.

Hitler began by treating his commanders to a prolonged rant on the nature of the Western alliance. This, the Führer told them, was sure to fall apart if struck a heavy strategic blow which would 'deprive the enemy of the belief that victory was certain,' and the coming offensive would do just that. Whether any of those listening believed that the Ardennes attack could succeed is doubtful: in their post-war accounts all state their belief that shortages of fuel alone would restrict their advance – although they might hope to overrun the American fuel dumps they had no idea if such dumps existed or exactly where they were.

On the other hand, they had enough fuel to get to the Meuse and inflict a heavy defeat on the US First Army, and that alone would be no mean achievement. Finally, as Hitler assured them, the weather would restrict the operations of the Allied air forces and although it would also restrict any support from the Luftwaffe they had learned to do without that in recent weeks. All in all, and having no choice, the German commanders prepared to do their best. So, over the next few days, under cover of bad weather and by night, the German forces moved up to their start lines in the Ardennes and by the evening of 15 December all was ready – with the Americans still, apparently, completely unaware of what was about to happen.

As is often the case, this belief was not entirely correct. On 15 December Bradley's intelligence officers produced an appreciation that declared they had detected the arrival behind the West Wall, somewhere between Dueren and Trier, of three or four enemy divisions. It was therefore possible that a limited offensive was pending, perhaps, as some German prisoners reported, in the hope of giving the Führer the recapture of Aachen as a Christmas present. Even as this appreciation was being typed out, the German panzers and no fewer than fourteen infantry divisions were rolling from the Schnee Eifel into Belgium, preceded by an artillery bombardment from 2,000 guns which started shelling the American line at 0530hrs on 16 December.

Jack Capell of the 4th Infantry Division recalls this time:

Some of my earliest recollections of the Bulge date to when we moved out of the Huertgen and went into position near Senningen in Luxembourg. We were to remain in that position long enough to give the Huertgen veterans a rest and let us absorb some replacements. I was elated to discover that as a D-Day veteran I would be one of the first to go back for a two-day rest in hospital at Arlon and we went back there in trucks on 15 December. Hot showers, beds with pillows, this was luxury... paradise. After breakfast next day I was ready to go out and explore the town but instead I stayed in camp to play table tennis and while I was doing that an officer came in and said we were immediately to load up our trucks and go back to our outfits.

This raised a mighty furore, all directed at the officer, who stomped out and was replaced by a colonel, who said that if we refused to go back we would all be considered as deserters and shot. So we loaded up our things and got in the trucks; it was about twenty below and the wind was blowing through the tarpaulin at the front of the truck. Shortly afterwards we arrived at a fuel dump and while the truck took on more gas we went into the shack and listened to the radio to hear a broadcast, I assume from the BBC. The voice was talking excitedly about this new German attack and this was a shock as we had heard nothing about this.

Outside, asking questions, they told us the 4th Division had been over-run and 'annihilated' and so we asked the driver 'If our unit has been annihilated where are you taking us?' The driver said that he had been ordered to take us back to Senningen and as we got closer we heard a lot of artillery and shellfire. In fact, the 4th Division was holding on at Senningen; we heard that Eternach had also been attacked and our division had taken heavy casualties. We were gathered in at Senningen, and given as much ammunition and as many grenades as we could carry, as well as blocks of TNT to blast foxholes in the frozen ground; although the ground was frozen hard it had not started snowing yet; that started about 28 December... but so ended my second day of scheduled rest.[5]

Whole books have been written about the 1944 Ardennes offensive and there is no space here to do more than describe the main events and their relevance to the overall situation. The most important points are what happened at the front in the first few days and what the commanders at Allied headquarters did about it.

For the first four days, the man most directly concerned with this problem, General Omar Bradley, commander of the 12th Army Group, did very little. Granted, on the evening of 16 December he sent in two armoured divisions from the flanking Ninth and Third Armies – but that was some twelve hours after the first reports of the attack had reached him. He then waited another full day before calling in the SHAEF reserve – the two US airborne divisions in Champagne – and another day before he ordered Patton to halt his pending offensive in the Saar; and he had still not established contact with his beleaguered First Army commander, Courtney Hodges. It was three days after the attack began before he withdrew divisions from the Aachen front to shore up the Ardennes, and he had still not produced any kind of overall defensive plan when the Supreme Commander intervened directly late on 19 December. While all this was going on the German armies were surging forward into his lines.

The first blow was delivered by the Fifth Panzer Army and fell on the three divisions of Middleton's corps south of St Vith. The 28th Division, attacked soon after dawn by no fewer than five German divisions, was quickly overwhelmed. Manteuffel's men then surged on to surround two regiments of the raw 106th Infantry Division in the Schnee Eifel. Though surrounded, these two regiments held their ground, but the way was now open to St Vith – although the other infantry division of the VIII Corps, the veteran 4th Infantry, still held on in the south.

To the north of VIII Corps the men of Gerow's V Corps, though equally surprised, gave a good account of themselves. The four divisions of V Corps were heading for their attack on the Roer dams when they ran into Sepp Dietrich's SS Panzer Army and halted the SS Panzer Grenadiers at Monschau. They also slowed the Panzer Army's infantry advance at Butgenbach, even though Dietrich promptly threw in the 12th SS Panzer Division (Hitler Jugend), to speed up the advance.

Following this encounter, Gerow applied to First Army HQ for permission to halt his push for the Roer and occupy a defensive position on the Butgenbach ridge, but General Hodges refused, apparently believing that the German attack had been put in with the precise intention of halting the V Corps thrust for the river; the true purpose and scale of the German attack had not yet been realised by Hodges, Bradley or SHAEF. Part of this failure was due to a lack of information: the German units were ripping up telephone wires and destroying signals units at every opportunity, and very little precise information was getting back to the relevant HQs.

South of Butgenbach, the 1st SS Panzer Division (Liebstandarte) broke through the US line and by nightfall the leading element, Kampfgruppe Peiper, commanded by Obersturmbannführer (Colonel) Joachim Peiper, a man who had built up a formidable reputation in Russia, had penetrated six miles into the US positions – and was about to commit a war crime.

The 1st SS Panzer Division had around 100 Mark IV or Panther tanks plus forty-two Tigers of the 501st Heavy Panzer battalion. This force was preceded by the 12th Volksgrenadier Division, which was supposed to open the way through the Schnee Eifel, but the volksgrenadiers failed to do this on the first day of the offensive and clogged up the narrow roads in the process.

Perhaps this delay frayed Peiper's nerves or put an edge on his men's uncertain temper. At around 1230hrs on 17 December, the second day of the attack, advanced elements of Kampfgruppe Peiper ran into the US 285th Field Artillery Observation Battalion on the move near the town of Malmedy. The artillery trucks were shot up, a number of American soldiers were killed and around ninety were taken prisoner. These prisoners were marched into a field and raked with machine-gun and machine-pistol fire until eighty-six of them had been killed, those who were merely wounded being finished off with a bullet in the head.

This was murder. Nor was it the first such incident involving Peiper's men that day. Later evidence confirmed that his SS kampfgruppe had also massacred sixty-seven other American prisoners earlier that day at Honsfeld and at the Bullingen fuel dump, which the SS had captured soon after dawn. At Bullingen the US prisoners were forced to refuel the German tanks before they too were murdered. News of these massacres spread quickly among the US units and stiffened their resolve to hang on and fight back – which they were already doing. At the end of the first day, the US units in the line were holding on, fighting hard, slowing the enemy down and doing well. The problem lay not with the soldiers in the field but with the situation at First Army and 12th Army Group HQ's – and not a little at SHAEF.

The basic cause of the dilemma gripping the US HQs was that those in command had not yet grasped the scale of the German attack, partly because it was so unexpected, partly because of poor communications, not least because

Bradley's HQ in Luxembourg, though close to Patton's Third Army, was a long way from the headquarters of Hodges' and Simpson's First and Ninth Armies north of the Ardennes. Hodges, the man closest to the action, seems to have been the most confused; he did not ask Bradley for reinforcements or, it appears, pass on any detailed information about the situation developing on his front to his Army Group commander.

This was a pity, for Bradley was with Eisenhower at Versailles, celebrating the latter's promotion to five-star general when, late in the afternoon of 16 December, some twelve hours after the attack began, vague reports about some German attack in the Ardennes began to filter in to SHAEF. Had the two commanders been able to agree about what was happening in the Ardennes that day, or been correctly informed about the details of this sudden attack, they were ideally placed to act.

However, though Eisenhower was 'immediately convinced that this was no local attack' – at least according to his post-war memoirs[6] – Bradley was equally convinced that this was a local attack, launched to halt Patton's pending offensive further south. This Bradley declined to do and Patton's attack was not cancelled until 18 December, three days into the Bulge offensive.

After some debate that evening, Eisenhower and Bradley did agree to send two armoured divisions into the Ardennes in support of VIII Corps, the 7th Armored from Simpson's Ninth Army and 10th Armored from Patton's Third Army – a unit currently engaged in battering away in the Saar. This order to divert an armoured division to help Hodges did not please General Patton, who ordered his other armoured unit, the 4th Armored Division, to get itself engaged with the enemy as quickly as possible, lest it too should be sent to the north – a typically Patton tactic. However – and this is now part of the Patton legend – it appears that Patton appreciated that this was no spoiling attack but a major offensive, and ordered his staff to prepare plans that could swing the Third Army ninety degrees to the north, into position for a rapid advance to the aid of Hodges' army.

Diverting divisions from other armies was the only option available to Eisenhower. In accordance with the broad front strategy, all his divisions were already fully engaged. The only 'reserve' immediately available was the 82nd and 101st Airborne Divisions, now resting and re-equipping at Rheims in Northern France after their battles in the aftermath of Market Garden. These two divisions were also ordered into the Ardennes and were on the move that night, in open trucks and using their headlights to make better time.

Getting more troops into the line was now becoming urgent. By the morning of 17 December, the German divisions of all three attacking armies were forging ahead everywhere, tearing the First Army front apart. Dietrich's leading elements were already twenty miles inside Belgium with Peiper's SS kampfgruppe at Stavelot, a few miles from Bradley's HQ at Spa and the two vast US petrol dumps containing some three million gallons of vital fuel.

This was worrying, but elsewhere US divisions, regiments, or battalions were still holding their ground, at Monschau and Elsenborn and Butgenbach, and also at St Vith, where Major-General Hasbrouck's 7th Armored Division had arrived in time to block the advance of the 1st SS Panzer Division. Blocked at St Vith, Peiper turned north only to find that US engineers had already destroyed one of the petrol dumps and were blowing bridges across the line of the German advance. Hasbrouck's division formed a bastion on the American line as units scattered by the German advance came into St Vith and took up their share of what, from its shape, came to be called the St Vith goose egg.

The American troops in the front line were doing well and had already taken much of the steam out of the German attack, but a form of chaos was rapidly developing at First Army and 12th Army Group HQs. This was largely due to the inability of the commanders – Hodges and Bradley – to find out what exactly was happening, a situation that would alarm and confuse any commander. Though the tenacity of their troops had delayed the German thrust towards the Meuse, all that Hodges knew was that German armour – and SS armour at that – had got through to Stavelot and was now nearing his headquarters at Spa. Hodges was seeking some way to block this progress when General James Gavin of the 82nd Airborne arrived at First Army HQ seeking orders.

Gavin had heard some news of the Ardennes attack on 16 December, but it was not until the evening of 17 December, thirty-six hours into the attack, that he was summoned to the telephone and told that, in the absence of the Corps Commander, General Matthew Ridgeway, he was to act as Corps Commander and get his division and the 101st Airborne into the Ardennes. Gavin duly issued his orders and left for Spa, arriving at Hodges HQ at 0900hrs on 18 December – D plus 2 of the German attack – to find Hodges 'a bit weary', which is hardly surprising after the events of the last two days.

Hodges' original intention had been to deploy the 82nd at Houffalize, to block the road from St Vith to Bastogne. Now, with the enemy west of Stavelot, he ordered Gavin to deploy his regiments at Werbemont and block any advance past that point. This was done but the road to Bastogne was left wide open to the onrushing tanks of the 2nd Panzer Division and Panzer Lehr of the Fifth Panzer Army. The intermediate town of Houffalize was the objective of 116th Panzer, which took it without difficulty – but the vital position in this sector was Bastogne, the centre of a road network, a place the Germans needed to occupy and the Americans had to retain.

On the morning of 18 December, two days into the attack, Bastogne contained only the headquarters of Middleton's VIII Corps and assorted stragglers from the battered 28th Division, who were streaming back into the town and being sorted out. Middleton had no orders to hold Bastogne, had no troops to hold it with, if he reached a personal decision to do so, and no information regarding any reinforcements. Fortunately, Middleton was no fool: realising the importance of Bastogne he decided to stay put and await events.

Reinforcements were coming, the 101st Airborne from Rheims, 100 miles away and Combat Command B (CCB) of the 10th Armored Division, rumbling down the forty miles of ice-bound road between Bastogne and Luxembourg. The first to arrive was CCB, at around 1800hrs, and was sent to block the roads from the east, pending the arrival of the 101st Airborne. Unable to contact Hodges, Middleton then petitioned Bradley for permission to hold the town even if cut off.

The race for Bastogne on 18 December was a close-run thing. By 2200hrs, elements of Panzer Lehr were probing the outskirts but not closely enough to impede the arrival of the 101st Airborne. The 101st, commanded by Brigadier General Anthony McAuliffe, began to dig-in overnight in the frost-hardened ground outside the town and the 101st troopers were bickering with the grenadiers of Panzer Lehr soon after daylight on 19 December. The German commander of the troops investing Bastogne, Lieutenant General Von Luttwitz, intended to circle Bastogne if he could not capture it, but found the wide deployment of US troops around the town denied him any access to the roads leading out of it to the west.

The Germans had not expected the US forces to act so quickly, or fight so hard, but Manteuffel was not willing to let resistance at Bastogne delay his advance to the Meuse. He ordered von Luttwitz to capture or contain Bastogne with his infantry and press on towards the Meuse with the panzer divisions. This decision had an immediate effect on the German strategic plan, which had assumed that Dietrich's Sixth SS Panzer Army would deliver the main weight of the attack in the north. This aim had been thwarted, for the Americans still held St Vith and Butgenbach, so Model suggested to von Rundstedt that the weight of the attack – and the available reinforcements, amounting to five divisions, two of them SS and three of them Panzer – should be put behind Manteuffel's attack in the south.

This would have been a wise decision, but as it involved reserves it had to be referred to the Führer, who decreed that the two SS divisions in reserve should be transferred to Dietrich for another blow in the north – though he did agree that the other divisions could be sent to Manteuffel, providing him with an armoured force to strike through the gap his army had already made in the US line.

At this point, two days into the action, it is necessary to return to the various US army headquarters. On 18 December, Patton had been ordered to halt his attack in the Saar and strike north into the flank of the Seventh Army 'as soon as possible'. Patton had been anticipating such an order and replied that he would have three divisions on the move within twenty-four hours. He also received an order to join Bradley, Devers, Eisenhower and Tedder at Verdun for a conference on the following day, 19 December.

Eisenhower began this meeting by telling his commanders that 'only cheerful faces were needed around the table' and that the situation should be viewed as an opportunity rather than a disaster. This view chimed in with Patton's thinking, the Third Army commander suggesting that the enemy should be allowed to go 'all the way to Paris before we cut him off and chew him up.'

Eisenhower then reviewed the situation in the light of current information on the enemy's position and intentions. The latter seemed to indicate that they were heading for Liège and Namur: they were in fact heading in the direction of Dinant, which lies well south of Namur. Eisenhower then decreed that the current policy was to shore up the line in the north and launch a counter-attack from the south – by Patton. When asked, Patton declared that he could attack in three days, on 22 December, as two of his divisions were already on the move.

To allow Patton to thin out his front for this attack, Devers was directed to take over the eastern edge of the Saar position, but this introduced another problem. It will be recalled that the attempt to eliminate the Colmar pocket had been thwarted when Eisenhower directed the Seventh Army to aid Patton's thrust for the Saar. This had left the elimination of the Colmar pocket to the French First Army in Devers' group – they were still heavily engaged in this task and the 6th Army Group was therefore fully stretched.

Eisenhower studied the map and told Devers that, if necessary, he could pull out of the Vosges for a while and even abandon the city of Strasbourg – which the French First Army had recently taken – to the enemy. This suggestion, if implemented, meant handing back some recently liberated French civilians to the Germans, who tended to take a harsh revenge on any of their former subjects who had recently been cheering on the Allies. Eisenhower's order to Devers therefore provoked a serious breach with de Gaulle, who ordered the French First Army to disobey any such order – to which Eisenhower replied that until the French Army obeyed his orders they would not receive a mouthful of food, a gallon of fuel or a round of ammunition – hardly a happy situation for the Allies at this time. This dispute was only resolved when de Gaulle gave way: but the French Army was directed to hang on to Strasbourg.

Having apparently got a grip on the situation Eisenhower then returned to SHAEF at Versailles, only to discover that matters had deteriorated considerably during his absence. Everywhere the Germans were surging forward and although Bastogne was holding, the Germans were flooding past it, heading for the open sector between Namur and Dinant on the Meuse. They were west of Bastogne, and had taken Houffalize, and in the north were racing towards Liège. Unless something was done, it appeared more than likely that the German panzers would be on or over the Meuse within the next twenty-four hours.

The problem facing Eisenhower was the usual one – what to do now? SHAEF had no reserves and Bradley was only able to assemble one by pulling in divisions from the Ninth and Third Armies, and they would not be available within the required twenty-four hours. Scratching around for troops, Eisenhower was forced to consider the unpalatable option of asking Field Marshal Montgomery what he had available? Montgomery replied that he had the four divisions of XXX Corps he had been bringing forward to attack the Reichswald – adding that he had already anticipated the need for support and had moved these divisions into a blocking position west of the Meuse. Montgomery did not add that he had also sent his liaison officers into the First Army area to find out what was going on, even to Hodges' HQ – all without informing Bradley.

The news that Monty was covering the Meuse bridges was comforting but the real problem was communications. Bradley was not in regular contact with any of his units north of the German breakthrough – the First and Ninth Armies – and as the Germans continued to press west, his communications became ever more tenuous, and would be broken entirely if Bastogne fell. One solution was for Bradley to move his Tactical HQ to Verdun, but this he refused to do, saying that any move would be taken as 'a sign of panic'.

In the circumstances this was a curious claim. Hodges had already shifted his headquarters north from Spa to Chaudfontaine near Liège, the roads were crammed with disorganised American units and retreating soldiers seeking a place to make a stand – it is hard to see how a sensible shift of Army Group headquarters to Verdun would have increased the current state of confusion.

Eisenhower might have been wise to insist on this move, for the alternative was even less attractive. By staying in Luxembourg, Bradley was out of touch with Hodges' new HQ near Liège and with Simpson's HQ further north. Meanwhile, radio communications were open to enemy ears and therefore unreliable, and telephone lines were already being cut. Both of these army commanders needed to be in regular, reliable contact with their group commander, especially if the current German thrust to the Meuse was supported by further thrusts from the north, between Aachen and the Maas. Delay was not an option – the American front had been torn open for thirty miles and the enemy was at least that far into the breach already, splitting the 12th Army Group in two. This action had, in effect, created two battles, one north and one south of the German 'bulge', and no means of controlling or co-ordinating the Allied response to such a move currently existed.

Slowly, a dire thought began to percolate into the higher minds at SHAEF. If one man was not able to control these two battles, then two men must be employed, one on either side of the enemy penetration – and the most obvious candidate to control the northern sector of the Bulge battle was Field Marshal Sir Bernard Law Montgomery.

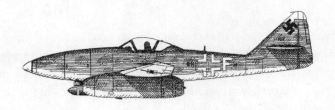

14 · MONTGOMERY INTERVENES
DECEMBER 1944 – JANUARY 1945

This won't do; the country would go mad. Write me a victory.

GENERAL SIR ARTHUR WELLESLEY,
ON RECEIVING BERESFORD'S REPORT ON THE BATTLE OF ALBUHERA, SPAIN, 1811

The German attack through the Ardennes on 16 December 1944 presented the American commanders with two immediate problems. Firstly, the First Army front had been torn open for thirty miles, at least one American division had been destroyed, German panzers were pouring through this vast breach, eventually to a depth of fifty miles, and causing the loss of some 75,000 American soldiers. Secondly, there was no way the US commanders could blame this alarming reverse on Field Marshal Montgomery.

At this point, and in view of what follows, it might be as well to consider what the reaction would have been had such a reverse fallen on 21st Army Group – always supposing that the 'cautious' Montgomery would have permitted such an opportunity to arise. It is fair to say that irresistible demands for Montgomery's head would have swept across the Atlantic from Washington to SHAEF and tales of 'Montgomery's greatest failure' would be common currency in military history down to the present day. In the event, the main reaction to the man chiefly responsible for this Ardennes debacle, General Omar Bradley, was a proposal from Eisenhower to Marshall that Bradley be promoted immediately to the rank of four-star general.

When Hitler's offensive fell on VIII Corps of the US First Army in

December, Montgomery was miles away and busy completing arrangements for his next offensive, Operation Veritable, an attack east through the Reichswald. The errors and miscalculations that permitted the Ardennes breakthrough were entirely American in origin and could not be blamed either on Montgomery or the British Second Army's frequently alleged 'timidity', 'caution' or 'slowness'. Fortunately for the US commanders, Monty soon came to their rescue, not simply on the battlefield but, as we shall see, with a spectacularly ill-advised speech to the Allied newspaper correspondents in early January that successfully diverted American public attention from their generals' recent disasters in the field.

In his *Memoirs* Montgomery states that 'the battle of the Ardennes, which began on 16 December 1944 and continued to 16 January 1945, has aroused such bitter feelings between the British and Americans that I cannot disregard it.'[1] Montgomery adds later: 'I think the less one says about this battle the better, for I fancy that whatever I do say will almost certainly be resented.'[2]

Montgomery's *Memoirs* did not appear until 1958 and most of those 'bitter feelings' he refers to appeared before that time, shortly after the war, in the published memoirs of the American commanders, accounts which never fail to condemn the Field Marshal for his various failings, personal and professional. On the matter of the Ardennes, their allegations are that Monty's interventions in the battle were by no means as important as he claimed, that he attempted to hog the credit for an American 'victory' and generally behaved like his usual arrogant self when dealing with the US Army commanders – and Bradley. The sub text of all this is an ill-concealed fury that during the battle Montgomery was placed in command of two American armies by the Allied Supreme Commander, General Eisenhower.

The Ardennes offensive – the Battle of the Bulge – contains many myths, the largest of which is the one peddled by the media and the film industry that the battle was a 'victory'. If so, it was a victory of the Phyrric kind. A more accurate assessment might aver that the Ardennes battle was at best a draw: the Allied winter offensive was disrupted and American losses – see above – were considerable.

On the other hand, the Germans were hurled back to their start line and their losses in manpower and *matériel* could not be made good. On that basis rests those claims of 'victory', which has happily concealed the various failures that caused the initial catastrophe and the subsequent division of command. This victory was won by the guts and tenacity of the ordinary American soldier: whether he was well served by his commanding generals during the battle is quite another matter.

According to the US Official History,[3] the first person to appreciate that some changes had to be made to the command structure of the US 12th Army Group was Eisenhower's Chief of Intelligence at SHAEF, Major-General Kenneth Strong. Unfortunately, General Strong was a British officer. On the evening of 19 December, picking up the situation on his return from the Verdun conference, Strong's information suggested that the main thrust of the German drive was due west, to the Meuse south of Namur, and if it continued the US forces would shortly be split in two. He therefore went to see Major-General Jock Whiteley, Deputy Chief of Staff for Operations at SHAEF – who, unfortunately, was yet another British officer – and proposed that two Commands should be created: Bradley commanding the US forces south of the Bulge, effectively the Third Army, and Montgomery taking charge of the US First and Ninth Armies to the north of it.

Whiteley agreed that in the circumstances this move was logical. Their next step was to take their proposal to Eisenhower's Chief of Staff, Walter Bedell Smith. Bedell Smith was less than enchanted with the idea of giving Montgomery any say whatsoever in the Ardennes battle and accused the two officers of abandoning their Allied responsibilities in favour of national and, even worse, British interests, telling them that they no longer had a place at SHAEF and would be sent back to Britain. Later that evening, having calmed down and considered the proposal, Bedell Smith admitted the plan had merit, and the following day he publicly apologised to Whiteley for his accusation of national bias.

Bedell Smith had already discussed the proposal with Eisenhower and Bradley. Bradley admitted that some command changes were necessary, adding that had the officer proposed been American and not someone who was British – and Montgomery to boot – he would have had no objections to the proposal. This comment says it all: the argument over this necessary appointment at a crucial juncture in the Ardennes battle was not on the basis of logic or competence, but on nationality and personality. The US History admits as much, stating that:

Eisenhower and Smith were acutely conscious of the smouldering animosity towards the British in general and Montgomery in particular which existed in the Headquarters of the 12th Army Group and Third Army, not to mention the chronic anti-British sentiments which might be anticipated from some circles in Washington.[4]

Since Bradley and Patton were known to be Anglophobic, one might wonder why those two British officers did not let these people sort out their own problems, without letting logic and military necessity get in the way. Fortunately for the Allied alliance, Eisenhower saw the sense in this proposal and, having discussed the situation with Bedell Smith, telephoned Bradley with his decision to split the command. Bradley protested and only stopped doing so when Eisenhower said bluntly, 'Well, Brad, those are my orders.'[5]

It was a decision both wise and timely, for the current situation on the First Army front was not encouraging. Many US units were putting up a stiff resistance and the commanders at regimental and divisional level were doing their best to coordinate the fight and slow down the enemy, but the current communications problem and the speed and force of the enemy attack had caught the senior commanders on the back foot. Units were being fed into the line as they arrived to shore up some perceived local weakness, but no coherent plan had yet evolved, either to stem the current attack or put in a counter-attack.

Eisenhower remarks, for example,[6] that the 101st Airborne had not been sent to Bastogne to hold that town but because it was a road junction from where the division could be deployed as necessary. The same reason is given for the decision to send the 7th US Armored Division to St Vith. The local commanders then took the decision to deploy these divisions for local defence: even by 19 December, three days into the offensive, no overall plan had emerged from 12th Army Group or SHAEF, other than the decision to send Patton's forces north to Bastogne. Overall, the Ardennes battle was in urgent need of grip.

General Hodges had yet to see Bradley or receive more than the sketchiest orders from his Army Group commander. Nor were his forces concentrated: apart from the wide dispersion in the Ardennes that had provoked this reverse, the rest of Hodges' command, four corps mustering twenty divisions, was still widely deployed. While the US forces confronting the enemy did their gallant best to stem the German tide, someone needed to restore a measure of control. Only then could the overwhelming strength of the American armies north and south of this penetration be brought to bear against the German forces in the Bulge.

Few Allied generals were more apt for this task than Bernard Montgomery. A belief in a tidy battle and a balanced army were an engrained part of Montgomery's basic military philosophy, one which accounted for much of his success – and many of the complaints of caution and slowness levied against him by his detractors. If the Americans wanted a different style of command they should have chosen somebody else.

On 20 December, Montgomery had sent a signal to Alanbrooke, telling him that the situation on the US front was:

> Not good... definite lack of grip and control. I have heard nothing from Ike or Bradley and had no orders or requests of any sort. My own opinion is that the American forces have been cut in half and the Germans can reach the Meuse at Namur without opposition. I have told Whiteley that Ike ought to place me in operational command of all troops on the northern part of the front. The situation needs to be handled very firmly and with a tight grip.

Alanbrooke agreed with this assessment but cautioned:

> Be careful what you say to Eisenhower himself on the subject of command set-up as it may do much more harm than good, as he is now probably very worried about the whole situation. It is a different thing to make suggestions to Whiteley as you have done, and this may bear fruit.

This it did. On the same day, Ike telephoned Montgomery and told him to take command of the First and Ninth Armies on the northern front. An announcement to this effect was duly issued to the armies and the press, unfortunately without mentioning that Montgomery was taking over these armies 'on a temporary basis' – an omission that should be noted, for it was to cause a great deal of grief later in the month.

On assuming command of these US forces Montgomery's first task was to find out what was going on; but he already had that task in hand. His team of liaison officers – captains and lieutenants – was despatched to the Ardennes front with orders to keep going forward and keep asking questions until they had an accurate grasp of the situation. By the time Montgomery arrived at Hodges' headquarters at Chaudfontaine, he knew more about the battle than the First Army commander.

Hodges knew of these enquiries and of what Montgomery had done and was already doing, and apparently raised no objections. The US History records[7] that at 0200hrs on 20 December – in other words, before Monty was ordered to take over command – a British major arrived in Hodges' bedroom and told the First Army commander that the British XXX Corps was moving up to secure the west bank of the Meuse with five divisions and that Liège, Namur, Huy and Givet were now a British responsibility; Hodges could concentrate on the enemy to his front as his rear was now secure.

Montgomery arrived at Hodges' headquarters at noon on 20 December, where he met the First Army commander and General Simpson of the Ninth Army. He was travelling in a staff car bearing his Field Marshal insignia and flying a Union Jack pennant – a fact that produced the inevitable accusation that Monty came to Hodges' HQ 'like Christ coming to cleanse the Temple', flaunting his authority over the US generals. It is hard to see what attitude Montgomery should have adopted at this time. It is hardly reasonable to suppose he should have approached the US Headquarters cap in hand and entered by the back door, but when people are determined to take offence, reasons to do so are rarely hard to find.

On the matter of his 'flag-draped staff car' the Field Marshal was simply being sensible. The shooting of US prisoners and the actions of Skorzeny's roving commandos had already forced General Eisenhower to stay at Versailles behind a heavily-armed guard and made US forces in the field very wary of the unusual: a strange, unmarked British staff car roaming about in the US sector would have been a great temptation for trigger-happy and nervous troops.

Nor is there any evidence that Hodges or Simpson were anything other than glad to see the Field Marshal. Montgomery was always genial with his subordinates, willing to help and ready to listen, and so it was here. The first requirement was to tidy up the front, so the three men studied their maps and concluded that the First Army should extend its front from Stavelot to Marche, while trying to assemble a strong corps, the VII Corps, under Montgomery's favourite US general, 'Lightning Joe' Collins, for a counter-attack north west of Marche when the German offensive ran out of steam.

Montgomery ordered that Simpson's Ninth Army should take over responsibility for the First Army's Roer front, releasing VII Corps. Montgomery also positioned British units behind the two US armies and, since the First Army again had no reserve – the airborne divisions having already been committed – he proposed that Hodges should withdraw units from some areas on the north shoulder of the Bulge, so shortening the line and enabling those divisions to come into reserve or be available for a counter-attack.

This suggestion of withdrawal did not go down well with General Hodges and Montgomery did not insist on it. The situation in the north was soon resolved by a signal from General Hasbrouck of the 7th Armored Division at St Vith, who stated that he was under attack on his right flank and while he could hold today – 20 December – he could not guarantee to be in position on the morrow. To resolve this difficulty, Montgomery proposed that XVIII Airborne Corps under Lieutenant General Matthew Ridgeway – currently only the 82nd Airborne and a Combat Command of the 3rd Armored Division – should advance to the line Malmedy–St Vith–Houffalize, straighten the line and make contact with the US forces in Bastogne.

Ridgeway slammed in an attack that night and succeeded in driving Peiper's kampfgruppe away from St Vith. However, with the dawn came the discovery that another German armoured division,116 Panzer, had outflanked XVIII Corps and taken St Vith. The II SS Panzer Corps of Dietrich's Sixth SS Army was now coming forward, just part of a force amounting to twelve German divisions, six of them panzer, which was now attacking First Army's extended front.

This new onslaught came in three waves. The first wave attacked the Malmedy sector on the morning of 21 December and kept battering at this sector of the US line until the afternoon of 23 December. The attack was held, but it took half the divisions of First Army to do it and keep the defensive line along the northern shoulder of the Bulge from collapsing.

The second attack drove the American 7th Armored Division out of St Vith and back across the River Salm. The 7th Armored Division made a classic retreat from this trap and in Montgomery's own words, 'They can come back with all honour. They can come back to more secure positions. They have put up a wonderful show.'

This was true, but the Germans had now opened the road to Houffalize and

St Hubert and General Hasbrouck's handling of his division did not meet with the approval of his corps commander who, on the morning of 22 December, relieved the general of his command, albeit briefly. General Hasbrouck was restored to his division just twelve hours later, but his short dismissal reveals the US reluctance to give up ground. While admirable in itself, this reluctance sometimes flew in the face of military realities: it was of no possible advantage to the Allied position if the fate of the 7th Armored Division had replicated that of the 106th Division, which had been destroyed on the first day of the offensive.

The US History records that while Hodges agreed to this withdrawal from St Vith, he was 'tired and worried from the strain he had been under since December 16'. It is also likely that he was worried over what his peers and superiors would make of any withdrawal, and only marginally comforted by the fact that the order to pull back had originated with Montgomery. American generals did not like withdrawing whatever the circumstances and, as the case of General Hasbrouck indicates the consequences for their reputations could be serious, blighting an entire career. Field Marshal Montgomery had no such inhibitions about withdrawing or defending or attacking. He did whatever made sense at the time and the sensible decision on 21 December was to withdraw the 7th Armored from St Vith.

The sum total of these events and the strong German attack between 21–23 December was that the German advance got to within four miles of Dinant on the Meuse – but the US divisions it encountered were still intact and still fighting, and the Meuse bridges and west bank were securely held by the British. Although it did not seem so at the time, by Christmas Eve the German Ardennes offensive had reached its high-water mark.

The main problems affecting the German armies were stout US resistance and a chronic shortage of fuel. By the evening of 17 December, it is arguable that the aim of Dietrich's Sixth Panzer Army – to cross the Meuse and head for Antwerp via Liège – was already an impossible dream. Manteuffel's leading divisions, Panzer Lehr and 2nd Panzer, were making good progress in the centre but they needed support and fuel. Manteuffel was already requesting both, but the Führer was insistent the offensive should be pursued by Dietrich and the SS, who would retain the follow-up forces and get the available fuel.

Manteuffel did his best and Panzer Lehr duly outflanked Bastogne, but on

21 December his fuel supplies ran out, stranding 2nd Panzer at Tenneville and bringing Kampfgruppe Peiper to a standstill at La Glaize. Had Hitler agreed to switch his last assets from the Sixth Panzer Army to the Fifth Army, it might have been very different. As it was, the time was rapidly approaching for an American counter-attack, one that the US commanders were very anxious to make.

Since taking over the northern battle, Montgomery had done what needed doing. He had tidied up the front, brought up fresh divisions and established a sound defence line. That done, he was content to wait until the Germans exhausted themselves against the stubborn American defences and ran out of men, ammunition and fuel – but anticipated yet another strong attack before they had done so.

This was a view he shared, somewhat surprisingly, with George Patton further south. Patton believed that the further the enemy forged west, the more of their forces his army would eventually destroy. 'The enemy', said Patton at Verdun on 19 December, 'have their head in the meat grinder and I have hold of the handle.' Montgomery was willing to wait for the right moment to strike, but this course of action did not appeal to Bradley or Hodges.

Unlike these two commanders, Montgomery had not been surprised or driven back by this Ardennes offensive. He could take an objective view of the present situation and wait on events. Not so the American commanders. They had been caught unawares and were very anxious to hurl the enemy back as quickly as possible, so restoring both their lines and their reputations before too many searching questions were asked in the US press or Congress.

The problem was that Hodges and Bradley could not have it both ways. Their reluctance to give up ground not only proved expensive in lives, it tended to unbalance the Allied line and prevented Hodges assembling divisions he needed for his much desired counter-attack. Therefore, on Christmas Eve, displaying reserves of tact the American generals never knew he had, Montgomery merely suggested that Hodges should pull Collins' VII Corps back as far as a line between Hotton on the River Ourthe and Andenne on the Meuse, west of Huy, a manoeuvre known in military circles as 'refusing a flank'. Hodges did not like this suggestion either, fearing that refusing a flank might be taken by his colleagues as refusing a fight.

Since the British held the Meuse bridges, this move would have shortened the US line at no strategic cost, but Hodges was most reluctant to comply and Montgomery again did not insist. Telling Collins to fall back slowly before the German pressure, Hodges intimated that Collins should attack whenever he felt able to do so. Montgomery, on the other hand, told Collins to keep his corps out of the battle until ordered to counter-attack – the difference in the two approaches could not be more starkly revealed.

While all this was going on in the north of the Bulge, the eyes of the world were fixed on Bastogne, that small town in the central Ardennes where the 101st Airborne were putting up a gallant and memorable fight. The 101st had narrowly won the race for Bastogne on 19 December and three days later they were still hanging on, denying the enemy armoured divisions – Panzer Lehr, 2nd and 116 Panzer – not only the road junctions in the town but the use of the surrounding roads, thereby slowing their progress and allowing Hodges to get a grip on his forces along the Ourthe.

The Germans then decided to eliminate the American defenders of Bastogne with artillery, bombing and tank and infantry assaults, but found the defences too hard to crack. The German commander, General Heinrich von Luttwitz of the XLVII Panzer Corps, then sent Brigadier General McAuliffe a summons to surrender, a demand to which McAuliffe made a terse, one-world reply – 'Nuts'. Thinking that von Luttwitz might not understand this, the US messenger explained kindly that this meant 'Go to Hell'.

Even as these exchanges were taking place the American position in Bastogne was improving. Clearing skies brought in transport aircraft to drop supplies, especially medical supplies and ammunition, and ground attack aircraft began to take a regular toll of German tanks, now starkly visible against the snowy ground. This was a relief as Patton's progress was being delayed by stubborn German resistance. By 23 December the artillery in Bastogne were rationed to ten rounds, per gun per day, and a strong attack that evening saw some German tanks roving the streets of the town. This attack went on for most of the night before the enemy was driven out.

Bastogne was a stone stuck in the Germans' throat, a choking obstruction that had to be cleared. On 23 December Manteuffel brought up the as yet uncommitted 15th Panzer Grenadier Division, raising the forces besieging Bastogne to three full divisions. Once again a race was on: could the Germans overrun the 'Battered Bastards of Bastogne' before Patton's forces broke through the siege lines and came to their relief? Preceded by bombing, the attack came in at 0200hrs on Christmas Day and scored some immediate if local successes, German tanks and infantry breaking into the town in several places.

The attack was renewed at dawn, but by now US tank destroyers were at work, picking off the German panzers and the panzergrenadiers had their hands full winkling the 101st troopers out of their well-prepared positions. The attack went on until the afternoon of 26 December but no further penetrations were made and on that day the leading tanks of Patton's relief force broke into the town.

Nor was this all. Everywhere along the front the German advance was coming to a halt as their tanks and trucks ran out of fuel, and that stubborn American resistance took its toll. On 23 December Kampfgrupppe Peiper disintegrated. Peiper and some 800 men – SS soldiers the US Army was very anxious to talk to about Malmedy – made their way back to the German lines, leaving behind some 1,200 men and all their equipment – thirty-nine tanks, seventy half tracks, thirty-three guns and all their supply lorries.

The 2nd Panzer Division got as far as the east bank of the Meuse at Dinant. There, almost out of fuel, it had to stop, though some elements were deployed to capture Rochfort. The 2nd Panzer were still engaged in this task when, unable to resist the opportunity to attack, Collins sent his 2nd Armored Division smashing in on their rear. Fighting went on around Rochfort and Dinant until 28 December and when it ended the Fifth Panzer Army had suffered a major defeat. German tanks would never again cross the Meuse – and Collins' action met with Montgomery's entire approval.

On 28 December Eisenhower and Montgomery had a meeting to discuss the development of a battle that was now gradually turning in the Americans' favour. Once again the discussion centred on how soon the US armies could move from defence to attack, with Eisenhower anxious that the move should not be delayed too long. Bradley was also eager to get his forces back to their former lines and proposed that the three US divisions now assembled as a SHAEF reserve should be used to attack the southern face of the Bulge, in concert with Third Army, while the First Army attacked from the north, so squeezing the Germans out of the Bulge.

Montgomery demurred, pointing out that German forces in the north still consisted of seven panzer divisions, and expressing doubts on whether the First

Army was yet ready to begin an offensive. The outcome of these discussions was that Patton should attack the south face of the Bulge as soon as possible and the First Army would attack the north face on 3 January – unless the Germans put in a spoiling attack before then.

Bradley and Patton were dismissive of such caution, complaining that the British were letting them do all the fighting and that the British XXX Corps of four divisions should have been injected into the First Army – this in spite of their constant arguments in recent months about not mixing up US divisions with British formations. This was an American battle, and had been from the moment the first shot was fired. If Bradley and Patton handled their forces correctly they should now be able to defeat the enemy without asking the British to intervene at all; and the British had already freed them from a major strategic worry by keeping their divisions in reserve on the west bank of the Meuse. Although subsequent US accounts make no mention of the fact, British divisions, including the 6th Airborne Division and the 52nd Lowland Division, were now fighting in the Ardennes, though the US divisions – without much help from Bradley or Hodges – had already done the necessary work of stemming the German advance.

Nor was Montgomery's caution unwise. The Führer was planning more offensives, telling Manteuffel that he intended to get his forces across the Meuse, after making a major thrust in the Saar and Alsace. This attack, by eight divisions, in Alsace, Operation Nordwind, began on New Year's Day and caused a great deal of concern at SHAEF, but was quickly repulsed by US resistance at the Saverne gap in the Vosges.

New Year's Day 1945 was also marked by Der Grosse Schlag, an all-out assault by the Luftwaffe on Allied airfields in Belgium and Northern France. This attack, by some 900 German aircraft, took the Allies completely by surprise and a large number of planes were destroyed on the ground, including Field Marshal Montgomery's personal C-47 Dakota. German losses amounted to over 360 aircraft, mostly fighters, which they could ill afford to lose.

Patton was attacking the south face of the Bulge on 2 January when the German assault anticipated by Montgomery came in – their final attempt to take Bastogne. This attack continued for the next two days and was only broken off when Montgomery's push against the north side of the Bulge on 3 January began to bear down on the German forces. By 7 January the Germans were in full retreat and on 8 January Hitler was forced to admit that his Herbstnebel offensive had failed – with the loss of some 81,000 German soldiers and a vast quantity of equipment.

By that time the Allied commanders were quarrelling again. The cause was another memorandum from Montgomery to Eisenhower, which arrived at SHAEF on 29 December, following a less-than-happy meeting between the two men the previous day. This letter restated the position Monty had been putting forward since the previous September – that he should again become Ground Force Commander and take charge of Bradley's group. Monty seems to have assumed that after the recent Ardennes reverses his claim for the field command was beyond dispute. The significant difference this time was that Montgomery's letter included a paragraph that he suggested Eisenhower should include in his next directive to Bradley, namely:

> Twelve and 21 Army Groups will develop operations in accordance with above instructions. From now onwards, full operational direction, control and coordination of these activities is vested in C-in-C, 21 Army Group, subject to such instructions as may be issued by the Supreme Commander from time to time.

Monty concluded his advice by commenting that 'I put the matter up to you again only because I am so anxious not to have another failure.' Monty's letter was extremely unwise. The US commanders had recently had a bad fright, losing a lot of men and a lot of ground, and their nerves were understandably somewhat frayed. They had also been obliged to ask Montgomery to intervene on their northern flank and take command of two US Armies. They did this because they had to, but it went against the grain.

Montgomery, on the other hand, felt this reverse justified all he had been saying for the last months: that the thin spread of units as a result of the broad front policy was a recipe for disaster, and that some central command set-up was needed to keep a day-to-day eye on affairs at the front. These views had been constantly dismissed or ignored, but when they proved correct and disaster duly appeared, Montgomery had been summoned to take charge. This being so, thought Monty, if he was good enough to take charge in hard times, surely he had earned the right to remain in charge thereafter?

The US commanders did not see it that way *at all*. Quite apart from their engrained antipathy to Montgomery and the British, they knew – as the media did not – that this transfer of command of two American armies had been arranged on a temporary basis and they were now most anxious to get back to the *status quo ante*: retake the ground lost, reinforce the divisions, drive back the enemy, and do everything possible to refute the idea that they had been caught napping, a notion which might lead to Congressional enquiries and various recriminations that would be hard to refute.

The matter was becoming crucial because the press, in Britain and the USA, were now moving away from covering the front-line dramas of recent days and starting to ask questions as to why this situation had arisen in the first place – and why Montgomery and the British had ever become involved? The US commanders in Europe and Washington were always extremely sensitive to press comment and criticism – far more so than their British colleagues who, by and large, paid no great attention to journalists.

Eisenhower had already tried to deflect any criticism away from Bradley by proposing that the 12th Army Group commander be promoted to four-star general, a promotion that required Congressional approval. Appointing Montgomery over Bradley's head now would excite just the kind of critical comment the US commanders in Europe were most anxious to avoid. On the other hand, the British media – all Montgomery partisans – were openly claiming the credit for the successes on Montgomery's behalf. Up to this time Montgomery had said nothing, having his hands full on the battlefield.

The sum total of all this was that Montgomery's letter arrived at SHAEF when American nerves were already raw and, urged on by Monty's most devoted foe, Air Marshal Sir Arthur Tedder, Eisenhower was ready for a showdown. With Tedder's eager help, he drafted a signal to the CCS in Washington, asking for permission to relieve Montgomery of his command. Marshall replied on 30 December, offering his full support for any action Eisenhower saw fit to take, adding that there would be widespread disapproval in the United States if a British general was given command of US ground forces.

Montgomery's head was therefore on the block on 31 December when his faithful and popular Chief of Staff, Major-General Freddie de Guingand, intervened. De Guingand was visiting SHAEF that day and Bedell Smith informed him that Eisenhower was determined that Montgomery must go. Bedell Smith was actually doubtful about the wisdom of this move, and supported de

Guingand when he begged Eisenhower and Tedder for a little time to sort Monty out. Bedell Smith was no lover of Montgomery, but he was no chauvinistic Anglophobe either, and far more politically astute than the Supreme Commander. After all, if Eisenhower sacked Montgomery now, what reason could he advance for doing so? Just seven days previously Ike had given Montgomery the field command of two US armies and, with the enemy falling back on every side, he could hardly claim that Montgomery had mishandled them.

Arguing with one's senior commander may be unwise, but it is hardly a sacking offence, and Montgomery was saying nothing he had not said many times before. The failures of recent weeks, those losses of men and territory listed above, could not be laid at Montgomery's door, and if Monty went and Bradley stayed – after the loss of much ground and 75,000 American soldiers – questions were certainly going to be asked by the British press and in parliament that higher minds at SHAEF would find very hard to answer. Sacking Montgomery would certainly cause an almighty row between the Allies. The US Congress and media would get involved. Certain senior officers at SHAEF were soon fervently hoping that de Guingand could smooth the path to reconciliation.

De Guingand flew back to Montgomery's headquarters and found the Field Marshal blissfully unaware of his pending dismissal. De Guingand quickly convinced Montgomery that this matter was serious and an alarmed Monty duly despatched an apologetic letter:

31 December 1944.

Dear Ike,

I have just seen Freddie and understand you are very worried by many considerations in these difficult days. I have given you my frank views because I have felt you like this. I am sure there are many factors which have a bearing beyond anything I realise. Whatever your decision may be you can rely on me one hundred per cent to make it work and I know Bradley will do the same.

Very distressed that my letter may have upset you and I would ask you to tear it up.

Your very devoted subordinate,

Monty

This large slice of humble pie apparently did the trick, and a telegram from Eisenhower put an end to the matter:

> Dear Monty,
>
> I received your telegram this morning. I truly appreciate the understanding attitude it indicates. With the earnest hope that 1945 will be the most successful of your entire career.
>
> As ever,
>
> Ike.

Common sense had apparently won the day. However, a broader reading of the situation indicates that had Montgomery been sacked the resulting explosion in military, political and public circles would have done Eisenhower and Bradley no good at all: in early January 1945 they needed to damp down public interest in the Ardennes debacle, not add to it. Sacking this successful Allied commander – the senior commander of America's closest ally – would need a better reason than any Eisenhower could currently advance and might provoke a searching enquiry into the causes – and losses – of the Ardennes offensive, which could hardly rebound to Bradley's credit. Ike was therefore wise to accept Montgomery's apology and hope the matter would go away.

This hope was to be realised in an unexpected way. On 7 January Montgomery elected to give a press conference on the Ardennes battle – a conference which various friends and advisers strongly urged him not to give. He should have followed their advice, for Monty's address was widely misquoted and gave grievous offence to Bradley and others at SHAEF who were always more than willing to take offence at anything Montgomery said or did.

In his memoirs Eisenhower writes: 'I doubt if Montgomery ever came to realise how resentful some American commanders were. They believed he had belittled them – and they were not slow to voice reciprocal scorn and contempt.'[8]

The full text of Montgomery's 7 January address actually gives little cause for offence. Though not without some typical Montgomery bombast, the address pays full credit to the American soldier:

> I first saw him in battle in Sicily and I formed a very high opinion of him. I saw him again in Italy. He is a brave fighting man, steady under fire and with that tenacity in battle which marks the first-class soldier. I have a great affection

and admiration for the American soldier. I salute the brave fighting men of America. I never want to fight alongside better soldiers. I have tried to feel that I am almost an American soldier myself so that I might take no unsuitable action or offend them in any way... Rundstedt was really beaten by the good fighting qualities of the American soldier and by the team work of the Allies.

This eulogy to the American soldier can surely give few grounds for complaint, and Montgomery was equally fulsome when he came to speak of General Eisenhower:

The captain of our team is Eisenhower. I am absolutely devoted to Ike; we are the greatest of friends. It grieves me when I see uncomplimentary articles about him in the British press; he bears a great burden, he needs our fullest support, he has the right to expect it and it is up to all of us to see that he gets it.

This is directed at current press comment, particularly in the British press, which praised Montgomery, was somewhat critical of the US commanders, and currently upsetting certain sensitive people at SHAEF and 12th Army Group. It should be remembered that this address was to war correspondents, for Montgomery concludes: 'And so I would ask all of you to lend a hand and stop that sort of thing; let us rally round General Eisenhower, the captain of our team, and so help win the match.'

So far, so good, but there were some omissions in this address that Montgomery's enemies were quick to seize on. First of all, there was no mention whatsoever of Bradley or Patton. Since neither officer ever missed a chance to denigrate Montgomery – or the British – and Bradley's performance had been less than impressive lately, this omission is understandable, if somewhat unwise. Secondly, there was a failure to stress that the major components in the forces Montgomery commanded in the Ardennes were the US First and Ninth Armies. Given the tissue-thin skin of most US commanders, these points should not only have been made but laid on with a trowel.

Finally, there was the matter of tone. Certain parts of Monty's address, that he found the battle 'one of the most interesting I have ever handled' for example, inevitably come over as patronising... and then the German propaganda chief, Dr Josef Goebbels, took a hand in the game. An edited version of Montgomery's speech, honing up any divisive aspects, was broadcast by German radio and then picked up as a source by the US radio stations. When it came to taking offence at Montgomery and disparaging the British even the enemy came in useful and Dr Goebbels' version gained wide currency and caused severe angst in US circles.

The one taking grievous offence was Bradley. His role in the Ardennes affair had been at best undistinguished and he was probably not unaware of the fact. Bradley chose to interpret Montgomery's speech as an attempt to claim the ultimate ending of the Ardennes affair as a triumph for the Field Marshal – and the British.

Though it is hard to see where Monty's words lend themselves to that interpretation, Bradley declared that they undermined his entire position and could lead to a loss of confidence with his leadership among the soldiers of the 12th Army Group. This sort of comment verges on the hysterical, but Montgomery should have been well aware by now of just how quick the Americans were to take offence at anything he said, and listened to those on his staff who were aware of how sensitive US–British relations were at this time.

Part of the trouble, yet again was the press, but the main problem was caused by SHAEF, which on 5 January had issued a statement saying that Montgomery's command of the US armies was 'only temporary'. This it was, and no one at SHAEF or 21st Army Group ever supposed otherwise, but one might ask why it was necessary to mention this fact in an official handout more than two weeks after Montgomery had taken charge of the First and Ninth Armies? The most obvious reason was to placate Bradley.

This information was neither secret nor embargoed; everyone, soldiers, press and the public in Britain and the USA, knew that Montgomery had been put in command of two US armies – but the press and the British public were not fully aware it was a 'temporary' appointment. This belated statement was therefore seized on by the British press as a slap in the face for their favourite commander, a general good enough to command Allied armies when the Americans had got themselves into trouble but one to be brushed aside again when the going got easy. These British papers found their way to SHAEF and Bradley's HQ and gave yet more offence. Montgomery's press conference on 7 January was an attempt to limit this damage and prevent such a thing happening again – an effort that was doomed from the start. In his *Memoirs* Montgomery states:

> I think now that I should never have held that press conference. So great
> were the feelings against me on the part of the American generals that whatever
> I said was bound to be wrong. I should therefore have said nothing.[9]

This is true, but it could also be argued that Montgomery's press conference, so widely reported and condemned at the time, proved very useful to the American commanders. Newspaper headlines and editorials in the USA promptly abandoned critical comment or enquiry into the causes of the Ardennes debacle to concentrate on this new allegation, that the detested Montgomery was attempting to hog the credit for the British and disparage the heroism and sacrifice of American soldiers – an accusation that is hardly borne out by the text of his address.

Bradley was sensitive to criticism because his actions before and during the Ardennes battle leave plenty of grounds for criticism. He had persistently allowed Patton to re-interpret Eisenhower's directives and so undermine the Supreme Commander's plans. He had thinned out his forces on the Ardennes front but claimed after the battle this was a 'calculated risk' enabling him to send more divisions north and south. He also claimed that the 'build-up of German forces in the Cologne area had been observed for some weeks and the possibility of an attack through the Ardennes had been thoroughly studied by me and my Staff.'

Evidence for this latter claim is lacking, but if correct it can only add to unkind suspicions that Bradley and his staff were simply incompetent. Even after Eisenhower had queried the thin state of the US line in the Ardennes, Bradley did nothing to thicken it up. All the factual evidence suggests that the Ardennes attack came as a complete surprise to Bradley, an attack for which no contingency plans whatsoever had been made by the 12th Army Group commander and his staff. Nor can Eisenhower escape criticism here. If he felt that the VIII Corps line across the Ardennes front was too thin, why did he not *order* Bradley to do something about it? Waving vaguely at the brooding Ardennes woods and then passing on to other matters was not going to solve the problem: a commander must command.

Nor did Bradley react swiftly or wisely after the attack. As related, his reactions were slow. Yes, two divisions were ordered in from the Ninth and Third Armies on 16 December, but it was another full day before he called for the SHAEF reserves. It was not until 18 December, two days into the breakthrough, that he halted Patton's pending offensive in the Saar and not until 19 December that he began pulling divisions out of the Roer offensive. During this time – four full days – Bradley had made little attempt to provide any of his army commanders with some overall strategic plan and yet he was annoyed when Eisenhower brought in Montgomery to command the northern flank on 20 December.

This post-action statement, delivered to the press on 9 January, should be seen for what it is: a feeble attempt to excuse some grave miscalculations in early December and at the start of the battle, and 'play the Montgomery card' with the US press and public, where any mention of the British Field Marshal provoked automatic derision.

Montgomery's military philosophy is quite clear. He believed in commanding a balanced army – one in which the fighting arm was fully backed up by the logistical component. Unless those two elements were balanced, the army would eventually grind to a halt, short of the wherewithal to carry on fighting. Before this happened, Montgomery would pause to bring the logistical support forward – a process he called 'bringing up the logistical tail' and so fighting a 'tidy battle'.

There was nothing wrong with this philosophy. Montgomery did not believe in ad-hoc, make-it-up-as-you-go-along strategies, but dealing with the logistical problem did entail periodic pauses. These gave the Americans an excuse for that endless bitching and whining about Montgomery's 'caution' and 'slowness' which has haunted his reputation ever since. The record shows that the US armies also paused; the difference is that Montgomery slowed before he outran his supplies, while Patton and his ilk stopped because they had outrun their supplies.

The point here is that the Americans and SHAEF already knew about Montgomery's philosophy and therefore how he would exercise command. If they had wanted a different command style, they should have appointed another commander: 'Lightning Joe' Collins of the VII Corps comes to mind. Montgomery believed in a tidy battlefield and his critics should have known that also. Instead, they chose to complain, but what they saw was what they got: Montgomery delivered order from confusion during the Ardennes battle and the restoration of order paved the basis for what has since been loudly claimed as an American victory. What is the problem with admitting that fact?

Any analysis of the Ardennes fighting shows that the real credit for halting and driving back the enemy in the Ardennes belongs to the American soldiers and to their commanders at corps, divisional and regimental level: men who kept their heads and held their ground and dragged victory out of defeat – at the cost of some 75,000 casualties *in one month*. This can be compared with the 125,000 US casualties taken during the successful three-month Battle of Normandy. The comparison is not to Bradley's credit.

Full credit should be given to General Eisenhower for having the strength of character to see what was needed at the crux of the battle and for appointing Montgomery to command the northern front of the Bulge, knowing his decision would be vastly unpopular at SHAEF and in Washington. The exercise of command is not a popularity contest; it is pleasant to be popular but more essential to be right, and in taking this decision Ike clearly was right.

With the ending of the Ardennes battle in mid-January 1945, the post-Normandy phase of the Allied drive to defeat the German Reich comes to a close. The battles in north-west Europe between September 1944 and January 1945, at Nijmegen, Arnhem, Walcheren, Aachen, in the Heurtgen Forest and the Ardennes, had been bitter, expensive and strategically inconclusive. Few, if any, of those optimistic, post-Normandy plans had been realised and when the Ardennes fighting petered out in mid-January, the Rhine was as far away as ever from the Allied armies in the north and centre.

Much heavy fighting lay ahead before these armies crossed the Rhine in March 1945, and it is arguable that had a better strategy been employed, and some firmer direction been given to the Allied armies as a whole, post-Normandy, they might have been across the Rhine in 1944 and in a better position to fight their way swiftly into Germany in 1945 – with all the post-war political advantages that might have offered.

The reasons why that objective was not achieved in 1944 and why those bitter battles did not add up to a coherent strategy have been given in this book. The root of the problem clearly lies in the various decisions over command and strategy taken – or not taken – at SHAEF, with the resulting effect on the armies in the field. Those decisions were coloured by political and logistical considerations. These may strike some readers as irrelevant to the argument, but it is unrealistic to suppose that military decisions can be taken in isolation, especially in an alliance where national considerations are sure to intervene.

It now only remains to review the actions of the Allied commanders and see what fair and reasonable conclusions can be reached about the four-month long battle for the Rhine.

15 · EPILOGUE

If there is one thing harder than fighting a war with Allies it is
fighting a war without them.

WINSTON S. CHURCHILL

The core arguments in this book have centred on two main topics, strategy and command, and the disputes over those matters between Eisenhower and Montgomery in the last months of 1944. The question to be addressed now is, who was right? There is no easy answer, and underpinning that question is another; had the right strategy been followed, had the right command structure been in place, is it possible that the Second World War in Europe would have been over by the end of 1944?

While euphoria was gripping the Allied commanders at the end of August 1944, many people thought the end of the war was in sight. However, Winston Churchill, that shrewd politician, was much more sceptical, declaring it more than probable that the war would continue into 1945, and if a German collapse did come, it would be due more to internal factors – another, more successful, assassination attempt on the Führer, perhaps – than any pressure exerted by the Allied armies in the West.

Even without the inestimable benefits of hindsight, this last assessment seems correct. Study the factors affecting the progress of the Western armies in the autumn of 1944, and any hopes that their actions would deliver a swift victory before the end of the year – with or without Soviet assistance from the East – are clearly revealed as a pipe dream. This is not to say that more could not have been achieved in 1944.

The road to victory stretched long and hard before the Allied armies in September 1944. Victory over Germany was a distant prospect, so more limited objectives had to be considered and the first major post-Seine step would have been a successful crossing of the River Rhine. It can be fairly argued that had it been achieved – and depending on *when* it was achieved – the Western armies would have been either well placed to push into Germany in the autumn and winter of 1944–5 or in a better position to resume their advance when the weather moderated in the spring of 1945.

This author's conclusion is that the war would not have ended in 1944, but that the Allies could have achieved more limited objectives and crossed the Rhine before the end of the year – had the right strategy been employed and had the various Army commanders put their shoulders to the same wheel. Their failure to do so can be largely attributed to Eisenhower's chronic lack of grip.

His first decision, whether to continue the rapid pursuit of the retreating armies or stop the Allied advance until Antwerp was open, should have been made in favour of rapid pursuit – such an opportunity to drive the enemy back, albeit, given the supply situation, on a narrow front, would not occur again. This narrow pursuit – recalling Market Garden – could have continued until a Rhine crossing had been achieved, probably on a line between Arnhem and Wesel. This Rhine bridgehead could then have been expanded, again as per the Market Garden plan, to the Zuyder Zee, allowing the armies across the Rhine to pivot their front to the east.

With that much achieved, the Scheldt should have been cleared and Antwerp opened to shipping, while the Arnhem corridor was widened and the German Fifteenth Army destroyed. Then, with supplies assured and more US divisions available, another broad front could have been established, one facing east rather than north, the armies tasked to clear both banks of the Rhine, with a possible pivot on Aachen. Had all gone well, the Allies would have been able to clear the west bank of the Rhine and begin the capture of the Ruhr.

Would this strategy have worked? Since only parts of it were tried, one cannot tell, but at least it resembles a *strategy*, a logical progression of events, and treats Eisenhower's steadily-expanding forces as a composite Allied army, not a disparate collection of Army Groups, all competing for supplies and attention. Indeed, some parts of this theoretical strategy were tried later, in the Veritable and Grenade offensives to clear the Reichswald, in the operations to clear the west bank of the Rhine and during the subsequent river crossings in 1945. It is at least arguable that had such a strategy been in place in 1944, it would have delivered those assets just that much sooner.

There were, of course, a large number of snags, not least the reaction of the Germans, the deteriorating autumn and winter weather inhibiting the use of the Allied air forces – and that old bugbear, national rivalries. The political snag with the strategy proposed above is that it places Montgomery's 21st Army Group in pole position across the Rhine, in position to garner a great deal of credit for the advance into Germany.

This would not have pleased General Marshall, but there was a solution to this dilemma. To carry out this strategy Montgomery would need more divisions; these could have been found by attaching Simpson's Ninth Army to Montgomery's Group – as was done in 1945. Simpson got on well with Montgomery and there would have been no problems there. This Ninth Army transfer would provide the Allies with an ecumenical force – American, British, Canadian – across the Rhine and the glory of overrunning the Ruhr could have been shared among the Allied nations.

In the event, the Rhine was not crossed until March 1945, six months after the Allied armies crossed the Seine; and a great many soldiers' lives were lost during that time. The reasons for that delay have been analysed and need not be reconsidered – but the focus of any argument on the campaign leads directly back to matters of command.

The question of command is easier to answer than that of strategy because the outcome of the argument was never in doubt. Given that the USA had more forces in the ETO, that General George C. Marshall, Chairman of the Combined Chiefs of Staff, wanted American generals to have the larger share of the action – and the subsequent credit – the notion that the British would ever get their hands on the levers of command at anything above Army Group level was another pipe dream. Even if the hands in question had not belonged to Field Marshal Montgomery, in any argument over the command set-up, the American view would prevail. To this can be added the fact that Monty was a good general but a poor advocate. By linking strategy to command he ensured his views on either subject would never get a fair hearing.

However, winning the argument is not the same as proving the case. The Americans won the command argument by *force majeure* and there is no point debating that Anglo-American argument yet again; it is far more important to put the nationality issue aside for the moment and consider which of the two generals was right – or mostly right – during the period in question. Given the arguments advanced in the previous pages, readers may be surprised that, in this author's opinion, Eisenhower was right to reject the idea of a Ground Force Commander on the Normandy model.

That opinion is largely founded on the question of scale. Circumstances alter cases and when Dever's 6th Army Group came under Eisenhower's command on 14 September 1944, circumstances had changed in both the number of armies under SHAEF command and the width of front involved. In Normandy, General Montgomery, while retaining control of his own 21st Army Group and taking a very personal interest in Dempsey's Second Army, also directed – or advised on – the operations of Bradley's First Army and, briefly, Bradley's 12th Army Group of two armies. At their strongest these two Allied groups consisted of four armies – two American, one British, one Canadian – all operating within one French province with a combined front of around 150 miles.

After 15 September the Allied front rapidly expanded to over 500 miles and the three Army Groups – the 21st, 12th and 6th – now contained the First Canadian Army, the British Second Army, the Ninth, First, Third and Seventh US Armies and the First French Army, a colossal force that eventually contained some four million soldiers. This was certainly too much for one man to handle but, equally, it was too large a force and too extended a front for a duplication of the Normandy system – again without discussing the problems inherent in employing Field Marshal Montgomery in this role.

Eisenhower's proposal, that each Army Group commander should be a commander-in-chief within his own operational area, therefore has merit. This system of command provides a great deal of field authority to the relevant C-in-C's and leaves the Supreme Commander with just three subordinates to deal with directly. Even a corporal commands more than three men and as command systems go, it should have worked… so why didn't it?

Where it went awry has little to do with Montgomery's oft-repeated argument that the system itself was at fault, and more to do with with Eisenhower's almost total failure to grip his subordinates, most notably Patton, and insist on compliance with his orders. To this should be added an apparent inability to decide on a firm strategy, dictated by the current situation, and stick to it for any period of time.

The Supreme Commander was responsible for strategy, but in his role of field commander, he also had to ensure his subordinates followed that strategy and made it work. This Eisenhower failed to do, probably because he was by nature a compromiser and conciliator, but also because he had enough on his plate without being dragged into the day-by-day chore of ensuring that his strategy and policies were not being tinkered with by his subordinates. In the final analysis, Ike simply did not have the time to check up on what his subordinates were doing.

For that task he did indeed need someone in the field, close to the action, checking that the Supreme Commander's orders were being obeyed. It is not hard to visualise a scenario in which General Eisenhower, with his penchant for meetings and conferences, briefs his three commanders-in-chief – and then adds that his deputy supreme commander, or better still, Bedell Smith, will be visiting their respective headquarters on a regular basis to see how they are getting on. The C-in-C's might not have liked this but their likes and dislikes are of no importance; the Supreme Commander has the right to ensure that his orders were not being altered, amended or compromised by independent action unless he was informed of such action and the reason for it – and approved.

Eisenhower proposed a perfectly workable command set-up, but it did not work because he lacked the grip and the experience of field command to make it work. Eisenhower was superb in his prime role as Allied Supreme Commander and nothing can detract from his success in that role. The problem is that Eisenhower also had another role, as ground force commander, and in that his performance was frequently lamentable. This was partly through a lack of experience and partly because of his conciliatory character, but also because two of his subordinates, Generals Bradley and Patton, were frequently disloyal and constantly undermined his orders – and he let them get away with it.

In such a situation errors are inevitable. It is no good having a viable command set-up without the strength of character to make it work. Like many good people, Eisenhower had the faults of his virtues: he was reasonable, open-minded, willing to listen – perhaps too willing to listen – to people who were often far from reasonable. He was perfectly capable of crushing opposition when confronted with it directly – as with de Gaulle over the Strasbourg issue – but a reasonable approach all too often won him round to a course of action that was inimical to his strategy and interests, and he failed to realise this.

The wider his responsibilities became – and they were always awesome – the more Eisenhower needed to devise and maintain a coherent strategy that took into account the changing exigencies of the time – logistics, manpower, weather, terrain, choice of objectives – and lead to some clear, attainable objectives. This did not happen during the period under examination and the results of that failure have already been described: delay, confusion, failure to achieve any major strategic objective.

On the matter of strategy, therefore, the balance of the argument lies with Montgomery. Montgomery is a much-criticised man, at least in US military circles, but according to the American historian Harold R. Winton, 'Monty was a better general than many historians, particularly American historians, are willing to admit.'[1] This is true, and Monty's record supports that claim, but Montgomery's many admirers must not be too quick to assume that he was always right – and should not overlook the fact that his character kept getting in the way of his abilities.

Ike and Monty faced different problems and Monty, notoriously single-minded, totally failed to comprehend that fact. From 1 September 1944, he was an Army Group commander; the winds and pressures that blew about that post were mild compared with those gales constantly battering the Supreme Commander, not least the blasts from Marshall in Washington and US public and political opinion. To simply award the strategic argument prize to Montgomery on the grounds of practical military expedience is taking the narrow view. National and political considerations affected almost every military proposal.

Nevertheless, while accepting those points, Montgomery was generally right over the strategic issue and equally right that the matter of strategy was closely linked to the matter of command. It is interesting to consider what would have happened if the commander-in-chief command system had worked – and Eisenhower had listened to Montgomery on matters of strategy.

During the period covered in this book, the broad front strategy was a mistake. By spreading his resources over a 600-mile front, Eisenhower ensured that his armies were not strong enough at any point to achieve the breakthrough necessary to reach the Rhine and perhaps cross it. Strategy is often a question of horses for courses, not of deciding what strategy is right but which strategy is right *now*. In the circumstances of late 1944, Montgomery's demands for a concentration of force were correct; had they been followed more would have been achieved, probably including a Rhine crossing.

To make his broad front strategy viable, Eisenhower needed more troops and a source of supply capable of maintaining those troops in the field. In the end, by the early spring of 1945, Eisenhower had finally obtained the facilities of Antwerp and more troops; with these assets to hand his broad front policy worked – and then, on the *post hoc, ergo propter hoc* argument so beloved by so many US historians, Eisenhower was awarded the palm of victory in the European war. In the end – but only in the end – Eisenhower won.

This undeniable fact has led some historians to the conclusion that Eisenhower was therefore always right, but that view is not supported by the facts. It is neither right nor sensible to cherry-pick those parts of the story that suit one particular argument. Eisenhower's strategy may have delivered the goods in the spring of 1945, but in the autumn of 1944 his strategy was little short of lamentable: to pretend otherwise is a denial of the facts. On the evidence presented during the months between the Normandy breakout and the end of the Bulge, the facts suggest that Eisenhower was a superb Supreme Commander but an indifferent field commander.

The central command and strategy argument having been extensively aired, it would be as well to look at some of the peripheral factors that seem to have played an important role in the post-Normandy campaign, and the first of these is Anglophobia.

Any recent love-in between the Anglo-American peoples should not conceal the fact that Anglophobia was a potent factor in their relations during the Second World War. Most US histories admit that Anglophobia was rife in Washington and at SHAEF, and the British are freely and frequently criticised in the memoirs of US commanders – criticism that is sometimes fully justified but is all too often based on a selective interpretation of the facts. Among the US officers at SHAEF Montgomery became the lightning rod for the more open manifestations of Anglophobia, but it seems to have been deeply engrained in many American officers and surfaces constantly in their post-war accounts. Anglophobia, open or covert, undoubtedly affected attitudes towards their

British colleagues and to any British proposal on the conduct of the campaign, whatever its merit.

Anglophobia has deep roots in American society. In the history of the United States it is Britain – or more often, England – which is seen as the traditional enemy of the Republic; not Germany, not Japan, certainly not Italy, but Britain, is constantly depicted as the United States' historic and implacable foe. The Americans look back on a history of actions against the British: Paul Revere's ride, 'The Shot Heard Round The World', the Boston Massacre, Bunker Hill, Saratoga, the War of 1812 – when the British burned down the White House – the Battle of New Orleans... the list is endless and the British are always the villains

One result of this is – or certainly was – a willingness to believe any slander about the devious, snobbish, cold-hearted British, a people always eager to disparage or deceive the honest, straight-talking American. When people are determined to take offence, reasons to do so are never hard to find. The curious thing is that this antipathy only went one way. The British may not have viewed their American allies as supermen or have been warmed by that glow of self-esteem with which many American generals and historians choose to surround themselves, but one will search widely to find evidence of any deep rooted anti-American feeling among the British.

On the other hand, one can make too much of this Anglophobia. Many Americans liked, even admired, their British comrades-in-arms. In the end, the Alliance worked and delivered an Allied victory. This author would also like to record that in over a quarter of a century of interviewing American and British front-line veterans he has *never* heard one disparaging word from one about the other. Front-line soldiers are too decent and too experienced to indulge in such behaviour.

However, reading the memoirs of the American generals and the comments passed from one to another, any friend of the USA is constantly saddened by how thin-skinned the US generals seemed to be, how eager to find fault and pass the blame for any failure to their British allies – undisturbed in most cases by the evidence. This attitude certainly affected the conduct of the European war and the decisions taken during the campaign.

In the end, brushing all other excuses aside, the US claim to total command and control was based on military demographics. They had more troops in theatre, they were calling the shots, and they would run the show.

This argument was the clincher and most people in Britain – including CIGS Field Marshal Alanbrooke – accepted the fact with as much grace as they could muster. Not so Montgomery, as Alanbrooke records:

> During the afternoon I had a talk with Monty before he returned to France. He still goes on harping over the command in France and the fact that the war is being prolonged. He has got this on the brain as it affects his own personal position and he cannot put up with not being the sole commander of the ground forces. I agree that the set-up is bad but not one that can be easily altered as the Americans now have the preponderating force in France and naturally consider they should have a major say in running the war. Perhaps when they see the results of dispersing their strength all along the front it may be easier to convince them that some drastic change is desirable.[2]

No such change came. Indeed, with Antwerp open and the American presence increasing and the British and Canadians running out of men, no change was deemed necessary. The US doctrine of attrition could be employed and from January of 1945 the Allied Armies – and the Soviets – gradually wore the enemy down. Victory in Europe came, and none too soon, on 8 May 1945 – VE Day. That happy outcome need not obscure the tangled events of late 1944 which this book has attempted to disentangle.

There are lessons to be learned from studying the Rhine campaign but it is very doubtful if those lessons will ever be applied in the future. American military dominance is now complete in the west, if not in the world. If the generals commanding armies totalling over a million British and Canadian soldiers fighting in north-west Europe could not get a hearing in 1944, it is unlikely that the commander of a light armoured division of two brigades – the maximum force Britain can now put in the field – will do any better today.

The major lessons of the post-Normandy campaign lie in the area of command and might be studied profitably by any military commander. A commander should not be bound by established doctrine; his actions should relate to the situation confronting him at the time. A commander who cannot control his subordinates cannot control a battle; a subordinate who will not obey orders should be axed. A commander must evolve a consistent, workable strategy and stick to it – order and counter-order inevitably lead to disorder.

Chauvinism and nationalism are a menace to allied operations, irrespective of the comparative size of the forces; it does not matter where an idea comes from, only whether it is right or wrong – or workable. The secret of applying any of these precepts lies in the use of grip. A commander who lacks grip should also be pole-axed.

If Eisenhower won in the end and has been awarded the palm of victory it seems only fair to let the much-maligned Field Marshal Montgomery have the last word – and a typically Montgomery word at that. Writing in the 21st Army Group log on 12 May 1945, four days after the war in Europe ended, Montgomery concluded:

> And so the campaign in North West Europe is finished. I am glad. It has been a tough business. When I review the campaign as a whole I am amazed at the mistakes we made. The organisation for command was always faulty. The Supreme Commander had no firm ideas as to how to conduct the war and was blown about in the wind all over the place. At that particular business he was quite useless.
>
> The Deputy Supreme Commander [Tedder] was completely ineffective; none of the Army Commanders would see him and growled if he appeared on the horizon... and SHAEF were completely out of their depth all the time. And yet we won.
>
> The point to understand is that if we had run the show properly the war could have been finished by Xmas, 1944. The blame for this must rest with the Americans. And yet, to balance this, it is merely necessary to say one thing; if the Americans had not come along and lent a hand we would never have won the war at all.

That seems fair and so, with something for everyone, we can leave this story there.

NOTES TO THE TEXT

CHAPTER 1

1   Bradley, *A Soldier's Story*, p. 398
2   See comments on Monty collected for the author's book *Eighth Army*, John Murray, 2004
3   Montgomery, *Memoirs*, p. 268
4   ibid, p. 268
5   Eisenhower, *Crusade in Europe*, p. 251
6   D'Este, *Eisenhower: A Soldier's Life*
7   Author's oral history collection, 2003
8   Montgomery, *Memoirs*, p. 52
9   ibid, p. 270
10 ibid, p. 269
11 US Official History, *The Siegfried Line Campaign*, p. 9
12 *Post-Neptune Courses of Action after Capture of the Lodgement Area; Main Objectives and Axis of Advance*, SHAEF, 1944

CHAPTER 2

1   British Official History, Vol. 11, *The Defeat of Germany*, p. 3
2   Correspondence with the author, 2004
3   Message, Model to Jodl, 4 September
4   Wilmot, *The Struggle for Europe*, p. 531
5   ibid, pp. 533–4
6   British Official History, Vol. 11, *The Defeat of Germany*, p. 9

CHAPTER 3

1   Van Creveld, *Supplying War*, p. 122
2   ibid, p. 221
3   Graham and Bidwell, *Coalitions, Politicians and Generals*, p. 203
4   ibid, p. 204
5   Author's oral history collection, 1994
6   ibid

7   Ruppenthal, *Command Decisions*, p. 327
8   Van Creveld, *Supplying War*, p. 226
9   ibid, p. 228
10 ibid, p. 230
11 ibid, p. 222
12 Wilmot, *The Struggle for Europe*, p. 525
13 US Official History, Vol. 2, *Logistical Support of the Armies*, pp. 10–11
14 Van Creveld, *Supplying War*, p. 227
15 ibid, pp. 226–7
16 US Official History, Vol. 2, *Logistical Support of the Armies*, p. 9
17 ibid, p. 9
18 D'Este, *Eisenhower: A Soldier's Life*, p. 587
19 ibid, p. 587
20 Gilbert, *Road to Victory: Winston S. Churchill 1941–1945*, p. 943
21 Wilmot, *The Struggle for Europe*, p. 537

CHAPTER 4

1   Thompson, *Ready for Anything*, p. 195
2   US Official History, *The Siegfried Line Campaign*, p. 120
3   Thompson, *Ready for Anything*, p. 208
4   ibid, p. 199
5   SHAEF Weekly Intelligence summary, 9 September 1944
6   Intelligence Survey 100
7   Operation Instruction No 24
8   US Official History, MacDonald, *The Decision to Launch Operation Market Garden*, Chapter 19
9   British Official History, Vol. 11, *The Defeat of Germany*, p. 31
10 US Official History, *The Siegfried Line Campaign*, p. 144

CHAPTER 5

1 US Official History, *The Siegfried Line Campaign*, p. 156
2 ibid, p. 168
3 Gavin, *On to Berlin*, p. 147
4 ibid, p. 150
5 US Official History, *The Siegfried Line Campaign*, p. 156
6 ibid, p. 162
7 ibid, p. 162
8 British Official History, Vol. 11, *The Defeat of Germany*, p. 97
9 Gavin, *On to Berlin*, p. 151
10 US Official History, *The Siegfried Line Campaign*, p. 162
11 ibid, p. 162
12 ibid, p. 163
13 ibid, p. 164
14 ibid, p. 164
15 ibid, p. 165
16 ibid, p. 165
17 ibid, p. 167
18 ibid, p. 166
19 ibid, p. 168
20 ibid, p. 173
21 ibid, p. 174
22 ibid, p. 175
23 ibid, p. 175
24 Gavin, *On to Berlin*, p. 171
25 US Official History, *The Siegfried Line Campaign*, p. 176
26 ibid, p. 179
27 *History of the Guards Armoured Division*, p. 229, and *History of the Royal Engineers*
28 Interview with the author, 2004
29 Gavin, *On to Berlin*, p. 181
30 ibid, p. 131
31 ibid, p. 132
32 US Official History, *The Siegfried Line Campaign*, p. 183
33 Lamb, *Montgomery in Europe 1943–1945*, p. 243
34 US Official History, *The Siegfried Line Campaign*, p. 185
35 ibid, p. 185

CHAPTER 6

1 Gavin, *On to Berlin*, p. 150
2 Conversation with the author, 1990
3 Instructions No. 1 – Operation Market Garden, to Major General R. E. Urquhart, DSO
4 Lamb, *Montgomery in Europe 1943–1945*, pp. 222–3
5 Urquhart, *Arnhem*
6 Thompson, *Ready for Anything*, p. 243
7 Major Charles Farrell, MC, 6th Guards Tank Brigade, conversation with the author, 2004
8 Otway, *Airborne Forces*

CHAPTER 7

1 Bryant, *Triumph in the West*, p. 291
2 Montgomery, *Memoirs*, p. 297
3 Letter to the author, 2003
4 British Official History, Vol. 11, *The Defeat of Germany*, p. 80
5 Wilmot, *The Struggle for Europe*, p. 604
6 Account supplied to the author, 2003
7 British Official History, Vol. 11, *The Defeat of Germany*, p. 69
8 ibid, p. 103
9 Account supplied to the author, 2003
10 British Official History, Vol. 11, *The Defeat of Germany*, p. 121
11 ibid, p. 128
12 Canadian Official History, *The Canadian army, 1939–1945*, p. 225

CHAPTER 8

1 Butcher, *My Three Years with Eisenhower*, p. 567
2 US Official History, *The Siegfried Line Campaign*, p. 14
3 ibid, p. 39
4 Wilmot, *The Struggle for Europe*, pp. 553–4
5 US Official History, *The Siegfried Line Campaign*, p. 46
6 Account supplied to the author
7 US Official History, *The Siegfried Line Campaign*, pp. 62–3
8 ibid, p. 77
9 ibid, pp. 89–90
10 Patton, *War as I Knew It*, p. 133

CHAPTER 9

1 Vol. 3, Autumn 2003
2 US Official History, *A Time for Trumpets*, p. 614
3 Wilmot, *The Struggle for Europe*, p. 590
4 Graham and Bidwell, *Coalitions, Politicians and Generals*, p. 205
5 de Guingand, *Operation Victory*, p. 413
6 Wilmot, *The Struggle for Europe*, p. 501
7 Eisenhower, *Crusade in Europe*, pp. 248–52
8 British Official History, Vol. 11, *The Defeat of Germany*, p. 78
9 Wilmot, *The Struggle for Europe*, p. 598

CHAPTER 10

1 US Official History, *The Siegfried Line Campaign*, p. 242
2 ibid, p. 251
3 ibid, pp. 256–7
4 ibid, p. 303
5 Montgomery, *Memoirs*, p. 284
6 Marshall, Hydrick and Lester, *The Papers of George C. Marshall*, p. 264
7 US Official History, Pogue, *The Supreme Command*, p. 297
8 US Official History, *The Siegfried Line Campaign*, pp. 377–80
9 ibid, p. 421
10 ibid, p. 426
11 *Conquer: The Ninth Army History*, p. 83
12 Account supplied to the author, 2004

CHAPTER 11

1 US Official History, *The Siegfried Line Campaign*, p. 332
2 ibid, p. 336
3 Account supplied to the author, 2004
4 US Official History, *The Siegfried Line Campaign*, p. 344
5 ibid, p. 364
6 Account supplied to the author
7 Account supplied to the author, 2004

8 US Official History, *The Siegfried Line Campaign*, p. 431
9 ibid, p. 493
10 US Official History, *The Battle of the Huertgen Forest*, p. 195

CHAPTER 12

1 Letter to the author, 2004
2 D'Este, *Patton: A Genius for War*, p. 649
3 US Official History, *The Lorraine Campaign*, p. 24
4 D'Este, *Patton: A Genius for War*, p. 650
5 Bradley, *A Soldier's Story*, p. 403
6 US Official History, MacDonald, *The Decision to Launch Market Garden*
7 Message from von Rundstedt, 7 September
8 Correspondence with the author, 2004

CHAPTER 13

1 Wilmot, *The Struggle for Europe*, p. 625
2 US Official History, *The Ardennes*, p. 650
3 ibid, p. 652
4 Wilmot, *The Struggle for Europe*, p. 642
5 Correspondence with the author, 2004
6 Eisenhower, *Crusade in Europe*, p. 374

CHAPTER 14

1 Montgomery, *Memoirs*, p. 299
2 ibid, p. 307
3 US Official History, *The Ardennes*, p. 423
4 ibid, p. 424
5 Wilmot, *The Struggle for Europe*, p. 660
6 Eisenhower, *Crusade in Europe*, p. 390
7 US Official History, *Ardennes*, p. 426
8 Eisenhower, *Crusade in Europe*, p. 389
9 Montgomery, *Memoirs*, p. 314

CHAPTER 15

1 Winton, *War in History*, Vol. 4, p. 228
2 Alanbrooke, *War Diaries*, entry for 9 November 1944

DOCUMENTS

Many of the following documents were provided to the author by Major Frank Clark of the Guards Armoured Division:

Operational Orders for Market Garden for British 1st Airborne Division, US 82nd Division and US 101st Division

Operational Orders for Nijmegen and Grave by Major-General James Gavin, US 82nd Airborne Division

Operation Market Garden, Script Scenario provided by Major George Thorne, MC, Grenadier Guards

Address by General James M. Gavin, Nijmegen, 1984

Operation Market Garden by Brigadier A. N. Breitmayer, Grenadier Guards

One Aspect of the Battle of Nijmegen by Major H. F. Stanley, Grenadier Guards

Les Britanniques dans la Bataille des Ardennes, publication Wallonie Bruxelles, 2000

Assorted articles, correspondence and letters in *The Guards Magazine* referring to Market Garden

Report on the Waal river crossing by Thomas Pitt, S-I, 504th Parachute Infantry Regiment, 82nd Airborne Division

Accounts from the National Archives, Washington DC, including correspondence between Generals Marshall and Eisenhower

Report by the Supreme Allied Commander to the Combined Chiefs of Staff on the Operations in Europe of the Allied Expeditionary Force, 6th June 1944 to 8th May, 1945

BIBLIOGRAPHY

Alanbrooke, Field Marshal Lord, *War Diaries, 1939–1945,* London, ed.

Danchev and Todman, 2001

Ambrose, Stephen, *The Supreme Commander*, London, 1970

Barnett, Corelli (ed.), *Hitler's Generals*, London, 1989

Bartov, Omar, *Hitler's Army*, Oxford, 1992

Bennett, Ralph, *Ultra in the West* London, 1980

Blair, Clay, *Ridgway's Paratroopers,* New York, 1985

Bland, Larry and Stevens, S. R. (eds.), *The Papers of George Catlett Marshall,* Vol. 4 *Aggressive and Determined Leadership*, Baltimore, 1996

Bracer, William M., *Storming Hitler's Rhine*, New York, 1985

Bradley, Omar N., *A Soldier's Story*, New York, 1951

Bradley, Omar N., and Blair, Clay, *A General's Life*, London, 1983

Brereton, Lewis H., *The Brereton Diaries*, New York, 1946

Bryant, Arthur, *Triumph in the West,* London, 1959

Butcher, Harry C., *My Three Years with Eisenhower*, New York, 1946

Cole, Hugh M., *The Lorraine Campaign*, US Official History, Department of the Army, Washington DC, 1950

Collins, J. Lawton, *Lightning Joe*, Baton Rouge, 1979

David, Saul, *Military Blunders; The How and Why of Military Failure*, New York, 1998

Delaforce, Patrick, *Marching to the Sound of Gunfire,* Stroud, 2003

Ehrman, John, *Grand Strategy: Oct.1944–Aug.1945 (Vol VI)*, British Official History, London, 1956

D' Este, Carlo, *Eisenhower: A Soldier's Life*, London, 2003

D' Este, Carlo, *Patton: A Genius for War*, London, 1995

De Guingand, Francis, *Operation Victory,* London, 1947

Eisenhower, Dwight D., *Crusade in Europe,* London, 1948

Eisenhower, John S. D., *The Bitter Woods: The Ardennes Offensive*, London, 1969

Ellis, L. F., *Victory in the West: The Defeat of Germany*, British Official History, London, 1968

Fraser, David, *Alanbrooke,* London, 1982

Gavin, James M., *On To Berlin*, London, 1978

Gilbert, Martin, *The Road to Victory: Winston S. Churchill, 1941–1945,* London, 1989

Graham, Dominick and Bidwell, Shelford, *Coalitions, Politicians and Generals*, London, 1993

Greenfield, Kent Roberts (ed.), *Command Decisions* (Prepared by the Office of the Chief of Military History, Department of the Army, Washington, DC) London, 1960

Hamilton, Nigel, *Monty: The Field Marshal, 1944–1976*, London, 1986

Harvey, A. D., *Arnhem*, London, 2001

Hobbs, Joseph P., *Dear General: Eisenhower's Wartime Letters to Marshall*, Baltimore, 1971

Howarth, T. E. B. (ed.), *Monty at Close Quarters,* London, 1985

Irving, David, *The War Between the Generals*, London, 1981

Lamb, Richard, *Montgomery in Europe, 1943–1945*, London, 1983

Lucas, James, *The Last Days of the Reich*, London, 1986

MacDonald, Charles B., *The Siegfried Line Campaign*, US Official History (Department of the Army), Washington DC, 1961

MacDonald, Charles B., *A Time for Trumpets: the Untold Story of the Battle of the Bulge*, New York, 1983

Merriam, Robert E., *The Battle of the Bulge,* New York, 1978

Middlebrook, Martin and Everitt, Chris, *The Bomber Command War Diaries, 1939–1945*, Leicester, 1985

Montgomery, Field Marshal Viscount, *From Normandy to the Baltic*, London, 1950

Montgomery, Field Marshal Viscount, *Memoirs,* London, 1958

Moorehead, Alan, *Montgomery*, London, 1946

Neillands, Robin H., *The Battle of Normandy 1944,* London, 2002

Neillands, Robin H., *The Conquest of the Reich*, London, 1995

Neillands, Robin H., *The Raiders: The Army Commandos*, London, 1989

Neillands, Robin H., *By Sea and Land: The Royal Marines Commandos*, London, 1987

Ottway, T. B. H., *Airborne Forces*, Imperial War Museum, 1990

Patton, George S., *War As I Knew It,* New York, 1948

Pogue, Forrest C., *The Supreme Command*, Washington, 1954

Powell, Geoffery, *The Devil's Birthday: The Bridges to Arnhem*, London, 1984

Ruppenthal, Roland G., *Logistical Support of the Armies*, US Official History (Department of the Army), Washington, 1959

Ryan, Cornelius, *A Bridge Too Far,* London, 1974

St George Saunders, Hilary, *The Red Beret: The Story of the Parachute Regiment at War, 1940–1945*, London, 1950

Sixsmith, E. K. G., *Eisenhower as Military Commander*, London, 1973

Stacey, C. P., *The Victory Campaign: Operations of the Canadian Army in North West Europe, 1944–5*, Ottawa, 1960

Thompson, Julian, *Ready for Anything: The Parachute Regiment at War*, London, 1989

Thompson, R. W., *The Eighty-Five Days: the Battle of the Scheldt,* London, 1957

Urquhart, Roy, *Arnhem,* London 1958

Van Creveld, Martin, *Supplying War: Logistics from Wallenstein to Patton,* Cambridge, 1977

Verney, Major-General G. L., *The Guards Armoured Division,* London, 1955

Weigley, Russell F., *Eisenhower's Lieutenants: The Campaign in France and Germany, 1944–1945,* New York, 1981

Whiting, Charles, *The Field Marshal's Revenge,* London, 2004

Wilmot, Chester, *The Struggle for Europe,* London, 1952

INDEX